AMERICAN JOURNAL of PUBLIC HEALTH
APRIL 2026
Issue 4

AJPH

A PUBLICATION OF THE
AMERICAN PUBLIC HEALTH ASSOCIATION

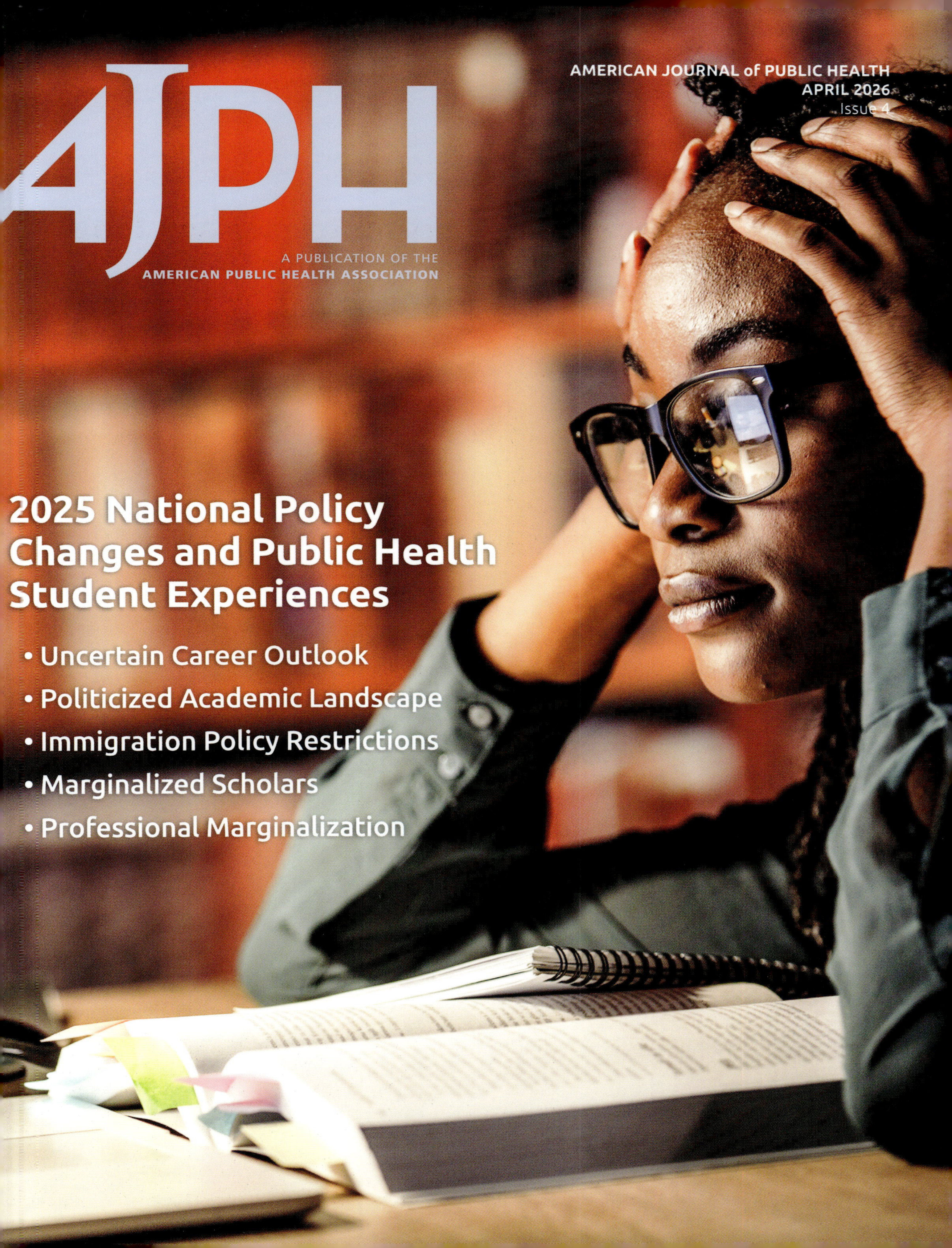

2025 National Policy Changes and Public Health Student Experiences

- Uncertain Career Outlook
- Politicized Academic Landscape
- Immigration Policy Restrictions
- Marginalized Scholars
- Professional Marginalization

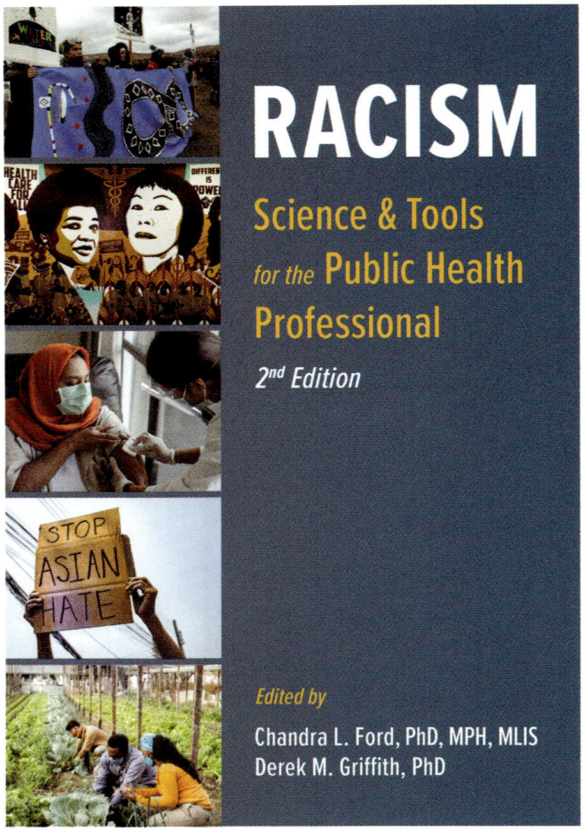

ISBN 978-0-87553-352-0, 600 PP.,
2025, SOFTCOVER

Racism: Science and Tools for the Public Health Professional, 2nd edition

Chandra L. Ford, PhD, MPH, MLIS, and Derek M. Griffith, PhD

Racism: Science and Tools for the Public Health Professional, 2nd edition enables public health professionals to address the health impacts of racism. This vital title also responds to the watershed events of the past five years: the COVID-19 pandemic and its intersection with overt forms of racism across all socioecological levels, the 2020 murder of George Floyd by Minneapolis police and the unprecedented domestic and global movements toward racial justice that transpired, and other major global events.

APHABOOKSTORE.ORG

APHA PRESS

AN IMPRINT OF **AMERICAN PUBLIC HEALTH ASSOCIATION**

AMERICAN PUBLIC HEALTH ASSOCIATION
For science. For action. For health.

AJPH®, published monthly, is the official Journal of the American Public Health Association®, 800 I St NW, Washington, DC 20001-3710; (202) 777- APHA; TDD (202) 777-2500. APHA is a nongovernmental professional society founded in 1872, representing all disciplines and specialties in public health.

The *American Journal of Public Health*® (*AJPH*) (print ISSN: 0090-0036; electronic ISSN: 1541- 0048), first published in 1911, is the official journal of the American Public Health Association® (APHA). The oldest and largest organization of public health professionals in the world, APHA represents approximately 30 000 members from more than 50 occupations of public health.

Submissions: Visit www.editorialmanager.com/ajph for online manuscript preparation and submission guidelines. Contributions of original unpublished research, social science analyses, scholarly essays, critical commentaries, departments, and letters to the editor are welcome. Questions? Write ajph.submissions@apha.org or call APHA at (202) 777-2469.

Print plus online subscriptions: Institutional price (print copy with online access) for a single institution and all authorized users, regardless of geographic location varies by size of organization; multiple campuses not permitted without special arrangement. To order, write apha.subscriptions@apha.org.

Online-only subscriptions: Institutional price for one US federal institution and its authorized users is $1,015–$1,510. To order, write apha.subscriptions@apha.org. For academic, non-US federal consortia, or multisite subscriptions, contact apha.subscriptions@apha.org or visit http://research.ebsco.com for pricing information.

Print-only subscriptions: Institutional price is US $970, $1,065 international.

Back print issues: A limited number of print issues are for sale. Single copies are US $80, $90 international (air delivery). Shipping and handling fees will apply; prepay only. To order, write apha.subscriptions@apha.org.

Reprints: For prices and ordering information on 50 or more reprints, check the Reprints section at www.ajph.org. To order smaller quantities of reprints (rush delivery), use the "Purchase Article" link on the article site itself.

Electronic access: Online articles more than 10 years old are available free for personal use at www.ajph.org. Recent articles are available through pay-per-view: single PDF article for $24, single issue access for 24 hours for $33, or entire site access for 24 hours for $38.

Postal information: Periodicals postage paid at Washington, DC, and additional mailing offices. Postmaster: Send address changes to American Journal of Public Health, 800 I St NW, Washington, DC 20001-3710.

Address changes: Send to AJPH, Membership Department (members) or AJPH Subscriptions (subscribers), APHA, 800 I St NW, Washington, DC 20001-3710. Or write to membership.mail@apha.org (members) or apha.subscriptions@apha.org (subscribers).

Indexes: Publications that index or abstract articles from *AJPH* include the following: Ageline, Assia (Applied Social Science Index and Abstracts), Biological Abstracts, Chemical Abstracts, CINAHL, Criminal Justice Abstracts, EMBASE, EMCare, Environmental Abstracts, e-psyche, ERIC, ETOH (Alcohol and Alcohol Problems Science Database), Excerpta Medica, Food Science and Technology, General Science Index, Grateful Med, Hospital Literature Index, Human Resources Abstracts, International Pharmaceutical Abstracts (IPA), Medline, Physical Education Index, Pollution Abstracts, Psychological Abstracts, PsychINFO, Safety Science Abstracts, Sage Family Studies Abstracts, Sage Human Resources Abstracts, Science Citation Index, SCOPUS, SIIC Data Bases, Social Work Research and Abstracts, and Statistical Reference Index (SRI)/LexisNexis.

AJPH

A PUBLICATION OF THE
AMERICAN PUBLIC HEALTH ASSOCIATION

COVER: The 2025 national policy changes are taking a toll on public health students. Federal policy decisions affect the trajectory of student educational paths and careers. This is particularly evident in graduate programs where grants are terminated and field placements disappear because of funding cuts and downsizing. And, as the field narrows, opportunities for Black, Indigenous, students of color, particularly Black women, are being eliminated at an alarming rate calling us to question the future of the public health field as well as the future health of the public.

Cover concept and selection by Aleisha Kropf. Photo by fotostorm/Getty. Printed with permission.

APHA
AMERICAN PUBLIC HEALTH ASSOCIATION
For science. For action. For health.

Promoting public health research, policy, practice, and education is the *AJPH* mission. As we widen our scope to embrace global issues, we also sharpen our focus to support the needs of public health practitioners. We invite contributions of original unpublished research, opinion and commentary, and letters to the editor.

The *Journal* is printed on acid-free recycled paper.

AJPH April 2026, Vol. 116, No. 4

OPEN ACCESS ONLINE ONLY PODCAST DATA SUPPLEMENT AVAILABLE

EDITOR'S CHOICE

405 Public Health Education in 2025 and Beyond: A Rose With Thorns
P. J. A Kelly

OPINIONS, PRACTICE, & EDUCATION

EDITORIALS FROM THE ACADEMICS

407 *AJPH* New Editorial Section: Voices of Public Health Academic Leaders
P. C. Erwin and D. T. Lau

408 How Damage to Our Public Health Emergency Preparedness System Impacts Public Health Students
J. A. Horney

VACCINE ACCESS

411 Health Plans as Public Health Leaders: Advancing Vaccine Access Through Evidence, Trust, and Collaboration
R. Kavasery

EDITORIALS

414 From Isolation to Inclusion: Using Community Infrastructure to Support Isolated Older Adults in Crises
M. A. Guest

417 Wage Theft: A Critical Labor Determinant of Health
J. P. Leigh

420 How the Federal Home Loan Bank Board Shared Home Owners' Loan Corporation Maps With Private Industry: Elucidating Redlining Causation in Public Health Research
J. Reaves, B. Newton, B. Boakye, and L. Brown

424 Swope et al. Respond
C. Swope, S. Markley, S. Whittaker, and A. Hillier

NOTES FROM THE FIELD

427 A Three-Year Evaluation of COVID-19 Vaccination and Testing Patterns Among Homebound Older Adults: Implications for Future Preparedness
K. E. Skinner, A. Stoever, J. R. Zakibe, C. Evans, J. Saunders Jr, and M. W. Kreuter

431 "The Agenda of the People": A Multisector Partnership for COVID-19 Mitigation in New York City
B. Rhodes-Bratton, M. Goodman, N.J. Williams, D. Shelley, E. Gill, E. Anastasiou, J. Reiss, M.A. Punter, A. Wallach, and L. E. Thorpe

437 Qualitative Evaluation of Health Department Measles Response Practices: Lessons Learned From 11 US Jurisdictions, March–October 2024
H. F. Wellham, S. Ravi, E.S. Toner, A. S. Fogarty, S. Gillani, E.A. Campbell, S. Soneja, and C. M. Rivers

443 Curriculum Approaches to Strengthen Public Health–Primary Care Collaboration: Northwest Leadership Institute, 2020–2024
J. G. Jones-Vanderleest, A. Angulo, and J. Z. Martelino

AJPH STUDENT THINK TANK

447 Insights on Recent National Policy Changes: Public Health Students' Experiences
A. K. Rodriguez, A. T. Ajamu, D. A. Adom, L. Angelo, T. Green, and C. White

452 Navigating Graduate Education in an Era of Policy-Driven Employment Pressures
F. Ahmed

455 Navigating a Politicized Landscape: The Imperative for Activist and Advocate Leadership in Public Health Education
P. A. Serrano

458 How the Escalating War on Immigrants Impacts Students' Mental Health and Well-Being
M. Zaragoza

460 A Generation at Stake: Master of Public Health Education, Workforce Decline, and the Future of US Public Health
D. Yagudayev, B. Bawa, A. Shaykevich, Z. Osiv, and M. Wojtowycz

463 Beyond Inclusion: Policy Shifts Reshaping Careers for Black Women in Public Health
N. Nzama, A. Scott-Davis, and J. C. Kerr

466 Precarious Futures: International Student Distress, Limited Training Pathways, and Career Uncertainty in Public Health
C. Chow and M. Chen

470 Public Health Students Confront New Career Realities: Will They Pass, Pivot, or Persist?
S. Krosin and R. Abouzaid

473 Between Gratitude and Advocacy: Navigating LGBTQ+ Public Health Research as Immigrant PhD Students
S. K. Sarker Rony, A. Adebanjo, and R. M. Combs

476 National Policy Changes Impacting Transgender Populations and Their Implications for Researchers and Public Health
G. Babbs, E. Balkan, R. Flores, and J. M. W. Hughto

479 When Your Research Is Devalued: Discovering Purpose in an Uncertain Academic Landscape
I. Willis

482 Bright Spot, Closing Door: Encouraging Innovation, Restricting Foreign Talent
Y. Zhu, M. W. Latshaw, and P. A. Locke

RESEARCH & ANALYSIS

OPEN-THEMED RESEARCH

485 Student Loan Debt Burden in the Public Health Workforce
J. P. Leider, M. Robins, N. McDaniel, R. Hare Bork, H. Doyle, and B. C. Castrucci

492 Protecting Low-Wage Workers From Exploitation: A Mapping Study of Wage Theft Laws in the 40 Largest US Cities
J. J. Lee, M. O'Connor, and J. Shen

502 US Black Women's Health Before and After the COVID-19 Pandemic: Socioeconomic and Temporal Patterns
B. A. Taddess, J. Tan, and S. A. Mojola

512 Disaggregating Gestational Diabetes and Hypertension Among Hispanic Mothers in Florida by Nativity and Country of Birth: 2004–2022
C. N. Lebron, M. Larson, M. Mitsdarffer, and T. von Ash

522 Effectiveness of a Participatory Voice Intervention on Psychological Well-Being Among Warehouse Workers: Results From the Fulfillment Center Intervention Study, United States, 2021–2023
K. F. Siebach, Y. Díaz-Linhart, L. D. Kubzansky, L. F. Berkman, M. Wang, L. Ge, A. M. Kowalski, H. Rahmandad, and E. L. Kelly

533 Context and Disclosure of Sexual Orientation and Gender Identity Information Among US Adults, 2021
T. E. Schlechter, B. T. Conner, A. C. Allen, A. T. Pho, N. Bates, R. Logan, A. Flentje, M. E. Lubensky, M. R. Lunn, and J. Obedin-Maliver

544 Navigating "Wicked" Disagreement in Public Health
S. A. Karim, R. Faden, A. Barnhill, V. A. Brown, J. Kahn, N. Kass, A. Mastroianni, S. Morain, V. Ravitsky, and R. Tuckson

552 Who Counts, Who's Accountable: Independent Scholarship and the Future of Carceral Mortality Oversight
D. H. Cloud, Z. Cullins, A. Armstrong, and L. Brinkley-Rubinstein

Public Health Education in 2025 and Beyond: A Rose With Thorns

Patrick J. A. Kelly, MPH
AJPH Student Editor
Department of Behavioral and Social Sciences
Brown University School of Public Health
Providence, RI

In April 2025, the editorial team of *AJPH* gathered in Washington, DC, amid a climate of escalating devaluation of public health. I had just begun my position as student editor of the *Journal*. On day one of our meeting, the challenges facing public health that were the backdrop to our meeting became even more personal. In alignment with President Trump's executive orders, the National Institutes of Health (NIH) announced a "civil rights" term and condition (http://bit.ly/4jsVGXo) on April 21, 2025, indicating that programs and research aligned with diversity, equity, and inclusion would be terminated. Accordingly, surrounded by our editorial team, I was notified that my NIH Predoctoral Fellowship to Promote Diversity in Health-Related Research (i.e., F31 diversity fellowship) would be terminated. My doctoral training suddenly became entangled with the turbulence of federal policy changes and chaos.

Among the many emotions I felt when receiving my termination notice was a realization that what was once the high point of my doctoral career was now the low point. I was also in disbelief at how nonsensical the termination was; an applicant's background plays a limited role in the review of F31 diversity fellowships relative to scholarly promise, scientific rigor, and the quality and feasibility of proposed training. I was eligible for a diversity award as a first-generation student who received a Federal Pell Grant and the Federal Free and Reduced Lunch Program growing up. For many terminated F31 diversity fellowships, including my own, the research was not disfavored and was aligned with a priority area of the Trump administration. My three-year grant is focused on using qualitative methods and artificial intelligence to understand xylazine, a health-harming adulterant to the unregulated fentanyl supply that the Trump administration considers a topic of concern. It appears many terminations resulted from elimination of diversity programming regardless of whether the science of the grant was disfavored or aligned with national priorities.

Fellowship terminations delay or eliminate scientific progress at a time when the health challenges faced by the United States need more, not less, scientific attention. Hundreds of F31 diversity fellows, including me, who should be invigorated by the nation's investment in their research, are contending with navigating the roulette of terminations and reinstatement while simultaneously strategizing how to continue their research without delay. I was focused and unwavering in my dedication to science and the opioid crisis. Yet, because of a capricious policy change targeting diverse students, none of that mattered.

The elimination of the F31 diversity fellowship funding mechanism is a sharp departure from decades of bipartisan federal investment in NIH training programs. NIH fellowships have launched the careers of thousands of scientists who have shaped the US reputation for producing world-class science. Expanding the breadth of backgrounds in our scientific workforce through the diversity fellowship is vitally important to improve public trust in science, maximize variation in research questions, and ensure that scientific evidence represents all populations. In this way, the elimination of the F31 diversity mechanism not only disadvantages the fellows but prevents a return on the investment of taxpayer dollars in solving the most complex and urgent health challenges of our time.

Federal grant terminations have not gone unchallenged. As a member of the American Public Health Association, I was represented in a lawsuit to restore terminated grants. On June 16, 2025, a federal judge in Boston, Massachusetts, reversed grant

AJPH April 2026, Vol. 116, No. 4

terminations stemming from Trump era NIH policy changes. Just before that decision, NIH rescinded the "civil rights" term and condition (https://bit.ly/3YyQJTk). The judge's decision resulted in the reinstatement of hundreds of research grants, including my own, notwithstanding federal government appeals. With a 5–4 decision announced August 21, 2025, the Supreme Court lifted the Boston judge's ruling to block the Trump administration's sweeping cuts to NIH research. How the high court's ruling will affect grants reinstated by NIH is yet to be understood, but for now, my research and training can continue. I certainly did not anticipate that my first NIH grant as the principal investigator would be terminated, let alone be included in a case before the Supreme Court.

My story is one of many represented in this *AJPH* issue's special section, which lays bare the intersectional difficulties public health students are experiencing on top of their existing responsibilities as principal investigators, clinicians, parents, and employees. As written in this special section, students face a precarious job market as well as legislative actions to restrict access to and the affordability of higher education. They are also contending with limited institutional support for students from marginalized backgrounds. These challenges are felt unequally, with students of color, immigrant students, transgender students, and students that self-fund their education weathering these challenges in multiplicative ways. A dampening of the passion that inspires bold scientific inquiry has occurred, with repercussions for public health and society that have not yet been fully realized.

I have not lost all hope. The outpouring of submissions we received for the special section signifies that we are a courageous and visionary generation. Also noteworthy are the faculty who supported our student authors, exemplifying the role of intergenerational knowledge in helping to chart a course forward in the shifting landscape of higher education. My generation understands that collective action, strong unions, and strategically wielding the pen are critical to protecting our careers and communities, safeguarding our science, and denying the erasure of our identities and the stifling of our passions. AJPH

DOI: https://doi.org/10.2105/AJPH.2025.308398

ORCID iD:
Patrick J. A. Kelly https://orcid.org/0000-0003-1462-1150

AJPH New Editorial Section: Voices of Public Health Academic Leaders

Paul C. Erwin, MD, DrPH, CPH, and Denys T. Lau, PhD

ABOUT THE AUTHORS

Paul C. Erwin is AJPH *associate editor and is with the School of Public Health, University of Alabama at Birmingham. Denys T. Lau is* AJPH *editor-in-chief and is with the Johns Hopkins University, Baltimore, MD, George Washington University, Washington, DC, and University of Illinois at Chicago.*

See also Horney, p. 408.

The *American Journal of Public Health* (*AJPH*) is committed to being one of the most trusted sources of scholarly, scientific information in public health.[1] To strengthen confidence in the *Journal* and enhance its relevance to the field, *AJPH* actively engages public health thought leaders, educators, practitioners, and policymakers to inform and shape its content. Among these voices, academic leaders play unique, critical roles in advancing evidence-based research, driving innovative policies and programs, translating science into practice, and educating the next generation of the public health workforce.

As part of its effort to engage stakeholders, *AJPH* is pleased to launch a new editorial section—*Editorials From the Academics*—beginning with the January 2026 issue. We will invite deans of schools of public health and directors of public health programs to either provide academic perspectives aligned with the special section's focus of each monthly issue or highlight innovative initiatives emerging from their schools or programs. For example, the inaugural editorial about the role of uncertainty in rebuilding trust in science was published in an issue that featured a special section on promoting trust and trustworthiness in public health.[2]

By elevating these voices, *AJPH* seeks to create a platform that directly and meaningfully bridges academic leadership and various public health professionals—including those in academic institutions, private sector businesses, nonprofit and community-based organizations, health care systems, and policymaking arenas at the local, national, and global levels. This forum also will showcase the breadth of public health, helping make university-based research and education more relevant to real-world public health practice.

Although public health academic leaders regularly convene at national meetings such as those sponsored by the American Public Health Association and the Association of Schools and Programs of Public Health, opportunities for sustained engagement through scholarly writing are far more limited and less frequent. These editorials will provide a dedicated platform for academic leaders to connect with one another across disciplines, share ideas, and articulate informed perspectives through the written word. Importantly, this discourse also offers an avenue for academic leaders to speak truth to power—a value that is as essential to public health as social justice, health equity, and science-driven evidence, and one that is being challenged in the current climate of dissolution.

Ultimately, we hope that *Editorials From the Academics* will inspire *AJPH* readers to reflect on their own roles in "creating the conditions in which people can be healthy,"[3] by strengthening communities, fostering meaningful engagement, enhancing the evidence base, and shaping health policy. We invite you to join us in this important endeavor. AJPH

CORRESPONDENCE

Correspondence should be sent to Denys T. Lau, Editor-in-Chief, *American Journal of Public Health*, 800 I St, NW, Washington, DC 20001 (e-mail: Denys.Lau@apha.org). Reprints can be ordered at https://www.ajph.org by clicking the "Reprints" link.

PUBLICATION INFORMATION

Full Citation: Erwin PC, Lau DT. *AJPH* new editorial section: voices of public health academic leaders. *Am J Public Health*. 2026;116(4):407.

Acceptance Date: January 13, 2026.

DOI: https://doi.org/10.2105/AJPH.2026.308418

CONTRIBUTORS

P. C. Erwin drafted the editorial. D. T. Lau revised the text.

CONFLICTS OF INTEREST

The authors declare no conflicts of interests.

REFERENCES

1. Lau DT. My vision for AJPH. *Am J Public Health.* 2025;115(9):1342–1343. https://doi.org/10.2105/AJPH.2025.308238
2. McCain K. The role of uncertainty in rebuilding trust in science. *Am J Public Health.* 2026;116(1):35–37. https://doi.org/10.2105/AJPH.2025.308317
3. Institute of Medicine. *The Future of Public Health.* Washington, DC: National Academy Press; 1988.

How Damage to Our Public Health Emergency Preparedness System Impacts Public Health Students

Jennifer A. Horney, PhD, MPH

ABOUT THE AUTHOR

Jennifer A. Horney is the Founding Chair of the Department of Epidemiology, University of Delaware, Newark.

See also Erwin and Lau, p. 407.

AJPH April 2026, Vol. 116, No. 4

Support for, and trust in, public health is at a nadir. Recent accomplishments include the rapid development and approval of a safe and effective COVID-19 vaccine, effective mpox response, declines in opioid overdose deaths through harm reduction, and evidence-based public health initiatives addressing root causes of gun violence. Despite these initiatives, which have significantly reduced the population-level impact of injury and illness, perceived missteps in the management of COVID-19, pervasive mis- and disinformation, increasing public distrust, and a lack of financial support have contributed to the deterioration of public health's ability to respond to disasters and emergencies. The impact of false narratives and disinvestments interrupt the public health workforce pipeline, denying students opportunities to be trained for and participate in public health emergency preparedness activities.

In 2003, I began my career as a disaster epidemiologist conducting household interviews for rapid needs assessments being conducted by the US Centers for Disease Control and Prevention (CDC), the North Carolina Division of Public Health, and the University of North Carolina following Hurricane Isabel. For more than two decades, I deployed with students in partnership with local, state, and federal public health agencies to respond to disasters and collect data that contributed to both the immediate and long-term mitigation of the negative health impacts of disasters.

This work, conducted in communities across the United States, is only possible because of a community's trust in public health agencies and individuals' willingness to share their postdisaster needs with our interview teams, which typically include a public health student and a local resident. The collection of perishable data in postdisaster contexts is challenging regardless of circumstance, and alterations have been made over time to ensure better representation of pregnant women, migrant workers, and rural populations in these postdisaster assessments. Yet, these assessments would not be possible at all without trusted connections between governmental agencies, academic public health, and disaster-affected communities.

POLITICIZATION THREATENS OUR ABILITY TO RESPOND

Politicization of disaster response and disaster assistance, and the mis- and disinformation that has now become prevalent around it, make it more difficult to collect these data. Following Hurricane Helene, one of my public health students at the University of Delaware worked with the western North Carolina nonprofit Sustaining Essential and Rural Community Healthcare to conduct key informant interviews and a Community Assessment for Public Health Emergency Response community survey. Both officials and residents reported that misinformation took time and attention away from response activities and disinformation led residents to distrust the response and recovery.

After the pandemic, we have a dramatically underresourced public health preparedness and response system, even in the face of more frequent and severe disasters and public health emergencies. These challenges will continue to mount as the Trump administration dismantles not only public health but also science more broadly. If the administration continues with their stated intent to dismantle the National Center for Atmospheric Research, this will further limit our ability to understand the human health impacts of extreme weather and weather-related hazards associated with climate change. This comes after significant damage to other federal agencies, including the CDC, the Environmental Protection Agency, and the Occupational Safety and Health

Administration, all of whom monitor and collect data on disasters caused by natural, biological, and technological or industrial hazards and risks.

A WEAKENED WORKFORCE PIPELINE

With the rapidly changing landscape, students are learning about "how things used to be," with an asterisk next to almost all federal disaster and public health policies and legal frameworks noting that the material could be outdated quickly. However, it is important that students are aware of the mechanisms and functionalities that have existed before this most recent political upheaval. For new public health professionals to help build back programs in more sustainable and resilient ways, it is vital that they have a comprehensive understanding of the policies that were dismantled, as well as their strengths and weaknesses. However, limited job opportunities and ongoing uncertainty will steer this generation of public health students away from governmental public health careers, leaving a long-term deficit of expertise.

The difference between an emergency and a disaster is that in an emergency, actions can be taken to avoid a disaster, which exceeds the capacity of an impacted community. The Federal Emergency Management Agency's (FEMA's) workforce is 20% smaller under the Trump administration, and mitigation grants through the Flood Mitigation Assistance and Building Resiliency Infrastructure and Communities programs have been eliminated. Reducing community capacity to manage social, systemic, and infrastructural risks through disaster risk reduction, mitigation, and anticipatory action will result in emergencies more frequently progressing into disasters. Furthermore, without federal capacity to respond in agencies like FEMA or CDC, the risks that a given emergency will become a disaster also drastically increase simply because of the ways resources are allocated. Students will no longer have the opportunity to participate in fieldwork when there are no federally supported disaster responses or to learn about disaster epidemiology when there is no longer funding for academic programs that teach students public health in complex emergencies and disaster epidemiology concepts. A safety net that is frayed in nondisaster times will simply unravel during a public health emergency.

Overall, it is critical for both the current and future public health workforce to continue to work to identify and understand the social drivers of health and the ways in which the current regulatory, technological, and political moment is affecting public health in both the short and long term. Discussing the ongoing stress impacts of the "triple disaster" in Japan in 2011 (i.e., earthquake, tsunami, and nuclear accident at the Fukushima power plant), Adam highlighted the importance of identifying and understanding the impacts of new and unexpected stressors on population health.[1]

A CALL TO ACTION

Borrowing from this framing, the next generation of public health professionals must now begin to engage in quantifying the public health impacts of these policies to generate the essential evidence base for the future reinvestment in, and reinvigoration of, public health emergency preparedness. Current public health students can begin to actively capture the baseline state of public health, commit to ongoing active surveillance and measurement, and engage with both objective measures of health and self-reported perceptions to track how the human-made and unexpected stressors like artificial intelligence, climate change, and political polarization may affect us.

While being "political" has often been seen as a negative for public health officials, now is not the time for public health students to be insular or isolated. Although engaging with the political, legislative, legal, and business sectors as a public health student or professional may feel daunting, public health must now more than ever engage with a variety of new partners and tools for public health practice. We cannot respond to the current attacks on public health in isolation. Businesses must speak up regarding how important a healthy and safe workforce is to their success. Local officials must advocate for the health of their residents and communities. The long-held sovereignty of local public health governance must give way to regional collaborations like the recently announced Northeast Public Health Collaborative, which brings together 10 states and New York City to work together on issues like vaccine policy, public health financing, and public health data collection, management, and analysis.

Public health has always had the impetus to protect previous achievements—vaccination, robust surveillance systems, workplace and environmental safety, maternal and child health, reducing health disparities—through monitoring and evaluation, education, regulatory enforcement, and other essential public health services. For public health students, now is the time to find your passion, engage with partners that can support you, and prepare to lead. AJPH

CORRESPONDENCE

Correspondence should be sent to Jennifer A. Horney, 100 Discovery Blvd, Suite 614, Newark DE 19713 (e-mail: horney@udel.edu). Reprints can be ordered at https://www.ajph.org by clicking the "Reprints" link.

PUBLICATION INFORMATION

Full Citation: Horney JA. How damage to our public health emergency preparedness system impacts public health students. *Am J Public Health*. 2026;116(4):408–410.

Acceptance Date: January 13, 2026.

DOI: https://doi.org/10.2105/AJPH.2026.308419

ORCID iD:

Jennifer A. Horney https://orcid.org/0000-0003-3060-0894

CONFLICTS OF INTEREST

There are no potential or actual conflicts of interest from funding or affiliation-related activities.

REFERENCE

1. Adam EK. Natural disasters as natural experiments: lessons for human stress science. *Proc Natl Acad Sci U S A*. 2023;120(44):e2316231120. https://doi.org/10.1073/pnas.2316231120

Health Plans as Public Health Leaders: Advancing Vaccine Access Through Evidence, Trust, and Collaboration

Ravi Kavasery, MD

ABOUT THE AUTHOR

Ravi Kavasery is with Blue Shield of California, Oakland, CA.

See also *AJPH*'s Vaccine Access Collection.

In a time of growing public skepticism and confusion, the role of health plans in safeguarding vaccine access and advancing public health has never been more critical. As a practicing physician and a chief medical officer of a leading health plan, I recognize the unique position of payers as public health actors with the capacity and responsibility to encourage vaccination, protect evidence-based scientific integrity, and collaborate across sectors to increase uptake.

HEALTH PLANS ARE PUBLIC HEALTH ACTORS COMMITTED TO ACCESS

Vaccines remain one of the most effective and cost-efficient public health interventions, preventing millions of deaths annually and reducing the burden of infectious disease across populations.[1,2] Yet access to vaccines is not guaranteed. In the absence of consistent guidance on vaccine coverage, health plans have stepped in to ensure coverage, even amid an environment in which clinicians and the general public express concern over the scientific justification for vaccine recommendations and insurers face uncertainty over the legal coverage implications of widespread changes to those recommendations.[3] This commitment reflects a broader public health responsibility to ensure that preventative care is not contingent on geography, insurance type, or socioeconomic status.

Major payers have stepped up to offer stability and peace of mind for Americans whose benefits they manage. Their coverage decisions should continue to support individuals' ability to access vaccines without financial or logistical barriers. By prioritizing no cost-sharing coverage for evidence-based vaccines, they reinforce the principle that vaccination should be universally accessible, regardless of a person's insurance type, geography, or socioeconomic status.

Moreover, health plans are uniquely positioned to act on population-level data with respect to the more than 300 million Americans who have health insurance. They can identify gaps in vaccination rates, target outreach to high-risk individuals and communities, and deploy interventions that increase uptake and reduce disparities. These efforts are not merely cost-containment strategies; they are essential to preventing outbreaks, protecting vulnerable populations, and contributing to healthier communities.

MAINTAINING PUBLIC TRUST BY ADHERING TO EVIDENCE

Public trust in vaccines—and trust in the institutions that promote them—has been eroding in recent years. Misinformation and inconsistent messaging have fueled confusion and hesitancy. According to a 2025 KFF poll,[4] doctors and health care providers remain the most trusted sources for information about vaccines (83%). Most people also still trust their local public health department (62%) and the US Centers for Disease Control and Prevention (CDC; 57%). But these percentages have been declining since 2023. The same survey found that less than half of the public trusted institutions like the CDC or the Food and Drug Administration to make decisions based on evidence rather than personal decisions or to act independent of personal interests.

Coverage decisions must be based on independent, evidence-based guidance. Their obligation is to follow the evidence—ensuring that coverage decisions reflect the best available data, clinical consensus, and ongoing rigorous evaluation as new evidence becomes available. When health plans follow this approach, they send a clear message: evidence drives our decisions on behalf of the people and populations we serve.

AJPH April 2026, Vol. 116, No. 4

When agencies like the CDC and its Advisory Committee on Immunization Practices (ACIP) issue recommendations grounded in rigorous evidence, and health plans consistently follow suit, the result is a coherent, trusted framework that provides clarity for individuals, the public, and health care professionals, and that supports vaccine access and uptake. This minimizes confusion for providers and patients, reinforces the credibility of public health messaging, and ensures that coverage decisions are predictable and equitable. However, plans must turn elsewhere to inform credible coverage determinations in cases where federal recommendations are deemed imprudent or unsupported by clinical evidence, in the opinion of major physicians groups and specialty societies.[5] For example, insurers (individually and in reliance on shared clinical expertise through trade associations such as the Blue Cross Blue Shield Association) already frequently review medical policies upon which the scope of coverage determinations are reached. Plans consult evidence-based, peer-reviewed clinical studies and available clinical data in reaching these determinations. Regional and state policymakers and public health departments can also offer guidance and expertise to inform plans' coverage determinations. In California, for example, lawmakers passed AB 144, which requires coverage of state-recommended vaccines irrespective of federal determinations. Through the West Coast Health Alliance, California and neighboring states have aggressively touted regional and state recommendations[6] following ACIP's change to its pediatric hepatitis B vaccine recommendation.

Health plans, in turn, must remain steadfast in their commitment to scientific rigor to preserve the integrity of public health.

COLLABORATING TO ENSURE VACCINE UPTAKE

No single stakeholder can solve the challenge of vaccine access alone. Health plans will continue to collaborate with clinicians, pharmacists, community leaders, policymakers, and public health agencies to drive uptake and build trust.

Clinicians remain the most trusted source of vaccine information. By streamlining reimbursement, reducing administrative burdens, and investing in provider education, health plans can empower clinicians to have meaningful conversations with their patients. Pharmacists, too, play a vital role—especially in rural and underserved areas, where they may be the most trusted and accessible health care professionals.

And it is more important than ever that these varied partners across the health system work together in a collaborative and consistent way to ensure access to vaccines for those who want them. To that end, the Common Health Coalition[7]—of which Blue Shield and many other leading health plans are members—is working to improve coordination across provider, payer, and public health organizations to translate the evidence-based justifications for vaccines into sound policy and action for patients.

Community-based organizations offer another critical avenue for engagement. Faith leaders, local advocates, and grassroots groups can help make vaccination efforts culturally and linguistically inclusive. They also support informed patient choices through shared decision-making, culturally sensitive communication, and meaningful community engagement. Health plans continue to invest in these partnerships, recognizing that trust is built locally.

Finally, we must consider the long-term implications of coverage decisions. Disruptions in vaccine access not only threaten public health, but they also jeopardize innovation. Manufacturers rely on predictable demand and reimbursement to invest in new vaccines. By maintaining stable coverage, health plans help sustain the ecosystem that drives scientific advancement.

CONCLUSION

A strong public health infrastructure is more vital than ever—and health plans are uniquely positioned to serve as key public health actors. By advancing vaccine access, upholding scientific integrity, and fostering cross-sector collaboration, they contribute directly to the stability and resilience of our public health system. Their collective action can serve as a stabilizing force. The future of vaccine access and the health of our communities depend on it. AJPH

CORRESPONDENCE

Correspondence should be sent to Ravi Kavasery, Blue Shield of California, 601 12th St, Oakland, CA 94607 (e-mail: Ravi.kavasery@blueshieldca.com). Reprints can be ordered at https://www.ajph.org by clicking the "Reprints" link.

PUBLICATION INFORMATION

Full Citation: Kavasery R. Health plans as public health leaders: advancing vaccine access through evidence, trust, and collaboration. *Am J Public Health*. 2026;116(4):411–413.

Acceptance Date: January 7, 2026

DOI: https://doi.org/10.2105/AJPH.2025.308406

ACKNOWLEDGMENTS

This article is part of a curated collection of editorial perspectives on vaccine accessibility, equity, and public health impact. Check out the rest of the series here: https://bit.ly/4I98J12

CONFLICTS OF INTEREST

The author has no conflicts of interest to report.

REFERENCES

1. Boccalini S. Value of vaccinations: a fundamental public health priority to be fully evaluated. *Vaccines (Basel).* 2025;13(5):479. https://doi.org/10.3390/vaccines13050479
2. Aviraj KS, Wasnik A, Gupta L, Ranjan A, Suresh H. Effectiveness of interventions to improve vaccine efficacy: a systematic review and meta-analysis. *Syst Rev.* 2025;14(1):105. https://doi.org/10.1186/s13643-025-02856-6
3. America's Health Insurance Plans (AHIP). AHIP statement on vaccine coverage. Available at: https://www.ahip.org/news/press-releases/ahip-statement-on-vaccine-coverage. Accessed December 18, 2025.
4. Kaiser Family Foundation. KFF tracking poll on health information and trust: COVID-19 vaccine update. August 1, 2025. Available at: https://www.kff.org/health-information-trust/kff-tracking-poll-on-health-information-and-trust-covid-19-vaccine-update. Accessed December 18, 2025.
5. American College of Physicians. Joint press statement: ACIP Hepatitis B—12-5-25. ACP Policy Library. December 5, 2025. Available at: https://www.acponline.org/sites/default/files/acp-policy-library/statements/Joint%20Press%20Statement%20ACIP%20Hep%20B-12-5-25.pdf. Accessed December 18, 2025.
6. California Dept of Public Health. Public health for all. December 15, 2025. Available at: https://www.cdph.ca.gov/Pages/public-health-for-all/publichealthforall.aspx. Accessed December 18, 2025.
7. Common Health Coalition. Aligning forces for health. Available at: https://commonhealthcoalition.org. Accessed December 18, 2025.

From Isolation to Inclusion: Using Community Infrastructure to Support Isolated Older Adults in Crises

M. Aaron Guest, PhD, MPH, MSW

ABOUT THE AUTHOR

The author is with the Center for Innovation in Healthy and Resilient Aging, Edson College of Nursing and Health Innovation, Arizona State University, Phoenix.

See also Skinner et al., p. 427.

AJPH April 2026, Vol. 116, No. 4

Public health crises draw bright lines around the places where our systems fail to function effectively. Yet, often these are the exact places where those working in the field have warned of impending concern. The COVID-19 pandemic exposed what many aging and public health practitioners have long known: homebound older adults are positioned at the edges of our already fragmented aging and public health systems.[1] Homebound individuals are often medically complex, socially isolated, and structurally disconnected from traditional health care systems.[2] At the same time, they are rarely recognized as a distinct population in preparedness planning.

Scholarship on isolation and aging has documented the very real health consequences of living alone and being disconnected from routine services. Isolated older adults are more likely to experience functional limitations, unmanaged chronic conditions, and unmet care needs.[3] They face higher risks of hospitalization and mortality.[4] Nevertheless, they remain a blind spot in many public health interventions, which often assume the ability to travel and acquire needed public health knowledge through social networks. What happens, though, when we reverse the direction of delivery and bring health resources to isolated older adults through the community services that already reach them?

In this issue of *AJPH*, Skinner et al. (p. 427) highlight the role of a COVID-19 self-test kit access program delivered as part of a meal delivery service. They also offer, quietly, a radical proposition. If we treat the home-delivered meal network as public health infrastructure, we can close long-standing gaps in access to public health technologies for individuals who rarely visit a clinic and often lack opportunities to engage with public health innovations or programs. Over a three-year period (2022–2024) of distribution of COVID-19 self-test kits alongside meals to low-income, homebound older adults, self-test use not only increased (from 28% to 39%) but reached parity with the national estimate for the general population (27%). This profound equity achievement was accomplished not by building a new system but by asking more of what we already have.

Preparedness efforts for disasters frequently assume that people can travel to specific locations and navigate websites or, if not, that they can obtain assistance from those in their support network.[5,6] Isolated older adults confound these assumptions. Often, their isolation is both social and geographic. They have few sources of social network support and limited ability to engage with traditional health services.

Skinner et al. emphasize that, without intentional strategies, isolated older adults are likely to be among the last to gain access to new health technologies and services such as at-home diagnostics. The intervention evaluated by the authors shows that this outcome is not inevitable. When self-test kits are carried the last mile by people and programs that engage with and have preexisting relationships with these populations—and, critically, do not have to identify them—isolated older adults can be reached effectively and at scale.

The findings from this and other work also invite a broader reevaluation of what constitutes public health infrastructure in the lives of older adults living in isolation.[7] The components of our aging support network, including meal delivery, transportation assistance, housing-based support, and home care, have been described as the scaffolding that supports people aging in place.[8] However, until recently, they have rarely been mentioned in formal and informal response plans.[9] As we see from this work, these services are not peripheral. They are the connective tissue through which crisis-responsive tools and resources can move. Equally important, however, is how these works address long-standing inequities while ensuring access to health technologies. Isolated and low-income older adults are often late adopters of emerging technologies, if they are reached at all. By showing that self-test use can match national levels when combined with a trusted program, the authors demonstrate a different pathway. The intervention operates as a kind of equalizer, not by asking people to change their behavior but by embedding new components within their existing services.

In reading Skinner and colleagues' work, I also note a tacit need for public health to consider new forms of governance for responding to public health crises. The program at the heart of this intervention sits at the margins of traditional public health authority, funded and regulated through various mechanisms rather than through a single core budget.[10] Yet, the partners involved in the intervention are indispensable in reaching those whose risk is compounded by isolation.

Public health systems need to move beyond episodic contracting and symbolic language toward more durable arrangements wherein aging services are integrated into planning, resource sharing, and decision making. Efforts implemented through Age-Friendly Public Health Systems that aim to better integrate local public health departments in recognizing and being a part of the aging support network in their community are already under way.[11] However, more still needs to be done. In public health, we must consider how to develop data-sharing and accountability structures that respect individuals' privacy while ensuring that isolated older adults are not left to weather the next emergency alone simply because they are known by one agency and not another.

Looking ahead, the implications of this work extend well beyond COVID-19. Climate change is driving an increase in the frequency and severity of extreme weather events. New infectious threats are likely to recur. In each case, isolated older adults will face amplified risks. Public health must adopt a more expansive view of where its infrastructure resides. Clinics, local public health departments, and hospitals remain indispensable, but they are not the only ones always on the front lines. A knock at the door from a meal driver, a home care worker, or a service coordinator is a frontline encounter, one that can carry not just food or basic assistance but timely tools for addressing public health crises. And we do not have to stop there. Research has shown that mail delivery drivers[12] can play important roles in observing and alerting when there are concerns for older adults. Other, often overlooked last-mile service providers such as sanitation workers and road workers may be able to fill similar roles.

Read this way, the Skinner et al. article serves as both demonstration and provocation. It shows that, with intentional design, community service delivery systems can function as last-mile health infrastructure for isolated older adults in times of crisis. At the same time, it prompts public health systems to envision preparedness not as a discrete set of activities in designated places but as an extension of existing programs and partnerships.

In doing so, the study helps outline a forward-looking research agenda, one in which comparative work is needed to understand how different forms of community infrastructure (e.g., housing-based support, neighborhood associations) can be configured as delivery systems for health tools under crisis conditions. Public health must reconcile with the reality that crises are no longer rare interruptions but recurring features in an unequal world. Skinner et al. offer a compelling starting point for such discussions. AJPH

CORRESPONDENCE

Correspondence should be sent to M. Aaron Guest, PhD, MPH, MSW, 550 N 3rd St, Suite 311, Phoenix, AZ 85004 (e-mail: aaron.guest@asu.edu). Reprints can be ordered at https://www.ajph.org by clicking the "Reprints" link.

PUBLICATION INFORMATION

Full Citation: Guest MA. From isolation to inclusion: using community infrastructure to support isolated older adults in crises. *Am J Public Health*. 2026;116(4):414–416.

Acceptance Date: January 7, 2026.

DOI: https://doi.org/10.2105/AJPH.2025.308405

ORCID iD:

M. Aaron Guest https://orcid.org/0000-0001-7356-3734

CONFLICTS OF INTEREST

The author has no conflicts of interest to declare.

REFERENCES

1. Yeh J, Holley L, Ford CD, Guest MA. Engagement and advocacy of community-based organizations serving older adults in Native American, rural, and homeless communities during the COVID-19 pandemic. *J Aging Soc Policy*. 2024;36(6):1626–1638. https://doi.org/10.1080/08959420.2022.2133317
2. Mather H, Kleijwegt H, Bollens-Lund E, et al. The heterogeneity of the homebound: a latent class analysis of a national sample of homebound older adults. *J Am Geriatr Soc*. 2023;71(7):2163–2171. https://doi.org/10.1111/jgs.18295
3. National Academies of Sciences, Engineering, and Medicine. *Social Isolation and Loneliness in Older Adults: Opportunities for the Health Care System*. National Academies Press; 2020.
4. Barnes TL, Ahuja M, MacLeod S, et al. Loneliness, social isolation, and all-cause mortality in a large sample of older adults. *J Aging Health*. 2022;34(6–8):883–892. https://doi.org/10.1177/08982643221074857
5. Hess JJ, Errett NA, McGregor G, et al. Public health preparedness for extreme heat events. *Annu Rev Public Health*. 2023;44:301–321. https://doi.org/10.1146/annurev-publhealth-071421-025508

6. Murthy BP, Molinari NM, LeBlanc TT, Vagi SJ, Avchen RN. Progress in public health emergency preparedness—United States, 2001–2016. *Am J Public Health.* 2017;107(suppl 2):S180–S185. https://doi.org/10.2105/AJPH.2017.304038
7. Smith ML, Steinman LE, Casey EA. Combatting social isolation among older adults in a time of physical distancing: the COVID-19 social connectivity paradox. *Front Public Health.* 2020;8:403. https://doi.org/10.3389/fpubh.2020.00403
8. Scharlach A, Diaz-Moore K. Aging-in-place. In: Bengston VL, Settersten RA, eds. *Handbook of Theories of Aging.* 3rd ed. Springer Publishing; 2016:407–425.
9. Bell SA, Singer D, Solway E, Kirch M, Kullgren J, Malani P. Predictors of emergency preparedness among older adults in the United States. *Disaster Med Public Health Prep.* 2021;15(5):624–630.
10. Juckett LA, Bunck L, Thomas KS. The Older Americans Act 2020 Reauthorization: overcoming barriers to service and program implementation. *Public Policy Aging Rep.* 2022;32(1):25–30.
11. De Biasi A, Wolfe M, Carmody J, Fulmer T, Auerbach J. Creating an Age-Friendly Public Health System. *Innov Aging.* 2020;4(1):igz044. https://doi.org/10.1093/geroni/igz044
12. Suzuki K, Dollery BE, Kortt MA. Addressing loneliness and social isolation amongst elderly people through local co-production in Japan. *Soc Policy Adm.* 2021;55(4):674–686. https://doi.org/10.1111/spol.12650

Wage Theft: A Critical Labor Determinant of Health

J. Paul Leigh, PhD

ABOUT THE AUTHOR

J. Paul Leigh is with the Department of Public Health Sciences, the Center for Poverty and Inequality Research, and the Center for Healthcare Policy and Research, all at the University of California, Davis.

See also Lee et al., p. 492.

Wage theft is a widespread but underrecognized feature of low-wage labor markets in the United States. Common forms of wage theft include unpaid overtime and wages below the legal minimum. Using the most recent estimates, Cooper and Kroeger found that employers stole roughly $15 billion per year through minimum wage violations in the mid-2010s.[1] By comparison, the FBI estimated that the combined value of all robberies, burglaries, larceny, and motor vehicle theft was $12.7 billion in 2015.[1] Minimum wage violations thus exceeded the total value of property crimes, yet only a small share of stolen wages is ever recovered.[2] Galvin estimates that 16.9% of low-wage workers reported minimum wage violations.[2] Despite these striking figures, wage theft remains understudied.[1,2] This gap may begin to close with the comprehensive data set on wage theft laws covering 40 cities and 25 states compiled by Lee et al. (p. 492) in this issue of *AJPH*, which I believe will be the gold standard for future research.

WAGE THEFT AS A DETERMINANT OF HEALTH

Wage theft should be understood as a social, or labor, determinant of health and, potentially, as a public health hazard. Like low, falling, and stagnant wages, wage theft undermines economic security in ways that are consequential for health. Falling and stagnating wages among lower- and middle-income workers have characterized the US economy for several decades. Figure 1 shows cumulative growth at five-year intervals in inflation-adjusted wages (including salaries) and per capita gross domestic product (GDP).[3] From 1979 through 2020 (data not available for 2025), wages rose by only 11.6% at the 10th percentile and 23.1% at the median, with most gains occurring between 2015 and 2020; wages at the lowest percentile declined from 1979 through 2010. By contrast, wages at the 95th percentile increased by 75.6% over the same period yet still lagged behind the per capita GDP growth of 89.1%.

The vertical gap between GDP and wage lines reflects income generated in the economy that did not accrue to workers in the bottom 95% of the wage distribution. Although some income accrued to workers above the 95th percentile, most flowed to capital owners through profits, capital gains, interest, dividends, and rents. The figure thus offers a wage-based perspective on the well-documented, decades-long increase in US income inequality. These patterns sharply contrast with those of 1945 through 1973, when wage percentiles and per capita GDP grew at similar rates—an era captured by John F. Kennedy's remark that "a rising tide lifts all boats" and described by some as a period when the United States was "Great."

Falling and stagnating wages for lower- and middle-income workers have been linked to many economic, social, and political problems, including the increasing gap between wages and productivity (had wages kept up with productivity, they would be approximately 45% higher today),[4] a perceived crisis in male identity, growing anti-immigrant sentiment, political polarization, decreasing affordability of basic goods and services, and heightened resentment among non–college-educated Americans toward college-educated Americans.[5] The wage trends may also influence US presidential election results. Wage theft is also an equity issue: relative to White men, disproportionate shares of women and Black and Hispanic people hold low-wage jobs and experience wage theft (Lee et al.).[5]

There are many public health implications of these wage trends. First, they have been associated with increasing "deaths of despair"—including liver cirrhosis, drug overdoses, and suicide—which began in the late 1990s and continue today.[5] These deaths resulted in US mortality rates increasing in the late 2010s even before the COVID-19 pandemic.[5] Second, wage theft and low wages increase reliance on the Supplemental Nutrition Assistance Program (SNAP), Medicaid, and Affordable Care Act subsidies and contribute to individuals' receipt of Social Security disability benefits.[1,5]

AJPH April 2026, Vol. 116, No. 4

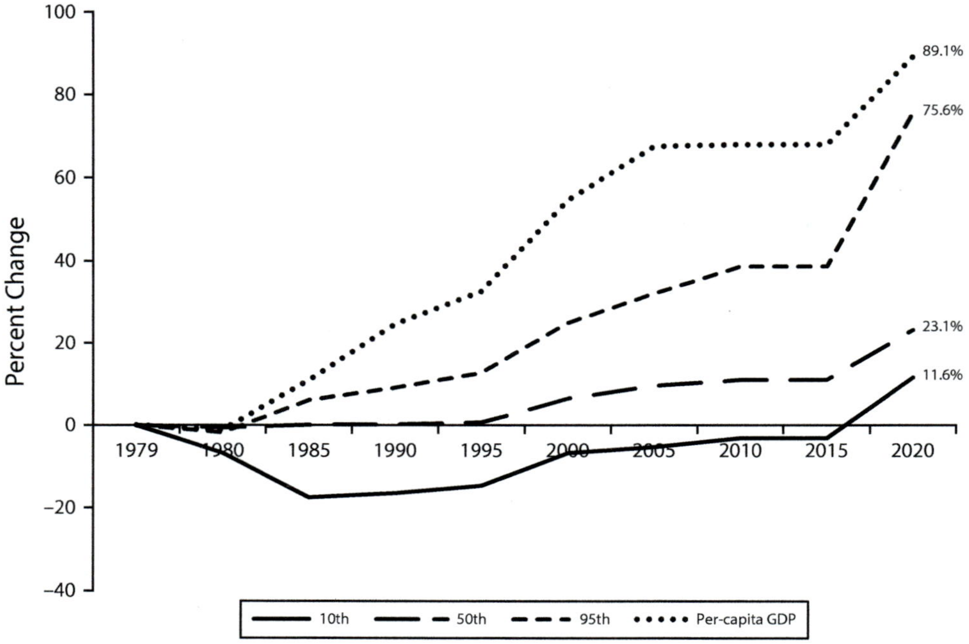

FIGURE 1— Cumulative Growth in Wage Percentiles and per Capita Gross Domestic Product (GDP)

Source. Economic Policy Institute[3]: United States.

AJPH April 2026, Vol. 116, No. 4

Cooper and Kroeger estimate that approximately one third of victims of wage theft rely on some form of public assistance.[1] US taxpayers—the funders of SNAP, Medicaid, and the subsidies—thereby subsidize businesses and corporations that benefit from keeping workers healthy yet profit from wage theft and low wages.[5] Third, falling and stagnating wages contribute to rising income inequality, which, in turn, might harm population health. Fourth, the Centers for Disease Control and Prevention identifies economic stability as one of five social determinants of health, noting that even people employed full-time often do not earn enough to afford health-promoting resources and activities.[6] Finally, low wages and wage theft may be health hazards, as several public health investigations into economic well-being, financial strain, and living wages suggest.[7]

These trends have numerous causes. The inflation-adjusted federal minimum wage has decreased over time: from $12.76 (in 2025 dollars) in 1980 to $7.25 today. By collectively bargaining for better pay, unions lift wages for their members and create competitive pressure for nonunion employers to raise theirs; conversely, declining union presence erodes this upward pressure, lowering standards. Unions also reduce, and sometimes eliminate, wage theft. Since 1980, union membership has been declining. Private-sector membership was 23% in 1980 but fell to 6% in 2024, a level lower than in 1929, during the presidency of Herbert Hoover. Lind attributes this decline to business-friendly policies enacted over these years.[5] Finally, wage theft may contribute to wage trends: when some employers engage in wage theft, they gain an unfair advantage by lowering labor costs, thereby pressuring ethical employers to lower wages and undermining workers' livelihoods.

There are ways to combat wage theft. First, the federal government and many state governments have labor departments with wage and hours divisions that can enforce wage theft laws and provide outreach to inform workers of their rights. Lee et al. suggest that educational outreach might be particularly effective. State and federal legislators could prioritize enforcement by providing these divisions with adequate funding. Second, states and the federal government could pass stronger laws governing wage theft. Galvin's study suggests that treble damages, that is, penalties equal to three times the amount of stolen wages, imposed on employers for violations are especially effective deterrents.[2] Lee et al. document variation across jurisdictions in the use of outreach and treble-damages provisions.

To date, a dearth of robust data sources has hindered a causal understanding of the link between wage theft and health. Lee et al. review the four most prominent public health studies and note that none use city-level data. A similar assessment applies to the economics and social science literatures, which include relatively few studies overall and only a handful that use city-level data.

FUTURE RESEARCH

Lee et al. assembled a data set based on systematic coding of local and state minimum wage and wage theft laws spanning January 2010 through April 2023. These data enable the examination of policy-relevant research questions. The authors examined approximately 85 criteria when reviewing each law and produced a data set with substantial variability, creating opportunities for future empirical inquiry.

First, Galvin's treble damages finding warrants further investigation. Second, researchers could construct a composite index—as Galvin did—to classify states or localities as having strong or weak laws by summing relevant provisions and logically weighting them (e.g., weighting treble damages more heavily than double damages).[2] Third, the two-way fixed-effects model—long the workhorse in minimum wage studies—has been found to generate bias; alternative approaches, including stacked regression, may yield less biased estimates.[8] Finally, wages should be the initial dependent variable investigated. Laws should reduce wage theft and thereby increase wages, and models intended to estimate health effects should first demonstrate effects on wages. If the models and data fail to detect wage effects, their estimated health effects are less credible. This test is analogous to those in minimum wage studies that establish wage effects before examining downstream health outcomes.[8]

Wage theft is a substantial but understudied labor determinant of health, operating through economic insecurity, inequality, and weakened protections for low-wage workers. A clearer empirical understanding of these mechanisms is essential for aligning labor policy with public health goals. AJPH

CORRESPONDENCE

Correspondence should be sent to J. Paul Leigh, Department of Public Health Sciences, University of California, Davis, One Shields Ave, Davis, CA 95618 (e-mail: pleigh@ucdavis.edu). Reprints can be ordered at https://www.ajph.org by clicking the "Reprints" link.

PUBLICATION INFORMATION

Full Citation: Leigh JP. Wage theft: a critical labor determinant of health. *Am J Public Health*. 2026; 116(4):417–419.

Acceptance Date: January 9, 2026.

DOI: https://doi.org/10.2105/AJPH.2025.308417

ACKNOWLEDGMENTS

I would like to thank the anonymous referee for insightful comments on this editorial.

CONFLICTS OF INTEREST

I have no conflicts of interest to declare.

REFERENCES

1. Cooper D, Kroeger T. Employers steal billions from workers' paychecks each year. May 10, 2017. Available at: https://www.epi.org/publication/employers-steal-billions-from-workers-paychecks-each-year. Accessed December 1, 2025.
2. Galvin DJ. Deterring wage theft: alt-labor, state politics, and the policy determinants of minimum wage compliance. *Perspect Polit.* 2016;14(2):324–350. https://doi.org/10.1017/S1537592716000050
3. Gould E, Kandra J. Wages grew in 2020 because the bottom fell out of the low-wage labor market. The State of Working America 2020 wages report. February 24, 2021. Available at: https://www.epi.org/publication/state-of-working-america-wages-in-2020. Accessed November 20, 2025.
4. Economic Policy Institute. The productivity-pay gap. January 16, 2026. Available at: https://www.epi.org/productivity-pay-gap. Accessed January 22, 2026.
5. Lind M. *Hell to Pay: How the Suppression of Wages Is Destroying America.* New York: Portfolio/Penguin; 2023.
6. US Department of Health and Human Services. Healthy People 2030. Available at: https://health.gov/healthypeople/priority-areas/social-determinants-health. Accessed November 30, 2025.
7. Nykiforuk CIJ, Belon AP, Scott LKA. Untangling concepts of financial circumstances for public health professionals and scholars: a glossary and concept map. *Am J Public Health.* 2024;114(1):79–89. https://doi.org/10.2105/AJPH.2023.307449
8. Leigh JP, Du J. Estimating minimum wage effects on alcohol abuse and wages with alternative likely affected samples and models. *Rev Econ Household.* 2025;1. https://doi.org/10.1007/s11150-025-09760-x

How the Federal Home Loan Bank Board Shared Home Owners' Loan Corporation Maps With Private Industry: Elucidating Redlining Causation in Public Health Research

Jehan Reaves, MHA, Bianca Newton, MEd, Brittney Boakye, MPH, and Lawrence Brown, PhD

AJPH April 2026, Vol. 116, No. 4

ABOUT THE AUTHORS

All authors are affiliated with the Center for Urban Health Equity (CUHE) at Morgan State University, Baltimore, MD. Jehan Reaves is a CUHE research associate, Lawrence Brown is a CUHE research scientist, and Brittney Boakye and Bianca Newton were CUHE research fellows at the time of this study.

See also Swope et al., p. 424.

In their article entitled "How and Why Does Redlining Matter for Present Day Health? Critical Perspectives on Causality, Cartography, and Capitalism," scholars Swope et al. remarked that there is "no existing evidence" that redlining maps were widely disseminated to private lenders.[1] Regarding the impact of Home Owners' Loan Corporation (HOLC) maps on lending practices, they argued:

> In addition, there is no existing evidence that its maps were widely disseminated, suggesting that they should not be viewed as directly shaping private lenders' practices, either. Assuming direct effects from HOLC grades diverts research away from questioning how redlining actually happened and identifying the true causal mechanisms that might shape present-day outcomes.[1(p773)]

As more than 50 studies now link HOLC grades to health outcomes, this argument has strong implications for the field of public health. At stake is whether public health researchers should be engaged in this line of inquiry at all, because it would be misleading to link HOLC grades to health outcomes if HOLC maps were never shared or distributed to private lenders.

Hence, it is important to review the existing evidence to show exactly "how redlining actually happened" and how HOLC maps were disseminated. Much of this evidence has been unearthed in the archival work of historians such as Kenneth Jackson, Louis Lee Woods II, Todd Michney, and Jennifer S. Light.[2–5] By studying their work and incorporating recent findings, public health researchers can better understand exactly what the Federal Home Loan Bank Board (FHLBB)—which commissioned the HOLC maps—shared with private lenders.

Researchers can then explain how the grades assigned on HOLC maps shaped private lenders' practices and, thus, produced contemporary outcomes.

MEDIUMS OF COMMUNICATION

First, there is evidence that physical copies of HOLC maps were widely spread in government circles. A FHLBB document located in the National Archives and Records Administration II (NARA II) outlines which government agencies received copies of the maps. The document is called "City Survey Program."[6(p1)] On pages 6 and 7, the FHLBB listed where they distributed copies of their maps:

- Federal Housing Administration—three complete sets
- United States Housing Authority—one complete set
- California Veterans' Welfare Board—set of the California maps
- The Commissioner of Banks of the State of Wisconsin—map of Milwaukee

Three more federal agencies are listed on page 8. Altogether, the FHLBB distributed their physical maps to seven different government agencies—five of them federal and two of them state.

Second, the FHLBB spread critical knowledge of HOLC maps to private industry. From 1934 to 1947, the Board published a monthly periodical called the *Federal Home Loan Bank Review* (the *Review*), which was described on the table of contents as the "Board's medium of communication with member institutions." In the August 1936 edition of the *Review*, the FHLBB published the landmark article "Security Maps for Analysis of Mortgage Lending Areas." The FHLBB lauded its Mortgagee Rehabilitation Division, which had "demonstrated [HOLC] maps to mortgage lenders around the country."[7(p389)] As a result, the FHLBB remarked:

> several hundred institutions which had never previously considered such an approach to their mortgage problems have begun to develop and maintain security maps. They will thus be in a better position than ever before to know in what neighborhoods they ought to seek loans and in what neighborhood they are over loaned.[7(p389)]

Not only did the FHLBB take credit for spreading HOLC maps to private industry, but they were also well aware of how mortgage lenders would use them to shape capital flows to neighborhoods nationwide. According to their fourth annual report, as of June 30, 1936, the FHLBB listed 3640 institutional members.[8(p15)] But they also noted that "Approximately 6000 copies of each edition of the Review are distributed."[8(p11)]

A New Basis for Facts

When providing instructions on replicating HOLC maps to private lenders, the FHLBB did more than just provide *techniques* and *logics* (i.e., how to make maps and their rationale for making them). The *Review* also pointed mortgage lenders to a specific data source called the Real Property Inventory (RPI), which was produced by the Works Progress Administration starting in 1933.

In the August 1936 *Review* article (Figure A, available as a supplement to the online version of this article at http://www.ajph.org), the FHLBB informed mortgage lenders of the RPI. "A real property inventory would show by blocks the number and type and construction of dwellings, their age and condition of repair, the material used in their construction, and the presence or absence of modern conveniences."[7(p390)] In a footnote, the Board also encouraged mortgage lenders to use the RPI as a survey instrument.

The FHLBB had previously introduced the RPI to mortgage institutions. In November 1935, the *Review* published two critical articles: "Neighborhood Standards as They Affect Investment Risk" and "A Practical Technic for Making a Real Property Survey." In the first article, the Board instructed its readers on how to spatially define neighborhoods. In the latter article, the FHLBB highlighted the data components of a Real Property Survey (another name for the RPI), which featured maps depicting various statistics compiled at the block level in cities. The Board emphasized to mortgage lenders:

> With such information for every block in the city, a home-financing institution will have a new factual basis for determining the desirability and risk of investment, for deciding the amount that can be safely invested, and for deciding where new building is justified.[9(p46)]

To prepare its HOLC maps, FHLBB local agents identified and partnered with scores of private map consultants. Using NARA II records, Boakye et al. identified more than 1100 private map consultants listed in 133 City Survey Reports.[10] Approximately 250 worked in the mortgage lending industry.

Therefore, beyond learning the FHLBB's general mapping techniques and logics, many private lenders were able to (1) access their city's RPI, (2) serve as FHLBB informants during their city's HOLC map creation, and (3) attend FHLBB demonstrations featuring HOLC maps.

Plans Visualized

Evidence of how the FHLBB's HOLC maps directly shaped private lenders' maps can be seen on a map published by Security-First National Bank of Los Angeles in the February 1938 edition of the *Insured Mortgage Portfolio*[11] (Figure B, available as a supplement to the online version of this article at http://www.ajph.org). Although printed in the monthly journal of the Federal Housing Administration (FHA), the Security-First National Bank's map featured the same four-area breakdown of urban space as the FHLBB spelled out in the August 1936 *Review*. Instead of the familiar Best (1), Still Desirable (2), Definitely Declining (3), and Hazardous (4) descriptions on HOLC maps, the Los Angeles bank used parallel categories named Growth, Maturity, Decline, and Decadence.

Even more tellingly, the bank's internal map used color. According to the bank's researcher L. Elden Smith, "The color scheme [we] used ranged from yellow for undeveloped areas through red, green, and blue to brown."[11(p10)] Aside from brown, the colors on the bank's internal map matched the colors depicted on HOLC maps. Notably, the FHA article reached a wide audience. In their fourth annual report, the FHA enumerated 5980 mortgage lender mortgagees in their mortgage insurance program[12(p48)] and stated that their journal "reaches all approved mortgagees."[12(p21)] As a consequence, the private bank's HOLC-inspired map was mailed to nearly 6000 mortgage lenders.

The printing of the HOLC-inspired map in the FHA journal was no accident. Archival records illuminate the close working relationship between the FHLBB and FHA. Historian Todd Michney uncovered collaborative exchanges between FHLBB and FHA, including the FHLBB sending the FHA a copy of the Atlanta HOLC map in April 1936 in his article "How HOLC Maps Were Made."[4] Recent archival work uncovered still more evidence that the FHA was an active collaborator in preparing HOLC maps. FHLBB City Survey Reports list 13 FHA chief valuators, underwriters, or state directors who served as map consultants in preparing HOLC maps.[13]

Given this, it is not surprising that maps produced by the FHLBB and FHA were closely aligned conceptually. HOLC Area Description forms underscore how the FHLBB designated red to indicate the "infiltration" of Negroes or colored people. Similarly, FHA maps tracked "any distinct racial, national, or income group that would be considered an undesirable element if introduced to other parts of the city."[14(p2)] Both agencies embedded a race-based tracking function into their maps, meaning that redlining boundaries were fluid and could be moved based on changing racial demographics.

OPERATIONAL EFFICIENCY

Archival records also shed light on another critical question raised by scholars. Did HOLC maps simply reflect preexisting private market preferences or did HOLC maps inaugurate race-based spatial mapping in the private industry? The evidence points toward the latter. As a result of the FHLBB's foreclosure rescues, mortgage terms were changed from three to five years in length with large final balloon payments to 10 to 15 years in length featuring full amortization starting in 1933. The new structure reduced monthly payments and eliminated balloon payouts for homeowners. Convinced that new appraisal methods were needed to assess risk over a longer mortgage term, the FHLBB initiated their mapmaking project on July 28, 1935.[8(p40)]

A New Day and Age

"It takes far better appraising and lending to make 10-year loans than short term loans,"[15(p11)] remarked FHLBB's Division of Research and Statistics director (Corwin Fergus) during his October 7, 1937, keynote address. Speaking before the Society of Residential Appraisers in Los Angeles, Fergus then announced: "The day of horse-back appraisals is over."[15(p12)]

The following month, the federally organized Joint Committee on Appraisal and Mortgage Analysis convened the National Appraisal Forum at the Mayflower Hotel in Washington, DC, on November 19 and 20. Eight of the 12 members of the Joint Committee were high-ranking officials from the FHLBB, FHA, Society of Residential Appraisers, and the American Institute for Real Estate Appraisers. During the Urban Land Use plenary session, director Fergus described HOLC maps and displayed the Dayton, Ohio, HOLC map.[16(p76)]

During his address, FHLBB general counsel Horace Russell reminded attendees that private industry appraisals were "wholly inadequate" before the FHLBB's work and that HOLC had "developed for the first time a nation-wide appraisal personnel consisting at one time of more than 8000 appraisers, trained that personnel, . . . and finally developed what has been recognized as one of the greatest appraisal organizations of all time."[17(p6)]

FHLBB administrators did not mince words. The Board had lengthened mortgage terms and inaugurated a nationwide appraisal system, supplanting the private industry's "wholly inadequate" appraisal system. As the Board insisted in the August 1936 *Review*: "To obtain an adequate picture, the balance sheet must be supplemented by a security map of the institution's lending area."[7(p389)] By openly demonstrating their HOLC maps to "several hundred institutions" and training more than 8000 appraisers, the Board schooled private industry. Indeed, the day of "horse-back appraisals" was over. The FHLBB ushered in a new day by spreading its mapping rubric far and wide.

Map Exhibitions

The FHLBB also displayed HOLC maps during the 1937 National Appraisal Forum. The large exhibit of appraisal tools spilled over from the Pan-American Room into the hotel lobby.[18] FHLBB maps included the following:

- Map of Detroit showing location of foreign racial groups; courtesy of Arthur A. May, Regional Appraiser, HOLC, Detroit
- School Census Map, Birmingham, Alabama, showing location of Negro school children; courtesy of Hill Ferguson, HOLC

AJPH April 2026, Vol. 116, No. 4

- Kansas City Atlas, HOLC Office, courtesy of James R. Barker, district appraiser

Even without distributing physical maps directly to private lenders, the FHLBB was clearly able to spread critical mapping knowledge to private industry and, as a result, influence mortgage lenders to create their own redlining maps. Private lenders' maps were likely to bear a striking resemblance to HOLC maps as demonstrated by the Security-First National Bank of Los Angeles map published in the February 1938 edition of the *Insured Mortgage Portfolio*.[11(p10)] Furthermore, building industry professionals who purchased the February 1938 edition of *The Architectural Forum* obtained a grayscale facsimile of a HOLC map.[19(p181)] Essentially, the FHLBB used *The Architectural Forum* as a vehicle to distribute physical copies of HOLC maps to private industry by proxy.

The Board did not need to hand out paper copies of HOLC maps to influence private lenders. Instead, the FHLBB

- Directed mortgage lenders to the Works Progress Administration's Real Property Inventory as a critical source of granular data and maps in the November 1935 *Review*
- Demonstrated to "several hundred institutions" how they could make their own maps as described in the August 1936 *Review*
- Provided written instructions to 3640 mortgage lenders on how to create HOLC-inspired maps in the August 1936 *Review*
- Trained more than 8000 appraisers and developed a nation-wide appraisal system by November 1937
- Exhibited several HOLC maps and displayed the Dayton redlining map at the National Appraisal Forum in November 1937
- Featured their mapping project in the February 1938 edition of *The Architectural Forum* including the de-identified HOLC map for Lima, Ohio
- Allowed mortgage lenders to visit FHLBB headquarters in Washington, DC, to view their city's map as written in the same 1938 magazine article
- Apprenticed more than 1100 private map consultants who contributed to the making of HOLC maps and reviewed final drafts between 1935 and 1940
- Displayed maps to private industry during keynotes delivered by Fergus between 1938 and 1940[20,21]

PUBLIC POLICY AND PUBLIC HEALTH

Based on this evidence, scholars can explain "how redlining actually happened" and identify "the true causal mechanisms" driving contemporary outcomes as Swope et al. recommended.[1] Simply put, the FHLBB intentionally embedded map-based appraisals in multiple private industries, including real estate, banking, appraisal, insurance, and home building. The Board and its officials demonstrated HOLC maps to "several hundred institutions," trained more than 1100 map consultants and 8000 appraisers, and mailed written instructions on creating HOLC-inspired maps to 3640 private mortgage lenders while specifying a concrete data source. Based on this federal proliferation, redlining as public policy soon became private practice.

Public health researchers should closely read and cite this extensive evidence to clearly elucidate causality when linking HOLC grades with contemporary health and environmental outcomes in future empirical studies. Researchers should also specify that redlining was designed to be an adaptive practice. This explains the finding by Markley and Holloway that neighborhood home values since 1970 are better predicted by Black population share than HOLC grade.[22] From their inception, redlining maps tracked and forecasted Black people's spatial movements. Hence, public health researchers should also develop new measures for identifying and countering contemporary redlining. AJPH

CORRESPONDENCE

Correspondence should be sent to Lawrence T. Brown, MSU Center for Urban Health Equity, 1700 E Cold Spring Lane, Baltimore, MD 21251. Reprints can be ordered at https://www.ajph.org by clicking the "Reprints" link.

PUBLICATION INFORMATION

Full Citation: Reaves J, Newton B, Boakye B, Brown L. How the Federal Home Loan Bank Board Shared Home Owners' Loan Corporation Maps With Private Industry: Elucidating Redlining Causation in Public Health Research. *Am J Public Health*. 2026;116(4):420–424.

Acceptance Date: October 19, 2025.

DOI: https://doi.org/10.2105/AJPH.2025.308342

ORCID iD:
Brittney Boakye https://orcid.org/0009-0002-6177-6569

CONTRIBUTORS

J. Reaves originated the study, engaged in archival acquisition, and co-drafted and revised the article. B. Boakye and B. Newton contributed to the design of the work and the archival acquisition of files cited in the piece and analyzed files for inclusion. L. Brown directed the archival research and also co-drafted and revised the article.

ACKNOWLEDGMENTS

The authors would like to thank CUHE for supporting the archival work that made this piece possible.

CONFLICTS OF INTEREST

The authors declare no conflicts of interest.

REFERENCES

1. Swope C, Markley S, Whittaker S, Hillier A. How and why does redlining matter for present-day health? Critical perspectives on causality, cartography, and capitalism. *Am J Public Health.* 2025;115(5):769–779. https://doi.org/10.2105/AJPH.2024.308000
2. Jackson KT. *Crabgrass Frontier.* New York, NY: Oxford University Press; 1985.
3. Woods LL II. The Federal Home Loan Bank Board, redlining, and the national proliferation of racial lending discrimination, 1921–1950. *J Urban Hist.* 2012;38(6):1036–1059. https://doi.org/10.1177/0096144211435126
4. Michney T. How the City Survey's redlining maps were made: a closer look at HOLC's Mortgagee Rehabilitation Division. *J Plan Hist.* 2021;20(4):318–344. https://doi.org/10.1177/15385132211013361
5. Light JS. Nationality and neighborhood risk at the origins of FHA underwriting. *J Urban Hist.* 2010;36(5):634–671. https://doi.org/10.1177/0096144210365677
6. Federal Home Loan Bank Board. City survey program. ca. 1942. National Archives and Records Administration II. Record Group 195, Entry 39, Series: City Survey Files, 1935–1940, Preliminary Inventory, College Park, MD.
7. Security maps for analysis of mortgage lending areas. *Federal Home Loan Bank Review.* Washington, DC: Federal Home Loan Bank Board; August 1936:389–391.
8. *Fourth annual report of the Federal Home Loan Bank Board.* Washington, DC: Federal Home Loan Bank Board; 1937.
9. A practical technic for making a real property survey. *Federal Home Loan Bank Review.* Washington, DC: Federal Home Loan Bank Board; November 1935:45–47.
10. Boakye B, Newton B, Reaves J, Brown L. Agents of the New Deal Mapping State: how private consultants shaped the New Deal's redlining maps. Mapping Inequality. 2025. Available at: https://dsl.richmond.edu/panorama/redlining/consultants. Accessed September 25, 2025.
11. Smith LE. Measuring the neighborhood risk. *Insured Mortgage Portfolio.* Washington, DC: Federal Housing Administration; February 1938:9–11, 22–23
12. *Fourth annual report of the Federal Housing Administration.* Washington, DC: Federal Housing Administration; 1938.
13. Brown LT, Reaves J, Newton B, Boakye B, Lansey A. FHLBB redlining evidence: How the FHLBB-HOLC created and spread security maps. American Apartheid Archive. 2024. Available at: https://storymaps.arcgis.com/stories/d71df00d4baa43668655ff3b977e6a21. Accessed September 25, 2025.
14. Hoyt H. The preparation of maps showing the dynamic factors of city growth. 1935:2. National Archives and Records Administration II. Record Group 207, Series: Economic Data System, 1936–1943, Entry PI 164 30, Box 1, College Park, MD.
15. Fergus CA. Real estate surveys as aids to mortgage lenders. 1937. National Archives and Records Administration II. Record Group 195, Entry 24, Series: Speeches and Press Releases, Box 6, College Park, MD.
16. Joint Committee on Appraisal and Mortgage Analysis. Proceedings of the general session and urban group meetings: National Appraisal Forum. 1937:75–76. National Archives and Records Administration II. Record Group 207, Series: General Records, 1935–1942, Box 7, College Park, MD.
17. Russell H. Appraisal data and the control of mortgage lending policy. 1937:6. National Archives and Records Administration II. Record Group 207, Series: General Records, 1935–1942, Box 7, College Park, MD.
18. Central Housing Committee. Exhibits—National Appraisal Forum. 1937. National Archives and Records Administration II. Record Group 207, Series: General Records, 1935–1942, Box 7, College Park, MD.
19. Searchlights for lenders. *The Architectural Forum.* February 1938:179–183.
20. Fergus CA. *Analyzing your market – Does it pay?* 1938. National Archives and Records Administration II. Record Group 195, Entry 24, Series: Speeches and Press Releases, Box 6. College Park, MD.
21. Fergus CA. Real estate and mortgage surveys. 1940. National Archives and Records Administration II. Record Group 195, Entry 24, Series: Speeches and Press Releases, Box 6, College Park, MD.
22. Markley SN, Holloway SR. Underestimating racism? Decoupling race and redlining. *Ann Am Assoc Geogr.* 2024;114(7):1464–1482. https://doi.org/10.1080/24694452.2024.2350993

Swope et al. Respond

Carolyn Swope, MPH, Scott Markley, PhD, MS, Shannon Whittaker, PhD, MPH, and Amy Hillier, PhD, MSW

ABOUT THE AUTHORS

Carolyn Swope is with the Urban Planning Program, Graduate School of Architecture, Planning and Preservation, Columbia University, New York, NY. Scott Markley is with the National Zoning Atlas, Washington, DC. Shannon Whittaker is with the Center for Innovation in Social Science, Boston University, Boston, MA. Amy Hillier is with the University of Pennsylvania School of Social Policy and Practice, Philadelphia.

See also Reaves et al., p. 420.

We read with interest the critique of Reaves et al. (p. 420) of our earlier article on the Home Owners' Loan Corporation (HOLC) redlining maps and causality in public health research. We appreciate the opportunity to respond. Reaves et al. focus primarily on our different understanding of how widely HOLC's maps were shared—a topic that urban historians have debated for several decades. Their critique reacts to our statement that "there is no existing evidence that [HOLC's] maps were widely disseminated, suggesting that they should not be viewed as directly shaping private lenders' practices."[1(p773)] They argue instead that "grades assigned on HOLC maps shaped private lenders' practices and thus produced contemporary outcomes." In this response, we explain why we do not view the evidence as supporting this argument. However, we emphasize that HOLC maps and area descriptions are nevertheless highly significant and useful for researchers.

For HOLC grades to be causal for the purposes of epidemiological analysis, private lenders' practices would need not only to have mirrored HOLC's graded areas on a widespread basis but to be directly shaped by them. Echoing the distinction of economist Price Fishback et al., there are two potential avenues through which this could occur: (1) "the effects of the specific borders drawn by the HOLC," that is, lenders had access to the maps and copied their graded areas; or (2) "the broader dissemination of mapmaking techniques" by the Federal Home Loan Bank Board (FHLBB)[2] if detailed instructions allowed lenders to replicate these exact borders. But neither avenue appears to have been possible: The distribution of HOLC maps was simply too limited to have had such influence, and the FHLBB's guidance was not sufficiently specific to reproduce HOLC-graded areas.

First, HOLC maps were almost entirely confidential. Work by historians LaDale Winling and Todd Michney,[3,4] as well as by Hillier, our article's senior author,[5,6] has documented extensive archival evidence of explicit policies to this end. They discuss the rationales for confidentiality, how even the survey's private consultants did not have access to the finalized maps, and how maps' distribution was tightly controlled even within HOLC. A summary of HOLC's information sharing is offered by Winling and Michney in their article reviewing most of the same evidence discussed by Reaves et al.: "Contrary to popular belief, HOLC never shared copies of the City Survey's finalized security maps outside select government circles" although "it did disseminate the theories and methodologies behind them in other ways,"[4(p63)] as we will discuss. Although there were several exceptions, they were just that, exceptions, proving the rule. The authors surprisingly do not acknowledge this pertinent evidence.

Reaves et al. state that the 1938 *Architectural Forum* article says that the FHLBB "allowed mortgage lenders to visit FHLBB headquarters in Washington, DC to view their city's map." However, in our reading, the article went on to explain that certain visitors would be allowed to view the accompanying reports but would be granted "only the most limited kind of peek," at only the data "not received in confidence." But "not for release to anybody as yet are the HOLC security area maps. The article explained why: Mortgage lenders who served as consulting informants shared information "in confidence for the obvious reason that some of it had competitive value, some of it was unfavorable." Further, publication of the maps "would tend to raise or depress the values of individual properties."[7(p46)]

Reaves et al. note several examples when, indeed, individual HOLC maps were publicly displayed on a one-off basis, including the *Architectural Forum* article and particular presentations. Yet it does not follow that private lenders in attendance would be able to use these examples to precisely replicate HOLC maps of their own cities. The authors suggest that such displays were more widespread, stating, "The FHLBB lauded its Mortgagee Rehabilitation Division which had 'demonstrated [HOLC] maps to mortgage lenders around the country,'" quoting from the *Federal Home Loan Bank Review* article. Thus, according to them, "the FHLBB t[ook] credit for spreading HOLC maps to private industry."

However, the text most closely approximating this statement in the source differs from the authors' quotation and is ambiguous: "The practical value of such maps" (referring to a discussion of hypothetical security maps generally, not HOLC's specifically) "in guiding lending policies and collection policies is being demonstrated to mortgage institutions throughout the country."[8(p389)] Although HOLC did sponsor technical conferences that emphasized neighborhood influences, including race, on appraisals[4,9] (perhaps what the *Review* is referencing), we know little about them at this time—an interesting topic for further research that could alter our understanding.

Reaves et al. also note that several copies of HOLC maps were distributed to other government agencies, which they describe as "widely spread." It is unclear how this relates to HOLC maps' effects on private sector practices. Regardless, we disagree that this constitutes "widely spread" distribution.

What, then, of the guidance offered by the FHLBB? To our knowledge, its subjective instructions on making security maps lacked the operationalization to allow lenders to precisely replicate the borders of HOLC-graded areas. Consider the guidance provided to identify A-graded areas in the *Federal Home Loan Bank Review* article discussed by Reaves et al., quoted here in its entirety:

> These areas, often spoken of by real-estate men as "hot spots," are just as clear in $5,000 neighborhoods as they are in $25,000 neighborhoods. Generally, "A" areas are comparatively new, well-located, uniformly developed; construction is sound and the pride of ownership is evidenced by the well-maintained properties; the type of dwelling is modern. In normal times, sales in these sections are active and sales resistance is low. If there is any appreciable amount of new construction in the town, these areas will be getting a substantial amount.[8(p389)]

For a lender seeking to produce their own maps, this guidance would surely raise a number of questions: how new is "comparatively," how does one assess how "well-maintained" a property is, and so on. Lenders attempting to follow it thus might reasonably decide to place graded areas' borders in different places. Indeed, HOLC's own rating practices varied locally—evident, for example, in the designation of an "A" rating for a Black neighborhood in Savannah, Georgia[3]—which would have made it all the more difficult to have precisely replicated HOLC-graded areas. One might also note the lack of instruction on how to address racial composition. In an epidemiological study seeking to demonstrate causality of HOLC maps—the type of study we were addressing in our original article—the precision of the similarity in how the graded areas were defined and drawn makes all the difference.

Finally, Reaves et al. declare that HOLC "inaugurate[d] race-based spatial mapping in the private industry." But the directions of influence are not clear-cut, especially given the "porous boundaries"[4(p58)] between public and private actors in real estate at the time. For example, J. M. Brewer created a Philadelphia, Pennsylvania, residential security map in 1934—predating HOLC's City Survey—with five categories of graded areas, from "A," "highest class residential," descending to "E" and denoting the presence of several racialized groups.[10] Brewer then later served as a consultant for HOLC's local survey.[5,6]

In sum, the evidence on "How the FHLBB Shared HOLC Maps With Private Industry" uncovered thus far suggests that they did so in only a very limited way. The picture is one of only rare and guarded access to the maps, coupled with high-level instructions about their approach, which is unlikely to have resulted in lenders' widespread direct replication of HOLC-graded areas to causally influence present-day outcomes. The hyperattention focused on these maps' supposed causal influence risks obscuring a broader understanding of the multiple mechanisms in racial capitalism that continue to drive racialized disinvestment, dispossession, and inequity today. Yet as discussed in our previous article, we view HOLC maps and their area descriptions as immensely valuable for researchers to explore how race and neighborhood value were coconstructed at a crucial point in time, even if they are only a proxy for actually practiced redlining. We thus emphatically disagree with the statement by Reaves et al. that "At stake is whether public health researchers should be engaged in this line of inquiry at all, because it would be misleading to link HOLC grades to health outcomes if HOLC maps were never shared or distributed to private lenders."

To be clear, we agree that the evidence indicates HOLC's culpability in promoting the use of racist security maps and the practice of redlining generally. But this is a different argument than what our original article responded to: the pervasive assumption in public health literature that HOLC's maps themselves are a primary direct cause of present-day geographic health inequities. We anticipate further generative debate as evidence continues to emerge. AJPH

CORRESPONDENCE

Correspondence should be sent to Carolyn Swope, MPH, Schermerhorn Extension 659, 1200 Amsterdam Ave, New York, NY 10027 (e-mail: cbs2164@columbia.edu). Reprints can be ordered at https://www.ajph.org by clicking the "Reprints" link.

PUBLICATION INFORMATION

Full Citation: Swope C, Markley S, Whittaker S, Hillier A. Swope et al. Respond. *Am J Public Health*. 2026;116(4):424–426.

Acceptance Date: November 15, 2025.

DOI: https://doi.org/10.2105/AJPH.2025.308365

ORCID iDs:

Carolyn Swope https://orcid.org/0000-0002-5982-5950

Scott Markley https://orcid.org/0000-0001-9004-6595

CONTRIBUTORS

C. Swope drafted and all authors critically reviewed and revised the editorial.

CONFLICTS OF INTEREST

The authors have no conflicts of interest to disclose.

REFERENCES

1. Swope CB, Markley S, Whittaker S, Hillier A. How and why does redlining matter for present-day health? Critical perspectives on causality, cartography, and capitalism. *Am J Public Health*. 2025;115(5):769–779. https://doi.org/10.2105/AJPH.2024.308000
2. Fishback P, Rose J, Snowden KA, Storrs T. New evidence on redlining by federal housing programs in the 1930s. *J Urban Econ*. 2024;141:103462. https://doi.org/10.1016/j.jue.2022.103462
3. Michney TM. How the city survey's redlining maps were made: a closer look at HOLC's Mortgagee Rehabilitation Division. *J Plan Hist*. 2021;21(4):316–344. https://doi.org/10.1177/15385132211013361
4. Winling LC, Michney TM. The roots of redlining: academic, governmental, and professional networks in the making of the New Deal lending regime. *J Am Hist*. 2021;108(1):42–69. https://doi.org/10.1093/jahist/jaab066
5. Hillier AE. Redlining and the Home Owners' Loan Corporation. *J Urban Hist*. 2003;29(4):394–420. https://doi.org/10.1177/0096144203029004002
6. Hillier AE. Residential security maps and neighborhood appraisals: the Home Owners' Loan Corporation and the case of Philadelphia. *Soc Sci Hist*. 2005;29(2):207–233. https://doi.org/10.1017/S014555320001292X
7. Searchlights for lenders. *Archit Forum*. 1938;68(2):179–183.
8. US Federal Home Loan Bank Board. Security maps for analysis of mortgage lending areas. *Federal Home Loan Bank Review*. 1936;2(11):389–391. Available at: https://fraser.stlouisfed.org/title/116/item/2025. Accessed January 29, 2026.
9. US Federal Home Loan Bank Board. Appraisal conferences and techniques. *Federal Home Loan Bank Review*. 1940;6(4):106–109. Available at: https://fraser.stlouisfed.org/title/federal-home-loan-bank-review-116/january-1940-2053?page=2. Accessed January 29, 2026.
10. Brewer JM. *Survey of Philadelphia*. Philadelphia, PA: Free Library of Philadelphia; 1934.

A Three-Year Evaluation of COVID-19 Vaccination and Testing Patterns Among Homebound Older Adults: Implications for Future Preparedness

Karen E. Skinner, MPH, Anneliese Stoever, MSW, John R. Zakibe, MSW, Carla Evans, BS, John Saunders Jr, BS, and Matthew W. Kreuter, PhD, MPH

See also Guest, p. 414.

COVID-19 self-test kits were distributed to low-income, homebound older adults with their home-delivered meals annually (2022–2024). A convenience sample of recipients completed follow-up surveys in 2022 (n = 271), 2023 (n = 295), and 2024 (n = 285). In 2023, 28% had ever used a COVID-19 self-test, which increased to 39% in 2024 and is comparable to a national study (27%). Through partnerships with trusted meal-delivery providers, homebound older adults can achieve rates of COVID-19 self-testing comparable to those of the broader population. (*Am J Public Health*. 2026;116(4):427–430. https://doi.org/10.2105/AJPH.2025.308349)

AJPH April 2026, Vol. 116, No. 4

Washington University in St. Louis, Missouri, collaborated with the City of St. Louis Department of Health, St. Louis Area Agency on Aging, and two local senior centers to provide iHealth COVID-19 self-tests to older adults in St. Louis. Initial program findings from 2022 have been previously published.[1] Here, we report findings for older adults from two senior centers for three time points—2022, 2023, and 2024—to describe how COVID-19 vaccination and testing changed as the COVID-19 pandemic evolved.

INTERVENTION AND IMPLEMENTATION

Health COVID-19 self-tests were provided by the City of St. Louis Department of Health, and local senior centers distributed them to older adults in St. Louis, Missouri each year from 2022 through 2024. Existing home-delivered meal clients received one COVID-19 self-test kit delivered to their home during routine meal delivery each year, in 2022, 2023, and 2024; timing was based on availability of test kits from our local public health partner.

PLACE, TIME, AND PERSONS

The evaluation included three cross-sectional samples that received COVID-19 self-tests with home-delivered meals in 2022 (n = 753), 2023 (n = 800), or 2024 (n = 877). Follow-up surveys were then administered to a convenience sample drawn from each set of self-test recipients (for 2022, n = 271; 2023, n = 295; 2024, n = 285). Some older adults responded to follow-up surveys in more than one year: 2022 and 2023 (n = 68), 2022 and 2024 (n = 34), 2023 and 2024 (n = 52), and 2022, 2023, and 2024 (n = 33).

PURPOSE

The federal COVID-19 public health emergency ended in May 2023.[2] However, COVID-19 remains a public health challenge requiring ongoing vaccination, testing, and treatment.[3] Testing and treatment are especially important for older adults who have a higher risk of severe disease,[4] where testing could lead to earlier treatment.

Prior government efforts to increase access to COVID-19 self-tests included mailing self-tests at no cost to those who requested them.[5] However, online ordering was a barrier for many older adults,[6] and demand for self-tests was lower in certain racial minority groups.[7] The iHealth COVID-19 self-testing initiative was supported by trusted senior centers to overcome barriers and ensure older adults' access to COVID-19 resources.

EVALUATION AND ADVERSE EFFECTS

Approximately one month after each annual distribution of COVID-19 self-tests (in 2022, 2023, and 2024), senior centers called a convenience sample of home-delivered meal clients to complete a 10-minute survey by telephone assessing COVID-19 vaccination status and thoughts about receiving a COVID-19 self-test.

Vaccination Status and Self-Test Kit Recall

In each annual survey, vaccination was evaluated by asking, "Have you received at least one dose of a COVID-19 vaccine?" (yes, no, or not sure). They were then asked about the COVID-19 self-test: "You should have received a self-test for COVID-19 in a recent meal delivery. Do you remember receiving a self-test for COVID-19?" Those who replied no or not sure to the self-test question were asked a prompted recall question: "It was an orange box about 3 inches by 6 inches in a Ziplock bag that came with your meal delivery. Do you remember seeing that?" (yes, no, not sure).

COVID-19 Self-Test Access and Use

Those who responded yes to the initial or prompted recall question were asked, "Did you have a COVID-19 self-test in your home before receiving the one with your meal delivery?" (yes, no, not sure). "What did you think about getting a COVID-19 self-test in your box of meals?" (I liked it, I didn't like it, I don't care either way, not sure). "Have you ever used a COVID-19 self-test?" (yes, no, not sure). In 2024, we also asked, "Did you use the self-test alone or did someone help you?" (by myself, with help, not sure).

Descriptive statistics (frequencies, proportions, means) are reported for 2022, 2023, and 2024. Characteristics of home-delivered meal clients were similar in each annual survey (Table 1). Approximately 60% were female, 75% to 80% were Black or African American, and average age was 73 years. Most had received at least one dose of a COVID-19 vaccine, with rates ranging from 84% in 2022 to 91% in 2024 (Table 1). Most recalled receiving a self-test with their meal delivery; recall ranged from 69% in 2022 to 82% in 2024.

In 2022, one in five respondents (21%) had a self-test in their home before receiving one with their meal delivery and approximately half had one in 2023 (50%) and 2024 (46%). In the subgroup of respondents who completed follow-up surveys in multiple years, 153 did so in consecutive years (i.e., 2022 and 2023 or 2023 and 2024) and 67 did so with a two-year gap (i.e., 2022 and 2024). In the consecutive year group, the proportion who already had a self-test increased 40% from the first to second year; in the two-year gap group, the proportion who already had a self-test increased 93% from 2022 to 2024.

The overall proportion who reported ever using a self-test was 28% in 2023 and 39% in 2024 (not assessed in 2022). In the subgroup of respondents who completed both 2023 and 2024 surveys, 26% had ever used a self-test in 2023 and 38% in 2024 (45% increase). Among 2024 participants who had used a self-test, 66% used it "by myself" and 33% "with help." The proportion who "liked" getting a self-test peaked at 97% in 2022 and fell to 83% in 2024.

Testing Preference

In the 2024 survey, home-delivered meal clients were also asked, "If you were feeling sick and had the choice of testing for an illness like COVID-19, the flu, or RSV [respiratory syncytial virus] either at home or at your doctor's office or a pharmacy, which would you prefer?" (test at home, test at a doctor's office or pharmacy, not sure, I wouldn't test).

More than half of 2024 respondents (51%) preferred to test at home if they were feeling sick; 44% preferred testing at a doctor's office or pharmacy. A χ^2 test was used to evaluate the association between past self-test use (yes or no) and testing preference (test at home, test at a doctor's office or a pharmacy; n = 223). Preference was associated with past self-test use ($\chi^2_1 = 32.3$; $P < .001$). Older adults who had ever used a self-test were more likely to prefer testing at home than those who had never used a self-test (57% vs 20%).

SUSTAINABILITY

Nearly all older adults served by these senior centers were vaccinated for COVID-19, and most remembered receiving a COVID-19 self-test kit each year. "Acceptability" is a key indicator of feasibility in public health pilot projects,[8] and nearly all older adults said they liked receiving a test kit.

This partnership increased access to COVID-19 self-tests at no cost to homebound older adults by overcoming barriers identified by prior research[9–11] without increasing costs for health systems and federal programs. We previously reported that few ordered freely available COVID-19 self-tests from the federal government and less than one third personally acquired a test before this program.[1]

Although the study did not assess how many self-test recipients experienced COVID-19 symptoms each year and thus might need to use the tests,

TABLE 1— Summary of COVID-19 Vaccination and Testing Among Older Adult Home-Delivered Meal Clients: St. Louis, MO, 2022–2024

	No. (%) or Mean ±SD		
	2022 (n = 271)	2023 (n = 295)	2024 (n = 285)[a]
Sex			
Male	107 (39)	115 (39)	117 (41)
Female	164 (61)	180 (61)	168 (59)
Race			
Black or African American	202 (75)	237 (80)	226 (79)
White (Hispanic or non-Hispanic)	67 (25)	54 (18)	57 (20)
Asian or Asian American	1 (0)	2 (1)	1 (0)
American Indian or Alaska Native	0 (0)	2 (1)	0 (0)
Unknown	1 (0)	0 (0)	1 (0)
Age, y	72 ±8	73 ±8	73 ±8
"Have you received at least one dose of a COVID-19 vaccine?" (yes)	227 (84)	260 (88)	260 (91)
"Do you remember receiving a self-test for COVID-19?" (yes)	187 (69)	215 (73)	235 (82)
"Did you have a COVID-19 self-test in your home before receiving the one with your meal delivery?"[b]	40 (21)	107 (50)	109 (46)
"What did you think about getting a self-test kit in your box of meals?"[b]			
Liked it	181 (97)	187 (87)	194 (83)
Didn't like it	1 (1)	5 (2)	4 (2)
Didn't care either way	4 (2)	22 (10)	32 (14)
Not sure/missing	1 (1)	1 (0)	4 (2)
"Have you ever used a COVID-19 self-test kit?" (yes)[b]	NA	60 (28)	91 (39)
"If you were feeling sick and had the choice of testing for an illness like COVID-19, the flu, or RSV either at home or at your doctor's office or pharmacy, which would you prefer?"[b]			
Test at home	NA	NA	121 (51)
Test at a doctor's office or pharmacy	NA	NA	103 (44)
Not sure	NA	NA	5 (2)
Wouldn't test	NA	NA	4 (2)

Note. NA = question was not included in the survey version; RSV = respiratory syncytial virus.
[a]One person was excluded from this analysis because of a duplicate identification number.
[b]Denominator is the number who recalled receiving a COVID-19 self-test (2022, n = 187; 2023, n = 215; 2024, n = 235).

28% and 39% reported using a self-test in 2023 and 2024, respectively. These rates are comparable to estimates of self-testing among older adults from a national study (27% among those aged ≥ 65 years[9]), although that study's sample was limited to those who ordered self-tests from COVIDTests.gov, whereas very few older adults in our sample could acquire self-tests online.[1] This finding suggests that targeted efforts to reach homebound older adults can achieve an impact comparable to that in the broader population.

PUBLIC HEALTH SIGNIFICANCE

Older adults liked receiving a COVID-19 self-test with their home-delivered meals, suggesting that bundling tests with other aging services might increase access to testing for higher-risk populations. Home-delivered meal clients have mobility challenges limiting how quickly and easily they can go to a testing site without assistance. This barrier can delay testing, put others at risk for infection, and risk untreated illness for the older adult. Self-tests support someone's autonomy or self-sufficiency to test when needed.

This program built upon existing community infrastructure among trusted partners who are well-known to homebound older adults for the range of services they provide. At a time when older adults are increasingly targeted for fraud[12] and being taught not to share information with unfamiliar sources, working with senior centers that older adults know and trust likely increased survey response rates and candor in responses about COVID-19 self-tests.

Those who had used a self-test preferred it over testing at a doctor's office or pharmacy. Although our experience may not be generalizable to other populations, partnership with an Area Agency on Aging or senior center is possible in virtually every community. Future research should explore barriers beyond self-test access, such as factors influencing decision-making on when to test and self-efficacy to use the test. Understanding these barriers could inform future efforts to promote self-testing for illnesses other than COVID-19, such as influenza.[13] Advancing self-testing could help older adults to test sooner than if they had to wait for an appointment with a health care provider. Adoption of self-testing behavior by older adults could lead to earlier treatment of respiratory illnesses as well as reduced morbidity and mortality. AJPH

ABOUT THE AUTHORS

Karen E. Skinner and Matthew W. Kreuter are with the Health Communication Research Laboratory, Washington University in St. Louis, St. Louis, MO. Anneliese Stoever and John R. Zakibe are with the St. Louis Area Agency on Aging, St. Louis City Department of Human Services. Carla Evans is with Five Star Center, Inc, St. Louis, MO. John Saunders Jr is with Wesley House Association, St. Louis, MO.

CORRESPONDENCE

Correspondence should be sent to Karen E. Skinner, MPH, WashU School of Public Health, 1 Brookings Dr, MSC 1303-40-03, St. Louis, MO 63130 (e-mail: Karen.Skinner@wustl.edu). Reprints can be ordered at https://www.ajph.org by clicking the "Reprints" link.

PUBLICATION INFORMATION

Full Citation: Skinner KE, Stoever A, Zakibe JR, Evans C, Saunders J Jr, Kreuter MW. A three-year evaluation of COVID-19 vaccination and testing patterns among homebound older adults: implications for future preparedness. *Am J Public Health*. 2026;116(4):427–430.

Acceptance Date: October 14, 2025.

DOI: https://doi.org/10.2105/AJPH.2025.308349

ORCID iDs:
Karen E. Skinner https://orcid.org/0000-0001-6591-2332

Carla Evans https://orcid.org/0009-0009-8561-2332

Matthew W. Kreuter https://orcid.org/0000-0001-7272-0785

CONTRIBUTORS

K. E. Skinner led the project management and analysis, contributed to the project conceptualization, development and implementation, and wrote the initial draft of the article. A. Stoever and J. R. Zakibe contributed to the project conceptualization, development, and implementation, and reviewed/edited the article. C. Evans and J. Saunders Jr assisted with the project coordination, data collection, and interpreting the findings, and reviewed/edited the article. M. W. Kreuter led the conceptualization and development of the project and assisted in writing the article.

ACKNOWLEDGMENTS

This research was funded in part by the National Institutes of Health (Agreement OT2HL158287).

Thank you to our partners at the St. Louis Area Agency on Aging for their support in increasing access to COVID-19 resources to older adults, and to the senior centers who were instrumental in implementing these programs: Five Star Center, Inc. and Wesley House Association. We also thank the Missouri Community Engagement Alliance team members who contributed to this project: City of St. Louis Department of Health: Matifadza Hlatshwayo-Davis and Craig Schmid; Washington University Health Communication Design Studio: Penina Acayo Laker and Christine Watridge.

Note. The views and conclusions contained in this document are those of the authors and should not be interpreted as representing the official policies, either expressed or implied, of the National Institutes of Health.

CONFLICTS OF INTEREST

The authors report no conflicts of interest.

HUMAN PARTICIPANT PROTECTION

The institutional review board (IRB) at Washington University in St. Louis deemed this project not human participant research because the purpose of data collection was program evaluation for the St. Louis Area Agency on Aging (IRB IDs: 202204070, 202305002, 202311210).

REFERENCES

1. Skinner KE, Stoever A, Zakibe JR, Butler T, Kreuter MW. Outreach to low-income homebound older adults to increase access to COVID-19 self-test kits, Missouri, 2022. *Am J Public Health*. 2024; 114(S1):S65–S68. https://doi.org/10.2105/AJPH.2023.307485
2. Centers for Disease Control and Prevention. End of the Federal COVID-19 Public Health Emergency Declaration. Available at: https://archive.cdc.gov/www_cdc_gov/coronavirus/2019-ncov/your-health/end-of-phe.html#:~:text=The%20federal%20COVID%2D19%20PHE,share%20certain%20data%20will%20change. Accessed May 1, 2025.
3. Silk BJ, Scobie HM, Duck WM, et al. COVID-19 surveillance after expiration of the Public Health Emergency Declaration—United States, May 11, 2023. *MMWR Morb Mortal Wkly Rep*. 2023;72(19):523–528. https://doi.org/10.15585/mmwr.mm7219e1
4. Kang SJ, Jung SI. Age-related morbidity and mortality among patients with COVID-19. *Infect Chemother*. 2020;52(2):154–164. https://doi.org/10.3947/ic.2020.52.2.154
5. Fact sheet: the Biden administration to begin distributing at-home, rapid COVID-19 tests to Americans for free [press release]. January 14, 2022. Available at: https://bidenwhitehouse.archives.gov/briefing-room/statements-releases/2022/01/14/fact-sheet-the-biden-administration-to-begin-distributing-at-home-rapid-covid-19-tests-to-americans-for-free/#:~:text=To%20help%20ensure%20Americans%20have,mailed%20directl. Accessed December 8, 2025.
6. Masters JL, Wilkinson LR, Kelly CM, et al. COVID-19 and the vulnerabilities of community-dwelling older adults: findings from a statewide survey of home-delivered meals recipients. *Gerontol Geriatr Med*. 2022;8:23337214221086465. https://doi.org/10.1177/23337214221086465
7. Rager JB, Kirch M, Singer DC, et al. Use of at-home medical tests among older US adults: a nationally representative survey. *Inquiry*. 2024; 61:469580241284168. https://doi.org/10.1177/00469580241284168
8. Bowen DJ, Kreuter M, Spring B, et al. How we design feasibility studies. *Am J Prev Med*. 2009;36(5):452–457. https://doi.org/10.1016/j.amepre.2009.02.002
9. Luisi N, Sullivan PS, Sanchez T, et al. Use of COVIDTests.gov at-home test kits among adults in a national household probability sample—United States, 2022. *MMWR Morb Mortal Wkly Rep*. 2023;72(16):445–449. https://doi.org/10.15585/mmwr.mm7216a6
10. Gavin K. Big gaps seen in home medical test use by older adults. Michigan Medicine, University of Michigan. October 2, 2024. Available at: https://www.michiganmedicine.org/health-lab/big-gaps-seen-home-medical-test-use-older-adults#:~:text=But%20even%20among%20older%20adults,trustworthy%20or%20a%20good%20value. Accessed November 15, 2024.
11. Kanyangarara M, Daguise V, Gual-Gonzalez L, et al. COVID-19 testing practices, preventive behaviors, and factors associated with test positivity: population-based statewide survey study. *JMIR Public Health Surveill*. 2023;9:e34579. https://doi.org/10.2196/34579
12. Burnes D, Henderson CR Jr., Sheppard C, Zhao R, Pillemer K, Lachs MS. Prevalence of financial fraud and scams among older adults in the United States: a systematic review and meta-analysis. *Am J Public Health*. 2017;107(8):e13–e21. https://doi.org/10.2105/AJPH.2017.303821
13. FDA authorizes marketing of first home flu and COVID-19 combination test outside of emergency use authorities [press release]. 2024. Available at: https://www.fda.gov/news-events/press-announcements/fda-authorizes-marketing-first-home-flu-and-covid-19-combination-test-outside-emergency-use. Accessed November 15, 2024.

"The Agenda of the People": A Multisector Partnership for COVID-19 Mitigation in New York City

Brennan Rhodes-Bratton, DrPH, Melody Goodman, PhD, Natasha J. Williams, EdD, MPH, Donna Shelley, MD, MPH, Emily Gill, MPH, Elle Anastasiou, MPH, Jeremy Reiss, MSc, Malcolm A. Punter, EdD, MBA, Andrew Wallach, MD, and Lorna E. Thorpe, PhD, MPH

We evaluated the effectiveness of a community research partnership focused on improving severe acute respiratory syndrome coronavirus 2 (SARS-CoV-2) testing for New York City residents during the pandemic. We employed interviews, a focus group, and a survey to evaluate partnership characteristics, engagement, and future collaboration. Qualitative analysis revealed five core themes: committee identity, collective goals, information sharing, adaptability, and trust. The findings highlight the importance of flexibility, shared goals, diverse representation, open communication, and trust in effective multisector community health partnerships. (*Am J Public Health*. 2026;116(4):431–436. https://doi.org/10.2105/AJPH.2025.308358)

AJPH April 2026, Vol. 116, No. 4

In September 2020, the National Institutes of Health launched the Rapid Acceleration of Diagnostics for Underserved Populations initiative (RADx-UP)[1] to ensure access to severe acute respiratory syndrome coronavirus 2 (SARS-CoV-2) testing and vaccination for all Americans, with a focus on impacted communities.[2–5] RADx-UP emphasized building partnerships grounded in community-based approaches.

STUDY OBJECTIVE

We evaluated the effectiveness of a community steering committee (CSC), established as part of the RADx-UP initiative,[1–5] in improving COVID-19 testing for New York City residents.

RESEARCH QUESTIONS

We aimed to assess whether the multisector partnership achieved its aims to (1) establish sustainable community engagement for SARS-CoV-2 testing, (2) assess inequities in SARS-CoV-2 testing and infection among residents living in New York City Housing Authority (NYCHA) housing, (3) collaborate with residents and community-based organizations (CBOs) to identify testing barriers, and (4) evaluate community-informed strategies to increase testing uptake through a cluster randomized controlled trial. We also explored which elements of the partnership, if any, were unique because of the pandemic and whether partners envisioned future collaborations beyond pandemic response.

PARTICIPANTS, SAMPLE, GEOGRAPHIC LOCATION, SETTING, AND YEAR OF STUDY

Between November 2020 and 2023, representatives from NYCHA, NYC Department of Health and Mental Hygiene, NYC Health + Hospitals, and six CBOs were convened monthly by the NYU Grossman School of Medicine (NYUGSoM) as the CSC to serve historically minoritized neighborhoods with high public housing density and persistently high levels of SARS-CoV-2 infection rates.[6] The CSC included 20 members from nine organizations, who were invited because of the services they provided in the prioritized communities.[7] The CSC was co-led by CBO partners and NYUGSoM staff. Two CBO partners cochaired monthly meetings, and a subgroup met weekly regarding cluster randomized controlled trial logistics and recruitment. Each CBO partner received a subaward from the academic partner to support recruitment, enrollment, and contributions to the CSC. Funds also supported resident navigators, and the CBO partners played a key role in identifying these navigators.

METHODS

We performed a mixed-methods evaluation in 2023 to assess whether and how CSC engagement effectively tailored the project to meet community needs and fostered long-term partnerships. This note presents the qualitative findings; the quantitative component is presented in the Appendix ("Quantitative Analysis" section, available as a supplement to the online version of this article at https://ajph.org).

All CSC members were e-mailed to schedule interviews; those who did not respond after three reminders were considered lost to follow-up (n = 10). The external evaluator conducted interviews (n = 10) in English to discuss the partnership's strengths and challenges. CSC members then participated in a focus group visioning session to collectively reflect on the partnership while envisioning the future of their collaboration. All qualitative data were collected remotely via videoconferencing, recorded, and transcribed with participants' verbal consent.

Three external evaluators conducted thematic analysis,[8] guided by the Patient-Centered Outcomes Research Institute principles.[9] Additional codes emerged through open coding of transcripts (conducted by two evaluators), revealing new themes. All analyses were conducted in English using Atlas.ti (version 24; ATLAS.ti Scientific Software Development GmbH, Berlin, Germany).

TABLE 1— Demographic Characteristics and Organizational Affiliations of Community Steering Committee Members in the RADx-UP SARS-CoV-2 Testing Project for NYCHA Residents

Demographic Characteristics	Mean ±SD or No. (%)
Age, y	48.6 ±0.5
Gender	
Man	4 (40)
Woman	6 (60)
Race/ethnicity	
Black or African American (e.g., Jamaican, Nigerian, Haitian, Ethiopian)	4 (40)
Hispanic or Latino/a (e.g., Puerto Rican, Mexican, Cuban, Salvadoran, Colombian)	2 (20)
White or European (e.g., German, Irish, English, Italian, Polish, French)	3 (30)
Prefer not to say	1 (10)
Affiliation	
Academic institution	1 (10)
Community-based organization	6 (60)
Government agency	2 (20)
NYCHA resident	1 (10)

Note. NYCHA = New York City Housing Authority; RADx-UP = Rapid Acceleration of Diagnostics for Underserved Populations; SARS-CoV-2 = severe acute respiratory syndrome coronavirus 2.

KEY FINDINGS

The CSC includes leaders from CBOs, government, and academia, and NYCHA residents (Table 1). Interviews were conducted with 10 members, and the focus group included nine members. We identified five themes: (1) committee identity, (2) collective goal, (3) information sharing, (4) adaptability, and (5) trust. Box 1 provides descriptions of the themes and subthemes. Several illustrative quotations are presented here.

- Committee identity: The CSC's unique identity was intentionally developed by centering its members' diverse expertise and equitable participation. "It's about making sure the partners are involved in the process and building out a process that is inclusive. From agenda design to program implementation and report-back facilitation, the partners led the meetings to be flexible to the coalition's needs" (CSC member 1).
- Collective goal: The shared commitment to ending health inequities related to SARS-CoV-2 unified the partnership, fostered purpose, and initiated collaboration among the individuals representing the multisectoral partners. The state of emergency brought together this unique group of people with the sole purpose of helping their community. CSC member 2 emphasized, "We were all from different walks of life; different educational backgrounds; different financial backgrounds. And we understood that we were not there for our agenda, but we were there for the agenda of the people."
- Information sharing: "The information they provided helped me be a better TA [tenant association] president. . . . I was more informed . . . and could give [my residents] facts while . . . so much misinformation spread that people didn't know what to believe. . . . as their elected leader, I [gave] them accurate information, and we were able to survive and move forward" (CSC member 3). The information shared between CSC members

BOX 1— Thematic Framework of the RADx-UP Community Steering Committee: A Qualitative Analysis of Partnership Dynamics, Trust, and Adaptive Strategies in Addressing SARS-CoV-2 Inequities Among NYCHA Residents

Core Themes	Subtheme	Definitions
Adaptability: The ability for the CSC to change and meet the needs of the CSC and their constituents	Digital tools	Videoconferencing, webinars, etc.
	Shifting focus to meet community needs	Shifting focus of information disseminated to meet community needs
	Language	Language as a barrier or facilitator of community engagement Positive: Example of how language was a facilitator of community engagement Negative: Example of how language was a barrier of community engagement
	Evolving membership	CSC members came into the project at different times
	Challenge	Example of issue, situation, or circumstance that was a barrier or limitation to achieving the RADx-UP goals
	Implement feedback	Examples of how feedback was incorporated into changes in the RADx-UP research activities or other activities related to SARS-CoV-2 in CSC members' respective organizations
Collective goal: The goal to end health inequities associated with SARS-CoV-2	Goal	Perception of RADx intention and desired outcomes
	Success	Description of the successes and outcomes of the partnership or project
	Commitment	Commitment to higher goals to alleviate health inequities among NYCHA residents; often an example of commitment that benefitted CSC and their constituents
	COVID-19–related issues	SARS-CoV-2–related in terms of the testing, vaccines, and the specific challenges unique to the pandemic
	Fear	Fear of SARS-CoV-2 outcomes, health concerns
	Collaboration	Description of collaboration, teamwork, sharing of resources, ideas, and information between organizations in RADx meetings or outside
	Future collaboration	Desire or plans for future collaborations between CSC members, or CSC members and NYU
Committee identity: The values, beliefs, and actions of the individual CSC members that collectively join to develop the identity of the CSC as its one entity	Sector	Mention of the type of sector the organization represents: government, CBO, academia, hospital, etc.
	Mission statement	Participant's description of their organization's mission statement
	Power	The amount of authority and input in the decision-making process
	Goals (organizational goal)	Organizational intention and perceived desired outcome of RADx
	Participation	Duration and level of participation in RADx project Invited: Clear invitation from NYU research team to join the partnership Recruited: Told to join the partnership from within CBO leadership
	Research activities	Description of activities that pertain to specific research-related aspects of the project
	Respect	Recognizing the worth of CSC members and admiring each other's expertise
	Competition	Competition between CSC organizations to meet research goals
	Funding	Funding support for RADx members which facilitated the partnership
	Community building of CSC	Supportive space and a sense of community was built between CSC members
	Expectations	Description of CSC's members' expectations of their experience on CSC

Continued

BOX 1— Continued

Core Themes	Subtheme	Definitions
Information sharing: Bidirectional dissemination of information (i.e., general information about SARS-CoV-2, the effects of prevention interventions, effective outreach strategies, and the effects of treatments like vaccination) between CSC members to achieve the goal of the partnership	Capacity building	Skills gained from the partnership
	Engagement strategies	Outreach strategies to engage and communicate with NYCHA residents
	Information as incentive	Bidirectional information sharing regarding SARS-CoV-2 updates from H+H and peer-to-peer learning as a primary motivation for meeting attendance
	Expertise	Highlighting skill or knowledge in a particular field that is relevant to the success of project
	Meeting dynamics	Description of communication style, method of meeting, agendas, or other information shared in RADx meetings
Trust: The activities and beliefs that contribute to building trust (within CSC and with community)	Trust	Trust or mistrust between communities, organizations, or government or health fields Positive: Example of how trust was built between CSC members or with community residents Negative: Examples of the presence of mistrust
	Misinformation	Changes in information throughout SARS-CoV-2 that were not effectively communicated or misinformation spread
	Appreciation	Expression of gratitude for the work, goal, or commitment of CSC members
	Community perception	Description of the community or neighborhood's perception of RADx or the organization

Note. CBO = community-based organization; CSC = community steering committee; H+H = New York City Health + Hospitals; NYCHA = New York City Housing Authority; NYU = New York University; RADx-UP = Rapid Acceleration of Diagnostics for Underserved Populations; SARS-CoV-2 = severe acute respiratory coronavirus 2.

was multifaceted and nuanced. Topics included community engagement strategies, community concerns and needs, community resources, SARS-CoV-2 infection prevalence, prevention strategies, and medical information.

- Adaptability: The partnership's focus shifted to meet community needs. This was evident in evolving outreach activities, shifting from relying solely on resident navigators for recruitment to working directly with CBOs. For example, "based on concerns about getting infected while there [SARS-CoV-2 testing site], we created site lines for people who had symptoms and lines for people who didn't, people who just wanted to get tested" (CSC member 4). This change significantly enhanced residents' sense of safety and trust.
- Trust: Effective trust-building included a commitment to follow through and open communication. However, tackling community mistrust, particularly regarding SARS-CoV-2 information, continued to pose challenges. "Some things I heard while in the street were just downright ridiculous . . . the best way to combat that is not to make them feel like they're foolish because they don't understand, but to provide enough information to dispel their fears" (CSC member 5). Because of these efforts, "They [the residents] welcome the vans to vaccinate us. They welcome the health department and everyone who came to educate us and assist us with being well. That couldn't have happened without [the PIs] and the steering committee, which is invaluable" (CSC member 3).

Feedback on the CSC was generally positive, but it faced challenges influenced by circumstances within their organizations, personal lives, and national discourse. Establishing the CSC during a public health emergency created significant hurdles. The fear and trauma from SARS-CoV-2 devastated many NYC neighborhoods[10,11] and impacted CSC members' lives. These issues may have limited some members' participation in the project. The sociopolitical context (including misinformation, changing guidelines, and collective fear), language barriers, and resource shortages were obstacles. CSC member 4 said, "I'm going to say out loud the answer to everything: money, right? We did not have endless funds. It would have been nice to have more money to purchase even more [SARS-CoV-2 test kits] or hire even more community advocates to go door to door." Therefore, effective outreach during a pandemic depended on public discourse, policy, and financial support. Finally, a strong desire to continue collaborating existed, but it could not be actualized without funding. Still, several members pursued new projects together.

EVALUATION, TRANSFERABILITY, AND ADVERSE EFFECTS

With this study, we aimed to evaluate the CSC partnership's strengths, weaknesses, and future using the SARS-CoV-2 pandemic as a learning opportunity. The mixed-methods approach offered a multifaceted understanding, where the quantitative results confirmed that the collaboration was highly effective, with high engagement, and the qualitative findings identified key elements like adaptability, shared purpose, strong identity, effective sharing, and trust. This provided a framework for understanding the partnership's dynamics and addressed the study's core questions about the effectiveness of this multisectoral collaboration.

The study's findings are subject to several limitations, including small sample size. The 10 survey respondents, 10 interview participants, and 12 visioning session attendees, while valuable, were not necessarily the same individuals, which complicated data triangulation. The partnership's natural evolution, including a shifting research focus and emphasis on socially isolated adults, also led to a more specialized subset of members over time. Attrition was compounded by the public's waning interest in SARS-CoV-2 as the pandemic became endemic. In addition, conducting the interviews only at the end may not have fully captured partnership dynamics during the pandemic's peak or when the CSC was most active.

The insights gained may not fully represent the experiences of other multisector partnerships or public housing communities. Furthermore, a self-selection bias may be present, as individuals who volunteer for research are often highly motivated and engaged, potentially skewing the results. Despite these limitations, the rich qualitative data provide a valuable, in-depth understanding of the CSC partnership's dynamics and offer a crucial framework for guiding future collaborations.

SCALABILITY

The CSC's core strategies—such as leveraging established CBO relationships, collaborating with public health agencies, and countering misinformation—closely aligned with national trends, validating the feasibility of the model despite the challenges of virtual engagement. Although the study was limited by its small sample size and specific geographic focus, the lessons learned regarding adaptive community building and partnership dynamics are scalable and applicable to future multisector public health collaborations.[12–17]

PUBLIC HEALTH SIGNIFICANCE

The experiences of the CSC partnership offer crucial lessons for strengthening community-based responses to future public health crises. By evaluating the collaboration's successes and challenges, we can develop a more robust framework for future partnerships.

The CSC's effectiveness leveraged NYUGSoM's preexisting relationships with CBOs by prioritizing and continuously investing in engagement. This approach was instrumental in fostering a trusted source of information and ensuring diverse representation to combat misinformation. The partnership also demonstrated the importance of an adaptable framework, which allows quick strategic shifts to maintain relevance.

Although, the study also highlighted key challenges. While virtual tools proved useful, they could not fully replace the value of in-person interaction. A hybrid approach is necessary for long-term engagement. The decline in participation as the pandemic became endemic underscores the need to address the challenge of sustaining momentum. Lastly, the evaluation highlighted the benefit of integrating qualitative assessments throughout a partnership's lifecycle, rather than only at the end, to provide a more dynamic understanding of its evolution and effectiveness. AJPH

ABOUT THE AUTHORS

Brennan Rhodes-Bratton, Melody Goodman, and Donna Shelley are with the School of Global Public Health at New York University, New York, NY. Jeremy Reiss is with Henry Street Settlement, New York, NY. Malcolm Punter is with the Harlem Congregations for Community Improvement, New York, NY. Andrew Wallach is with NYC Health + Hospitals, New York, NY. Emily Gill, Elle Anastasiou, Natasha Williams, and Lorna Thorpe are with the New York University Grossman School of Medicine's Department of Population Health, New York, NY.

CORRESPONDENCE

Correspondence should be sent to Brennan Rhodes-Bratton, 708 Broadway, 9th Floor, New York, NY 10003 (e-mail: br2451@nyu.edu). Reprints can be ordered at https://www.ajph.org by clicking the "Reprints" link.

PUBLICATION INFORMATION

Full Citation: Rhodes-Bratton B, Goodman M, Williams NJ, et al. "The agenda of the people": a multisector partnership for COVID-19 mitigation in New York City. *Am J Public Health*. 2026;116(4): 431–436.

Acceptance Date: October 30, 2025.

DOI: https://doi.org/10.2105/AJPH.2025.308358

ORCID iDs:

Brennan Rhodes-Bratton https://orcid.org/0000-0003-4901-262X

Melody Goodman https://orcid.org/0000-0001-8932-624X

Emily Gill https://orcid.org/0000-0003-1893-8278

CONTRIBUTORS

B. Rhodes-Bratton, M. Goodman, and N. Williams conceptualized and designed the study. B. Rhodes-Bratton was responsible for data collection and received substantial assistance from E. Gill. B. Rhodes-Bratton conducted the analyses and drafted the initial article. All authors contributed to interpreting the findings, critically revised the article for intellectual content, and approved the final version for submission.

ACKNOWLEDGMENTS

We would like to acknowledge the community partners and the New York City residents served by the National Institutes of Health's Rapid Acceleration of Diagnostics for Underserved Populations New York City Housing Authority initiative. Thank you, Tess Cottrell, for your assistance in the evaluation.

CONFLICTS OF INTEREST

All authors declare no competing interests.

HUMAN PARTICIPANT PROTECTION

The study was approved by the New York University Grossman School of Medicine institutional review board.

REFERENCES

1. Tromberg BJ, Schwetz TA, Pérez-Stable EJ, et al. Rapid scaling up of Covid-19 diagnostic testing in the United States—the NIH RADx Initiative. *N Engl J Med.* 2020;383(11):1071–1077. https://doi.org/10.1056/NEJMsr2022263
2. Abedi V, Olulana O, Avula V, et al. Racial, economic, and health inequality and COVID-19 infection in the United States. *J Racial Ethn Health Disparities.* 2021;8(3):732–742. https://doi.org/10.1007/s40615-020-00833-4
3. Clouston SA, Natale G, Link BG. Socioeconomic inequalities in the spread of coronavirus-19 in the United States: a examination of the emergence of social inequalities. *Soc Sci Med.* 2021;268:113554. https://doi.org/10.1016/j.socscimed.2020.113554
4. Singu S, Acharya A, Challagundla K, Byrareddy SN. Impact of social determinants of health on the emerging COVID-19 pandemic in the United States. *Front Public Health.* 2020;8:406. https://doi.org/10.3389/fpubh.2020.00406
5. Van Dorn A, Cooney RE, Sabin ML. COVID-19 exacerbating inequalities in the US. *Lancet.* 2020;395(10232):1243–1244. https://doi.org/10.1016/S0140-6736(20)30893-X
6. Williams NJ, Gill E, Punter MA, et al. Rapid community engagement in response to SARS-CoV-2 funding opportunities: New York City, 2020–2021. *Am J Public Health.* 2022;112(suppl 9):S904–S908. https://doi.org/10.2105/AJPH.2022.307072
7. Gill E, Hall Z, Thorpe LE, et al. COVID-19 testing experiences and attitudes among young adults and socially isolated older adults living in public housing, New York City (2022). *Front Public Health.* 2025;13:1484473. https://doi.org/10.3389/fpubh.2025.1484473
8. Braun V, Clarke V. One size fits all? What counts as quality practice in (reflexive) thematic analysis? *Qual Res Psychol.* 2021;18(3):328–352. https://doi.org/10.1080/14780887.2020.1769238
9. Forsythe LP, Carman KL, Szydlowski V, et al. Patient engagement in research: early findings from the Patient-Centered Outcomes Research Institute. *Health Aff (Millwood).* 2019;38(3):359–367. https://doi.org/10.1377/hlthaff.2018.05067
10. Thompson CN, Baumgartner J, Pichardo C, et al. COVID-19 outbreak—New York City, February 29–June 1, 2020. *MMWR Morb Mortal Wkly Rep.* 2020;69(46):1725–1729. https://doi.org/10.15585/mmwr.mm6946a2
11. Wadhera RK, Wadhera P, Gaba P, et al. Variation in COVID-19 hospitalizations and deaths across New York City boroughs. *JAMA.* 2020;323(21):2192–2195. https://doi.org/10.1001/jama.2020.7197
12. Marsh EE, Kappelman MD, Kost RG, et al. Community engagement during COVID: a field report from seven CTSAs. *J Clin Transl Sci.* 2021;5(1):e104. https://doi.org/10.1017/cts.2021.785
13. Eder MM, Millay TA, Cottler LB. A compendium of community engagement responses to the COVID-19 pandemic. *J Clin Transl Sci.* 2021;5(1):e133. https://doi.org/10.1017/cts.2021.800
14. Afolabi A, Ilesanmi O. Community engagement for COVID-19 prevention and control: a systematic review. *Public Health Toxicol.* 2022;2(2):1–17. https://doi.org/10.18332/pht/149230
15. Burgess RA, Osborne RH, Yongabi KA, et al. The COVID-19 vaccines rush: participatory community engagement matters more than ever. *Lancet.* 2021;397(10268):8–10. https://doi.org/10.1016/S0140-6736(20)32642-8
16. Nutbeam D. The vital role of meaningful community engagement in responding to the COVID-19 pandemic. *Public Health Res Pract.* 2021;31(1):3112101. https://doi.org/10.17061/phrp3112101
17. Goodman MS, Ackermann N, Bowen DJ, Thompson V. Content validation of a quantitative stakeholder engagement measure. *J Community Psychol.* 2019;47(8):1937–1951. https://doi.org/10.1002/jcop.22239

Qualitative Evaluation of Health Department Measles Response Practices: Lessons Learned From 11 US Jurisdictions, March–October 2024

Haley F. Wellham, MPH, Sanjana Ravi, PhD, MPH, Eric S. Toner, MD, Alanna S. Fogarty, MPH, MSc, Sarah Gillani, MPH, Elizabeth A. Campbell, PhD, MS, MPH, Sutyajeet Soneja, PhD, and Caitlin M. Rivers, PhD, MPH

We conducted a qualitative evaluation of health department measles response practices from March to October 2024. Focus group sessions with public health officials from 11 jurisdictions revealed that despite resource constraints and evolving challenges, health departments enhanced surveillance and response capabilities by prioritizing community engagement, data modernization, and continuous quality improvement. Key lessons include the importance of real-time data tracking, the value of established protocols and training, and the need for standardized metrics to evaluate response effectiveness across jurisdictions. (*Am J Public Health*. 2026;116(4):437–442. https://doi.org/10.2105/AJPH.2025.308392)

AJPH April 2026, Vol. 116, No. 4

Measles has emerged as an urgent public health issue around the globe, including in the United States.[1] By July 2025, US measles cases exceeded the annual total for any year since the virus was declared eliminated in 2000.[2] As of November, 1753 cases have been confirmed and three deaths reported,[2] the first measles fatalities in the United States in a decade.[3] National vaccination rates declined during COVID-19 and have not rebounded to the 95% coverage needed to prevent community transmission,[4] with only 5% of states reporting vaccination coverage rates of 95% or more,[2] leaving the nation vulnerable to additional measles outbreaks.

STUDY OBJECTIVE

With a single measles case capable of generating more than a hundred contacts[5] and 12 to 18 secondary cases,[6] the efficiency of a health department to detect and respond to measles is critical. To understand current practices and identify opportunities for improvement, we conducted a qualitative evaluation of measles preparedness and response in US health departments. This evaluation examines how 11 jurisdictions approached measles surveillance, response coordination, and performance evaluation, focusing on challenges, strengths, and lessons learned.

RESEARCH QUESTIONS

This evaluation was conducted by the Center for Outbreak Response Innovation (CORI)[7] at the Johns Hopkins Bloomberg School of Public Health. CORI developed three primary research questions to explore health department measles response practices: (1) How do health departments adapt their response strategies and evaluation practices to improve outbreak preparedness and management? (2) What lessons can benefit other jurisdictions implementing outbreak response improvements? (3) What systemic needs remain to improve the national environment for health departments to respond to measles more effectively and efficiently?

PARTICIPANTS, SAMPLE, GEOGRAPHIC LOCATION, SETTING, AND YEAR OF STUDY

From March to October 2024, we conducted focus groups with public health officials from 11 state and local health departments across the United States, representing diverse geographic regions, public health governance, and population sizes (Table 1). Participants included medical directors, epidemiologists, program managers, emergency preparedness coordinators and planners, communicable disease nurses, and equity officers from state, city, and county health departments (Tables A and B, available as supplements to the online version of this article at https://ajph.org). The sample included both urban and rural jurisdictions. Eight out of the 11 health departments interviewed responded to measles (73%) in the previous 12 calendar months, which included managing cases, or cases and contacts. Two out of the three health departments were revisiting measles preparedness because of cases in nearby jurisdictions.

TABLE 1— Sample Characteristics of the 11 Participating Health Departments: United States, 2024

Characteristics and Category	Frequency (%)
HHS region	
1	0
2	0
3	3 (27)
4	2 (18)
5	3 (27)
6	0
7	0
8	0
9	2 (18)
10	1 (9)
Jurisdiction	
State	3 (27)
Tribal	0
Territorial	0
Regional	0
County	6 (54)
City	2 (18)
Public health governance[a]	
Centralized or largely centralized	1 (9)
Shared or largely shared	2 (18)
Mixed	2 (18)
Decentralized or largely decentralized	6 (54)
Size of population served[b]	
100 000–499 999	2 (18)
500 000–899 999	3 (27)
900 000–1 299 999	1 (9)
1 300 000–1 699 999	2 (18)
≥ 1 700 000	3 (27)

Note. HHS = US Department of Health and Human Services.
[a]Public health governance is reported at the state level for all participants because of the limited accessibility of public health governance descriptions for local and city health departments. Note: Centralized or largely centralized states are ones in which local health units are primarily led by the employees of the state and the state retains fiscal authority. In shared or largely shared states, local health units may be led by employees of the state or local government. If they are led by state employees, then local government has the authority to make fiscal decisions or issue public health orders. In mixed systems, some local health units are led by employees of the state and some are led by employees of the local government. In decentralized or largely decentralized jurisdictions, local health units are primarily led by the employees of the local governments and the local governments retain authority of most fiscal decisions.[8]
[b]The size of the population served by participating health departments is reported for the jurisdictions served based on US Census Bureau population estimates as of July 1, 2024.[9]

METHODS

To develop the interview guide, staff with three or more years of experience in epidemiology and emergency response conducted an informal scan through Google and Google Scholar with search terms including "measles response," "measles outbreak response," and "measles process improvement," which resulted in a review of publications, health department websites, and news articles. Questions were organized into a semistructured outline, and conversations were tailored to individual agencies' priorities and experiences.

Participants were recruited using a convenience sampling strategy[10] through a call to action for health departments advertised in a routine, public-facing newsletter with more than 40 000 subscribers composed of health department officials that include epidemiologists and decision-makers, as well as the public.[8] From this outreach, five health departments volunteered to participate. Supplemental targeted outreach was conducted to recruit experienced public health contacts through personal contacts and e-mails to jurisdictions reporting a measles outbreak in 2024. From this targeted outreach, six of the nine jurisdictions volunteered. In total, 11 health departments elected to participate. At least one focus group session was conducted for each health department. Three additional focus group sessions were conducted with one large participating health department to allow participation across the vaccine-preventable, communicable disease, and public health preparedness and response offices. In total, 14 sessions were held with 63 participants. Focus groups were conducted on a not-for-attribution, and all participants consented to recording.

Five coders (H. F. W., C. M. R., A. S. F., E. A. T., and S. R.) conducted thematic coding of transcripts to identify the key public health activities, operational challenges, and successes that they experienced or expected to experience when managing measles. Codes were initially derived based on a priori knowledge from an informal literature review, and additional codes were added iteratively to the framework as emergent themes were identified from the interview transcripts. Each transcript was coded by at least two staff. Measures of interrater agreement were not appropriate for this analysis, given the collaborative methods utilized for analysis.[9] Results were shared with all focus group participants for feedback, and no themes were modified or added.

KEY FINDINGS

Our analysis revealed three key findings: (1) real-time data tracking systems are essential for effective response coordination and quality improvement, (2) established protocols and regular training were foundational to successful outbreak responses, and (3) standardized metrics are critically needed but inconsistently implemented across jurisdictions (Box 1).

Real-Time Data Tracking Systems

Across jurisdiction types, health departments with robust real-time data tracking capabilities reported superior response coordination and continuous improvement. Departments emphasized the value of automated systems for monitoring data quality and identifying areas for improvement. Real-time tracking tools proved valuable for task management and coordination during active responses, helping departments manage the increased communication and coordination demands. In jurisdictions with resource limitations, Excel (Microsoft, Redmond, WA) was used to support real-time data tracking; however, some jurisdictions reported using more advanced tools, such as Research Electronic Data Capture (REDCap; Vanderbilt University, Nashville, TN), to standardize and streamline tasks such as symptom monitoring by automating daily, text-based surveys. Departments also highlighted ongoing challenges with data system integration and the administrative burden of maintaining data quality across multiple platforms, particularly when referring to integrating case investigation notes with state-wide surveillance systems.

Established Protocols and Training

Across jurisdiction types, established protocols and regular training emerged as fundamental infrastructure for effective response. Health departments confident in their ability to respond effectively emphasized their reliance on standard operating procedures, particularly when responding to infrequent events like measles outbreaks. Participants stressed the importance of maintaining readiness through regular engagement with protocols and training, recognizing that skills and familiarity diminish without practice, and stated that exercises are especially important with staff turnover.

Standardized Metrics for Response Evaluation

All health departments expressed significant need for standardized metrics but demonstrated inconsistent implementation across jurisdictions, with one state (Health Department B) and one county (Health Department A) testing a formal framework, while others reported ad hoc data collection. Communication gaps about data needs and expectations emerged as a significant challenge, with departments often learning about required metrics only after responses were complete. Two jurisdictions reported testing standardized metrics like the 7-1-7 target,[11] demonstrating growing recognition of the value of consistent performance measurement. However, both departments used these metrics retroactively rather than during an active response and noted significant challenges in defining and operationalizing key metrics, especially around temporal measurements central to response evaluation. Some departments were beginning to track resource utilization as a key performance indicator, recognizing the importance of understanding the true cost and burden of outbreak responses.

EVALUATION, TRANSFERABILITY, AND ADVERSE EFFECTS

Our findings may be applicable in other US public health departments. It is important to view measles preparedness

BOX 1— Key Findings Themes and Supporting Quotations: Qualitative Evaluation of Health Department Measles Response Practices, United States, 2024

Theme	Subtheme	Supporting Quotations
Real-time data tracking systems	Automated data quality monitoring	"We have some automated processes that our analytics and informatics team have been doing around data quality missingness . . . [we have been] thinking about ways that we can monitor this over time, [for example,] whether the number of errors are decreasing, or if it is shifting to something else." –Health Department A
	Task management and coordination	"We found that having spreadsheet tracking 'what tasks need to be done today? Who is doing it?' and getting the status on that in a line list was very helpful, because through the e-mails you could get on a regular day anywhere from 20–100 e-mails. And then, when we go into an incident command that can easily increase the number of e-mails and questions that we are getting from multiple groups." –Health Department A
	REDCap comprehensive data collection	"REDCap is for our own personal data tracking and is very comprehensive. We have built it out to capture any piece of data that we could ever imagine being asked for, we should easily be able to pull that straight from REDCap—even if there is a delay in getting cases entered into the state system." –Health Department B
	REDCap integration with text surveys	"We are using Twilio . . . it has the capability to send out text-based surveys . . . for our purpose we plan on sending out daily surveys for symptom monitoring to our exposed contacts. . . . Twilio is a third-party site that integrates with REDCap." –Health Department B
	REDCap dashboards and prioritization	"We had 9 different dashboards, and the [contact tracing] staff knew when they came in that day they needed to start with dashboard one, complete that, and then go to 2, 3 all the way down to 9 . . . we were able to set up dashboards within the system to show specifically people that were X number of days out from their exposure, and had not completed a survey that day and were unvaccinated or unknown vaccination status." –Health Department C
	REDCap contact list management	"We were able to import contact lists . . . [the provider office with the source case] was able to send us lists of everyone that was in the waiting room during the same time as another kid and as a measles case, and we were able to import those directly into REDCap to save some of the data entry burden on our side." –Health Department C
	REDCap passive monitoring	"We were able to do some passive monitoring, using REDCap . . . REDCap also allowed us to send out e-mails to contacts . . . while we had large [numbers of] staff on the phone, the folks that [elected to be e-mailed] did not need to be called so it helped to trim that list." –Health Department C
	Data system integration challenges	"The things that we more regularly track are around completeness of data, because we have two data systems within our local and the state database. We have to do regular quarterly reconciliation between these data systems." –Health Department A
Established protocols and training	Standard operating procedures (SOPs)	"We love our SOPs, especially if it is something that we have not seen in a while or seen before. So, I know we are revisiting our measles SOP." –Health Department D
	Maintaining readiness	"You feel pretty rusty when you have to do the next one, so we really try to plug [exercises] in wherever we can. So certainly, [we do these] for planned events as well as responses." –Health Department D
	REDCap training and preparedness	"We actually have scheduled a training on the [measles] REDCap project here in just a couple of weeks so that we can train people all across the state on how to use it. . . . We plan to record that training as well to make it available for a just in time training." –Health Department B
	Provider and laboratory relationships	"We have a very good relationship with one of the labs. The infection control and the lab director both called and said, 'I am sending a sample again.'" –Health Department E
	Real-time improvement processes	"We have just applied [process improvement] to any response that we ever do, because you start improving as soon as you start responding. Capturing that [information] from the very beginning is the only change we made. Instead of waiting till the end, or until a hot wash, you just start capturing it early, so you can hit the choke points before they become major choke points." –Health Department F

Continued

BOX 1— Continued

Theme	Subtheme	Supporting Quotations
Standardized metrics for response evaluation	Need for standard metrics	"It would be nice to have some kind of standard metrics that you know people find useful, or that are evaluated at the end of those responses." –Health Department F
	Communication gaps	"'I had no idea you ever needed that' . . . [this is something that we hear] all the way from the top, back down to the local level and vice versa. Sharing why the data are important at [every] level so that everybody understands why they are gathering it, that would be very helpful." –Health Department F
	Implementation of 7-1-7 metrics	"We are implementing the 7-1-7 metric across multiple outbreaks in [the state]. So, we collect some summary data on all kinds of outbreaks. . . . And we are implementing some additional measures into our project that tracks outbreak response to look at that 7-1-7 metric specifically." –Health Department B
	Operationalization challenges	"We have talked a lot about how we want to define time to detection and then also time to public health response, to actually get at those, the sevens on either end of the 7-1-7 . . . that is something we are working on." –Health Department B
	Resource utilization tracking	"We have asked people to code to a specific combo code for the hours that they spent on the measles response, understanding that it [still] underestimates the total amount of financial cost to the department." –Health Department A

Note. REDCap = Research Electronic Data Capture.

and response with a capability-based approach, which can inform both a standard and flexible process for preventing large-scale outbreaks. Future work should engage state, local, tribal, and territorial health departments in US Department of Health and Human Services regions 1, 2, 6, 7, and 8, whose perspectives were not represented in the convenience sample but are essential to understanding national implications.

SCALABILITY

Despite limitations, study findings may suggest clear targets for large-scale interventions, including technical assistance programs for automated data systems, national training curricula for measles response protocols, and standardized evaluation frameworks. Interview methodology could be adapted for structured data collection from a larger, nationally representative sample of health departments to quantify the prevalence of different response practices and establish baseline metrics for improvement initiatives.

PUBLIC HEALTH SIGNIFICANCE

The results of this evaluation have critical importance for public health practice for local, state, and national health agencies given the ongoing measles crisis.[2] At the state and local level, our findings provide health departments with strategies and tools to improve their outbreak response capabilities through three actionable areas: implementing real-time data tracking systems, strengthening protocols and training programs, and adopting standardized evaluation metrics. The findings from this work have resulted in the compilation of a publicly available resource repository for measles outbreak response, which includes surveillance and communication templates and resources for clinicians, as well as plans, workflows, and tabletop exercises tested by frontline responders.[12] These results and resources are immediately applicable for health departments currently preparing for or responding to outbreaks.

More broadly, our results highlight the variability in measles outbreak preparedness reported by state and local health departments, exposing a fundamental gap in public health emergency preparedness. To address this gap, we recommend the US Centers for Disease Control and Prevention, as well as other national and regional entities, lead improvements in outbreak response infrastructure that incorporate lessons learned from state and local health departments. Given the current risk of the United States losing measles elimination status, these findings offer a roadmap for system-wide improvements that could help prevent future large-scale outbreaks and maintain the country's elimination status through more effective and efficient response capabilities. AJPH

ABOUT THE AUTHORS

Haley F. Wellham, Sanjana Ravi, Eric S. Toner, Alanna S. Fogarty, Sarah Gillani, Elizabeth A. Campbell, Sutyajeet Soneja, and Caitlin M. Rivers are with the Johns Hopkins Bloomberg School of Public Health Center for Outbreak Response Innovation and the Johns Hopkins Bloomberg School of Public Health Center for Health Security, Baltimore, MD.

CORRESPONDENCE

Correspondence should be sent to Haley Wellham, Johns Hopkins Center for Outbreak Response Innovation, 700 E Pratt St, Suite 900, Baltimore, MD 21202 (e-mail: hfarrie1@jh.edu). Reprints can be ordered at https://www.ajph.org by clicking the "Reprints" link.

PUBLICATION INFORMATION

Full Citation: Wellham HF, Ravi S, Toner ES, et al. Qualitative evaluation of health department measles response practices: lessons learned from 11 US jurisdictions, March–October 2024. *Am J Public Health*. 2026;116(4):437–442.

Acceptance Date: December 8, 2025.

DOI: https://doi.org/10.2105/AJPH.2025.308392

ORCID iDs:

Haley F. Wellham https://orcid.org/0009-0001-8380-7410

Eric S. Toner https://orcid.org/0000-0001-5292-9450

Alanna S. Fogarty https://orcid.org/0009-0009-2366-5340

Elizabeth A. Campbell https://orcid.org/0000-0002-4665-3117

Sutyajeet Soneja https://orcid.org/0000-0003-4914-2432

CONTRIBUTORS

C. M. Rivers, E. S. Toner, S. Ravi, H. F. Wellham, and A. S. Fogarty contributed substantially to the study's conceptualization, interpretation of the data, and writing of the article. H. F. Wellham, C. M. Rivers, E. S. Toner, S. Soneja, and A. S. Fogarty collected and analyzed the data. H. F. Wellham, C. M. Rivers, E. S. Toner, A. S. Fogarty, S. Gillani, E. A. Campbell, and S. Soneja significantly contributed to writing drafts of the article and interpretation of the data. C. M. Rivers obtained the funding for this project. All authors reviewed and approved the final version of the article.

ACKNOWLEDGMENTS

This analysis was supported by the US Centers for Disease Control and Prevention (CDC; cooperative agreement NU38FT000004).

The authors acknowledge our state and local health department partners for inspiring this research. We would like to thank the Alameda County Health Department, Chester County Health Department, Los Angeles County Department of Public Health, Marathon County Health Department, Public Health–Dayton and Montgomery, Public Health–Seattle and King County, South Carolina Department of Health, Tennessee Department of Health, and additional state and local health departments that remain anonymous, for supporting this initiative. The research team would like to acknowledge the CDC Insight Net Program for supporting this work.

Note. The funders had no input or oversight over the conduct of this work.

CONFLICTS OF INTEREST

C. M. Rivers has received personal payments for professional writing, including a trade book, newsletter, and essays in major media outlets.

HUMAN PARTICIPANT PROTECTION

The Johns Hopkins Bloomberg School of Public Health institutional review board determined this evaluation did not constitute human participant research and was therefore classified as exempt.

REFERENCES

1. World Health Organization. Measles – Region of the Americas. April 28, 2025. Available at: https://www.who.int/emergencies/disease-outbreak-news/item/2025-DON565. Accessed August 1, 2025.
2. Centers for Disease Control and Prevention. Measles cases and outbreaks. July 9, 2025. Available at: https://www.cdc.gov/measles/data-research/index.html. Accessed July 11, 2025.
3. Branswell H. US measles cases break 33-year record, "kind of a new normal." STAT. July 9, 2025. Available at: https://www.statnews.com/2025/07/09/measles-america-breaks-33-year-record-anti-vaccine-sentiment-key-factor-behind-outbreaks. Accessed July 11, 2025.
4. Seither R, Yusuf OB, Dramann D, et al. Coverage with selected vaccines and exemption rates among children in kindergarten—United States, 2023–24 school year. *MMWR Morb Mortal Wkly Rep*. 2024;73(41):925–932. https://doi.org/10.15585/mmwr.mm7341a3
5. Saldanha Resendes D, Tomás A, Pinção Cardoso M, et al. Contact tracing management of a measles case in a paediatric hospital: experience of the local public health unit, Portugal, January 2024. *Euro Surveill.* 2024;29(17):240022. https://doi.org/10.2807/1560-7917.ES.2024.29.17.240022
6. Guerra FM, Bolotin S, Lim G, et al. The basic reproduction number (R0) of measles: a systematic review. *Lancet Infect Dis.* 2017;17(12):e420–e428. https://doi.org/10.1016/S1473-3099(17)30307-9
7. Center for Outbreak Response Innovation. Johns Hopkins University's Bloomberg School of Public Health. Available at: https://cori.centerforhealthsecurity.org. Accessed July 12, 2025.
8. Rivers C. Force of infection. Substack. November 2, 2025. Available at: https://caitlinrivers.substack.com. Accessed November 15, 2025.
9. Byrne D. A worked example of Braun and Clarke's approach to reflexive thematic analysis. *Qual Quant.* 2022;56(3):1391–1412. https://doi.org/10.1007/s11135-021-01182-y
10. Convenience sampling—an overview. ScienceDirect. Available at: https://www.sciencedirect.com/topics/computer-science/convenience-sampling. Accessed June 12, 2025.
11. Frieden TR, Lee CT, Bochner AF, Buissonnière M, McClelland A. 7-1-7: an organising principle, target, and accountability metric to make the world safer from pandemics. *Lancet.* 2021;398(10300):638–640. https://doi.org/10.1016/S0140-6736(21)01250-2
12. Center for Outbreak Response Innovation. Measles outbreak response. Available at: https://cori.centerforhealthsecurity.org/resources/measles-outbreak-response. Accessed November 5, 2025.

Curriculum Approaches to Strengthen Public Health–Primary Care Collaboration: Northwest Leadership Institute, 2020–2024

Jennifer G. Jones-Vanderleest, MD, MSPH, Antoinette Angulo, MPH, and Janelle Z. Martelino, RN, PhD, MN

We describe a novel curriculum designed to build capacity for public health and primary care collaboration. Since the Northwest Public Health & Primary Care Leadership Institute began in 2020, 119 participants have completed the seven-month hybrid curriculum. Application of knowledge and skills learned to workplace or community projects was reported by 84% of participants. Case-based learning and the critical friends group were valued learning methodologies. A cross-sectoral leadership curriculum can promote public health and primary care integration. (*Am J Public Health*. 2026;116(4): 443–446. https://doi.org/10.2105/AJPH.2025.308377)

AJPH April 2026, Vol. 116, No. 4

More than 20 years ago, the National Academy of Medicine released their report, *Primary Care and Public Health: Exploring Integration to Improve Population Health*, highlighting the importance of building relationships between public health and primary care sectors.[1] Without meaningful and ongoing collaboration, clinical and public health systems remain siloed, leading to miscommunication, fragmented care, inefficient use of resources, and missed opportunities for comprehensive care for communities.[2] The recent pandemic and other public health emergencies have required rapid changes to public health and primary care service delivery—including using strengths and resources across these sectors—further underscoring the need for primary care and public health integration.[3]

Establishing learning networks and training at regional, state, and local levels that cater to the specific needs of the area's public health and primary care workforce have been recommended to promote cross-sectoral integration.[1,4] However, there are few leadership development opportunities available to meet the diverse needs of both public health and primary care leaders as they work toward these goals.

INTERVENTION AND IMPLEMENTATION

In 2019, the University of Washington's Northwest Center for Public Health Practice partnered with the Northwest Regional Primary Care Association to create a community of practice focused on the leadership-training needs of public health and primary care workers in Health Resources and Services Administration Region X—Alaska, Idaho, Washington, and Oregon. The Northwest Public Health & Primary Care Leadership Institute ("the Institute") was launched in 2020.[5]

The Institute's curriculum is based on extensive input from public health practice partners, primary care providers, and administrators at federally qualified health centers throughout the region. Results from a region-wide workforce survey of leaders, managers, and frontline staff in state, local, and tribal health departments also informed the curriculum design.[6] The program prioritizes competencies in adaptive leadership, population health, systems thinking and health care transformation, and community engagement and collaboration. Corresponding learning objectives include understanding and using data effectively, managing interorganizational relationships, leading teams of diverse and competent staff and stakeholders, and addressing structural issues undergirding inequities (Box 1). The curriculum overview, including the theories of learning,

BOX 1— Core Competencies and Select Learning Objectives of the Northwest Public Health & Primary Care Leadership Institute

Core Competencies	Learning Objectives
Adaptive leadership	Apply systematic problem-solving and adaptive skills to identify, analyze, and manage emerging issues, particularly those with ambiguous causes and solutions.
	Identify effective channels and strategies to communicate complex health information with diverse public and professional audiences.
	Describe the importance of challenging the status quo to create paradigm shifts in systemic and organizational policy and practice.
Population health and health equity	Describe conditions that promote health and contribute to population health outcomes.
	Identify significant sources of valid, reliable data to analyze and compare trends in health status and outcomes at local, state, and national levels.
	Identify effective approaches for assessing equity in health care systems and communities.
Systems thinking and health care transformation	Describe the relationships of factors affecting the health of a community (e.g., income, education, environment, demographic trends, and legislation) by performing a root cause analysis.
	Discuss novel opportunities for individuals and organizations, including nontraditional or unconventional partners, collaborating to improve community health.
	Identify opportunities where public health and health care organizations can partner around funding, such as through accountable care structures and the move to value-based payment to improve the health of populations.
	Analyze internal and external facilitators and barriers that may affect implementation of population health policies, programs, and services.
Community engagement and collaboration	Describe approaches to meaningful collaboration with communities, utilizing information to assess community health needs, and developing, implementing, evaluating, and improving policies, programs, and services.
	Identify opportunities for building multisectoral partnerships to improve health in a community (e.g., relationships among hospitals, health departments, community health centers, primary care providers, schools, community-based organizations, jails/prisons, and other types of organizations).
	Identify approaches to building trust and sharing power with communities and stakeholders to support them as they develop strategies, programs, and services that will improve the health and well-being of their communities.

AJPH April 2026, Vol. 116, No. 4

instructional strategy, and desired positive outcomes of the program, are listed in Box 2.

The program offers didactic, experiential, reflective, and peer-to-peer learning opportunities, including faculty mentor consultations and critique of leadership and health system transformation efforts. Scholars participate in group and individual activities, panels, lectures, webinars, and discussions and use case-based learning to explore real-life situations leaders face in the field. Faculty have diverse academic and community-based clinical and foundational public health experiences across urban, suburban, and rural settings. Guest presenters provide case studies, promising practices, and lessons learned to illustrate the application of skills and program leadership competencies.

Case-based learning and the reflective learning process called "critical friends group"[7] are learning methods used to strengthen an individual's leadership skills. The Institute's planning committee assigns scholars to small learning groups that remain the same throughout the program. In case-based learning, scholars discuss the complexities of real-world public health challenges and how to create intentional partnerships to address them facilitated by senior faculty. In the critical friends group, scholars learn cooperatively from one another as they share and invite their group members to help them address a challenging situation or problem. The critical friends group process lends itself well to cross-sectoral understanding and collaboration by providing the structure for scholars to establish trusting professional relationships, practice reflective learning, and broaden and deepen their understanding of leadership across sectors.

Additionally, scholars propose a leadership project that explicitly includes a cross-sector integration component to apply leadership principles and skills learned during the program that are workplace relevant, approved by their supervisors, and implemented in consultation with their experienced faculty mentors. Past leadership projects that have highlighted aspects of integration include the reduction of community health risks associated with poor air quality, the

BOX 2— Curriculum Overview of the Northwest Public Health & Primary Care Leadership Institute

Content Focus	Model/Theory of Learning	Instructional Strategy	Desired Positive Outcomes
Collaborative leader behaviors	Competency models, Bandura's social learning theory	Mentorship, group learning, presentations, panels, debrief	Skills: reflective practice, bidirectional communication, network and systems awareness, empowerment of others
Real-world complex health and social issues	Experiential learning	Leadership project, problem-based learning/case studies, guest speakers (storytelling)	Skills: problem-solving, teamwork
Public health and primary care collaboration	Transformative learning theory	Leadership project, problem-based learning/case studies, panel discussions, shared learning (peer to peer), critical friends group	Viewpoint: Shift individuals' consciousness about self, other (sector), and their world Development: Establish and strengthen network after time at Leadership Institute
Population health, equity, and health care transformation topics	Cognitive learning	Lecture, directed readings, workshops	Knowledge: Confidence in knowledge about content areas
Personal leadership development	Reflective learning	Personal development plan	Skills: Awareness of leadership development during and after program participation

Note. The Northwest Public Health & Primary Care Leadership Institute is a partnership between the University of Washington's Northwest Center for Public Health Practice and the Northwest Regional Primary Care Association.

expansion of services in school-based clinics, and the primary prevention of food insecurity. Taken together, these curriculum features aim to position sector leadership to work together.

PLACE, TIME, PERSONS

The Institute has a seven-month program with monthly virtual sessions and two in-person sessions. It is open to mid-career primary care, public health, and tribal or community health emerging leaders from across Health Resources and Services Administration Region X states. From 2020 to 2024, the Institute graduated five scholar cohorts (119 participants), with 50% working in primary care, 47% in public health, and 3% in tribal or community health. Public health scholars were from local, state, and tribal health departments and included program directors in environmental health, community engagement, public health modernization, and organizational learning and change, as well as epidemiologists and economists. Primary care scholars were a mix of physicians, nurses, and administrators, with the majority from clinical and administrative leadership in primary care programs.

PURPOSE

After 16 years conducting the Northwest Public Health Leadership Institute, the Northwest Center for Public Health Practice initiated this collaboration with the Northwest Regional Primary Care Association. Together, the organizations sought to align their efforts at leadership development and to build cross-sector prevention systems between public health and primary care.[4] In 2020, the inaugural Institute cohort was launched and continues to train emerging public health and primary care leaders to drive more proactive, equitable, and effective approaches to improving population health.

EVALUATION AND ADVERSE EFFECTS

Over the first five years of the Institute, 84% of respondents indicated that they applied the knowledge or skills gained through the Institute to other projects in their workplace or community. Most scholars (78%) indicated that case-based learning helped them identify new ways to collaborate across sectors. The critical friends group method was used to reflect and collaborate on professional growth; 89% of participants ranked this as "very useful" or "useful." One scholar stated that participating in the Institute helped them "get a better understanding of the BIG picture connecting public health, primary care, value-based care, and health equity innovation." Another said:

> It was extremely helpful to hear from primary care folks. We are all working to make people healthier, and it was important to [hear their] perspective, to know their challenges and how public health can support them. I will know in the future who to connect with and what types of things to ask.

SUSTAINABILITY

Cross-sectoral collaboration and integration are necessary for the fields of public health and primary care—particularly in community health center settings—to be resilient and politically sustainable in the face of government budget cuts and disinvestments in our country's health and health care infrastructure today and into the future. Innovative, apolitical funding mechanisms are needed to sustain leadership development in primary care and public health collaboration and across other sectors, supporting ongoing training of the next generation of health leaders in shared frameworks and common population health goals.

In a 2023 survey, 75% of Institute alumni indicated that they were willing to participate in an ongoing peer learning and networking community. Institute faculty and alumni cocreated monthly virtual sessions focused on hot topics at the intersection of public health and primary care. Although participation in the sessions was steady, these efforts were challenged by a lack of dedicated funding to support this ongoing practice.

PUBLIC HEALTH SIGNIFICANCE

The Institute is a novel, efficacious, and feasible program that can be adapted to existing single-discipline leadership development programs to promote collaboration between primary care and public health. Evaluation data demonstrate that after program completion, participants have a better understanding of public health and primary care cross-sector roles, they expanded their networks with contacts beyond their sector, and their confidence in adaptive leadership increased.[4] Qualitative data collected in collaboration with the Institute suggest that reports of cross-sector communication, relationship-building, and leader self-efficacy held up to 20 months after program completion (J. Martelino, interview data, January 2023). These curriculum components, which explicitly focus on integration and collaborative activity between primary care and public health, support the integration of public health and primary care sectors. Scaling up and adapting these programs to focus on collaboration between two sectors can enhance integration in communities across the United States. AJPH

ABOUT THE AUTHORS

Jennifer G. Jones-Vanderleest and Antoinette Angulo are with the Department of Health Systems and Population Health, University of Washington School of Public Health, Seattle. Jennifer G. Jones-Vanderleest is also with Public Health–Seattle & King County, Seattle, WA. Janelle Z. Martelino is with the Department of Child, Family and Population Health Nursing, University of Washington School of Nursing, Seattle.

CORRESPONDENCE

Correspondence should be sent to Jennifer Jones-Vanderleest, MD, MSPH, University of Washington Northwest Center for Public Health Practice, Box 351621, Seattle, WA 98195 (e-mail: jjvander@uw.edu). Reprints can be ordered at https://www.ajph.org by clicking the "Reprints" link.

PUBLICATION INFORMATION

Full Citation: Jones-Vanderleest JG, Angulo A, Martelino JZ. Curriculum approaches to strengthen public health–primary care collaboration: Northwest Leadership Institute, 2020–2024. *Am J Public Health.* 2026;116(4):443–446.

Acceptance Date: November 30, 2025.

DOI: https://doi.org/10.2105/AJPH.2025.308377

ORCID iDs:

Jennifer G. Jones-Vanderleest https://orcid.org/0000-0001-6560-0208

Antoinette Angulo https://orcid.org/0000-0003-0324-4281

Janelle Z. Martelino https://orcid.org/0000-0002-1133-7608

CONTRIBUTORS

The authors contributed equally to the work.

ACKNOWLEDGMENTS

The Northwest Public Health and Primary Care Leadership Institute is supported by the Health Resources and Services Administration (HRSA) of the US Department of Health and Human Services (HHS; grant UB6HP31690) and the Washington State Health Care Authority.

We thank our colleagues for their contributions to the Leadership Institute: Betty Bekemeier, Barbara Rose, Megan Rogers, Seth Doyle, and Bruce Gray.

Note. This information or content and conclusions are those of the authors and should not be construed as the official position or policy of, nor should any endorsements be inferred by, HRSA, HHS, or the US government.

CONFLICTS OF INTEREST

The authors have no relevant financial or nonfinancial interests to disclose.

HUMAN PARTICIPANT PROTECTION

University of Washington procedures were used to determine that this was not human participants research.

REFERENCES

1. Institute of Medicine. *Primary Care and Public Health: Exploring Integration to Improve Population Health.* Washington, DC: National Academies Press; 2012. https://doi.org/10.17226/13381
2. Veenema TG, Toner E, Waldhorn RE, et al. The integration of primary care, public health, and community-based organizations: a federal policy analysis. February 2024. Available at: https://centerforhealthsecurity.org/sites/default/files/2024-03/240212-1540-pc-ph-report.pdf. Accessed September 1, 2025.
3. Veenema TG, Toner E, Waldhorn R, et al. Integrating primary care and public health to save lives and improve practice during public health crises: lessons from COVID-19. December 2021. Available at: https://centerforhealthsecurity.org/sites/default/files/2023-02/211214-primaryhealthcare-publichealthcovidreport.pdf. Accessed September 10, 2025.
4. Brandert K, Alperin M, Lloyd LM, et al. Learning to lead: 3 models to support public health leadership development. *J Public Health Manag Pract.* 2022;28(suppl 5):S203–S211. https://doi.org/10.1097/PHH.0000000000001519
5. Northwest Center for Public Health Practice. Northwest Public Health & Primary Care Leadership Institute. Available at: https://www.nwcphp.org/training/northwest-public-health-leadership-institute. Accessed September 10, 2025.
6. de Beaumont Foundation. Building skills for a more strategic public health workforce: a call to action. Available at: https://debeaumont.org/wp-content/uploads/2019/04/Building-Skills-for-a-More-Strategic-Public-Health-Workforce.pdf. Accessed September 10, 2025.
7. Michigan State University. Office of Faculty and Academic Staff Development. Critical friends: a process built on reflection. Available at: https://ofasd.msu.edu/wp-content/uploads/2020/09/criticalfriends-1.pdf. Accessed September 5, 2025.

Insights on Recent National Policy Changes: Public Health Students' Experiences

Alexandra K. Rodriguez, MPH, Amen T. Ajamu, Bpharm, Dorcas Ama Adom, MPH, Lois Angelo, BS, Taylor Green, BS, and Carmen White, MPH

ABOUT THE AUTHORS

Alexandra K. Rodriguez is with the University of Florida College of Public Health and Health Professions, Gainesville. Amen T. Ajamu is with the University of Louisville School of Public Health & Information Sciences, Louisville, KY. Dorcas Ama Adom is with the Louisiana State University Health Sciences Center, New Orleans. Lois Angelo is with the New York University School of Global Public Health, New York, NY. Taylor Green is with the Rutgers School of Public Health, Piscataway, NJ. Carmen White is with the University of South Carolina Arnold School of Public Health, Columbia. All authors are members of the AJPH *Student Think Tank 2025–2026 Cohort.*

See also *AJPH* Student Think Tank, pp. 452–484.

Policies shape communities at the macrolevel and dictate resource allocation, priorities, and access, all of which can have direct or indirect impacts on individuals. These impacts extend into health outcomes, educational opportunities, and even professional development. As national public health priorities in the United States continue to shift, students at foundational stages in their public health careers experience evolving curricula, financial constraints, and career uncertainties firsthand.

This special section examines the multifaceted implications of recent federal regulatory and policy changes in 2025 on the experiences of public health students in the United States, particularly those enacted or promulgated by the executive branch. For instance, executive orders from the most recent administration—such as Executive Order 14151, which restricts diversity, equity, and inclusion initiatives—have affected the grant-based financial support of public health students and have also often complicated or halted research undertakings.[1–3] Despite growing interests in the consequences of these policy changes, a notable gap remains in the scholarly literature concerning students and trainees in public health educational programs.[4–6] Even more underdeveloped is the literature that considers lived experiences and informed perspectives of public health students.[7] This collection, curated by the *AJPH* Student Think Tank, highlights lived experiences to better understand how national policy decisions have cascading implications and shape the future public health workforce.

PRESSURES ON PUBLIC HEALTH CAREER PATHWAYS

The COVID-19 pandemic brought national attention to the field of public

Continued on page 448...

HISTORY CORNER

11 YEARS AGO

A Call to Action: Training Public Health Students to Be Effective Agents for Social Change

We need to train public health leaders by providing students with the opportunity to: (1) develop the skills needed to successfully address problems that require societal change to solve, and (2) address social, economic, and environmental problems as part of a global community. We need to help all public health students develop these skills, including students in resource-constrained environments. . . . We developed a partnership between the Fielding School of Public Health (FSPH) at the University of California Los Angeles (UCLA) and the Division of Environmental Health in the Los Angeles County Department of Public Health (LACDPH) to propel regional climate action planning. . . . Too often, doctoral students are tightly focused on conducting their own research and do not get to interact substantively with public health practitioners who bring important perspectives to public health problems and a wealth of real-world experience. The opportunity to work directly with staff from LACDPH provided the doctoral students who participated in the workshop series with invaluable insights into perspectives of public health professionals and the constraints that health departments face.

From *AJPH*, Supplement 1, pp. S34–S35

health, increasing student awareness of a discipline defined by service, evidence, and collective protection. That surge reflected a growing appreciation for the role of the field in population health and national security. Unfortunately, recent policy shifts could erode the conditions needed to convert interest into durable careers. Budget contractions, executive actions antagonistic to science and equity, and instability in student financing have combined to weaken the training pipeline.

Yagudayev et al. (p. 460) discuss how these effects are particularly telling at the graduate level of education. Cuts and freezes at the National Institutes of Health (NIH) and the Centers for Disease Control and Prevention do not simply reduce the volume of funded projects. The cuts interrupt mentoring chains, stall dissertations, delay publications, and narrow the scope of permissible inquiry. Doctoral students feel the immediate consequences of these cuts most acutely. Research agendas are reshaped by funding exclusions that may render entire topics off-limits, including reproductive health, climate change, and health disparities. When data access is restricted and grants vanish midstream, students are forced to rethink timelines and even the viability of academic careers.

Graduate education at the master's level is equally affected. Scholarships and traineeships have been suspended. Field placements disappear as community partners downsize. Students absorb higher debt while receiving less applied training, a tradeoff that undermines readiness for governmental roles. Also, caps on federal borrowing and the elimination of graduate PLUS loans further compress access, particularly for students from low- and middle-income backgrounds. The result is a more expensive degree with fewer experiential returns.

Nzama et al. (p. 463) highlight how the field is also grappling with the narrowing of who belongs. Restrictions on diversity, equity, and inclusion have consequences beyond symbolism. For Black women and other scholars whose work centers on equity, policy shifts translate into restricted funding, constrained research questions, and fewer academic and federal employment pathways. Health equity research is reframed as ideological rather than essential, pushing students to dilute or abandon lines of inquiry they had hoped to pursue and thus resulting in losing talent and knowledge production, which leaves public health workers less capable of addressing the populations most at risk.

Chow and Chen (p. 466) discuss how the path for international students to contribute to US public health research and analytics is increasingly becoming more convoluted. Visa volatility, limited eligibility for federal fellowships, and citizenship requirements for public sector jobs converge to make long-term planning nearly impossible. The policy churn generates psychological distress that is often overlooked or missed.

Serrano (p. 455) highlights how the contraction of financial support for graduate public health education creates a dual burden of scholarship and employment to maintain financial stability for students. Consequently, time once allocated to research assistance, mentorship, conferences, and community engagement is consumed by wage labor. Equity gaps widen, as those with fewer safety nets shoulder the heaviest load.

When job security is uncertain, benefits shrink and public trust in institutions

Continued on page 449...

HISTORY CORNER

34 YEARS AGO

Habits and Attitudes of Public Health Students

In May of 1990 an anonymous two-page questionnaire was sent to all students at [Harvard School of Public Health]. . . US public health students at Harvard are politically "liberal" regarding public health issues. They overwhelmingly supported legal abortions (96%), seatbelt laws 87%), national health insurance (76%), and handgun bans (75%); they opposed the death penalty. Compared with the US students, those from abroad were more likely to smoke and less likely to wear a seatbelt. They were more likely to favor national health insurance and handgun restrictions. Overall, however, US and foreign HSPH students were found to be more similar to each other than to the general or college-educated US population. . . . If they had it to do over, 92% of the students would again seek public health training. The findings indicate that public health students have clear common interests although are a disparate group. Widespread agreement exists among them on many health-related policy issues, and compared even with American medical students, their personal behavior seems very healthy. Few appear to regret their decision to seek a public health education.

From *AJPH*, March 1992, p. 464

falters, making students more likely to move. Krosin and Abouzaid (p. 470) discuss how evidence indicates a shift away from governmental public health toward private and for-profit roles. This trend collides with a workforce facing historic shortages and high turnover. The damage, however, is not irreversible. The economic case for investment is clear, as are the documented returns of prevention. What is missing is policy alignment with these realities.

ADVOCACY IN A POLITICIZED ACADEMIC LANDSCAPE

Federal policy decisions increasingly shape not only public health systems but also the professional futures of students preparing to enter the field. As demonstrated across the contributions in this special section, policy environments influence how public health careers are valued, supported, and sustained, and advocacy offers a viable strategy to address current challenges.

Willis (p. 479) uses student experiences to illustrate how regulatory shifts and the rollback of equity-focused initiatives contribute to feelings of professional marginalization, diminished institutional support, and uncertainty about long-term career viability. These pressures are manifested through disrupted research opportunities, reduced funding streams, and constrained academic freedom, prompting students to question whether their training and commitment to public health are adequately recognized in the current policy climate. With this framing, the author issues a call to action for both strategic advocacy and coalition building.

Serrano also center advocacy as they highlight how public health students are actively responding to policy-driven instability by recalibrating career goals and advocacy strategies. The article underscores how executive actions and changing federal priorities influence access to internships, fellowships, and early career employment, often steering students toward nontraditional or private-sector pathways. Although these adaptations reflect resilience and innovation related to advocacy, they also reveal structural weaknesses in the public health workforce pipeline.

Together, these articles demonstrate that policy-driven pressures extend beyond abstract governance decisions, shaping lived experiences and career trajectories in ways that may ultimately affect the diversity, capacity, and preparedness of the future public health workforce.

IMMIGRATION POLICY AND ITS CASCADING IMPACTS

Recent federal immigration policies have simultaneously constrained how students access and translate public health training into practice while deepening the mental and emotional strain on students whose lives and work are intertwined with immigrant communities. Centering immigration policy as a throughline reveals how federal decisions reverberate across workforce development and well-being in ways that will shape the future of public health.

Zhu et al. (p. 482) highlight a stark paradox at the heart of current federal priorities. Agencies such as the Food and Drug Administration, the Environmental Protection Agency, and the NIH are championing human-relevant new approach methods to replace or reduce animal testing and improve the predictive value of preclinical research. This shift promises new training and employment opportunities across academia, government, and industry, especially for early career professionals. At the same time, immigration restrictions are closing the door on many of the international trainees who disproportionately populate new approach methods: relevant science, technology, engineering, mathematics, and public health disciplines. Policy changes such as pauses in visa interview scheduling, enhanced security screening, visa revocations for certain nationalities, and proposed visas with fixed admission periods destabilize international students' academic continuity and mobility. Layered onto these disruptions are hiring freezes across the executive branch, downsizing at key health agencies, elimination of scientific offices, and threats to long-standing programs. These intertwined policies risk a sharp decline in international enrollment, causing "brain drain" from US institutions and long-term losses in scientific capacity and innovation.

Zaragoza (p. 458) shifts the lens from structural barriers to the lived experiences of students working in the current policy climate. Building on evidence that punitive immigration policies generate intergenerational and community-wide mental health harms, the article shows how public health students who identify as immigrants, come from mixed-status families, or focus their research and practice on immigrant communities face heightened risks of vicarious trauma, stress, and burnout. Fears of deportation raids at campuses and field sites, coupled with federal funding restrictions on equity-focused work, directly affect immigrant-centered research and undermine students' sense of safety and intellectual freedom. In the absence of robust institutional structures, students are left to manage their own safety, protect community partners, and cope with the psychoemotional toll of their work, often with limited formal support.

Together, these articles show that immigration policy functions as a powerful structuring force in public health education and workforce development. Restrictions on immigrant communities narrow who can train and remain in the United States, and enforcement and funding climates intensify emotional burdens and safety concerns. Both articles urge aligning policy and practice with public health values through scientific roadmaps, including immigration strategies, and trauma-informed institutional cultures that offer mental health support and protect against enforcement threats.

IMPACT ON MARGINALIZED PUBLIC HEALTH SCHOLARS

As evidenced across the articles in this special section, the effects of recent policies extend into the health outcomes, educational opportunities, and even professional development of public health students. Unfortunately, marginalized public health scholars may be experiencing the effects of national policy changes disproportionately, creating intensified vulnerabilities.

Two articles specifically consider these inequitable impacts on LGBTQ+ (lesbian, gay, bisexual, transgender/-sexual, queer or questioning, and all subsets) populations. Sarker Rony et al. (p. 473) consider the intersectionality of identifying as both an immigrant and LGBTQ+ student, the vulnerability of immigrant scholars on visa status, and the need to frame academic freedom as integral to health. The authors also underscore how protecting equity-driven research is necessary for advancing population-level health. Babbs et al. (p. 476) consider the impacts of the executive order that declared the policy of the United States is to recognize only two sexes. The authors assert that the executive order acted as a formal erasure of trans communities from federal policy as well as an act that directly and systematically dismantles infrastructure for studying trans health.

Kelly (p. 405) explores how the termination of NIH-funded research has extended to the elimination of diversity programming, such as F31 diversity fellowships, regardless of scientific rigor or whether the grant aligned with or was disfavored by national priorities. The article further explains that the policy shift away from scientific funding is a clear departure from long-standing bipartisan investment in NIH training programs, which have historically catalyzed the careers of scientists who continue to lead research innovation in the United States. The elimination of diversity funding mechanisms, therefore, not only disadvantages the public health workforce pipeline but also limits the return on investment for taxpayers in addressing the pressing issues of our time.

As discussed in the previous section, in *"Pressures on Public Health Career Pathways,"* Nzama et al. also considers intersectionality by positioning lived experience as applied to the context of social justice and health equity. In addition to their focus on career pathway pressures, the authors offer discrete recommendations for navigating a climate that views health equity as unfavorable, such as suggesting that institutions should refrain from forms of overcompliance with anti–diversity, equity, and inclusion state and federal policies, as this can further marginalize students of color.

This collection of articles documents a tumultuous period in public health and in the nation as recent policies have reverberated through public health education, shaping who trains, what research is viable, and how careers are structured. Each article draws much-needed attention to the experiences of public health students—the future generation of leaders committed to safeguarding the nation's health—as they navigate mounting threats to public health. Importantly, this special section also centers lived experience alongside evidence-based data to convert critical insights. As health equity is devalued across federal funding mechanisms, immigration policies, and national agendas, marginalized public health students are disproportionately affected. To safeguard the future public health workforce, institutions and policymakers must prioritize equity, protect immigrant scholars, and uphold academic freedom. Mobilizing rigorous evidence and lived experience for advocacy in this moment is critical—not only to counter current challenges but also to uphold the future of public health. AJPH

CORRESPONDENCE

Correspondence should be sent to Alexandra K. Rodriguez, 1225 Center Dr, Suite 4101, Gainesville, FL 32611 (e-mail: alexandrarodrig@ufl.edu). Reprints can be ordered at https://www.ajph.org by clicking the "Reprints" link.

PUBLICATION INFORMATION

Full Citation: Rodriguez AK, Ajamu AT, Adom DA, Angelo L, Green T, White C. Insights on recent national policy changes: public health students' experiences. *Am J Public Health.* 2026;116(4): 447–451.

Acceptance Date: January 17, 2026.

DOI: https://doi.org/10.2105/AJPH.2026.308425

ORCID iDs:

Alexandra K. Rodriguez https://orcid.org/0000-0001-9254-3392

Amen T. Ajamu https://orcid.org/0000-0002-3545-1800

Dorcas Ama Adom https://orcid.org/0009-0005-8014-0656

Lois Angelo https://orcid.org/0009-0005-8427-3181

Taylor Green https://orcid.org/0009-0000-2946-6427

Carmen White https://orcid.org/0009-0002-8903-6220

CONTRIBUTORS

The authors contributed equally to the editorial.

ACKNOWLEDGMENTS

We wish to thank Denys Lau, the editor-in-chief of *AJPH*, and the *AJPH* editorial staff for their support of the *AJPH* Student Think Tank. Additionally, we thank Robert J. Kim-Farley and Patrick Kelly for support with this special section.

CONFLICTS OF INTEREST

The authors have no conflicts of interest to disclose.

REFERENCES

1. US Government. Executive Order 14151: ending radical and wasteful government DEI programs and preferencing. January 29, 2025. Available at: https://public-inspection.federalregister.gov/2025-01953.pdf. Accessed July 22, 2025.
2. Morabia A. *AJPH* and the threat of political interference in scientific publishing. *Am J Public Health.* 2025;115(5):626–627. https://doi.org/10.2105/AJPH.2025.308100
3. Gonzalez-Guarda RM, Williams JR, Alexander KA. Uncertainty in science and among early career investigators. *JAMA Health Forum.* 2025;6(4):e251946. https://doi.org/10.1001/jamahealthforum.2025.1946
4. Greer SL, Jarman H, Kulikoff R, Yaver M. Trump's second presidency begins: evaluating effects on the US health system. *Lancet Reg Health Am.* 2025;48:101173. https://doi.org/10.1016/j.lana.2025.101173
5. Woolf SH, Galea S, Williams DR. The potential impact of the Trump administration policies on health research in the USA. *Lancet.* 2025;405(10495):2114–2116. https://doi.org/10.1016/S0140-6736(25)01016-5
6. Jackson M. The impact of anti-DEI legislation on higher education pedagogy. *J Coll Character.* 2025;26(1):61–73. https://doi.org/10.1080/2194587X.2024.2442717
7. Abell-Selby E. The impacts of ongoing higher education legislation on university instruction: perspectives from an anthropology graduate student in the state of Florida. *Teach Learn Anthropol J.* 2024. Available at: https://www.academia.edu/123783163. Accessed February 12, 2026.

Navigating Graduate Education in an Era of Policy-Driven Employment Pressures

Fauwad Ahmed, MPH

ABOUT THE AUTHOR

Fauwad Ahmed is with the School of Public Health, LSU Health Shreveport, Shreveport, LA.

See also *AJPH* Student Think Tank, pp. 447–484.

At 6:30 AM, I review patient charts before my shift as an assistant practice manager begins. I spend my day running clinic operations, managing staff, and coordinating patient care until 6:00 PM, when I start my graduate studies. I dedicate my evenings and weekends to completing coursework for my master's program. For a growing number of students, federal changes to student loans, fellowship funding, and institutional support systems[1] have made it nearly impossible to avoid working while attending school. This new, policy-driven reality does more than create personal difficulties; it damages the quality of public health education and endangers the development of the professionals our country urgently needs.

A POLICY-DRIVEN REALITY

My personal experience is illustrative of a broader phenomenon. While many graduate programs, particularly those leading to a doctorate, provide stipends and prohibit outside work, the reality for master's-level students, who comprise the vast majority of the future public health workforce, is starkly different. We are the students who typically finance our own education or rely on limited institutional assistance. For us, a job is not a choice but a prerequisite for continued education. It is from this perspective, as a student–professional, that this editorial speaks.

The dual challenge of working full-time while pursuing graduate studies has become increasingly common. Under newly proposed federal borrowing limits, 20% of master's students would exceed allowable loan amounts, forcing them to fund their education primarily through employment.[2,3] This creates a difficult choice between accumulating educational debt and working long hours as education expenses rise and federal funding for graduate education decreases. The consequences extend beyond personal financial management. The Association of Schools and Programs of Public Health, our national training system, faces immense challenges in preparing professionals under these conditions. Students working more than 40 hours per week while managing a full course load inevitably experience a breakdown in performance. Moreover, cornerstones of public health training, including voluntary practicums, research internships, and immersive community experiences, are often forgone when students face the challenge of balancing academic enrichment with financial realities.

FUNDING CUTS AND STRUCTURAL BARRIERS

Graduate public health training is now endangered by an impossible situation created by recent policy changes. The "One Big Beautiful Bill Act" established new borrowing limits for graduate students, lowering their total debt capacity from $138 500 to $100 000 and setting annual borrowing limits at $20 500.[2] This policy threatens to halt the education of students who need to pursue multiple or expensive degrees. Compounding this financial pressure, the Department of Education's recent consensus decision to redefine "professional degree" programs has excluded public health degrees from this designation.[4] While students pursuing medicine, dentistry, or law degrees remain eligible for $200 000 in federal loans, MPH and DrPH students are now capped at the lower $100 000 limit, a decision that overlooks decades of precedent recognizing these degrees as professional credentials essential to protecting community health. Further intensifying these challenges, the educational system has cut back on the fellowship programs that students rely on. The National Science Foundation Graduate Research Fellowship Program, for instance, awarded roughly 1000 fellowships in 2025, less than half the number from two years before.[5] The cancellation of vital National Institutes of Health training programs has created new barriers, particularly for students from minority groups.[6]

AJPH April 2026, Vol. 116, No. 4

The effects are immediate. Students must divide their focus between academic work, research, and professional growth. The time I once spent in laboratories and community health centers now belongs to my job. The holistic training model, which integrates theory with practice, research, and mentorship, becomes difficult to sustain when survival necessitates full-time work. These pressures force students to make difficult choices: skipping conferences, declining research assistantships, or postponing publications. These missed opportunities may not appear on a financial ledger, but they critically shape a student's competitiveness for fellowships and leadership roles after graduation.

THE TOLL ON STUDENT WELL-BEING AND EQUITY

The psychological toll is immense. Research on graduate student populations more broadly shows that depression and anxiety affect 41% and 39% of students, respectively, compared with 6% in the general population.[7] Burnout symptoms affect up to half of the graduate student population.[8,9] The struggle to maintain a work–life balance is constant, as policy changes have intensified workloads.[10] Graduate students now devote approximately 55% of their time to working between 41 and 60 hours per week, with 25% working 61 to 80 hours.[11] Combining these hours with academic and practicum responsibilities creates an unsustainable burden. The equity implications are profound. Students from lower-income, first-generation, and international backgrounds face the greatest impact. At the same time, the diversity, equity, and inclusion (DEI) initiatives designed to support them face new obstacles, creating structural barriers that diminish workforce diversity and performance.[12]

Ultimately, the United States faces a dangerous pipeline gap in its public health workforce. Universities have already reduced admissions to some funded doctoral programs, while traineeships and scholarships are paused or downsized. Students are losing internships and field placements that build practical skills and professional networks, while promised stipends are paused or downsized. This trend is alarming, as the Health Resources and Services Administration already predicts multiple health professional shortages by 2037, and the Department of Health and Human Services' own workforce has decreased by 20 000.[13,14] Students who graduate under these conditions begin their careers with burnout and financial strain, having missed the vital research and policy experiences that develop leaders. The dismantling of DEI programs further exacerbates this crisis, threatening to increase health disparities by reducing workforce diversity and community preparedness.[12,15]

A PATH FORWARD

The future requires a whole new mindset about how we support our next generation of public health professionals. Will we continue along a path of policies actively discouraging qualified students from pursuing a career in public health, or can we develop an infrastructure supporting their success? The choice has serious implications for our readiness for the next public health challenge. The response requires earnest, comprehensive, and multisectoral effort. Congress needs to update graduate lending policies to account for modern graduate school finance trajectories and implement flexible fellowships to support working graduate students. The Department of Education must also reverse its decision to exclude MPH and DrPH degrees from professional degree designation, restoring the recognition these programs have historically received and ensuring students have access to adequate federal loan limits. Next, the federal government, in collaboration with philanthropic partners, must secure training grants, especially for those from underrepresented backgrounds. Finally, universities must become more responsive to the needs of a working graduate student population. Safeguarding DEI initiatives is as essential as upgrading lending policies; it is a vital step in cultivating a workforce that can earn public trust and ameliorate health disparities.

It is well past midnight as I shut down from my studies, after a long day running a health care practice. The burden of this double life is evident. But so, too, is our unswerving dedication. Our resolve, however, is not a renewable resource. We are the future of America's public health infrastructure. The most important health care investment our nation can make is in us. AJPH

CORRESPONDENCE

Correspondence should be sent to Fauwad Ahmed,1020 Brand Ln, Apt 1213, Stafford, TX 77477 (e-mail: fauwadwali@gmail.com). Reprints can be ordered at https://www.ajph.org by clicking the "Reprints" link.

PUBLICATION INFORMATION

Full Citation: Ahmed F. Navigating graduate education in an era of policy-driven employment pressures. *Am J Public Health*. 2026;116(4): 452–454.

Acceptance Date: January 16, 2026.

DOI: https://doi.org/10.2105/AJPH.2026.308420

ORCID iD:
Fauwad Ahmed https://orcid.org/0009-0009-6805-2986

CONFLICTS OF INTEREST

The author declares no conflicts of interest.

REFERENCES

1. Executive Office of the President. Ending radical and wasteful government DEI programs and preferencing. *Federal Register*. January 29, 2025. Available at: https://www.federalregister.gov/documents/2025/01/29/2025-01953/ending-radical-and-wasteful-government-dei-programs-and-preferencing. Accessed September 10, 2025.
2. Turner C. What borrowers should know about student loan changes in the One Big Beautiful Bill. NPR. July 24, 2025. Available at: https://www.npr.org/2025/07/24/nx-s1-5477646/student-loan-repayment-forgiveness-trump. Accessed September 10, 2025.
3. Lalljee J. What to know about Senate bill's major changes to student loans. *Axios*. July 2, 2025. Available at: https://www.axios.com/2025/07/02/student-loans-house-big-beautiful-bill. Accessed September 10, 2025.
4. Association of Schools and Programs of Public Health. Department of Education proposal excludes public health degrees from "professional degree" definition. November 12, 2025. Available at: https://aspph.org/department-of-education-proposal-excludes-public-health-degrees-from-professional-degree-definition. Accessed January 3, 2026.
5. Barbu B, Boerner LK. NSF halves graduate fellowship awards. *Chem Eng News*. 2025;103(11):12–13. https://doi.org/10.1021/cen-10311-polcon1
6. Palmer K. NSF, NIH slash support for early-career scientists. Inside Higher Ed. April 10, 2025. Available at: https://www.insidehighered.com/news/quick-takes/2025/04/10/nsf-nih-slash-support-early-career-scientists. Accessed September 10, 2025.
7. Evans TM, Bira L, Gastelum JB, Weiss LT, Vanderford NL. Evidence for a mental health crisis in graduate education. *Nat Biotechnol*. 2018;36(3):282–284. https://doi.org/10.1038/nbt.4089
8. Satinsky EN, Kimura T, Kiang MV, et al. Systematic review and meta-analysis of depression, anxiety, and suicidal ideation among Ph.D. students. *Sci Rep*. 2021;11(1):14370. https://doi.org/10.1038/s41598-021-93687-7
9. Aubin KCM, Thachet TA, Hotston I, Thompson AME, Hellemans KGC. Mental health and coping among graduate students during the COVID-19 pandemic: a gender-based analysis. *Front Psychiatry*. 2025;16:1532987. https://doi.org/10.3389/fpsyt.2025.1532987
10. Bolotnyy V, Basilico M, Barreira P. Graduate student mental health: lessons from American economics departments. *J Econ Lit*. 2022;60(4):1188–1222. https://doi.org/10.1257/jel.20201555
11. Kivimäki M, Kawachi I. Work stress as a risk factor for cardiovascular disease. *Curr Cardiol Rep*. 2015;17(9):630. https://doi.org/10.1007/s11886-015-0630-8
12. Nair A. DEI funds and the future: what's in store for the next 5 years? Enago Academy. March 25, 2025. Available at: https://www.enago.com/academy/dei-funding-future-next-5-years. Accessed September 14, 2025.
13. Health Resources and Services Administration. Projecting health workforce supply and demand. Bureau of Health Workforce. March 2024. Available at: https://bhw.hrsa.gov/data-research/projecting-health-workforce-supply-demand. Accessed September 10, 2025.
14. US Department of Health and Human Services. HHS announces transformation to Make America Healthy Again. March 27, 2025. Available at: https://www.hhs.gov/press-room/hhs-restructuring-doge.html. Accessed September 10, 2025.
15. Johnson R. The impact of DEI ban on clinical research ecosystem. *Appl Clin Trials*. 2025;34(2). Available at: https://www.appliedclinicaltrialsonline.com/view/the-impact-of-dei-ban-on-clinical-research-ecosystem. Accessed September 14, 2025.

Navigating a Politicized Landscape: The Imperative for Activist and Advocate Leadership in Public Health Education

Pedro A. Serrano, MPH

ABOUT THE AUTHOR

Pedro A. Serrano is with the School of Community and Global Health, Claremont Graduate University, Claremont, CA.

See also *AJPH* Student Think Tank, pp. 447–484.

Public health faces profound shifts driven by policy decisions constituting political interference against established domestic and global health agendas.[1] This editorial asserts that these actions undermine the field's foundational principles, necessitating a paradigm shift in doctor of public health (DrPH) education toward activism to prepare leaders for ideological encroachment.

Federal changes,[1] specifically Executive Orders 14151 and 14168, have restricted diversity, equity, and inclusion initiatives and labeled HIV and lesbian, gay, bisexual, trans, and queer (LGBTQ+) health research as "wasteful." Consequently, scholars face funding terminations, forcing layoffs and endangering community partnerships.[2] This climate threatens scientific infrastructure, risks eroding community trust, and endangers the visa status of international colleagues.[3] The broader scientific community has expressed concern regarding administrative actions that threaten to weaken the national scientific infrastructure, warning that without robust support for institutions like the National Institutes of Health, our defenses against genuine health threats may crumble.[4] Reports indicate significant cancellations of grants and indirect cost caps, further constraining the academic enterprise.[1]

Beyond financial considerations, policies like Florida's Senate Bill 266 constrain academic freedom by scrutinizing discussions on race and gender, compelling faculty to modify curricula to avoid legal repercussions.[5] This environment undermines the historical role of higher education as a forum for exploring challenging ideas. It thereby restricts the scope of what can be taught and debated, including theoretical frameworks such as Critical Race Theory and intersectionality, as well as related arguments such as racism as a public health crisis.[5] The cumulative effect is a direct disregard for well-established, evidence-based public health practice and research priorities, neglecting both professional experts and aspiring trainees.[4] This situation, marked by layoffs and a scramble for increasingly limited career opportunities, signals a crisis for the public health workforce, affecting workers in federal, local, higher education, and nonprofit sectors, as well as trainees at the undergraduate, graduate, and doctoral levels.[1]

At this critical juncture, the distinctive role of the DrPH degree becomes particularly salient.[6] The DrPH is recognized as the advanced, terminal professional degree for public health practice, emphasizing leadership in applying evidence-based solutions to complex public health challenges.[7,8] Unlike the more research-oriented doctor of philosophy (PhD) degree, the DrPH focuses on translating research into practice, providing leadership to execute core public health functions, and solving multifaceted problems in real-world settings.[7,8] Although the DrPH degree has historically faced challenges in establishing a consistent identity and standardization across programs,[7,8] the current sociopolitical climate underscores an urgent need for its unique practice-oriented leadership.

A significant barrier to DrPH graduates engaging in public service, especially within governmental or nonprofit sectors, is the substantial student debt incurred during their education.[9] A recent study indicated that over 70% of current DrPH students lack any funding support for their degree, with student debt affecting the career choices of nearly 60% of students and 29% of alumni.[9] This financial burden often steers graduates toward higher-paying private sector roles, thereby exacerbating the existing workforce shortages in vital public health areas.[9] The absence of comprehensive loan forgiveness programs for DrPH graduates, comparable to those available for other clinical providers, further compounds this issue.[9]

Given the gravity of these challenges, an immediate call to action is warranted. Public health students and practitioners, particularly those pursuing or holding a DrPH, should embrace activist and advocate orientations to address the inherent political dimensions of our work. The notion that public health is an apolitical[10] endeavor is a misconception that this moment demands we confront. It is no longer sufficient for DrPH graduates to possess only technical expertise; they must be prepared to lead, advocate, and effect change in contentious environments.

This urgent call for an activist orientation is not merely theoretical; it is already being modeled by a public health sector mobilizing in its own defense. In response to the current crisis, we are witnessing a multilevel organizational response. Established bodies, such as the American Public Health Association, are issuing direct condemnations of political interference and workforce reductions. Concurrently, new state-level alliances are forming to create parallel, evidence-based systems independent of federal guidance, while grassroots networks like Defend Public Health and the Health and Power Organizing Project[11] are organizing to resist specific harmful policies.

These emerging efforts, however, require the exact leadership competencies, policy advocacy, intersectoral coalition building, and crisis management that are central to DrPH training. The programmatic changes outlined in this editorial are therefore essential to formally prepare DrPH graduates to lead and sustain these vital movements, ensuring that they are not just participants but courageous and effective architects of the public health resistance.

To address these exigencies, DrPH training programs must implement focused programmatic changes. This period mandates swift, actionable steps to enhance preparedness, complementing necessary long-term strategic planning efforts.

1. Reform curricula for advocacy and resilience. DrPH programs must enhance curricula to provide robust training in crisis and change management, equipping future leaders to adapt and respond to unforeseen public health emergencies and policy shifts.[8] A strong emphasis on advanced applied communication skills is crucial, enabling graduates to effectively translate complex scientific information to diverse audiences, including policymakers and the public.[8] Furthermore, comprehensive training in mixed-methods analysis, strategic leadership, and policy advocacy is essential for navigating intricate intersectoral challenges and influencing policy decisions.[8]
2. Integrate practice-experienced faculty. DrPH programs must recruit and support faculty who possess extensive practical experience in public health, enabling them to serve as authentic mentors and academic advisors for students grappling with real-world problems.[8,12] This would help bridge the perceived gap between theoretical coursework and systematic, practice-based approaches often sought by students outside their formal programs.[8]
3. Enhance and centralize practice experiences. DrPH programs must ensure that robust, structured practice-based experiences, akin to residencies or immersive engagements, are central to the curriculum, rather than peripheral or concluding components.[8,12] This approach aligns with the demand for developing transdisciplinary leaders capable of navigating multisector partnerships and addressing conflicting interests.[8]
4. Embed core public health values. DrPH programs must ensure that the curriculum explicitly integrates antiracism principles, global health equity, and climate change as foundational pillars of DrPH training.[8,12] This commitment extends to preparing graduates to engage in ethical deliberation and advocacy for social justice and health equity, moving beyond traditional disease-centric interventions to address the root causes of health inequalities.[12]
5. Address financial barriers. DrPH programs, academic institutions, and funding bodies must prioritize mechanisms to alleviate the financial burden on DrPH students. This includes advocating for expanded loan forgiveness programs specifically for DrPH graduates committed to public service, increasing scholarships, and creating more fully funded positions to enable talented individuals to pursue public health leadership without career-limiting debt.[9]

Ultimately, public health leaders, including those in academic, governmental, and nonprofit sectors, must act decisively within their jurisdictions. This necessitates embracing cross-sectoral coalition building and movement organizing to collectively safeguard the mission of public health.[12] We must acknowledge that preventing, promoting, and protecting the health of the public is an inherently political act, and our educational systems must reflect this reality by preparing a generation of leaders who are not merely competent but courageous activists and advocates for health equity. The integrity of our scientific endeavors and the well-being of the populations we serve depend upon it. AJPH

CORRESPONDENCE

Correspondence should be sent to Pedro A. Serrano, 167 N Green St, 4th Fl, Chicago, IL 60607 (e-mail: pedro.serrano@cgu.edu). Reprints can be ordered at https://www.ajph.org by clicking the "Reprints" link.

PUBLICATION INFORMATION

Full Citation: Serrano PA. Navigating a politicized landscape: the imperative for activist and advocate leadership in public health education. *Am J Public Health*. 2026;116(4):455–457.

Acceptance Date: January 6, 2026.

DOI: https://doi.org/10.2105/AJPH.2025.308402

ORCID iD:
Pedro A. Serrano https://orcid.org/0000-0001-9504-5647

ACKNOWLEDGMENTS

I acknowledge the students, staff, and faculty of the Doctor of Public Health Program at Claremont Graduate University's School of Community and Global Health for their dedication to public health education. I am also deeply grateful to the university for its generous support through the DrPH Fellowship and the Felix and Helen Juda Endowed Fellowship. Additionally, I thank the Crossing Boundaries Research Award, which is funded by the Richter Memorial Funds Master Code, Bank of America, N.A., Trustee.

CONFLICTS OF INTEREST

The author declares that he has no known competing financial interests or personal relationships that could have appeared to influence the work reported in this editorial.

REFERENCES

1. Greer SL, Jarman H, Kulikoff R, Yaver M. Trump's second presidency begins: evaluating effects on the US health system. *Lancet Reg Health Am*. 2025;48:101173. https://doi.org/10.1016/j.lana.2025.101173
2. Patel VR, Liu M, Jena AB. Clinical trials affected by research grant terminations at the national institutes of health. *JAMA Intern Med*. 2026;186(1):126–128. https://doi.org/10.1001/jamainternmed.2025.6088
3. Hightow-Weidman L, Hosek S. The adolescent medicine trials network for HIV interventions as a driver of NIH's mission to end the HIV epidemic. *J Adolesc Health*. 2026;78(1):17–18. https://doi.org/10.1016/j.jadohealth.2025.09.026
4. Altice FL. The viral playbook threatening the National Institutes of Health: a call to inoculate the immune system of American science. *Lancet Reg Health Am*. 2025;47(:101145. https://doi.org/10.1016/j.lana.2025.101145
5. Jackson M. The impact of anti-DEI legislation on higher education pedagogy. *J Coll Character*. 2025;26(1):61–73. https://doi.org/10.1080/2194587x.2024.2442717
6. Schneider GE, McCann J, Foster A. From deficit to action: rebuilding policy and advocacy capacity in the public health workforce. *Health Aff Sch*. 2025;3(12):qxaf232. https://doi.org/10.1093/haschl/qxaf232
7. Calhoun JG, McElligott JE, Weist EM, Raczynski JM. Core competencies for doctoral education in public health. *Am J Public Health*. 2012;102(1):22–29. https://doi.org/10.2105/AJPH.2011.300469
8. Park C, Delgado C. Analysis of the doctor of public health (DrPH) training and identity needs in the United States: a qualitative study. *BMC Health Serv Res*. 2023;23(1):1216. https://doi.org/10.1186/s12913-023-10227-x
9. Park C, Coles E. The impact of student debt on career choices among doctor of public health graduates in the United States: a descriptive analysis. *Int J Environ Res Public Health*. 2022;19(8):4836. https://doi.org/10.3390/ijerph19084836
10. Cross RI, Huynh J, Rogers TB, Bradford NJ, Sharif MZ. CBPR is indeed political. *Lancet Reg Health Am*. 2025;51:101293. https://doi.org/10.1016/j.lana.2025.101293
11. McMurtry CL, Givens ML, Bailey ZD, et al. Why building power is key to protecting academic public health and advancing health equity. *Am J Public Health*. 2025;115(11):1783–1788. https://doi.org/10.2105/AJPH.2025.308210
12. Sullivan LM, Weist EM, Barrington WE, et al. Education for public health 2030: transformation to meet health needs in a changing world. *Front Public Health*. 2023;11:1269272. https://doi.org/10.3389/fpubh.2023.1269272

How the Escalating War on Immigrants Impacts Students' Mental Health and Well-Being

Michelle Zaragoza, MSW, LCSW

ABOUT THE AUTHOR

Michelle Zaragoza is a doctoral student at the School of Social Welfare, University of California, Berkeley.

See also *AJPH* Student Think Tank, pp. 447–484.

AJPH April 2026, Vol. 116, No. 4

In their timely editorial, Borrell and Kapadia[1] examine how the Trump administration's increasingly exclusionary immigration policies have deepened health disparities for immigrant communities. They emphasize how this "escalating war on immigrants" has created a public health crisis that demands urgent, multifaceted responses. Although they situate the impact of immigration policy on immigrant health as a crisis unfolding outside the walls of academia, their analysis equally applies to the reality faced by many public health students who themselves are immigrants or engage with immigrant communities. The same forces undermining immigrant health also infiltrate the environments of everyday student life (e.g., universities, hospitals, community organizations), leaving students to navigate the dual burden of managing the emotional labor of ensuring the safety of their community and themselves. Responding to Borrell and Kapadia's urgent call for public health action requires acknowledging the impact of immigration policies on students' mental health and well-being. Addressing this impact is critical if we aim to nurture and sustain a more compassionate workforce dedicated to health equity.

MENTAL HEALTH AND ETHICAL CONCERNS IN IMMIGRANT RESEARCH

Students like me, who engage with immigrant communities through our identities, research, or practice, frequently confront trauma and systemic violence. Research suggests that punitive immigration policies have far-reaching mental health impacts, extending beyond individuals to cause intergenerational trauma in families[2] and heightened anxiety and psychological distress in the broader community, particularly among those with social ties to immigrants.[3] Mental health impacts weigh heavily on students, who face heightened risks of vicarious trauma, stress, and burnout from repeated exposure to harm in their research and personal lives.[4] Yet managing this harm requires significant emotional labor as students navigate the psychosocial burdens of an aggressive immigration climate while balancing ethical and safety concerns in community-engaged research.

Students engaged in immigrant-centered research face numerous challenges, often with limited institutional guidance and support. They carry the responsibility of ensuring their own safety and that of the communities they engage with.[5] This requires the conscientious and intentional adoption of trauma-informed research practices that extend beyond traditional ethical frameworks, such as the Belmont Report of 1979, to avoid perpetuating systemic harm. Students must carefully navigate research procedures to protect and empower immigrant communities historically excluded from research and distrustful of institutions. These efforts are further complicated by fears of deportation and the presence of Immigration and Customs Enforcement (ICE) on campuses and in hospitals and community centers.[6] At the same time, federal restrictions on funding for equity-focused research create a chilling effect on scientific discourse, undermining intellectual safety and constraining efforts to address health disparities among immigrant communities.[7] In the absence of strong institutional support, students disproportionately shoulder the psycho-emotional toll of this work, balancing compassion and responsibility with awareness of the social and political realities harming immigrant communities.

TOWARD COLLECTIVE RESPONSIBILITY AND HOPE

Public health institutions must take shared responsibility to build institutional mechanisms that address the mental health and safety concerns that students face in their work with immigrant communities. Strategies to support students may include providing training and mentorship in trauma-informed research practices, embedding student wellness supports and debriefings into research protocols, securing nonfederal funding for equity-centered research, and strengthening protections to safeguard students from ICE presence on campuses.

Ultimately, promoting the well-being of students and immigrant communities depends on collective responsibility and a commitment to hope. To hope is to envision a future in which public health fosters justice, equity, and dignity for all, even amid shifting social and political realities.[8] By recognizing and addressing the challenges faced by students engaged in immigrant-focused work, we can foster a more resilient and compassionate workforce equipped to advance health equity. AJPH

CORRESPONDENCE

Correspondence should be sent to Michelle Zaragoza, PhD Student, School of Social Welfare, University of California, Berkeley, Haviland Hall, Berkeley, CA 94709 (e-mail: michellezaragoza@berkeley.edu). Reprints can be ordered at https://www.ajph.org by clicking the "Reprints" link.

PUBLICATION INFORMATION

Full Citation: Zaragoza M. How the escalating war on immigrants impacts students' mental health and well-being. *Am J Public Health*. 2026;116(4):458–459.

Acceptance Date: December 26, 2025

DOI: https://doi.org/10.2105/AJPH.2025.308401

ORCID iD:

Michelle Zaragoza https://orcid.org/0009-0008-5424-5499

CONFLICTS OF INTEREST

The author has no conflicts of interest to disclose.

REFERENCES

1. Borrell L, Kapadia F. The escalating war on immigrants is a public health crisis. *Am J Public Health.* 2025;115(8):1220–1221. https://doi.org/10.2105/AJPH.2025.308158
2. Rojas-Flores L, Clements ML, Hwang Koo J, London J. Trauma and psychological distress in Latino citizen children following parental detention and deportation. *Psychol Trauma.* 2017;9(3):352–361. https://doi.org/10.1037/tra0000177
3. Pinedo M, Valdez CR. Immigration enforcement policies and the mental health of US citizens: findings from a comparative analysis. *Am J Community Psychol.* 2020;66(1-2):119–129. https://doi.org/10.1002/ajcp.12464
4. Sprang G, Ford J, Kerig P, Bride B. Defining secondary traumatic stress and developing targeted assessments and interventions: lessons learned from research and leading experts. *Traumatology (Tallahass Fla).* 2019;25(2):72–81. https://doi.org/10.1037/trm0000180
5. Syeed E, Rosas A, Hammam F, Shen S, Zeferino F. Challenging "citizen science": liminal status students and community-engaged research. *Soc Sci.* 2022;11(2):66. https://doi.org/10.3390/socsci11020066
6. Martinez-Alvarado S. Undocumented students are living in fear on college campuses. The effects of campus raids. EdTrust. March 19, 2025. Available at: https://edtrust.org/blog/undocumented-students-are-living-in-fear-on-college-campuses-the-effects-of-campus-raids. Accessed September 10, 2025.
7. Coronado ZK, Koenders SL, Knight KR, Lechuga J, López AM, Martinez C. How anti-immigrant policies impact research among Latinx and undocumented people who use drugs. *Am J Public Health.* 2025;115(11):e1–e10. https://doi.org/10.2105/AJPH.2025.308234
8. Zaragoza M. A love letter to hope. *Am J Public Health.* 2025;115(5):681–681. https://doi.org/10.2105/AJPH.2024.307977

A Generation at Stake: Master of Public Health Education, Workforce Decline, and the Future of US Public Health

David Yagudayev, Banpreet Bawa, MS, Aaron Shaykevich, MPH, Zoreslava Osiv, MBA, and Martha Wojtowycz, PhD

ABOUT THE AUTHORS

The authors are with the Department of Public Health & Preventative Medicine, Norton College of Medicine, SUNY Upstate Medical University, Syracuse, NY.

See also *AJPH* Student Think Tank, pp. 447–484.

AJPH April 2026, Vol. 116, No. 4

At the height of the COVID-19 pandemic, the United States learned a critical lesson: public health infrastructure saves lives. Yet, scarcely four years later, Congress has now passed HR 1, also known as the "Big Beautiful Bill." We believe that this law will, among other issues, create long-term damage to public health education.

As master of public health students, we write from lived experience. The pressures students face are already immense. The proposed termination of the Graduate PLUS loan program, coupled with drastic cuts to the budgets of the National Institutes of Health (NIH) and the Centers for Disease Control and Prevention (CDC), will severely affect our education. These policies risk our future trajectories as public health workers and could disrupt the public health workforce, compromising the health and safety of every community in this country.

For decades, Graduate PLUS loans have allowed aspiring professionals to finance their education and basic living expenses. Unlike unsubsidized loans capped at $20 500 annually for graduate students, Graduate PLUS loans have no fixed annual or aggregate limits and cover the costs of attendance without a rigid borrowing ceiling.[1] Thus, for students admitted to programs involving costs well over the unsubsidized loan ceiling, these loans have often been the only way to continue their studies. HR 1 would end this program effective July 1, 2026. In addition, maximum graduate borrowing would be capped at $100 000 for master's programs and $200 000 for professional degrees, irrespective of the actual cost of attendance.[2] This shift would perpetuate and deepen the barriers to pursuing various fields of study such as law, medicine, business, and public health, making attendance inaccessible to students from low- and middle-income backgrounds.

Consequently, with the elimination of Graduate PLUS loans, students' only recourse would be private loans, many of which carry high interest rates and require strong credit or cosigners. Such loans may not be an option for first-generation students, those from low-income households, or those without family safety nets. In practice, this means that fewer students from diverse socioeconomic backgrounds will enter public health. This is not merely a financial issue; it is a workforce issue with profound long-term consequences. Previous studies have shown that student loans not only cause stress, anxiety, and depression but also negatively affect a person's well-being.[3] Having an additional stressor on top of a demanding academic program can exacerbate the burden on students, leading to adverse health outcomes over time. When students are preoccupied with the financial burden of school, they may find it difficult to devote sufficient attention to their studies. For many, this pressure leads them to seek part-time jobs to cover living expenses, despite the already rigorous demands of full-time graduate study.

Public health graduates already face a mismatch between educational debt and earnings. National data show that the average graduate degree holder carries $102 790 in federal student loan debt.[3] The median debt for master of public health graduates is $52 263, whereas median postgraduate first-destination earnings are only $48 866.[4] The economics of pursuing this path are already daunting; further restrictions on federal aid will make the decision irrational for many.

For students who enter public health despite these obstacles, the debt burden can feel like a trap. University tuition across the country continues to rise.[5] Federal support is shrinking, and trends over the years point to declining interest in the public health field. With 500 000 workers in the year 2000 and only 300 000 today, a 40% decrease, the return on investment is far lower than in comparable health professions.[6] In candid conversations among peers, the same message is repeated: "I want to pursue a career in public health and love the field, but I honestly don't know if I can afford to." If Congress truly intends to strengthen the nation's health and future preparedness, undermining the workforce pipeline is a grave mistake.

In addition, the timing could not be worse. State and local health departments need at least 80 000 additional full-time staff members, an astonishing 80% increase, just to provide minimum services.[7] Yet the authors of a previous study warned that 129 000 public health workers, 57% of the public health workforce, were projected to leave the field by 2025.[8] Instead of expanding capacity, Congress is cutting it. The 2026 budget proposes a 40% cut to the NIH (from $46 billion to $27.9 billion) and a 50% cut to the CDC (from $9.2 billion to $4.2 billion).[9] These reductions would eliminate or severely weaken the National Institute on Minority Health and Health Disparities, the Fogarty International Center, the Global Health Center, and many others. The result will be widening health disparities, reduced global collaboration, and slower progress in addressing chronic disease, injury prevention, environmental health, and mental health.

The crisis is not only fiscal; it is cultural. Public trust in health institutions has plummeted since 2020. A 2025 KFF poll showed that only 61% of Americans trust the CDC "at least a fair amount."[10] Public health professionals, once celebrated as essential, now face skepticism, hostility, and even harassment. Figures such as Secretary of Health and Human Services Robert F. Kennedy Jr. have undermined confidence in vaccines and public health institutions, eroding the foundation on which public health depends: public trust. For students training to enter this workforce, the message is dispiriting. The combination of limited job prospects, diminished institutional credibility, and overwhelming debt contributes to anxiety and burnout. Graduate students are already six times more likely than the general population to experience depression and anxiety.[11] Cutting financial support and workforce funding has the potential to intensify the mental health crisis among graduate students training for public health careers.

The HR 1 cuts also strike at the heart of equity. Eliminating the National Institute on Minority Health and Health Disparities, for example, would halt critical research on disease risk, morbidity, and mortality among underrepresented populations.[12] Studies in these areas have been indispensable in identifying patterns of health disparities and developing interventions. Without them, disparities will widen, and vulnerable populations will bear the brunt of policy neglect. The equity issue is just as urgent within the student body itself. Students from underrepresented backgrounds disproportionately rely on Graduate PLUS loans. Limiting or eliminating this resource will reduce diversity in graduate programs and, ultimately, in the public health workforce. A less diverse workforce will be less equipped to respond to the needs of marginalized communities, exacerbating disparities at multiple levels.

Public health is not partisan. Ensuring access to preventive care, protecting communities from infectious diseases, and reducing health inequities are fundamental responsibilities that serve every population. To safeguard the future, Congress should preserve and expand federal loan programs for graduate students, invest in loan forgiveness programs, and protect the research infrastructure that drives innovation and equity. Rebuilding trust in institutions will require transparent communication, genuine community partnerships, and stronger mental health support for graduate students. Education must remain a ladder, not an unclimbable wall.

Across the country, students are questioning whether a master of public health degree is worth it. Many are now forced to weigh public service against unsustainable debt. If current trends continue, we risk losing an entire generation of public health professionals. Public health is the backbone of resilience. Supporting students is not optional; it is essential. America's future, and the health of every community, depends on it. AJPH

CORRESPONDENCE

Correspondence should be sent to David Yagudayev, 2263 Weiskotten Hall, 766 Irving Ave, Syracuse, NY 13210 (e-mail: yagudayd@upstate.edu). Reprints can be ordered at https://www.ajph.org by clicking the "Reprints" link.

PUBLICATION INFORMATION

Full Citation: Yagudayev D, Bawa B, Shaykevich A, Osiv Z, Wojtowycz M. A generation at stake: master of public health education, workforce decline, and the future of US public health. *Am J Public Health*. 2026;116(4):460–462.

Acceptance Date: December 26, 2025

DOI: https://doi.org/10.2105/AJPH.2025.308399

ORCID iDs:

David Yagudayev https://orcid.org/0009-0008-7296-9036

Banpreet Bawa https://orcid.org/0009-0003-1771-9740

Aaron Shaykevich https://orcid.org/0000-0001-6917-0815

Zoreslava Osiv https://orcid.org/0009-0005-9968-4370

Martha Wojtowycz https://orcid.org/0009-0000-9374-2887

CONTRIBUTORS

D. Yagudayev conceived the editorial, developed the central arguments, and drafted the majority of the editorial. B. Bawa contributed to background research and assisted with the drafting of the editorial. A. Shaykevich assisted with the drafting and revision of the editorial. Z. Osiv and M. Wojtowycz served as faculty advisers and provided guidance and critical reviews of the editorial. All of the authors reviewed the final version.

CONFLICTS OF INTEREST

The authors report no conflicts of interest.

REFERENCES

1. Federal Student Aid. Grad PLUS loans. Available at: https://studentaid.gov/understand-aid/types/loans/plus/grad. Accessed September 11, 2025.
2. US Congress. One Big Beautiful Bill Act. Available at: https://www.congress.gov/bill/119th-congress/house-bill/1. Accessed September 11, 2025.
3. Education Data Initiative. Student loan debt statistics 2025. Available at: https://educationdata.org/student-loan-debt-statistics. Accessed September 11, 2025.
4. Beck AJ, Leider JP, Krasna H, Resnick BA. Monetary and nonmonetary costs and benefits of a public health master's degree in the 21st century. *Am J Public Health*. 2020;110(7):978–985. https://doi.org/10.2105/AJPH.2020.305648
5. Wood S. A look at 20 years of tuition costs at national universities. Available at: https://www.usnews.com/education/best-colleges/paying-for-college/articles/see-20-years-of-tuition-growth-at-national-universities. Accessed September 11, 2025.
6. Krasna H, Fried L. Generation public health: fixing the broken bridge between public health education and the governmental workforce. Available at: https://pmc.ncbi.nlm.nih.gov/articles/PMC8489610/pdf/AJPH.2021.306317.pdf. Accessed September 11, 2025.
7. de Beaumont Foundation. Staffing up: investing in the public health workforce. Available at: https://debeaumont.org/staffing-up. Accessed September 11, 2025.
8. Leider JP, Castrucci BC, Robins M, et al. The exodus of state and local public health employees: separations started before and continued throughout COVID-19. *Health Aff (Millwood)*. 2023;42(3):338–348. doi:https://doi.org/10.1377/hlthaff.2022.01251
9. The White House. The president's FY 2026 discretionary budget request. Available at: https://www.whitehouse.gov/omb/information-resources/budget/the-presidents-fy-2026-discretionary-budget-request. Accessed November 3, 2025.
10. KFF. KFF Tracking Poll on Health Information and Trust: January 2025. Available at: https://www.kff.org/health-information-trust/kff-tracking-poll-on-health-information-and-trust-january-2025. Accessed September 11, 2025.
11. Evans TM, Bira L, Gastelum JB, Weiss LT, Vanderford NL. Evidence for a mental health crisis in graduate education. *Nat Biotechnol*. 2018;36(3):282–284. doi:https://doi.org/10.1038/nbt.4089
12. National Institute on Minority Health and Health Disparities. Community health and population science. Available at: https://www.nimhd.nih.gov/research/extramural-research/community-health-and-population-science. Accessed September 11, 2025.

Beyond Inclusion: Policy Shifts Reshaping Careers for Black Women in Public Health

Nqobile Nzama, MPH, Amanda Scott-Davis, MPH, and Jelani C. Kerr, PhD

ABOUT THE AUTHORS

Nqobile Nzama, Amanda Scott-Davis, and Jelani C. Kerr are with the School of Public Health and Information Sciences, University of Louisville, Louisville, KY.

See also *AJPH* Student Think Tank, pp. 447–484.

The COVID-19 pandemic, which was declared a national emergency in the United States on March 13, 2020, and the co-occurring social upheaval have helped shape the research interests of public health students and practitioners. Specifically, the pandemic coincided with high-profile instances of state violence (e.g., Breonna Taylor's death on March 13, 2020, and George Floyd's death on May 25, 2020), which escalated the visibility of and participation in the Black Lives Matter (BLM) movement. The intersection of COVID-19 and the BLM movement revealed racial and socioeconomic injustices that disproportionately affect communities of color. These events became accelerants for a movement toward greater social justice and diversity, inclusion, and equity (DEI). As a concept, social justice has influenced the scope of culturally competent public health, broadened traditional methodologies and career opportunities, and increased commitment to community-engaged research grounded in the social determinants of health.[1]

In response to the COVID-19 pandemic and its deleterious social and health impacts, the Biden administration continued to invest in health equity and social justice. Although public health has shifted more toward a health equity paradigm in the United States, the field continues to face challenges, particularly within a political climate characterized by hostility toward equity during Trump's second term, beginning in January 2025. Donald Trump began writing executive orders (EOs) on the first day of his second term, revoking most Biden-era EOs and actions, which he called "deeply unpopular, inflationary, illegal, and radical practices." Some of Trump's EOs halted or rescinded federally funded research projects.[2] This has threatened secure employment for researchers and public health students supported by federal grants. The drastic changes in administrations have left a lingering question of whether there is still room for Black women students to thrive in a health equity–focused lens of public health under contemporary sociopolitical agendas.

POSITIONALITY OF BLACK WOMEN PHD STUDENTS

A social justice and health equity perspective is on the rise in the discipline of public health, including higher education institutions that offer this area as a concentration for public health programs.[3] Inclusive research and educational practices necessitate that the most affected communities are involved in equity processes. Thus, as students who are members of a marginalized group (Black women), we have received academic training emphasizing health equity and community-engaged research. This training has shifted from the field's typical interest in telling stories of minority populations through a colonial framework to the utilization of asset-based, culturally informed approaches. One coauthor, a PhD candidate who identifies as a Black woman, spent the first two years in her PhD program learning about the impact of HIV and mass incarceration on the African American community in Kentucky. Her utilization of a health equity paradigm amplified the voices and identities of the affected individuals. Although the study mainly involved quantitative data collection, the research team engaged in focus groups and knowledge translation events to establish steps to address the impact of mass incarceration and HIV vulnerability for African Americans. On projects such as this one, she learned that diversity is a strength, helping her understand how the tenets of health equity can be translated into practice while centering affected populations. However, directives such as EO 14151 ("Ending Radical and Wasteful Government DEI Programs and Preferencing") reframed intentionality in diversity as adverse to government or societal goals.[2]

Another coauthor is a PhD candidate who also identifies as a Black woman and a maternal health researcher whose work examines adverse health outcomes within a sociohistorical context. She recognizes this time as a pivotal moment in history. Current federal policies limit funding for her area of research, which has now been classified as DEI, thereby creating fewer career prospects because of decreased diversity efforts. To further her career in the current sociopolitical climate, she is exploring the autonomy of utilizing her expertise while also considering sustainability to support her livelihood. Her job search is hampered by the limited number of academic positions and private sector jobs in public health. Students' original career goals have been upended since they enrolled in their programs. The unique sociopolitical climate and challenges in public health leave uncertainty about future career possibilities and the populations that will be affected by scholarly work. In addition, she feels there is a lack of academic training to incorporate the new politically accepted language to account for unforeseen changes in health equity research. Changes during this striking moment leave students with limited guidance and uncertainty to secure prospective employment.

RESTRICTIVE CAREER EXPLORATIONS IN PUBLIC HEALTH

The sociopolitical climate in the United States has restricted health equity research and marginalized social justice scholars. Morabia[4] discusses the threat of political interference in scientific publishing. A central point of this piece is that politics can have a significant impact on censorship in academia and the distribution of funding, thus resulting in the neglect of critical areas of research and intervention. However, it falls short of acknowledging the influence of politics in shaping the trajectory of students' careers. This is especially important for public health students researching health disparities, who are experiencing funding cuts because of subject matter (e.g., maternal and child health) or population of interest (e.g., sexual and gender minorities).

Recently, students have been forced to comply with EOs and state policies (such as Kentucky House Bill 4)[5] that undermine efforts to ensure diversity. Some public health student researchers have encountered training barriers caused by EOs that have eliminated funding that supports predoctoral students and promotes workforce diversity (e.g., Predoctoral Individual National Research Service Awards [F31]). It is essential that, as political changes occur, students receive guidance from faculty and administration to help them remain within funding guidelines while also ensuring that academic freedom is maintained. Although the field of public health is challenged with reduced funding and restrictions on health equity–focused research, public health students' hopes for careers in the government sector are also filled with uncertainty, as evidenced by the recent layoffs within agencies such as the Centers for Disease Control and Prevention and the National Institutes of Health.[6] This is especially concerning for educated Black women, given the greater opportunity for middle-class jobs conferred by federal employment offerings (relative to the private sector).[7] Clearly, there is a need for intervention to assist Black women in public health to secure economic opportunity within a rapidly changing public health employment landscape. As public health students face challenges in research and career trajectories, higher education institutions should provide students with necessary tools for success. Administration, faculty, and career service offices have a shared responsibility to provide guidance and resources for students to succeed in future roles.

NEXT STEPS

Next steps in this sociopolitical climate include higher education institutions taking a greater responsibility to inform students about their approaches to academic freedom and the ways institutions are handling new changes that affect researchers. This includes helping students understand how newly implemented policies and EOs affect their work and creating a transparent trail of the steps institutions are developing to maintain academic freedom and inclusivity. This is especially relevant for students involved in health equity research, who must adapt to comply with new federal policy guidelines for public health research and practice. Students are looking to institutional leadership and professional organizations to urgently lead the way to the future of public health employment and guidance in navigating a newly ambiguous public health landscape. Collective statements highlighting the deleterious impact of attacking diversity and lawsuits preserving academic freedom help in this mission. At the same time, while practicing in "safe" public health spaces, students will not be stripped of their research interests and identities. Furthermore, institutions should refrain from overcompliance with state and federal policies that could further marginalize the voices of students of color. Lastly, institutions or programs (primarily those focusing on health equity and social justice) should develop and adapt education and training to help students navigate the job market, which is affected by an anti-DEI environment.

CONCLUSION

The changes in the current political climate, particularly in research funding and public health employment opportunities, have a negative impact on the trajectories of students of color who are dedicated to health equity. Specifically, there are considerable concerns regarding a lack of job opportunities because of a weakening of the public health infrastructure in research and practice. More efforts are needed to support students as they enter a more precarious public health employment marketplace. Academic institutions are key to this effort, particularly for Black women. AJPH

CORRESPONDENCE

Correspondence should be sent to Nqobile Nzama, 485 E Gray St, Louisville, KY 40202 (e-mail: nqobile.nzama@louisville.edu). Reprints can be ordered at https://www.ajph.org by clicking the 'Reprints" link.

PUBLICATION INFORMATION

Full Citation: Nzama N, Scott-Davis A, Kerr JC. Beyond inclusion: policy shifts reshaping careers for Black women in public health. *Am J Public Health*. 2026;116(4):463–465.

Acceptance Date: January 1, 2026.

DOI: https://doi.org/10.2105/AJPH.2025.308400

ORCID iD:

Nqobile Nzama https://orcid.org/0009-0002-9338-2230

CONTRIBUTORS

N. Nzama led the manuscript development, review, and revisions. A. Scott-Davis contributed to the manuscript development, review, and revisions. J. C. Kerr contributed to the manuscript development and revisions.

CONFLICTS OF INTEREST

The authors declare that they have no conflicts of interest.

REFERENCES

1. Knight E, Bogan C. What 2020 taught us about the politics and teaching of public health. *Dela J Public Health*. 2021;7(2):64–67. https://doi.org/10.32481/djph.2021.03.014
2. Federal Register. Presidential documents: ending radical and wasteful government DEI programs and preferencing. Executive Order 14151 of January 20, 2025. *Fed Regist*. 2025;90(19):8339–8441. Available at: https://www.federalregister.gov/documents/2025/01/29/2025-01953/ending-radical-and-wasteful-government-dei-programs-and-preferencing. Accessed September 10, 2025.
3. PublicHealthDegrees.org. Health equity concentration in public health. November 18, 2022. Available at: https://www.publichealthdegrees.org/specializations/health-equity. Accessed September 15, 2025.
4. Morabia A. AJPH and the threat of political interference in scientific publishing. *Am J Public Health*. 2025;115(5):626–627. https://doi.org/10.2105/ajph.2025.308100
5. Pinski H. Kentucky's new anti-DEI law is now in effect. How colleges, universities are complying. *Courier-Journal*. July 1, 2025. Available at: https://www.courier-journal.com/story/news/politics/2025/06/30/anti-dei-law-now-in-effect-in-kentucky-how-colleges-are-complying/82234702007. Accessed September 15, 2025.
6. Dietrich DR, Von Aulock S, Bal-Price A, et al. The alarming consequences of workforce reductions at the FDA, EPA, NIH and CDC in the United States. *Arch Toxicol*. 2025;99(6):2239–2241. https://doi.org/10.1007/s00204-025-04065-5
7. Childers C. Disinvestment in the public sector undermines opportunities for Black women across the South. Economic Policy Institute. Available at: https://www.epi.org/blog/disinvestment-in-the-public-sector-undermines-opportunities-for-black-women-across-the-south-trump-cuts-further-threaten-key-services-for-working-people-across-the-nation. Accessed September 15, 2025.

Precarious Futures: International Student Distress, Limited Training Pathways, and Career Uncertainty in Public Health

Cheng Chow, MPhil, and Meiyan Chen, MSW

ABOUT THE AUTHORS

Cheng Chow is with the School of Social Work and the Population Research Center, University of Texas at Austin. Meiyan Chen is with the School of Social Work, University of Texas at Austin.

AJPH April 2026, Vol. 116, No. 4

See also *AJPH* Student Think Tank, pp. 447–484.

In 2023 through 2024, the United States hosted 1 126 690 international students, an all-time high, including record graduate enrollment and continued growth in Optional Practical Training (OPT).[1] OPT, a federal program authorizing temporary employment directly related to a student's field of study, serves as a key bridge between academic training and practical experience. International students constitute a meaningful share of US higher education, especially in science, technology, engineering, and mathematics (STEM) and health-related fields that feed public health research and practice. Yet these students study amid rapid federal policy shifts, particularly executive actions and agency rules that regulate eligibility for training, funding, and employment.

This volatility has three compounding effects for international public health students: visa-related distress that undermines well-being and academic progress, constricted pathways to federally supported training and mentorship, and career uncertainty, especially with respect to roles in public service. These structural dynamics reveal how national policies shape the next generation of the US public health workforce.

VISA-RELATED DISTRESS AS STRUCTURAL VULNERABILITY

Policy churn, referring to rapid and recurring policy shifts, makes legal status seem contingent rather than cumulative. Routine academic milestones, such as internships, practicum placements, and conference travel, are bound up with documentation deadlines and the risk of policy reversal. OPT authorizes up to 12 months of postcompletion employment, with a 24-month STEM extension requiring employer attestations and recurring evaluations.[2] These administrative requirements, such as multistep authorization and time-sensitive reporting before initiation of internships, are largely invisible to international students' domestic peers and reduce time for scholarship and skill development.

Nevertheless, postgraduation employment offers no greater stability. H-1B employment hinges on a capped lottery. For fiscal year 2026, US Citizenship and Immigration Services received 343 981 eligible H-1B registrations for a statutory quota of 85 000, leaving many qualified graduates without a timely employment pathway aligned with training timelines.[3] In 2025, more than 6000 student visas were revoked, and a presidential proclamation attempted to suspend entry for students at Harvard University before being halted in court.[4,5] During such episodes, international students described checking immigration news obsessively each morning, fearing that their academic journey might be terminated without explanation.[6] This type of anxiety is well documented in research linking policy uncertainty to psychological distress and difficulties transitioning from school to work and undermines institutional investments in workforce diversity.[7]

Draft regulations circulated in 2025 proposed replacing duration of status with fixed admission periods, requiring international students to apply for extensions even if they were continuously enrolled and in good standing.[8] These proposals, whether finalized or not, signal instability that undermines students' ability to commit to multiyear projects and partnerships. Such shifts consume time and attention that could otherwise support research and training.

LIMITED PATHS TO FEDERALLY SUPPORTED TRAINING

The United States recruits global talent into graduate programs yet excludes many international students from keystone federally funded training pipelines. Two examples are the National Science Foundation Graduate Research Fellowship Program and the National Institutes of Health Ruth L. Kirschstein National Research Service Award fellowships and training grants, which require US citizenship or permanent residency at the time of application or award.[9,10] Although eligibility requirements for fellowships are grounded in statutory intent, they nevertheless limit access for qualified international trainees. These restrictions constrain who can pursue risk-tolerant research questions, secure formative mentorships, and obtain early career credentials despite international students contributing substantially to the US research enterprise.

Executive Order 14151 (Ending Radical and Wasteful Government DEI Programs and Preferencing) was signed on January 20, 2025, and published in the *Federal Register* on January 29, 2025, signaling retrenchment that affects mentoring networks and training environments.[11] When these executive actions restrict diversity, equity, and inclusion efforts inside federal agencies, the mentoring programs, affinity networks, and informal pipelines that have offset these exclusions can also weaken. These shifts have discouraged open discussion of certain topics. International students report avoiding topics such as structural racism and LGBTQ+ (lesbian, gay, bisexual, transgender, or queer) health disparities, fearing that these subjects might jeopardize their visa status or future employment. Editorial leaders in public health have warned that political interference in science endangers the research climate that trainees inhabit.[12]

CAREER UNCERTAINTY IN THE PUBLIC SECTOR AND BEYOND

The consequences of these training limitations extend beyond campuses. Many public health students aspire to careers in public service. Federal hiring rules, however, generally require US citizenship for competitive service positions, limiting access for international graduates at precisely the moment when agencies seek to expand capacity.[13] Predictably, graduates pivot to private-sector roles, health systems, or academia or they depart the United States altogether. This pattern produces measurable losses for governmental public health at a time when national reports describe persistent workforce gaps and an urgent need to strengthen pipelines and retention.[14]

LIVED EXPERIENCE WITHIN AN UNSETTLED RESEARCH CLIMATE

As current doctoral students navigating training, work authorization, and fellowship restrictions, we have experienced and witnessed among peers the pervasive uncertainty that structures daily academic life. Discussions around international students' training and well-being are not abstract. They reflect lived realities of monitoring visa updates daily, planning research timelines around regulatory deadlines, and balancing academic progress with policy anxiety. Commentaries in leading journals describe a climate of uncertainty that threatens early career investigators' ability to establish and sustain scientific programs, with cascading effects for trainees whose funding and mentorship depend on those programs.[15] Public health leaders have warned that recent federal actions could destabilize research infrastructure nationally, elevating the importance of editorial independence and science and governance safeguards to protect students and trainees as well as the evidence base.[12]

It is tempting to treat these challenges as private struggles to be managed with grit. They are structural indicators that national policies are undermining the sustainability of the public health workforce pipeline. The paradox is stark. The United States attracts global talent to strengthen its health system, yet it builds policy bottlenecks that strain well-being, suppress opportunity, and scatter graduates.

ACTIONS TOWARD STABILITY AND INCLUSION

Several coordinated actions can strengthen stability, inclusion, and well-being for international students.

Reform Fellowship Eligibility or Create Parallel Tracks

Federal science agencies could pilot merit-based graduate fellowships open to all qualified trainees regardless of citizenship in areas of declared public health workforce need. In instances in which statutes prevent change, agencies and Congress could establish parallel mechanisms or public–private partnerships to support international trainees alongside their domestic peers.

Stabilize Training Authorizations

OPT and STEM OPT should be preserved as predictable on ramps to supervised practice, reporting should be streamlined to focus on educational outcomes, and the relevance of epidemiology, biostatistics, and informatics roles within STEM-designated training pathways should be made explicit.

Expand Transparent Public-Sector Pathways

Given longstanding citizenship requirements in the United States and similar norms elsewhere, programs should clearly communicate eligibility and conversion rules at the outset. Agencies can expand adjacent public service contributions through extramural fellowships, cooperative agreements, and contractor roles that place trainees within public health agencies without formal federal appointments.

Invest in Mental Health Support

Campus services should include visa-aware counseling and peer groups. Graduate programs should train advisors to recognize policy-linked distress and help students plan around OPT and H-1B timelines. Evidence linking policy uncertainty to student stress justifies treating this issue as a programmatic challenge, not an individual failing.

Protect the Research Environment

Editorial independence, stable grant processes, and insulation from political interference matter for students because they determine the ground under their feet.

CONCLUSION

International public health students are building data systems, evaluating interventions, modeling outbreaks, and analyzing structural drivers of health. Policy shifts and uncertainty spanning visas, fellowship eligibility, and public-sector hiring too often render these contributions provisional. The international students who sustain US research and public health pipelines deserve the predictable pathways, supportive environments, and freedom from discrimination afforded to their domestic peers.

The solutions are within reach. High-impact training opportunities based on merit should be established, predictable and educationally meaningful work authorizations should be maintained, processes related to lawful access to early-career public service should be clarified, and the research environment that underpins training should be protected. A stable and inclusive policy environment is not charity; it is a prerequisite for the resilience of public health itself. Public health thrives when talent and opportunity align, and students should not have to choose between their science and their future. AJPH

CORRESPONDENCE

Correspondence should be sent to Cheng Chow, MPhil, Texas Social Work, University of Texas at Austin, 405 W 25th St, Stop D3500, Austin, TX 78705 (e-mail: chengchow@utexas.edu). Reprints can be ordered at https://www.ajph.org by clicking the "Reprints" link.

PUBLICATION INFORMATION

Full Citation: Chow C, Chen M. Precarious futures: international student distress, limited training pathways, and career uncertainty in public health. *Am J Public Health*. 2026;116(4):466–469.

Acceptance Date: December 12, 2025.

DOI: https://doi.org/10.2105/AJPH.2025.308388

ORCID iDs:
Cheng Chow https://orcid.org/0000-0002-2981-9728

Meiyan Chen https://orcid.org/0009-0003-1283-5961

CONTRIBUTORS

C. Chow conceptualized and drafted the editorial and led revisions in response to peer reviews. M. Chen reviewed and revised the editorial through substantive intellectual feedback across multiple drafts.

ACKNOWLEDGMENTS

We extend gratitude to Catherine Cubbin, who provided valuable feedback during the development of this editorial.

CONFLICTS OF INTEREST

The authors declare no conflicts of interest.

REFERENCES

1. Institute of International Education. United States hosts more than 1.1 million international students at higher education institutions, reaching all-time high. Available at: https://www.iie.org/news/us-hosts-more-than-1-1-million-intl-students-at-higher-education-institutions-all-time-high. Accessed September 4, 2025.
2. US Citizenship and Immigration Services. Policy manual volume 2—nonimmigrants, part F—students, chapter 5—practical training. Available at: http://uscis.gov/policy-manual/volume-2-part-f-chapter-5. Accessed September 2, 2025.
3. US Citizenship and Immigration Services. H-1B electronic registration process. Available at: https://www.uscis.gov/working-in-the-united-states/temporary-workers/h-1b-specialty-occupations/h-1b-electronic-registration-process. Accessed December 23, 2025.
4. The White House. Fact sheet: President Donald J. Trump restricts foreign student visas at Harvard University. Available at: https://www.whitehouse.gov/fact-sheets/2025/06/fact-sheet-president-donald-j-trump-restricts-foreign-student-visas-at-harvard-university. Accessed August 25, 2025.
5. Faguy A. US State Department revokes 6,000 student visas. Available at: https://www.bbc.com/news/articles/cz93vznxd07o. Accessed August 25, 2025.
6. Feng E. International students face visa cancellations despite no criminal records. Available at: https://www.npr.org/2025/04/22/nx-s1-5366021/international-students-face-visa-cancellations-despite-no-criminal-records. Accessed September 2, 2025.
7. Park C, Shimada S. The impact of changing nonimmigrant visa policies on international students' psychological adjustment and well-being in the United States during the COVID-19 pandemic: a qualitative study. *BMC Public Health*. 2022;22(1):2227. doi:https://doi.org/10.1186/s12889-022-14698-1
8. Department of Homeland Security. Establishing a fixed time period of admission and an extension of stay procedure for nonimmigrant academic

students, exchange visitors, and representatives of foreign information media. Available at: https://www.federalregister.gov/documents/2025/08/28/2025-16554/establishing-a-fixed-time-period-of-admission-and-an-extension-of-stay-procedure-for-nonimmigrant. Accessed December 23, 2025.

9. National Science Foundation. NSF Graduate Research Fellowship Program: GRFP program solicitation. Available at: https://www.nsf.gov/funding/opportunities/grfp-nsf-graduate-research-fellowship-program/nsf24-591/solicitation#elig. Accessed August 25, 2025.

10. National Institutes of Health. Ruth L. Kirschstein National Research Service Award individual predoctoral fellowship. Available at: https://grants.nih.gov/grants/guide/pa-files/PA-25-422.html#_Section%20III.%20Eligibility%20Information. Accessed September 2, 2025.

11. Executive Office of the President. Executive Order 14151—Ending Radical and Wasteful Government DEI Programs and Preferencing. Available at: https://www.whitehouse.gov/presidential-actions/2025/01/ending-radical-and-wasteful-government-dei-programs-and-preferencing. Accessed August 20, 2025.

12. Morabia A. *AJPH* and the threat of political interference in scientific publishing. *Am J Public Health.* 2025;115(5):626–627. doi:https://doi.org/10.2105/AJPH.2025.308100

13. USAJOBS. Employment of non-citizens. Available at: https://help.usajobs.gov/working-in-government/non-citizens. Accessed August 21, 2025.

14. National Center for Health Workforce Analysis. State of the US health care workforce, 2024. Available at: https://bhw.hrsa.gov/sites/default/files/bureau-health-workforce/state-of-the-health-workforce-report-2024.pdf. Accessed August 21, 2025.

15. Gonzalez-Guarda RM, Williams JR, Alexander KA. Uncertainty in science and among early career investigators. *JAMA Health Forum.* 2025;6(4):e251946. doi:https://doi.org/10.1001/jamahealthforum.2025.1946

Public Health Students Confront New Career Realities: Will They Pass, Pivot, or Persist?

Sara Krosin, MPP, and Reda Abouzaid, MS

ABOUT THE AUTHORS

Sara Krosin and Reda Abouzaid are with the Richard M. Fairbanks School of Public Health, Indiana University, Indianapolis.

See also *AJPH* Student Think Tank, pp. 447–484.

AJPH April 2026, Vol. 116, No. 4

Despite straining an already shrinking US public health workforce, the COVID-19 pandemic inspired a new generation of students to pursue a future in the field of public health.[1,2] Applications to schools of public health soared as young people watched epidemiologists, data scientists, and public health leaders step into the spotlight to protect communities and guide the response. For a moment, public health seemed like the place to be: a mission-driven career teeming with meaning and impact. However, shifting political tides risk limiting the opportunity this new interest provides toward reinvigorating the pipeline of students. Sustaining momentum will require navigating an environment where the value of science and academia is increasingly questioned.

PUBLIC HEALTH RESEARCH AND GRADUATE TRAINING

Students entering public health graduate programs are joining a field experiencing major shifts. More specifically, executive orders curbing diversity and equity initiatives, cuts to National Institutes of Health (NIH) and the Centers for Disease Control and Prevention (CDC) budgets, and heightened scrutiny on training programs translate into daily uncertainty for students' immediate training experiences and, in turn, future career outlooks. The scale of disruption is significant. NIH funding, which totaled over $36 billion in Fiscal Year 2024, ground to a halt as peer review stopped for months in early 2025, delaying or canceling grant cycles and leaving universities in limbo.[3]

As public health research grants and evaluation contracts suffer from abrupt shifts in federal priorities, some universities have reduced graduate admissions by as much as 20% to 50%.[4] Johns Hopkins, the largest private employer in Maryland and a major anchor institution in Baltimore, announced 2200 layoffs attributed directly to declining federal research funding.[5] For students preparing to enter the field, these losses reinforce uncertainty about the viability and standing of public health careers. Sweeping reductions in funding—combined with changing access to public data sets and websites, new data restrictions limiting the collection and reporting of population demographics, and censored research agendas—send a chilling message to students, and the message sounds like "your work may not be valued, your expertise may not be respected, and your careers may be politicized before they even begin." Some students may be forced to redesign their thesis or dissertation projects after losing access to key demographic data sets, further disrupting training timelines and undermining their research goals.

THE DOCTORAL STUDENT PERSPECTIVE

Doctoral students experience these disruptions acutely. Research and teaching are central to the training of doctoral students in public health, positioning graduates for careers in academia, research, and applied scientist positions in government agencies like the CDC. However, shifts in national policy are reshaping the training environment in ways that could alter doctoral students' career trajectories. The massive reductions in financial support to universities' research activities mean fewer opportunities to receive mentorship and training, gain teaching experience, present research to stakeholders, and publish findings that can affect population health and policy. Without stable funding and accessible data, projects halt. Timelines for critical milestones, such as qualifying exams or dissertation defenses, are put at risk, leaving students to make decisions amid uncertainty.[6]

The challenges extend beyond funding. Perhaps most disillusioning, many doctoral students discover that research areas they are passionate about are no longer supported or even allowed according to funding restrictions. For example, research on reproductive health, racial, gender, and ethnic disparities, or climate change may be restricted or defunded, forcing students to abandon or redirect work in which they have already invested significant time and hope. For some, entire dissertation projects are suddenly rendered untenable when faculty mentors lose grants and funding, or when university policies that have aligned with changing agendas and institutional review boards hesitate to approve studies that may trigger political scrutiny.[6–8] The instability erodes confidence in an academic or public health scientist career plan, pushing some trainees to reconsider whether their investment in research training will ultimately yield stable employment.

IMPACTS AT THE MASTER'S LEVEL

The master's-level experience illustrates another dimension of these challenges: students preparing for public health careers face obstacles in accessing the practical training and support that make them workforce-ready. Graduates trained at the master's level are often the individuals that governmental public health agencies are looking to recruit to the workforce. These students are particularly vulnerable to the immediate effects of federal policy shifts as their training relies heavily on scholarships, traineeships, and field placements that connect classroom learning to real-world practice. For example, disruptions such as delayed visa approvals or sudden work authorization issues further constrain access to these opportunities for international students. Recent scrutiny of diversity-focused scholarships has led some institutions to suspend awards for students from underrepresented backgrounds, raising concerns about affordability, access, and equity.[8] At the same time, grant freezes and other funding disruptions have reduced opportunities for practice-based training. This is in part because community organizations, including public health nongovernmental partners and governmental agencies, have had to cut staff, reducing their capacity to mentor students in required internships and applied learning experiences. This ultimately stresses students looking for internship placements and limits their opportunities for some of the types of internships that would help them prepare for desired careers.[4]

These changes make the pursuit of a public health degree more costly and less comprehensive, with implications for both students and the workforce. Graduates with more student loans and fewer applied public health experiences may choose to pursue positions outside public health where their skills will be of value or among settings that offer the highest salaries, which are often not governmental public health agencies. Graduate students who might have been considering the field may just look elsewhere.

CAREER PROSPECTS IN TRANSITION

Faced with these realities, students and graduates may be recalibrating their paths in ways that not only reshape individual careers but also weaken the future governmental workforce pipeline[9] at a time when these professionals are most needed. Public health graduates have options for where, and how, they can serve.[10] Historically, the majority of graduates take jobs in the private sector, nonprofit organizations, and universities.[9] For those who seek and secure jobs in governmental public health, decisions often hinge on job security, work–life balance, health insurance, and salary.[1] Yet each of these foundations is threatened by the current administration's policy changes, including prolonged funding disruptions, selective defunding of public health initiatives, and return to office requirements.[4] When those work benefits erode or disappear, it can be expected that employee dissatisfaction and burnout will rise, accelerating turnover and further weakening the workforce.[2,11]

The shift may already be underway. A Columbia University study found that between 2012 and 2016, the odds of public health graduates entering for-profit jobs jumped 23%, while government hiring flatlined or fell.[12] Those shifts are colliding with an already weary workforce: among early career public health employees aged younger than 35 years, more than one in three say they plan to leave their agency within a year—a churn rate even higher than the overall workforce average of one in four.[11]

MEETING THE MOMENT

Still, the damage is not irreversible. Public health students remain deeply motivated by the chance to prevent disease, protect communities, and advance health equity, but they are watching developments closely. National policies do more than set budgets; they send signals about what matters, what is possible, and what tomorrow's leaders can achieve. Right now, the message is muddled, but the economic case for restoring public health research funding is clear. NIH funding yields strong returns, generating over twice its value in economic activity.[4] Proposed cuts could cost the nation an estimated $16 billion in economic output and 68 000 jobs.[4] On the practice side, every dollar invested in public health interventions targeting common chronic conditions saves at least $5 in health care costs.[4] Despite this compelling return on investment, public health has historically been chronically underfunded, and the current disruptions threaten to compound this historic neglect.

If we want the best and brightest to dedicate their futures to public service, governmental public health jobs must provide security while also cultivating opportunities for growth, collaboration, innovation, and diversity.[11,13] Students entering the field today face a choice: pass on public health practice and research entirely, pivot to sectors and research areas where their expertise is valued, or persist despite the challenges. Public health has always demonstrated a remarkable capacity to adapt, rebuild, and thrive amid evolving demands. Critical moments like these reveal just how vital the work really is and how deeply communities depend on it. Student decisions will shape not just their own careers but the nation's capacity to protect the public's health for generations. AJPH

CORRESPONDENCE

Correspondence should be sent to Sara Krosin, Indiana University Indianapolis Richard Fairbanks School of Public Health, Department of Health Policy & Management, 1050 Wishard Blvd, RG 6144, Indianapolis, IN 46202 (e-mail: sakros@iu.edu). Reprints can be ordered at https://www.ajph.org by clicking the "Reprints" link.

PUBLICATION INFORMATION

Full Citation: Krosin S, Abouzaid R. Public health students confront new career realities: will they pass, pivot, or persist? *Am J Public Health*. 2026; 116(4):470–472.

Acceptance Date: December 12, 2025

DOI: https://doi.org/10.2105/AJPH.2025.308387

ORCID iD:

Sara Krosin https://orcid.org/0009-0003-5031-0584

CONTRIBUTORS

Both authors contributed equally to the research and writing of this editorial.

ACKNOWLEDGMENTS

The authors gratefully acknowledge Valerie A. Yeager, DrPH, for mentorship and guidance in the development of this editorial.

CONFLICTS OF INTEREST

The authors have no conflicts of interest to report.

REFERENCES

1. Yeager V. 2024 state of the evidence: employment choices of recent public health graduates. Consortium for Workforce Research in Public Health. 2024. Available at: https://cworph.umn.edu/products/2024-state-evidence-employment-choices-recent-public-health-graduates. Accessed September 10, 2025.
2. Leider JP, Yeager VA, Kirkland C, Krasna H, Bork RH, Resnick B. The state of the US public health workforce. *Annu Rev Public Health.* 2023;44: 323–341. https://doi.org/10.1146/annurev-publhealth-071421-032830
3. Hudson W. Federal funding cuts devastate academic public health programs. EDU Ledger. May 30, 2025. Available at: www.theeduledger.com/home/article/15747285/federal-funding-cuts-devastate-academic-public-health-programs. Accessed January 27, 2026.
4. Association of Schools and Programs of Public Health. Broken lifelines: the economic consequences of defunding academic public health. 2025. Available at: https://aspph.org/advocacy/broken-lifelines. Accessed September 10, 2025.
5. Saul S. Johns Hopkins to cut more than 2,000 workers funded by federal aid. *New York Times.* March 13, 2025. Available at: https://www.nytimes.com/2025/03/13/us/trump-cuts-johns-hopkins-university-layoffs.html. Accessed September 10, 2025.
6. Tham W, Staudt A, Perlman J, Cheng Y. Scientific talent leaks out of funding gaps. *arXiv* preprint. February 11, 2024. https://arxiv.org/abs/2402.07235
7. Ledford H, Basilio H. Postdocs and PhD students hit hard by Trump's crackdown on science. *Nature.* 2025;639(8053):13–14. https://doi.org/10.1038/d41586-025-00550-0
8. Kozlov M. Exclusive: NIH still screens grants in process a judge ruled illegal. *Nature.* June 27, 2025. https://doi.org/10.1038/d41586-025-02024-9
9. Leider JP, Burke E, Nguyen RHN, et al. Trends in degree conferrals, debt, and employment outcomes among public health graduates, 2001–2020. *Am J Public Health.* 2023;113(1):115–123. https://doi.org/10.2105/AJPH.2022.307113
10. Plepys CM, Krasna H, Leider JP, Burke EM, Blakely CH, Magaña L. First-destination outcomes for 2015–2018 public health graduates. *Am J Public Health.* 2021;111(3):475–484. https://doi.org/10.2105/AJPH.2020.306038
11. Kang I-G, Kim N, Injeian A, Chaney BH, Lee HY. Factors associated with turnover intention among early-career US governmental public health employees. *J Public Health Manag Pract.* 2025;31(5):E267–E275. https://doi.org/10.1097/PHH.0000000000002176
12. Krasna H, Kornfeld J, Cushman L, Ni S, Antoniou P, March D. The new public health workforce: employment outcomes of public health graduate students. *J Public Health Manag Pract.* 2021;27(1): 12–19. https://doi.org/10.1097/PHH.0000000000000976
13. Locke R, McGinty M, Guerrero Ramirez G, Sellers K. Attracting new talent to the governmental public health workforce. *J Public Health Manag Pract.* 2022;28(1):E235–E243. https://doi.org/10.1097/PHH.0000000000001336

Between Gratitude and Advocacy: Navigating LGBTQ+ Public Health Research as Immigrant PhD Students

Samir Kumar Sarker Rony, MSc, Ayobamidele Adebanjo, MPH, and Ryan M. Combs, PhD, MA

ABOUT THE AUTHORS

Samir Kumar Sarker Rony, Ayobamidele Adebanjo, and Ryan M. Combs are with the Department of Health Promotion and Behavioral Sciences, School of Public Health and Information Sciences, University of Louisville, Louisville, KY.

See also *AJPH* Student Think Tank, pp. 447–484.

As immigrant doctoral students committed to addressing mental health disparities among lesbian, gay, bisexual, transgender, and queer (LGBTQ+) youths and other disadvantaged communities, we began our studies in the United States with gratitude for the opportunity and readiness to confront difficult subjects and methodological challenges. However, we were unprepared for the ways in which significant domestic policy shifts would influence our work. For immigrant students like us, these changes carry extra weight. We pursue education in the United States because it is known as a country of opportunity, and public health training typically employs a health equity lens. Yet, in the current political context, the precarious nature of our visa status makes advocacy for health equity feel risky, even when our work is grounded in rigorous science.

CHILLING EFFECT OF ANTI-DIVERSITY, EQUITY, AND INCLUSION POLICIES

Recent policy developments signal the mounting influence of politics over academic discourse. Executive Order 14151 and similar directives state that they seek to "de-politicize" federal offices, policies, activities, and programs related to diversity, equity, and inclusion (DEI).[1] Grant guidelines have subsequently been reframed to constrain DEI-related aims and terminology. Critics argue that these directives threaten academic freedom, weaken university DEI policies and resources, disrupt research agendas, and reduce the opportunities available to underrepresented students.[2,3] This may put at risk public health's ability to maintain a diverse workforce.[4] All the while, research demonstrates that discriminatory state laws targeting LGBTQ+ communities adversely impact health care institutions and clinicians.[5] On the ground, researchers are reconsidering whether topics are "safe" to pursue.

The practical implications extend beyond funding or semantics. Early career scholars rely heavily on mentorship, grant opportunities, and collaborations to establish themselves in the field. When political climates shift, so do the boundaries of what is fundable, publishable, or even worth discussing in professional spaces. As a result, immigrant students like us find ourselves navigating not only the usual pressures of doctoral study but also the added burden of anticipating how our projects might be interpreted through political lenses. This anticipation requires constant recalibration of language, framing, and even choice of research questions, effectively reshaping the scientific agenda from the top down. Some of us have even gone so far as to change dissertation topics to avoid having our work framed within the DEI narrative.

What is most unsettling is witnessing institutions in our state remove DEI-friendly language under Kentucky HB 4, a process that penetrates academic life and reshapes institutional priorities.[6,7] Corridors that once embodied inclusivity and respect for diverse communities now reflect constraints that limit vision and narrow opportunity. As we are on F-1 immigration status, these changes feel like the clipping of wings and restrict our capacity to pursue equity-driven scholarship with confidence. Such shifts do not merely alter terminology; they dampen enthusiasm, constrain advocacy, and weaken our ability to advance health and well-being for those who are most marginalized and in the greatest need.

THE PRECARITY OF IMMIGRANT SCHOLARS

Tensions between new state and federal policies as well as public health's commitment to equity have been playing out in collaboration with our colleagues. For example, we encountered resistance to conducting research focusing on LGBTQ+ populations. The rationale was pragmatic: LGBTQ+

research could be perceived as politically charged and closely tied to DEI initiatives now subjected to intense scrutiny. While leading a scoping review examining mental health service utilization among LGBTQ+ youths, team members encouraged us to replace the term *LGBTQ+* with the more neutral sounding *sexual and gender minorities*. A colleague concerned about the potential repercussions withdrew from the project, transforming what should have been a collaborative, meaningful inquiry into a cautious negotiation.

This kind of experience illustrates the silencing effect of political pressures. Instead of devoting time to refining methodologies or deepening theoretical insight, much of our energy is spent negotiating terminology and reassuring collaborators that the work will not jeopardize their reputations or future prospects. Over time, these negotiations chip away at both productivity and morale, producing a chilling effect where projects are shaped more by risk avoidance than by scientific necessity. The tension is particularly pronounced for immigrant scholars who are already balancing gratitude for opportunities with vulnerability tied to visa status. For us, the stakes feel existential: the wrong word in a proposal or the wrong framing in a publication could carry implications not only for funding but also for our academic futures.

IMPACT ON MENTAL HEALTH, BELONGING, AND MINORITY STRESS

Research framed in politically "safe" terms fails to capture the full scope of health challenges of populations experiencing health disparities. These policy shifts are not abstract; they directly affect our ability to conduct research, to advocate for issues about which we are passionate, and to develop interventions to provide the resources necessary for people facing health inequity to thrive.

Specific to the LGBTQ+ community, policy exclusion may increase stigma, while the lack of new research perpetuates structural barriers to equitable care. Indeed, a recent study found that harmful legislation correlated with pervasive mental health distress among LGBTQ+ youths.[8] Research on minority stress highlights how stigma-related stressors disproportionately affect LGBTQ+ youths, undermining mental health outcomes.[9] These effects compound among those holding intersecting marginalized identities such as LGBTQ+ immigrants whose layered minority stress is shaped by xenophobia, homophobia, and systemic marginalization. Furthermore, studies reveal that LGBTQ+ students face notably high emotional abuse compared with their cisgender, heterosexual peers—upending mental health equity efforts.[10] A study by Bostwick et al.,[11] examining depressive symptoms, suicidal ideation, and suicide attempts among racially and ethnically diverse sexual minority youths, found that LGBTQ+ youths consistently reported poorer mental health outcomes than their heterosexual peers across all racial and ethnic groups. These disparities are further amplified by overlapping social and structural challenges that affect the daily lives and well-being of LGBTQ+ youths.

Research helps guide how we address these issues. For example, we know that inclusive environments matter profoundly. Research indicates that school climates that affirm students' identities can reduce suicide risk among sexual minority youths.[12] Likewise, exposure to inclusive language has demonstrable positive effects on the well-being of transgender individuals in occupational settings, illustrating the broader value of affirming terminology.[13]

ACADEMIC FREEDOM, CAREER PATHWAYS, AND THE SILENCING EFFECT

The intersection of our immigrant status and our desire to advocate for the LGBTQ+ community has shaped the topics we choose to pursue. There is growing concern that restrictive climates may deter emerging scholars from engaging in equity-focused research. As international students, we feel this tension acutely. There have been countless instances of international students' speech resulting in punishment.[14] International students report being warned that a social media post could risk visa revocation, seeing peers lose visas over minor infractions, and even censoring their own research.[15] While we are committed to pursuing equity-focused research, we are mindful of the vulnerabilities attached to our status. The possibility that our advocacy could be misinterpreted or that our chosen terminology might be deemed controversial makes every research decision feel weightier than it should.

Immigrant students often negotiate competing priorities and values. We feel gratitude to the United States for its openness to hosting international students, to the University and our department for supporting us personally and academically, and to our mentors and professors for investing in our growth throughout our doctoral studies. We do not want to risk our place in the program because of political objections to the topics we choose to research. This tension can lead to hesitation, self-censorship, or the pursuit of "safer" topics.

At the same time, policies that make such practices unsafe undermine both student success and the quality of our collective scholarly work. As Kierstead et al.[8] demonstrate, avoiding critical issues leaves urgent health disparities—in this case, mental health disparities—unaddressed and risks silencing the very voices public health needs to amplify. Adding to our hesitation, topics that are safe today may not be safe tomorrow. The years of effort we spend gaining expertise in our dissertation topic area can vanish in an instant. However, good science demands that we follow data, not ideology.

CONCLUSION

Balancing gratitude with the imperative to address systemic inequities creates tensions that shape immigrant scholars' reflexivity, research practices, and advocacy. When policy decisions make the environment for health equity research more difficult, we risk slowing down our progress, sacrificing critical inquiry for an ideology in conflict with the approach of the public health profession. We must accurately name populations and the health disparities they face, design responsive interventions, and convey our findings transparently. Freedom to conduct studies without political interference is foundational for advocacy. These values are central to ethical and impactful public health scholarship. For immigrant doctoral students, the erosion of DEI through censorship and fear not only harms mental health but also imperils research choice—the very core of higher education's mission. To ensure research remains robust and equitable, institutions must support and not silence work that uplifts historically oppressed voices. AJPH

CORRESPONDENCE

Correspondence should be sent to Samir Kumar Sarker Rony, Department of Health Promotion and Behavioral Sciences, School of Public Health and Information Sciences, University of Louisville, 485 E Gray St, Louisville, KY 40202 (e-mail: s0sark09@louisville.edu). Reprints can be ordered at https://ajph.org by clicking the "Reprints" link.

PUBLICATION INFORMATION

Full Citation: Sarker Rony SK, Adebanjo A, Combs RM. Between gratitude and advocacy: navigating LGBTQ+ public health research as immigrant PhD students. *Am J Public Health*. 2026;116(4):473–475.

Acceptance Date: December 12, 2025.

DOI: https://doi.org/10.2105/AJPH.2025.308383

ORCID iDs:

Samir Kumar Sarker Rony https://orcid.org/0000-0002-3142-6624

Ryan M. Combs https://orcid.org/0000-0002-7609-0925

CONTRIBUTORS

All authors made substantial contributions to the conceptualization and design of the work. S. K. Sarker Rony and A. Adebanjo drafted the initial article. S. K. Sarker Rony and R. M. Combs critically revised the article for important intellectual content. All authors reviewed and approved the final version of the article and agree to be accountable for all aspects of the work.

ACKNOWLEDGMENTS

The authors thank the School of Public Health and Information Sciences at the University of Louisville for institutional support.

CONFLICTS OF INTEREST

The authors declare no potential or actual conflicts of interest related to funding or affiliation-related activities.

REFERENCES

1. Trump DJ. Ending radical and wasteful government DEI programs and preferencing. *Fed Regist*. 2025;90(19):8339–8343. Available at: https://www.federalregister.gov/documents/2025/01/29/2025-01953/ending-radical-and-wasteful-government-dei-programs-and-preferencing. Accessed November 13, 2025.
2. Gottlieb AS, Jagsi R. Removing diversity, equity, and inclusion infrastructure in medicine, public health, and science: the cost of overcorrection. *BMJ*. 2025;388:r468. https://doi.org/10.1136/bmj.r468
3. Stich AE, Malik A, Walker WB Jr, Callan IN, Cooper C, Rodriguez J. The rapid suppression of diversity, equity, and inclusion in United States higher education. *J Res Innov High Educ*. 2025;6(1):119–141. Available at: https://rihe-journal.com/index.php/rihe/article/view/62. Accessed November 13, 2025.
4. Aaron DG, Stanford FC, Emery AE. Law and policy efforts to dismantle diversity, equity, and inclusion. *Am J Public Health*. 2025;115(7):1008–1013. https://doi.org/10.2105/AJPH.2025.308081
5. Underhill K, Earnshaw VA, Nelson KM. The synergistic health threats of state laws targeting marginalized groups in the United States. *Am J Public Health*. 2024;114(12):1335–1343. https://doi.org/10.2105/AJPH.2024.307830
6. BillTrack50. Kentucky House Bill 4 (2025): an act relating to diversity, equity, and inclusion in postsecondary education. 2025. Available at: https://www.billtrack50.com/billdetail/1830728. Accessed October 29, 2025.
7. Pinski H. Kentucky's new anti-DEI law is now in effect. How colleges, universities are complying. *Courier-Journal*. June 30, 2025. Available at: https://www.courier-journal.com/story/news/politics/2025/06/30/anti-dei-law-now-in-effect-in-kentucky-how-colleges-are-complying/82234702007. Accessed October 29, 2025.
8. Kierstead EC, Yoon SN, Iskra ML, Schillo BA, Kreslake JM. Cigarette and e-cigarette use among LGBT+ youths and young adults according to strength of state-level LGBT+ equality protections. *Am J Public Health*. 2025;115(6):945–953. https://doi.org/10.2105/AJPH.2025.308008
9. Ream GL. Minority stress and intersectionality in LGBTQIA+ youth mental health disparities. *Am J Public Health*. 2024;114(7):669–671. https://doi.org/10.2105/AJPH.2024.307676
10. Mittleman J. Adverse childhood experiences among LGBTQ+ high school students: national evidence from the 2023 Youth Risk Behavior Survey. *Am J Public Health*. 2025;115(7):1137–1145. https://doi.org/10.2105/AJPH.2025.308094
11. Bostwick WB, Meyer I, Aranda F, Russell S, Hughes T, Birkett M, Mustanski B. Mental health and suicidality among racially/ethnically diverse sexual minority youths. *Am J Public Health*. 2014;104(6):1129–1136. https://doi.org/10.2105/AJPH.2013.301749
12. Hatzenbuehler ML, Birkett M, Van Wagenen A, Meyer IH. Protective school climates and reduced risk for suicide ideation in sexual minority youths. *Am J Public Health*. 2014;104(2):279–286. https://doi.org/10.2105/AJPH.2013.301508
13. Perales F, Ablaza C, Elkin N. Exposure to inclusive language and well-being at work among transgender employees in Australia, 2020. *Am J Public Health*. 2022;112(3):482–490. https://doi.org/10.2105/AJPH.2021.306602
14. Weninger O. Revoking visas, silencing dissent: how Trump's crackdown on international students endangers academic freedom and US global standing. Human Rights Research Center. August 12, 2025. Available at: https://www.humanrightsresearch.org/post/revoking-visas-silencing-dissent-how-trump-s-crackdown-on-international-students-endangers-academi. Accessed September 15, 2025.
15. Ukaonu A. *Land of the Censored, Home of the Silenced: How Trump's Immigration Crackdowns Undermine the Virtues of American Higher Education*. BA report. University of Chicago; 2025. https://doi.org/10.6082/uchicago.15131

National Policy Changes Impacting Transgender Populations and Their Implications for Researchers and Public Health

Gray Babbs, MPH, Em Balkan, MSW, Rey Flores, MA, and Jaclyn M. W. Hughto, PhD, MPH

ABOUT THE AUTHORS

Gray Babbs, Em Balkan, Rey Flores, and Jaclyn M. W. Hughto are with Brown University School of Public Health, Providence, RI.

See also *AJPH* Student Think Tank, pp. 447–484.

AJPH April 2026, Vol. 116, No. 4

In January 2025, the President of the United States issued an executive order declaring it the policy of the United States to recognize only two sexes—male and female—and to define sex as an immutable biological classification.[1] This executive order attempted to create a political reality in which transgender, nonbinary, and gender-expansive (or trans) people do not exist. The signing of the executive order not only erased trans communities from federal policy but also set in motion a systematic dismantlement of the infrastructure for studying trans people's health.

IMPACTS: ACADEMIC ACTIVITIES AND RESEARCH

In the United States, public health research depends overwhelmingly on federal funding, much of which comes from National Institutes of Health (NIH) grants. The NIH's stated mission is to serve the public by enhancing health,[2] not to promote any political party or ideology. Historically, changes in presidential administrations altered little about the day-to-day functioning of public health research. Under the current administration, however, political influence has become overt and explicitly ideological.

Federal funders have deprioritized, delayed, and terminated proposals that reference gender identity and the health of lesbian, gay, bisexual, trans, and queer (LGBTQ+) communities.[3] Before the cuts, research focused on sexual orientation and gender identity constituted less than 1% of the NIH's overall research portfolio, a majority being HIV research.[4] Even this limited funding is now at risk. By declaring research on trans people ideological and no longer worthy of study—with the telling exceptions of detransition and conversion therapy[5]—the federal government is disrupting legitimate science.

Federal agencies now have limited access to robust epidemiological and demographic data, which are used to track disease progression, develop policies to prevent disease, and advocate for marginalized groups. US federal agencies removed thousands of publicly available data sets, many of which were later restored after legal challenges; however, some sexual orientation and gender identity variables and corresponding data were subsequently altered or omitted to align with executive orders.[6] Furthermore, the Centers for Medicare and Medicaid Services (CMS) mandated that Data Use Agreements no longer use the word "gender" or acknowledge trans people (E. Riebel-Paszkiewicz, e-mail, March 21, 2025). The CMS severed a key avenue for analyzing disparities in outcomes and service utilization in trans populations—the very tools needed to address health inequities.

IMPACTS: TRANS SCHOLARS, FIELDWORK, AND COMMUNITIES

Policy attacks and the withdrawal of federal grant funding have restricted researchers' ability to study the health of trans populations, impeding scientific inquiry. Students and professionals at all levels rely on grant funding and accessible, comprehensive data to monitor disease burden, inform policy, and communicate lived experiences to broader audiences. These actions severely limit the work of trans health researchers, obstructing career pathways and silencing emerging voices in the field.

Because academic institutions depend on grants to fund faculty, train students, and advance knowledge, researchers—particularly emerging faculty and doctoral students—are discouraged from pursuing trans health research out of fear that doing so could jeopardize their careers.

When questioning the status quo is a career risk, public health becomes a more homogenized environment, both in the subjects studied and in its workforce. Withdrawal of grant funding creates a chilling effect that will have lasting repercussions for public health professionals across all career stages. This causes researchers to exclude trans people from research out of fear, beyond the bounds of current policy changes and after they are repealed. By stunting research and suppressing the development of expertise, this administration is suppressing knowledge and restricting interest and investment in trans health for decades to come.

When the US federal government denies the existence of trans people, their health needs are rendered invisible as well. Yet trans people still experience disproportionate rates of mental health concerns and chronic conditions,[7] while facing persistent barriers to care—from insurance denials to explicit provider discrimination.[8] As a result of relentless political and legal attacks, trans people may be more reluctant to "out" themselves for fear of discrimination and the emotional burden of minoritized stress.[9] This fear is compounded for those with intersecting marginalized identities or living in conservative regions. Increasing antitrans policies and sentiments will almost certainly exacerbate disparities in health, health care access, and health care quality for trans individuals. As a result of the dismantled research infrastructure, we are unable to fully measure, document, or respond to these profound harms.

IMPLICATIONS: CALLS TO ACTION

Despite attempts at erasure, trans people will not disappear; however, society's collective capacity to study, understand, and provide care for this population has been constrained. By restricting grant funding, deleting and censoring data, and interrupting the academic trainee pipeline, the US federal government is suppressing trans health research from multiple directions. Public health professionals and academic institutions have an ethical responsibility to respond to these discriminatory federal actions by actively supporting trans health education, scholarship, and people.

Academic institutions have a responsibility to preserve academic freedom. This includes continuing to provide coursework and research opportunities for students to study LGBTQ+ health. Institutions have a responsibility to scholars whose research has been affected by NIH funding cuts and data deletion. They can provide support through bridge funding to affected scholars and offer additional time on dissertation, promotion, and tenure timelines.

Public health professionals and academic institutions should base decisions on science. A robust body of research shows that gender-affirming care, including medical gender affirmation and receiving care in affirming environments, is associated with improved mental health outcomes[10] and is cost-effective.[11] Contrary to current federal government claims, this evidence is rooted in rigorous scientific methods, and it is the rigor of prior research that led every major medical organization in the United States to consider gender-affirming care medically necessary.[12] Institutions should guarantee insurance coverage for gender-affirming care for employees, students, and dependents. Health services on university campuses should maintain medical and psychological services for trans and other LGBTQ+ people. Institutions should adopt or maintain other research-backed trans-inclusive policies, including access to gender-inclusive restrooms, nondiscrimination policies that include gender identity, and the ability to change one's name in internal records without a legal name change.[13]

As trans students and a mentor to trans students, we are aware of the grave times in which we live. We have lost research funding, been forced to change research topics, and watched as trans rights were used as a bargaining chip in institutional negotiations to regain federal research funding. For those of us who are trans, we feel less safe and included in our institutions than we did a year ago. Although we recognize the pressures facing our institutions, they need to hold their ground.

The moment we find ourselves in has precedent. In May 1933, Nazi-led student groups burned the library of the Institute of Sexual Science in Berlin, which destroyed the majority of the world's academic research on sexual and gender diversity.[14] Soon after, the institute was forced to close because of its "un-German spirit." By obliterating the knowledge production centers of the lives of people whom we would now call queer, intersex, or trans, the Nazi party set understanding of these communities back decades. Today, we are witnessing epistemic arson in practice.

Now is the time to collaborate, build community, and center diverse and marginalized voices. Institutions must uplift the very people they claim to serve—students, scholars, and the broader community—which always have and always will include trans and other LGBTQ+ individuals. We are not going anywhere. AJPH

CORRESPONDENCE

Correspondence should be sent to Gray Babbs, 121 S Main St, Providence, RI 02906 (e-mail: gray_babbs@brown.edu). Reprints can be ordered at https://www.ajph.org by clicking the "Reprints" link.

PUBLICATION INFORMATION

Full Citation: Babbs G, Balkan E, Flores R, Hughto JMW. National policy changes impacting transgender populations and their implications for researchers and public health. *Am J Public Health*. 2026;116(4): 476–478.

Acceptance Date: December 12, 2025

DOI: https://doi.org/10.2105/AJPH.2025.308386

ORCID iDs:

Gray Babbs https://orcid.org/0000-0003-4060-571X

Em Balkan https://orcid.org/0009-0001-0333-9312

Rey Flores https://orcid.org/0000-0003-4073-8328

Jaclyn M. W. Hughto https://orcid.org/0000-0003-4722-8179

CONTRIBUTORS

All authors made substantial contributions to the conceptualization of the work and provided final approval for publication. G. Babbs, E. Balkan, and R. Flores drafted the manuscript, and J. M. W. Hughto critically revised the manuscript for important intellectual content. G. Babbs, E. Balkan, and R. Flores contributed equally and should be considered co-first authors of the manuscript.

CONFLICTS OF INTEREST

The authors have no conflicts of interest to report.

REFERENCES

1. Trump DJ. Defending women from gender ideology extremism and restoring biological truth to the federal government. January 21, 2025. Available at: https://www.whitehouse.gov/presidential-actions/2025/01/defending-women-from-gender-ideology-extremism-and-restoring-biological-truth-to-the-federal-government. Accessed January 22, 2025.
2. National Institutes of Health. Mission and goals. January 10, 2025. Available at: https://www.nih.gov/about-nih/mission-goals. Accessed September 13, 2025.
3. Mueller B. Trump administration slashes research into LGBTQ health. *New York Times*. May 4, 2025. Available at: https://www.nytimes.com/2025/05/04/health/trump-administration-slashes-research-into-lgbtq-health.html. Accessed November 4, 2025.
4. Weideman BCD, Ecklund AM, Alley R, Rosser BRS, Rider GN. Research funded by National Institutes of Health concerning sexual and gender minoritized populations: a tracking update for 2012 to 2022. *Am J Public Health*. 2025;115(3):374–386. https://doi.org/10.2105/AJPH.2024.307913
5. Bhattacharya J. Advancing NIH's mission through a unified strategy. August 15, 2025. Available at: https://www.nih.gov/about-nih/nih-director/statements/advancing-nihs-mission-through-unified-strategy. Accessed September 11, 2025.
6. Pillai D, Hill L, Artiga S. Disappearing federal data: implications for addressing health disparities. KFF. September 23, 2025. Available at: https://www.kff.org/racial-equity-and-health-policy/disappearing-federal-data-implications-for-addressing-health-disparities. Accessed November 19, 2025.
7. Dragon CN, Guerino P, Ewald E, Laffan AM. Transgender Medicare beneficiaries and chronic conditions: exploring fee-for-service claims data. *LGBT Health*. 2017;4(6):404–411. https://doi.org/10.1089/lgbt.2016.0208
8. Mahowald L, Gruberg S, Halpin J. The state of the LGBTQ community in 2020. Center for American Progress. 2020. Available at: https://www.americanprogress.org/article/state-lgbtq-community-2020. Accessed October 11, 2023.
9. Babbs G, Wolfe HL, Ulrich MR, Raifman J, Lipson SK. Sexual and gender minority university students report distress due to discriminatory health care policies. *Stigma Health*. 2024;9(4): 601–604. https://doi.org/10.1037/sah0000459
10. Hughto JMW, Gunn HA, Rood BA, Pantalone DW. Social and medical gender affirmation experiences are inversely associated with mental health problems in a US non-probability sample of transgender adults. *Arch Sex Behav*. 2020;49(7): 2635–2647. https://doi.org/10.1007/s10508-020-01655-5
11. Padula WV, Heru S, Campbell JD. Societal implications of health insurance coverage for medically necessary services in the US transgender population: a cost-effectiveness analysis. *J Gen Intern Med*. 2016;31(4):394–401. https://doi.org/10.1007/s11606-015-3529-6
12. GLAAD. Medical association statements in support of health care for transgender people and youth. June 26, 2024. Available at: https://glaad.org/medical-association-statements-supporting-trans-youth-healthcare-and-against-discriminatory. Accessed September 12, 2025.
13. Goldberg AE, Beemyn G, Smith JZ. What is needed, what is valued: trans students' perspectives on trans-inclusive policies and practices in higher education. *J Educ Psychol Consult*. 2019;29(1): 27–67. https://doi.org/10.1080/10474412.2018.1480376
14. Tracey L. 90 years on: the destruction of the Institute of Sexual Science. JSTOR Daily. May 31, 2023. Available at: https://daily.jstor.org/90-years-on-the-destruction-of-the-institute-of-sexual-science. Accessed August 21, 2025.

When Your Research Is Devalued: Discovering Purpose in an Uncertain Academic Landscape

India Willis, MPH, MSN

ABOUT THE AUTHOR

India Willis is an advanced practice registered nurse and a PhD student at the School of Medicine and Health Sciences, George Washington University, Washington, DC.

See also *AJPH* Student Think Tank, pp. 447–484.

Recent policy shifts have created a disorienting and challenging environment for emerging public health scholars.[1,2] Rapid-fire policy changes have at times devalued evidence-based scientific inquiry.[3] For instance, when a White House Memorandum incorporates terms like "wasteful spending" to describe evidence-based research,[4] the consequences extend beyond rhetoric: they influence research priorities, funding allocations, and ultimately the health of populations that rely on this work.[5] These policy decisions implicitly signal which research questions are deemed worthy of pursuit and which communities receive scientific attention. They also shape perceptions of whose expertise is valued. For early-career researchers, these shifts can undermine confidence in the legitimacy and purpose of their work.

As a clinician, my research trajectory began with caring for communities disproportionately affected by structural inequities. My work in sexual health, evidence-based medicine, and HIV prevention led me to foundational questions: Who generates the evidence that informs prevention and care? How can I contribute meaningfully to advancing health equity? And how do we ensure that communities historically excluded from research are centered in future scientific inquiry? These questions took on greater urgency as policy changes increasingly threatened the infrastructure necessary to answer them.

The transition from clinician to scholar requires considerable adaptation, persistence, and commitment. That process became more complicated when trusted sources of clinical and research guidance were abruptly disrupted. As an adolescent medicine clinician focused on HIV prevention, I experienced significant uncertainty when the Adolescent Trials Network was temporarily suspended in early 2025.[6] Although the network was later reinstated,[7] the episode highlighted the precariousness of research environments shaped by shifting political priorities. This moment raised broader concerns not only about my own academic trajectory but also about the young people whose health depends on sustained, evidence-based research. It prompted a deeper reflection on how emerging scholars maintain commitment when the credibility of their research area can be so readily questioned.

In a research climate marked by constant change and volatility,[8] early-career researchers may be especially vulnerable to heightened imposter syndrome,[9] often manifesting as pervasive self-doubt. I frequently reassess my literature reviews and research aims, anticipating the possibility that my focus on HIV prevention, harm reduction, clinician education, and translational science could be misinterpreted as misaligned with broader political narratives.[4] Despite clear evidence of persistent gaps in the literature and clinical practice that my research seeks to address, I sometimes hesitate to reach out to mentors, concerned about competing demands on their time and the uncertainty they themselves face within this shifting landscape.

Yet these challenges have reinforced rather than diminished my commitment. My persistence reflects the interconnected identities I hold as a Black woman, a nurse practitioner, and a doctoral student. Intersectionality, as articulated by Lisa Bowleg, PhD, provides a framework for understanding how individual experiences mirror broader structures of power.[10] Historically, Black women have transformed imposed resilience into purposeful resistance.[11] Nurses have continued to advocate for patient care despite workplace violence,[12] nurse practitioners have fought for professional autonomy,[13] and faculty and PhD students of color have navigated isolation and stereotype-driven expectations to assert their intellectual authority.[14] Positioned at the intersection of these identities, I draw on multiple traditions of perseverance. Rather than amplifying vulnerability, this intersectionality strengthens my resolve to pursue research that advances equity and addresses the needs of marginalized communities. Continuing this work is a deliberate and necessary act of advocacy.

When systems of knowledge production are contested,[15] those who recognize their importance must respond with clarity and purpose. The devaluation of particular research domains emphasizes their necessity; the populations whose needs are deprioritized are often those most vulnerable to structural neglect. My professional trajectory will likely continue to involve demonstrating capability, articulating relevance, and ensuring that historically marginalized perspectives have a place within scientific discourse.

I now view imposter syndrome not as a deficit to overcome but as an indicator of the boundaries I am working to expand. The discomfort reflects a broader political moment in which those in power influence which populations are considered worthy of care, and which research questions are considered worthy of answers. Perhaps insisting we ask these "worthless" questions is what is most needed.

To fellow PhD students and recent graduates: we are navigating a scholarly landscape that diverges from what our program orientations prepared us for. We anticipated academic rigor, not existential questions about whether our fields merit recognition or support. Yet this unexpected environment also presents an opportunity. When traditional research structures become unstable, new possibilities emerge for reimagining how knowledge is produced and whose perspectives are centered.

We stand at a critical juncture, one that requires advancing science, health promotion, and disease prevention in areas where resistance is strongest. Doing so will depend on scholarly solidarity and collective perseverance. Emerging researchers can build alliances across institutions, collaborate with peers whose work faces similar vulnerabilities, and seek support from philanthropic organizations committed to health equity.[2] Expanding funding strategies beyond politically sensitive federal mechanisms can strengthen resilience,[2] and creating alternative dissemination pathways, including community partnerships, can ensure that scientific findings translate into real-world impact.[2]

Most importantly, we must recognize that research conducted in devalued or contested domains is not simply academic work. It is a form of advocacy that future scholars and the communities they serve will depend upon. The research environment may differ from what we expected, but it may be exactly where we are needed: not only as scholars defending intellectual inquiry but as clinicians and public health practitioners upholding our commitment to promote well-being, especially for those whose health depends on answers others deem unworthy of pursuit. AJPH

CORRESPONDENCE

Correspondence should be sent to India Willis, MPH, MSN, 225 E. Chicago Ave, Box 161 B, Chicago, IL, 60611 (e-mail: india.willis@gwmail.gwu.edu). Reprints can be ordered at http://www.ajph.org by clicking the "Reprints" link.

PUBLICATION INFORMATION

Full Citation: Willis I. When your research is devalued: discovering purpose in an uncertain academic landscape. *Am J Public Health*. 2026; 116(4):479–481.

Acceptance Date: December 12, 2025

DOI: https://doi.org/10.2105/AJPH.2025.308385

ORCID iD:
India Willis https://orcid.org/0009-0000-8843-0571

ACKNOWLEDGMENTS

Thank you, Sabrina Figueiredo, PhD; Randi B. Singer, PhD; Natasha Crooks, PhD; and Karen Schlumpf, EdD, for your continued support and mentorship.

CONFLICTS OF INTEREST

The author declares no potential or actual conflicts of interest from funding or affiliation-related activities.

REFERENCES

1. Woolf SH. How should health care and public health respond to the new US administration? *JAMA*. 2025;333(14):1197–1198. https://doi.org/10.1001/jama.2025.1218
2. Gonzalez-Guarda RM, Williams JR, Alexander KA. Uncertainty in science and among early career investigators. *JAMA Health Forum*. 2025;6(4): e251946. https://doi.org/10.1001/jamahealthforum.2025.1946
3. Austin SB, Cohen JE, Cooper S, et al. Standing up for core principles in departments of social and behavioral sciences in public health: department chairs speak out. *Am J Public Health*. 2025; 115(11):1767–1772. https://doi.org/10.2105/AJPH.2025.308283
4. The White House. Radical transparency about wasteful spending. 2025. Available at: https://www.whitehouse.gov/presidential-actions/2025/02/radical-transparency-about-wasteful-spending. Accessed December 22, 2025.
5. KFF. Analysis of USAID's active and terminated awards list: how many are global health? 2025. Available at: https://www.kff.org/global-health-policy/analysis-of-usaids-active-and-terminated-awards-list-how-many-are-global-health. Accessed December 22, 2025.
6. STAT News. NIH cuts include HIV prevention programs for teens and young adults. March 25, 2025. Available at: https://www.statnews.com/2025/03/25/nih-cuts-include-hiv-aids-prevention-program-for-adolescents. Accessed December 22, 2025.
7. Chronicle of Higher Education. An NIH grant is restored, with a catch: cut a study on trans youth. 2025. Available at: https://www.chronicle.com/article/an-nih-grant-is-restored-with-a-catch-cut-a-study-on-trans-youth. Accessed December 22, 2025.
8. Morabia A. AJPH and the threat of political interference in scientific publishing. *Am J Public Health*. 2025;115(5):626–627. https://doi.org/10.2105/AJPH.2025.308100
9. Merino M. Impostor syndrome in postgraduate research: the guilt isn't your fault. Oxford Scientist. 2023. Available at: https://oxsci.org/impostor-syndrome-in-postgraduate-research. Accessed December 22, 2025.
10. Bowleg L. The problem with the phrase women and minorities: intersectionality—an important

theoretical framework for public health. *Am J Public Health.* 2012;102(7):1267–1273. https://doi.org/10.2105/AJPH.2012.300750

11. Hughes R. The things about normalizing: black women, resilience, and superpowers. The EDU Ledger. 2022. Available at: https://www.theeduledger.com/opinion/article/15294497/the-things-about-normalizing-black-women-resilience-and-superpowers. Accessed December 22, 2025.
12. Jones CB, Sousane Z, Mossburg S. Addressing workplace violence and creating a safer workplace. AHRQ Patient Safety Network. October 31, 2023. Available at: https://psnet.ahrq.gov/perspective/addressing-workplace-violence-and-creating-safer-workplace. Accessed December 22, 2025.
13. Kleinpell R, Myers CR, Schorn MN. Addressing barriers to APRN practice: policy and regulatory implications during COVID-19. *J Nurs Regul.* 2023;14(1):13–20. https://doi.org/10.1016/S2155-8256(23)00064-9
14. Walkington L. How far have we really come? Black women faculty and graduate students' experiences in higher education. *Humboldt J Soc Relat.* 2017;1(39):51–65. https://doi.org/10.55671/0160-4341.1022
15. Beidas RS, Aarons GA, Geng EH, et al. Implementation science grant terminations in the United States. *Implement Sci.* 2025;20(1):20. https://doi.org/10.1186/s13012-025-01434-7

Bright Spot, Closing Door: Encouraging Innovation, Restricting Foreign Talent

Yiguang Zhu, ScM, BS, Megan Weil Latshaw, PhD, MHS, and Paul A. Locke, DrPH, JD, MPH

ABOUT THE AUTHORS

Yiguang Zhu is a doctoral candidate in the Department of Environmental Health and Engineering at the Johns Hopkins Bloomberg School of Public Health, Baltimore, MD. Megan Weil Latshaw is an associate teaching professor in the Department of Environmental Health and Engineering at the Johns Hopkins Bloomberg School of Public Health. Paul A. Locke is a professor in the Department of Environmental Health and Engineering at the Johns Hopkins Bloomberg School of Public Health.

See also *AJPH* Student Think Tank, pp. 447–481.

AJPH April 2026, Vol. 116, No. 4

Even in an era marked by political divisions, a remarkable consensus cutting across party lines has emerged within federal public health agencies: the future of preclinical and toxicological research lies in human-relevant, technology-driven New Approach Methods (NAMs). The Food and Drug Administration's (FDA's) April 2025 announcement to phase out animal testing requirements for monoclonal antibodies and other drugs, followed by the National Institutes of Health's (NIH's) historic commitment to prioritize human-based research technologies, represent a significant shift in health research under the current administration.[1]

THE BRIGHT SPOT: PUSHING HUMAN-RELEVANT RESEARCH

The shift is more than just administrative rhetoric. FDA Commissioner Martin Makary released the Roadmap to Reducing Animal Testing in Preclinical Safety Studies; NIH Director Jay Bhattacharya established the Office of Research Innovation, Validation, and Application to "expand funding and training in nonanimal approaches and awareness of their value" (https://bit.ly/46c1hvE); and Environmental Protection Agency (EPA) Administrator Lee Zeldin also revived previously shelved plans to phase out animal testing.[1] At a July 2025 FDA–NIH workshop, Acting NIH Deputy Director Nicole Kleinstreuer announced that the agency will no longer seek research proposals limited to animal experiments. Instead, all new funding calls will require the inclusion of nonanimal methods, finally lifting a long-standing constraint on innovation.

These initiatives promise to improve drug development and chemical safety assessment through NAMs (e.g., organ chips, 3D organoids, computational modeling). NAMs have the potential to offer more human-relevant predictions than traditional animal models, addressing the reality that more than 90% of drugs entering clinical trials fail to gain regulatory approval despite passing preclinical animal tests, with lack of efficacy and unexpected toxicity being primary reasons for attrition.[2]

For next-generation public health leaders, this shift necessitates a specialized workforce, creating training and employment opportunities across academia, government, industry, and nonprofit organizations. Expertise in human-relevant methods will be needed to develop assays, interpret nonclinical evidence, and support regulatory decision-making. Integrating NAMs concepts into public health curricula will ensure trainees are well-positioned to break through institutional inertia that favors animal experiments and move toward nonanimal approaches that can lead to innovative cures, save lives, and better protect public health. However, this bright spot faces a looming threat.

THE CLOSING DOOR: MOBILITY CRISIS FOR INTERNATIONAL TALENT

As federal agencies embrace alternatives to animal testing, success hinges on developing expertise throughout public health and allied science, technology, engineering, and mathematics (STEM) fields. International trainees, who earn 36% of all US STEM PhDs, are poised to play an essential role in this transformation. In fields critical to NAMs development, they account for 31% of PhD recipients in biomedical fields, 44% in NAM-relevant engineering, 56% in computational disciplines, 34% in toxicology and pharma, 21% in biology and physiology, and about 20% across public health majors.[3] Yet, just as the United States needs to widen this talent pipeline, immigration and visa rule changes and practices are narrowing access to a talented pool of students.

In May 2025, right after foreign students received their admission decisions from US institutions, the US Department of State directed embassies and consulates worldwide to halt scheduling new visa application interviews. After a month-long pause, overseas posts resumed appointments and added stricter screening requirements including social media review. Many in STEM fields were diverted into open-ended "administrative processing" that can take months. Starting October 2025, most interview waivers ended, pushing more applicants into longer queues.[4]

Enrolled international students find themselves on shifting sands, too. In May 2025, Secretary of State Marco Rubio announced that the United States would start revoking visas held by students of certain nationalities.[5] According to an April 2025 Associated Press report, more than 1200 international students had their legal status terminated since late March. Documented cases also show valid visa holders denied reentry at US ports, which fuels a fear of traveling abroad for conferences, fieldwork, or even family visits.[6] The Department of Homeland Security (DHS) also proposes replacing "duration of status" with fixed four-year limits for F and J visa holders, imposing uncertainties for multiyear projects common in STEM fields.[7] Compounding these pressures, the current administration had already terminated billions of dollars in NIH and National Science Foundation funding, resulting in deep cuts to higher-education and research opportunities.

At the same time, international trainees who finish their degrees face a narrowing path to employment. The first bottleneck appears in public-sector employment. Executive Order 14170 imposed a hiring freeze across the Executive Branch in January 2025, extended twice through October 15, 2025.[8] The Department of Health and Human Services is restructuring with a downsizing from 82 000 to 62 000 full-time employees.[9] EPA is eliminating its 1500-employee Office of Research and Development, the agency's core scientific branch, through a reduction in force, firing up to 75% of its staff and reassigning others.[10] These actions create a cascading effect. Thousands of displaced federal scientists are now flooding the private-sector job market, effectively reducing opportunities for new graduates. International jobseekers bear the brunt. They comprise 19% of today's STEM workforce, rising to 37% of the workforce at the master's level and 43% at the doctorate level.[11] If the trend continues, these percentages will likely shrink considerably.

In this increasingly intense competitive environment, international graduates face a unique disadvantage. The visa programs designed to retain US institution-trained talent are being dismantled. US Citizenship and Immigration Services director Joseph Edlow has discussed ending the Optional Practical Training (OPT) program, which would close the door for new graduates who rely on this program to start their careers in the United States.[12] DHS drafted a rule to change the H-1B working visa selection from a lottery to a wage-ranking system, potentially disadvantaging early career professionals in emerging fields like NAM development.[13] Furthermore, record-high green card processing time and multiyear backlogs for certain countries have made the immigration pathway increasingly unstable, jeopardizing international trainees' job security, research continuity, and career opportunities. If the path from student to employee narrows, the talent pool narrows with it.

These mounting pressures are already driving young professionals away from US universities. A report estimates that new international student enrollment could drop by 30% to 40% in fall 2025.[14] Because international students earn a disproportionate share of US STEM advanced degrees, even a single-year decline can cause long-term losses in research and innovation capacity. This "brain drain" risks not only humane research alternatives but also the entire American scientific research infrastructure that depends on diverse, global expertise. Foreign-born scientists have earned 40% (45 of 112) of US Nobel Prizes since 2000.[15]

MOVING FORWARD: ALIGNMENT OF POLICY WITH PURPOSE

As international students and professionals committed to public health education and practice, we urge policymakers to establish a transparent, fair, workable system so that international students have opportunities to learn, practice, and add to US scientific research and innovation. International students who came to the United States deserve the chance to contribute their passion, knowledge, and energy to advancing science and public health here. This better way forward starts with three recommendations.

Science Roadmap–Workforce Pipeline Alignment

Federal agencies embracing scientific advancements like NAMs should explicitly acknowledge the need to retain international talent. Create funded traineeships and bridge positions accessible to competitive foreign-born professionals, with structured pathways that serve US scientific priorities while maintaining some flexibility in immigration requirements. Publish scientific initiatives alongside plans for international recruitment, specify the required skill sets, and advocate for visa allocations to match. In this way, the United States can continue to attract the best and the brightest from around the world.

Stabilize the Channel From Campus to Career

International students are investing time, effort, and resources in the US education system and as a quid pro quo deserve predictability. Keep OPT and STEM OPT extension policy transparent and stable. Align H-1B cap season timing with academic calendars so that new graduates and employers can make informed decisions. When new visa vetting procedures are introduced, agencies should provide clear guidance and timelines so affected individuals can plan accordingly. Clear, consistent guidelines for nonimmigrant visa holders would allow them to organize life events and research commitments without living in constant fear of denial at ports of entry or visa revocation over minor administrative or technical infractions.

Let Science and Scientists Inform Policy

Safeguard the specific government units that translate scientific advances into regulatory practice and prioritize essential research activities including method validation, guidance development, and educational events. Agencies' roadmaps toward human-relevant research can succeed only if federal research branches have the capacity to review and adopt NAMs, and widespread imposition of reductions in force and position cutbacks will narrow this channel. Researchers, including international trainees, should not watch their efforts become obsolete because the regulatory system lacks qualified personnel.

The bright spot of NAMs innovation need not dim behind closing immigration doors. It is time to explicitly acknowledge that scientific roadmaps require corresponding talent pipelines, bolstered by concrete plans to welcome and retain international talent. Better public health innovation demands access to global talent, not barriers that drive it away. The path forward is clear. AJPH

CORRESPONDENCE

Correspondence should be sent to Yiguang Zhu, 615 N Wolfe St, W7034J, Baltimore, MD 21205 (e-mail: yzhu99@jh.edu). Reprints can be ordered at https://ajph.org by clicking the "Reprints" link.

PUBLICATION INFORMATION

Full Citation: Zhu Y, Latshaw MW, Locke PA. Bright spot, closing door: encouraging innovation, restricting foreign talent. *Am J Public Health*. 2026;116(4): 482–484.

Acceptance Date: December 12, 2025.

DOI: https://doi.org/10.2105/AJPH.2025.308384

ORCID iDs:

Yiguang Zhu https://orcid.org/0000-0002-7954-9105

Megan Weil Latshaw https://orcid.org/0000-0001-5291-7644

Paul A. Locke https://orcid.org/0000-0002-5350-2819

CONTRIBUTORS

Y. Zhu originated and drafted the article. M. Weil Latshaw and P. A. Locke provided conceptual guidance, helped frame the problem and writing strategy, and contributed to substantive revisions of the article's structure and language.

CONFLICTS OF INTEREST

The authors report no conflicts of interest.

REFERENCES

1. Reardon S. The US wants to phase out animal research. Are the alternatives ready? *Science (1979)*. 2025;389(6761). https://doi.org/10.1126/SCIENCE.Z37GLKY
2. Smietana K, Siatkowski M, Møller M. Trends in clinical success rates. *Nat Rev Drug Discov*. 2016;15(6):379–380. https://doi.org/10.1038/NRD.2016.85
3. National Center for Science and Engineering Statistics. Doctorate recipients from US universities: 2024 data tables. 2025. Available at: https://ncses.nsf.gov/surveys/earned-doctorates/2024. Accessed September 7, 2025.
4. US Department of State. Interview waiver update September 18, 2025. September 18, 2025. Available at: https://travel.state.gov/content/travel/en/News/visas-news/interview-waiver-update-sept-18-2025.html. Accessed January 22, 2026.
5. US Department of State. New visa policies put America first, not China. May 28, 2025. Available at: https://web.archive.org/web/20251026135411/https://www.state.gov/releases/office-of-the-spokesperson/2025/05/new-visa-policies-put-america-first-not-china. Accessed January 21, 2026.
6. Ma A. More than 1,000 international students have had visas or legal status revoked. *Associated Press*. April 18, 2025. Available at: https://apnews.com/article/f1-visa-international-college-student-trump-9d4d900d328a0c205503c1178e70f1d5. Accessed September 6, 2025.
7. US Department of Homeland Security. Establishing a fixed time period of admission and an extension of stay procedure for nonimmigrant academic students, exchange visitors, and representatives of foreign information media. *Federal Register*. August 28, 2025. Available at: https://www.federalregister.gov/documents/2025/08/28/2025-16554/establishing-a-fixed-time-period-of-admission-and-an-extension-of-stay-procedure-for-nonimmigrant. Accessed September 6, 2025.
8. The White House. Ensuring accountability and prioritizing public safety in federal hiring. Presidential Memoranda. July 7, 2025. Available at: https://www.whitehouse.gov/presidential-actions/2025/07/ensuring-accountability-and-prioritizing-public-safety-in-federal-hiring. Accessed September 8, 2025.
9. US Department of Health and Human Services. HHS announces transformation to Make America Healthy Again. March 27, 2025. Available at: https://www.hhs.gov/press-room/hhs-restructuring-doge.html. Accessed September 7, 2025.
10. Lofgren Z, Amo G. Letter to Administrator Zeldin. Congress of the United States, House of Representatives. Committee on Science, Space, and Technology, Subcommittee on Environment. May 27, 2025. Available at: https://democrats-science.house.gov/imo/media/doc/SST%20RM%20Lofgren%20Amo%20-%20Letter%20to%20Administrator%20Zeldin%20-%20ORD%20Labs%20-%205.27.25.pdf. Accessed September 8, 2025.
11. National Science Board, National Science Foundation. Science and engineering indicators 2024: the state of US science and engineering 2024. 2024. Available at: https://ncses.nsf.gov/pubs/nsb20243. Accessed September 8, 2025.
12. Senate Judiciary Committee. Nomination of Joseph Edlow to be director of the United States Citizenship and Immigration Services questions for the record. 2025. Available at: https://www.judiciary.senate.gov/imo/media/doc/2025-05-21_qfrresponses_edlow.pdf. Accessed September 6, 2025.
13. US Department of Homeland Security, US Citizenship and Immigration Services. Weighted selection process for registrants and petitioners seeking to file cap-subject H-1B petitions. 2025. Available at: https://www.reginfo.gov/public/do/eAgendaViewRule?pubId=202504&RIN=1615-AD01. Accessed September 7, 2025.
14. NAFSA: Association of International Educators. Fall 2025 international student enrollment outlook and economic impact. 2025. Available at: https://www.nafsa.org/fall-2025-international-student-enrollment-outlook-and-economic-impact. Accessed September 7, 2025.
15. National Foundation for American Policy. Immigrants and Nobel Prizes: 1901–2023. 2023. Available at: https://nfap.com/research/immigrants-and-nobel-prizes-1901-2023. Accessed September 10, 2025.

Student Loan Debt Burden in the Public Health Workforce

Jonathon P. Leider, PhD, Moriah Robins, MPH, Nicole McDaniel, MPH, Rachel Hare Bork, PhD, Hunter Doyle, MPH, and Brian C. Castrucci, DrPH

Objectives. To characterize the national landscape of student loan debt for state and local public health staff and consider the potential roles of loan forgiveness and repayment in workforce development.

Methods. This study analyzed data from the nationally representative 2024 Public Health Workforce Interests and Needs Survey, which had 57 000 respondents in the United States. We calculated descriptive statistics and performed an interval regression to assess correlates of student loan balance.

Results. More than 40% of the workforce has a student loan balance: $48 000 on average, among those with any debt. Differences are observed by age, race/ethnicity, and level of academic degree.

Conclusions. As in other fields, governmental public health is experiencing high rates of turnover while having difficulty with recruitment. Lack of competitive pay and benefits makes it difficult to find and retain staff who may have a public service inclination but also have bills to pay. High on that list of bills, for many, are student loans.

Public Health Implications. Loan forgiveness and repayment represent important policy tools to address the ongoing workforce shortage and may be adversely affected by recent federal legislation.
(*Am J Public Health*. 2026;116(4):485–491. https://doi.org/10.2105/AJPH.2025.308290)

Governmental public health has been saddled with underinvestment and stagnant wages, making recruitment into the sector challenging.[1,2] Prior to the onset of the COVID-19 pandemic, the governmental public health workforce was in decline, losing approximately 40 000 staff between 2009 and 2013 and never fully recovering by the onset of COVID-19.[1] An increase in staffing numbers was seen through hiring for pandemic response, although it is unclear whether that growth is sustainable.[3,4] Moreover, the COVID-19 pandemic exposed the gravity of worsening health disparities in the United States.[5,6] Recruitment and retention issues in governmental public health have become paramount.

Although governmental public health pays reasonably well overall, it is generally viewed as uncompetitive with the health care and tech sectors, which often capture recent graduates and recent hires.[7] The growing concern of student loan debt, coupled with compensation challenges, presents a significant barrier to service in governmental public health.[8] A recent survey on first-destination outcomes for public health graduates indicated that only 10% of bachelor's degree graduates and 19% of master's degree graduates chose to enter the field of governmental public health; most graduates' first job after school is in health care organizations or for-profit corporations.[9] With often-uncompetitive pay[10] and flagging traditional benefits, student loan repayment or forgiveness represents an important potential avenue to increase recruitment and retention of the governmental public health workforce.

In the context of pandemic response, and building on several previous failed attempts to create a public health–specific student loan program, the 2022 Public Health Workforce Loan Repayment Program (PHWLRP) was created as a means of improving the recruitment of the next generation of public health workers.[11] However, like its predecessors, it was not funded, and authorization expired in 2025. As passed, the PHWLRP would pay up to $50 000 for eligible loans.[12] Beyond the PHWLRP and other occupation-specific loan repayment programs, the broader Public Service Loan Forgiveness (PSLF) program is a major pathway for remediating student loan debt.[13] PSLF is a popular path to student loan debt forgiveness established by the federal government to promote and reward careers in public service, one that expanded dramatically under the Biden administration and has been curtailed by the Trump administration.[14,15] Recent changes owing to the One Big Beautiful Bill Act may significantly affect graduate and professional education in the United States, including in public health.[16] Limitations around total student loan debt and the elimination of the Graduate PLUS loan, in particular, may complicate pursuing a degree in public health and the health sciences more broadly.[16]

Student loan debt is an issue affecting 1 in 6 adult Americans, with the average debt at $26 000 for bachelor's degree holders, $68 000 for master's degree holders, and $77 000 for research doctorate holders.[17] Despite the pervasiveness of student loan debt, its level and overall burden on governmental public health staff have not been previously described. Current College Scorecard data offer a snapshot of the total loan burden of students graduating from schools of public health, but the data do not provide an accurate cumulative picture, nor do they show the amount of debt remaining.[18] The objectives of this study were to characterize student loan debt burden and its correlates among public health workers.

METHODS

To characterize student loan debt among governmental public health staff, this study used the 2024 Public Health Workforce Interests and Needs Survey (PH WINS), fielded from September 9, 2024, to January 10, 2025.[19] PH WINS is a US national survey capturing perspectives from individual governmental public health workers on workplace engagement, morale, intent to leave, training needs, and infrastructure, as well as demographic information. Details on the survey methodology have been previously described.[19] Additionally, in 2024, questions around student loan debt were added by the project team to understand its burden on governmental public health workers.

Approximately 159 627 people were invited to participate in the 2024 PH WINS across 48 state health agencies and nearly 1200 local health departments in the United States. Of those, 56 595 responded, a 37% response rate, after accounting for those who had left their position or were otherwise unreachable. All staff at participating health departments were invited to complete the survey via Qualtrics, an online platform. Employees were sent an invitation e-mail and 4 to 6 reminder e-mails depending on the date of the initial invitation e-mail.

Measurement

Specific to this analysis, PH WINS asked respondents to ascertain total student loan disbursements, remaining balances, and types of loans taken out. PH WINS asked questions around student loan disbursement and remaining balance using ranges in increments of $10 000 up to $200 000. We generated descriptive characteristics for student loan disbursements and balances by demographics and worker characteristics. We calculated PSLF "eligibility" based on years in public health practice. Other requirements of the program[20] were not measured, so estimates should be viewed as an upper bound. Similarly, we assessed PHWLRP "eligibility" based on years since graduation (and staff work at a governmental public health agency).[12]

Analytic Approach

We made inferential comparisons by using design-adjusted Wald tests. We generated a survey-weighted interval regression with the dependent variable as remaining student loan balance. Independent variables included age, educational attainment, gender, race/ethnicity, and supervisory status. Because of low rates of missingness, we excluded records with missing data from the final model. Variance inflation factor analysis did not indicate collinearity concerns for the final model. We generated nationally representative survey weights based on participation of staff from agencies, stratified by size of population served and Department of Health and Human Services (HHS) region. We performed statistical analysis in Stata 18 (StataCorp LP, College Station, TX) and created visualizations in Microsoft Excel (Microsoft Corporation, Redmond, WA).

RESULTS

The majority of public health workers secured student loans, varying largely by age of respondent and educational attainment (Table 1; Table A, available as a supplement to the online version of this article at http://www.ajph.org), with 70% reporting ever taking out loans and 40% of those staff having a nonzero balance. Among those aged 35 years and younger, 70% secured student loans, compared with 75% of those aged 36 to 49 years, 66% of

TABLE 1— Student Loans Taken Out and Remaining by Age Among PH WINS Respondents: United States, 2024

	Student Loan Amounts, %				
Age, y	**$0**	**$1–$20 000**	**$20 001–$40 000**	**$40 001–$100 000**	**> $100 000**
Loans taken out					
≤ 35	30	16	19	28	7
36–49	25	17	16	31	10
50–64	34	23	15	21	7
≥ 65	41	29	11	14	5
Loans remaining					
≤ 35	43	18	15	19	6
36–49	58	13	9	14	6
50–64	71	10	6	9	4
≥ 65	86	5	3	4	2

Note. PH WINS = Public Health Workforce Interests and Needs Survey. Percentage of PH WINS respondents with "student loans taken out" was calculated based on the total number of PH WINS respondents; percentage of respondents with "student loans remaining" was calculated based on the number of respondents that ever took out student loans (i.e., had > $0 balance).

those aged 50 to 64 years, and 59% of those aged 65 years and older (online Figure A). Forty percent of the workforce (including those who never took out loans) reported a $0 student loan balance, including approximately 43% of those aged 35 years and younger (online Table B). Remaining student loan balance varied by race/ethnicity, with 11% to 17% of American Indian/Alaskan Native employees, Asian employees, Hispanic employees, White employees, and Middle Eastern and North African (MENA) employees maintaining a balance above $40 000. By comparison, 35% of Black/African American employees, 20% of Native Hawaiian and Pacific Islander employees, and 20% of multiracial/multiethnic employees reported a balance above $40 000.

We estimated mean remaining loan burden within reported intervals in 2 ways: (1) an overall estimate including staff with a $0 balance and those who never took out loans, and (2) an estimate only for those with a balance remaining. In total, we estimated a mean student loan balance of $19 000 among all staff nationally, including those with a $0 balance. Among those with a balance remaining, the average owed was estimated at $48 000. For employees with loans, those with a doctoral degree had the greatest mean loan balance at $86 000, followed by master's degree holders at $67 000 and bachelor's degree holders at $38 500. Across demographic categories, American Indian staff reported a mean loan balance of $43 500 and Black/African American staff reported a mean of $60 500, compared with $51 000 for Asian staff, $42 000 for Hispanic/Latino staff, $50 000 for MENA staff, $51 000 for Hawaiian or Pacific Islander staff, $44 500 for White staff, and $47 500 for multiracial/multiethnic staff. Those in supervisory or management positions reported greater loan balances, with managers reporting an average of $60 000. Among individuals considering leaving their organization within the next year, the average loan amount was $24 000, compared with $18 000 among those not considering leaving ($P < .001$). We also looked at loan balance as a percentage of total disbursements (Table 2, online Figures B and C). Overall, 22% of those who ever had student loans had a remaining loan balance of more than 75% of the initial disbursement, whereas 14% of borrowers had a balance of more than 100%.

We built an interval regression model to examine correlates of student loan debt (Figure 1). All else being equal, those aged 35 years and younger and 36 to 49 years had higher debt ($10 000; 95% confidence interval [CI] = $9000, $11 000; $P < .001$) than those aged 50 to 64 years ($5500; 95% CI = $4500, $6500; $P < .001$). Compared with bachelor's degree holders, master's graduates had $14 500 more debt (95% CI = $13 500, $15 500; $P < .001$) and doctoral graduates had $18 000 more (95% CI = $15 000, $21 500; $P < .001$). Compared with White graduates, all racial/ethnic groups except Asian staff had higher remaining student loan balances (American Indian and MENA staff differences were not

TABLE 2— Remaining Student Loan Balance Among PH WINS Respondents as a Percentage of Initial Disbursement, by Age: United States, 2024

	% of Loan Disbursement Remaining					
Age, y	**0**	**1–24**	**25–49**	**50–74**	**75–99**	**≥ 100**
≤ 25	9	5	8	13	34	31
26–30	14	5	10	14	31	27
31–35	24	7	9	14	27	18
36–40	39	6	8	12	19	15
41–45	47	7	8	9	17	12
46–50	50	7	7	10	15	10
51–55	52	6	7	11	15	9
56–60	61	5	6	7	12	9
61–65	67	5	5	7	10	7
> 65	80	3	3	5	5	3
Total	44	6	7	11	19	14

Note. PH WINS = Public Health Workforce Interests and Needs Survey. Percentage of respondents with loan disbursement remaining was calculated on the basis of the number of respondents that ever took out > $0 student loans.

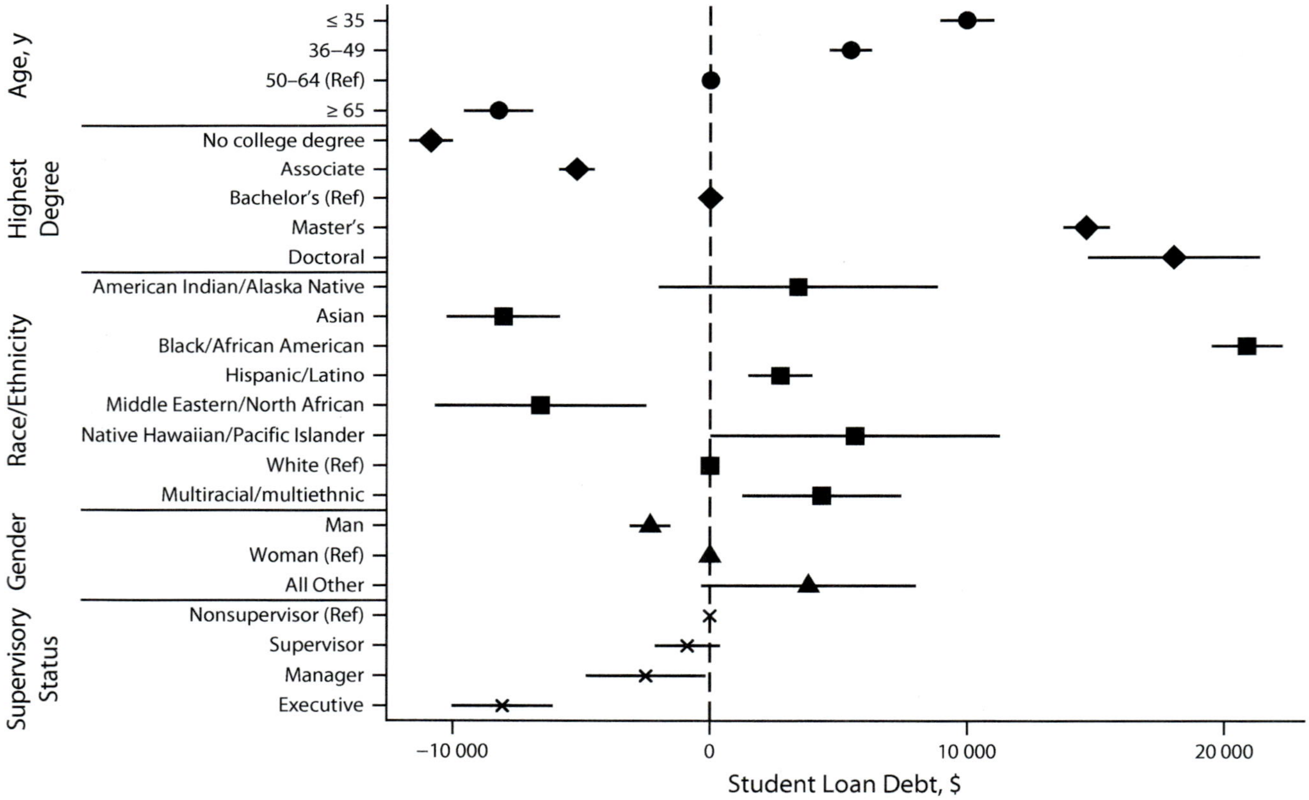

FIGURE 1— Correlates of Remaining Student Loan Debt Among Governmental Public Health Workers: United States, 2024

Note. Estimates represent additional remaining student loan debt relative to the reference population, all else being equal. Error bars represent 95% confidence intervals.

statistically significant). All else being equal, men had lower student loan debt than women (−\$2500; 95% CI = −\$1500, −\$3000; $P<.001$), and staff indicating any other gender had more (\$4000; 95% CI = −\$500, \$8000; $P=.065$).

There are multiple avenues for taking out student loans, including for dependents via the Parent Loan for Undergraduate Students (PLUS; online Figure D). Among those younger than 50 years, 72% of respondents' balance came from federal direct loans. However, for those older than 50 years, Federal Parent PLUS loans were approximately 20% of respondents' balance. Private loans remained relatively constant by age (12%−16%), although some groups had higher proportions (Asian and MENA staff at 19%).

Table 3 shows the upper bound of employees theoretically eligible for PSLF, based on years in public health. Also shown are those who would theoretically be eligible for the PHWLRP based on years since graduation and current employment in public health. Up to 9% of employees might have been eligible for PSLF (notwithstanding any nontenure-related requirements, such as on-time payments and annual certification). Potentially, 16% of staff might have been eligible for PHWLRP as passed, with 4% of staff potentially being eligible for both PSLF and PHWLRP based on tenure and years since graduation. Eleven percent of staff with student loan debt did not appear to be eligible for either, whereas 60% of staff did not have student loan debt.

A final area of analysis was the relationship between levels of student loan debt and intent to leave. Overall, among those not considering leaving, student loan debt was \$18 000, compared with \$24 000 among those considering leaving ($P<.001$). Among White staff not considering leaving, the mean student loan balance was \$15 000, compared with \$20 000 among those considering leaving ($P<.001$). Among staff not considering leaving who identified as Black, Indigenous, or people of color, the mean student loan balance was \$23 000, compared with a mean balance of \$30 000 among those considering leaving.

DISCUSSION

Among governmental public health staff, student loan debt is common and, for the 95 000 staff estimated from this study to have student loan debt, it is substantial. Among those with any student loan balance, the average owed is \$48 000. Student loans are a burden, one that magnifies inequities already present in the system. Younger employees, Black and African American employees, Native Hawaiian or Pacific Islander employees, and multiracial/multiethnic employees all reported relatively higher levels of remaining debt. Student loan debt is a problem not only for younger employees but for older employees as well. Not previously described is the burden of Parent PLUS loans on the public health workforce; overall, Parent PLUS loans represent approximately 11% of student loan debt. For those with any Parent PLUS loans, that debt is approximately 51% of the total. Previously, these loans were eligible for forgiveness under PSLF.[16] With recent changes to PSLF from the One Big Beautiful Bill Act, this is no longer the case. It is too soon to know the impact on the workforce of new lifetime caps on graduate loans, the elimination of certain student loan programs, changes to the PSLF structure, eligibility changes, the removal of

TABLE 3— Potential Loan Eligibility by Public Service Loan Forgiveness (PSLF) and Public Health Workforce Loan Repayment Program (PHWLRP) Among State and Local Public Health Staff PH WINS Respondents: United States, 2024

	Neither	PSLF Only	PHWLRP Only	Both PSLF and PHWLRP	No Balance
Total balance, \$	1 022 000 000	941 000 000	1 905 000 000	598 000 000	
Mean balance, \$	41 500	44 000	51 500	61 500	
Federal direct loans, %	64	53	76	74	
PLUS federal student loans for parents, %	11	18	7	8	
Estimated no.	25 000	22 500	38 000	10 000	142 500

Note. PH WINS = Public Health Workforce Interests and Needs Survey; PLUS = Parent Loan for Undergraduate Students. PSLF has requirements (e.g., 120 on-time payments, 10 annual certifications of eligible employment) that were not measurable directly and based on pre–Big Beautiful Bill standards; this estimate should be seen as an upper bound of program-specific student loan debt burden. Similarly, PHWLRP has its own potential rules if implemented, not all of which are measurable in PH WINS.

Parent PLUS from repayment programs, and changes to other repayment requirements. However, it seems unlikely that these challenges will improve recruitment or retention of the workforce. Some combination of tuition reductions, scholarships, and taking on more private student loan debt are the likely future for prospective applicants. Given the financial state of academic public health, the first 2 options appear somewhat unlikely, and the third would result in higher lifetime costs and student loan burden for graduates.

High levels of debt represent a prudential challenge to employers, given extreme turnover during the COVID-19 response and relatively high continuing turnover since then.[21] Disparities among those who carry student loan debt reduce equality of opportunity but also are highly associated with turnover.[1] Although the United States has more than 45 000 public health graduates a year, relatively few go into governmental employment.[9,22] Salary and benefits are a primary concern.[23–25] Additionally, across all industries, difficulties in paying student loan debt weigh heavily as financial concerns for borrowers.[26] Loan forgiveness and repayment programs have historically played an important role in the financial security of those eligible,[26] and data in this analysis show there is a statistically meaningful relationship between intent to leave and student loan balance.

Limitations

The primary limitations in this analysis relate to potential nonresponse in PH WINS. As with all surveys, those who choose to respond and those who do not may be different. Previous research has shown that nonparticipants are more likely to be in nonpublic health clerical positions, facilities positions, and certain clinical positions (e.g., emergency medical technicians, home health aides) than participants.[27] Additionally, some agencies choose not to participate in PH WINS. In 2024, 2 state health agencies and many local health departments chose not to participate. The staff working in these agencies may be different from those in agencies that chose to participate. However, survey weights were implemented to create nationally generalizable estimates.

Another potential limitation relates to imprecision in a respondent's student loan balance. Staff were asked both their total initial disbursements of student loans and current balance. This was done in intervals, rather than point estimates. Research suggests that survey respondents are generally more comfortable with intervals and point estimates for questions that relate to salary and debt.[28] Interval regression was used to create point estimates; although this is a reliable approach at a population level, variation between estimated and actual student loan debt at an individual level is expected.

Conclusion

Student loan debts among the public health workforce exceed $4.5 billion, almost $50 000 on average among those with a balance. Compounded by salaries that may not be competitive with the private market, this financial burden represents a meaningful policy target for recruitment and retention; on average, staff making $55 000 or less with any loans have a $38 000 balance. For decades, loan repayment and forgiveness have been tools used to try to close workforce gaps in other health science areas. Reasonable questions present about what is practical or possible under a presidential administration that has voiced concern about student loan debt forgiveness. Workforce challenges persist, however, and constituencies exist that may be able to highlight the critical importance of tackling this policy issue. Student loan burden is known, solutions exist, but the questions of political priority will remain. AJPH

ABOUT THE AUTHORS

At the time of the study, Jonathon P. Leider, Nicole McDaniel, and Hunter Doyle were with the Center for Public Health Systems, Division of Health Policy and Management, University of Minnesota School of Public Health, Minneapolis. Moriah Robins, Rachel Hare Bork, and Brian C. Castrucci were with the de Beaumont Foundation, Bethesda, MD.

CORRESPONDENCE

Correspondence should be sent to Jonathon Leider, D312 Mayo Bldg, MMC 729, 420 Delaware St SE, Minneapolis, MN 55455 (e-mail: leider@umn.edu). Reprints can be ordered at https://www.ajph.org by clicking the "Reprints" link.

PUBLICATION INFORMATION

Full Citation: Leider JP, Robins M, McDaniel N, Hare Bork R, Doyle H, Castrucci BC. Student loan debt burden in the public health workforce. *Am J Public Health*. 2026;116(4):485–491.

Acceptance Date: September 7, 2025.

DOI: https://doi.org/10.2105/AJPH.2025.308290

ORCID iDs:

Jonathon P. Leider https://orcid.org/0000-0001-9905-476X

Nicole McDaniel https://orcid.org/0009-0004-1989-4101

Rachel Hare Bork https://orcid.org/0000-0002-4523-8819

Hunter Doyle https://orcid.org/0009-0005-0571-4365

CONTRIBUTORS

M. Robins, R. Hare Bork, and B. C. Castrucci fielded and analyzed PH WINS. J. P. Leider conceptualized the study. J. P. Leider and H. Doyle performed data analysis. All authors participated in writing and critical review.

ACKNOWLEDGMENTS

This project was supported by the Centers for Diseases Control and Prevention (CDC) and the Health Resources and Services Administration (HRSA; awards U81HP47167 and UR2HP47371).

We thank Jocelyn Leung, Heather Krasna, Adriane Casalotti, and staff at the National Health Service Corps for their advice and assistance on this project.

Note. The contents are those of the authors and do not necessarily represent the official views of, nor an endorsement by, the HRSA, the CDC, the Department of Health and Human Services, or the US government.

CONFLICTS OF INTEREST

The authors have no financial interests to disclose.

HUMAN PARTICIPANT PROTECTION

This study was deemed exempt by the Western Copernicus Group institutional review board (#117945631).

REFERENCES

1. Leider JP, Yeager VA, Kirkland C, Krasna H, Bork RH, Resnick B. The state of the US public health workforce: ongoing challenges and future directions. *Annu Rev Public Health.* 2023;44:323–341. https://doi.org/10.1146/annurev-publhealth-071421-032830
2. Beatty K, Hunt Trull L, Minnick C, Al Ksir K, Surles K, Meit M. Expanding options to recruit, grow, and retain the public health workforce. *Health Aff Sch.* 2024;2(12):qxae115. https://doi.org/10.1093/haschl/qxae115
3. Leider JP, Balio CP, Hogg-Graham R, et al. Enumeration 2024: what we know and what we wish we knew about the governmental public health workforce in a COVID-19 recovery landscape. *Am J Public Health.* 2025;115(5):707–715. https://doi.org/10.2105/AJPH.2024.307960
4. Hall K, Brees K, McCall TC, Cunningham MC, Alford AA. 2020 forces of change: the COVID-19 edition. National Association of County and City Health Officials. 2022. Available at: https://www.naccho.org/uploads/downloadable-resources/2020-Forces-of-Change-The-COVID-19-Edition.pdf. Accessed January 24, 2025.
5. Mackey K, Ayers CK, Kondo KK, et al. Racial and ethnic disparities in COVID-19–related infections, hospitalizations, and deaths. *Ann Intern Med.* 2021;174(3):362–373. https://doi.org/10.7326/M20-6306
6. Magesh S, John D, Li WT, et al. Disparities in COVID-19 outcomes by race, ethnicity, and socioeconomic status: a systematic review and meta-analysis. *JAMA Netw Open.* 2021;4(11):e2134147. https://doi.org/10.1001/jamanetworkopen.2021.34147
7. Yeager VA, Krasna H. When money is not enough: reimagining public health requires systematic solutions to hiring barriers. *Health Aff (Millwood).* 2024;43(6):840–845. https://doi.org/10.1377/hlthaff.2024.00020
8. Krasna H, Fried L. Generation public health: fixing the broken bridge between public health education and the governmental workforce. *Am J Public Health.* 2021;111(8):1413–1417. https://doi.org/10.2105/AJPH.2021.306317
9. Plepys CM, Krasna H, Leider JP, Burke EM, Blakely CH, Magaña L. First-destination outcomes for 2015–2018 public health graduates: focus on employment. *Am J Public Health.* 2021;111(3):475–484. https://doi.org/10.2105/AJPH.2020.306038
10. Krasna H, Venkataraman M, Patino I. Salary disparities in public health occupations: analysis of federal data, 2021–2022. *Am J Public Health.* 2024;114(3):329–339. https://doi.org/10.2105/AJPH.2023.307512
11. Smith T, Collins S, Booker C, Murkowski L, Lowery R. US senators introduce bipartisan legislation to rebuild public health workforce amidst shortages. Tina Smith, US senator for Minnesota. January 14, 2022. Available at: https://www.smith.senate.gov/u-s-senators-tina-smith-susan-collins-cory-booker-and-lisa-murkowski-introduce-bipartisan-legislation-to-rebuild-public-health-workforce-amidst-shortages. Accessed January 26, 2025.
12. 42 USC 295f-1: Public Health Workforce Loan Repayment Program. Available at: https://uscode.house.gov/view.xhtml?req=(title:42%20section:295f-1%20edition:prelim). Accessed January 26, 2025.
13. Davis CS, Meyers P, Bazemore AW, Peterson LE. Impact of service-based student loan repayment program on the primary care workforce. *Ann Fam Med.* 2023;21(4):327–331. https://doi.org/10.1370/afm.3002
14. Briones DA, Ruby N, Turner S. Waivers for the public service loan forgiveness program: who could benefit from take-up? *J Policy Anal Manage.* 2024;43(4):1004–1033. https://doi.org/10.1002/pam.22566
15. Lonas Cochran L. Biden announces last round of student debt forgiveness. The Hill. January 16, 2025. Available at: https://thehill.com/homenews/education/5090323-biden-student-debt-relief-loan-forgiveness. Accessed March 28, 2025.
16. Robledo A. What will student loans look like after Trump's spending bill is signed? *USA Today*. July 3, 2025. Available at: https://www.usatoday.com/story/news/education/2025/07/03/trump-spending-bill-student-loans/84466499007. Accessed July 4, 2025.
17. Congress.gov. A snapshot of federal student loan debt. Available at: https://www.congress.gov/crs-product/IF10158. Accessed July 17, 2025.
18. Tait M, Burke E, Leshan T, Casalotti A, Krasna H, Leider JP. Federal student loan debt in public health and the opportunities for loan repayment programs. *Public Health Rep.* 2024;139(4):512–518. https://doi.org/10.1177/00333549231223712
19. Robins M, Popalis M, Burton-Anderson L et al. Surveying the state and local government public health workforce: the design and evolution of PH WINS 2024. *J Public Health Manag Pract.* 2026; 32(suppl 1):S33–S44. https://doi.org/10.1097/PHH.0000000000002248
20. Public Service Loan Forgiveness. Edfinancial Services. Available at: https://edfinancial.studentaid.gov/public-service-loan-forgiveness. Accessed January 26, 2025.
21. Leider JP, Castrucci BC, Robins M, et al. The exodus of state and local public health employees: separations started before and continued throughout COVID-19. *Health Aff (Millwood).* 2023;42(3):338–348. https://doi.org/10.1377/hlthaff.2022.01251
22. Leider JP, Burke E, Nguyen RHN, et al. Trends in degree conferrals, degree-associated debt, and employment outcomes among undergraduate public health degree graduates, 2001–2020. *Am J Public Health.* 2023;113(1):115–123. https://doi.org/10.2105/AJPH.2022.307113
23. Liss-Levinson R. 35 and under in the public sector: why younger workers enter and why they stay (or don't). MissionSquare Research Institute. 2023. Available at: https://research.missionsq.org/content/media/document/2023/8/FINAL%20WorkforceSurveyReport35andYounger.pdf. Accessed January 26, 2025.
24. Sellers K, Leider JP, Lamprecht L, Liss-Levinson R, Castrucci BC. Using public health workforce surveillance data to prioritize retention efforts for younger staff. *Am J Prev Med.* 2020;59(4):562–569. https://doi.org/10.1016/j.amepre.2020.03.017
25. Johnson CL, O'Neill B, Worthy SL, Lown JM, Bowen CF. What are student loan borrowers thinking? Insights from focus groups on college selection and student loan decision making. *J Financ Couns Plan.* 2016;27(2):184–198. https://doi.org/10.1891/1052-3073.27.2.184
26. Caldwell I, Conkling T, Garrett W, Gibbs C, Luce C, Murto M. Insights from the 2023 – 2024 Student Loan Borrower Survey. Consumer Financial Protection Bureau. November 2024. Available at: https://files.consumerfinance.gov/f/documents/cfpb_Insights-from-the-2023-2024-Student-Loan-Borrower-Survey_Report.pdf. Accessed July 17, 2025.
27. Krasna H, Venkataraman M, Robins M, Patino I, Leider JP. Standard occupational classification codes: gaps in federal data on the public health workforce. *Am J Public Health.* 2024;114(1):48–56. https://doi.org/10.2105/AJPH.2023.307463
28. Moore JC, Stinson LL, Welniak EJ. Income measurement error in surveys: a review. *J Off Stat.* 2000;16(4):331–361.

Protecting Low-Wage Workers From Exploitation: A Mapping Study of Wage Theft Laws in the 40 Largest US Cities

Jennifer J. Lee, JD, Maggie O'Connor, JD, and Jiahui Shen, JD

See also Leigh, p. 417.

Objectives. We measured key features of local and state wage theft laws in the 40 largest US cities to assess the added value of local legislation and to create scientific legal data for use in evaluating the health impact of wage theft laws.

Methods. We adapted standard policy surveillance methods to collect and code local and state minimum wage and nonpayment of wages theft laws from January 1, 2010, to April 15, 2023.

Results. Compared with state laws, local wage theft legislation was proportionally more likely to contain features that facilitated worker complaints and to provide flexible enforcement tools. Only 4 of the 40 largest cities were totally preempted from enacting local wage theft legislation.

Conclusions. Local wage theft laws provide an opportunity for innovative mechanisms to support complaint filing and enforcement. More cities could enact wage theft laws without preemption concerns.

Public Health Implications. Ensuring that low-wage workers are fairly paid is important to health and health equity. Our research provides scientific legal data for use in evaluating the health effects of these widely applied protections. (*Am J Public Health.* 2026;116(4):492–501. https://doi.org/10.2105/AJPH.2025.308351)

AJPH April 2026, Vol. 116, No. 4

Wage theft is the practice of employers failing to pay wages after workers have earned them.[1] Some employers engage in wage theft by failing to pay minimum, promised, or overtime wages. Other employers use more subtle tactics, such as taking unauthorized deductions, failing to account for all hours worked, or paying daily or weekly rates to obfuscate the calculation of overtime.

Wage theft is illegal. Two kinds of laws regulate wage theft: (1) minimum wage laws and (2) nonpayment of wages laws. Minimum wage laws regulate the payment of minimum and overtime wages. Nonpayment of wages laws regulate the payment of promised wages, which may exceed the minimum wage. The Fair Labor Standards Act is the federal minimum wage law. Most states also regulate minimum wage and nonpayment of wages, which are typically found in separate laws.

Although wage theft is difficult to measure, several studies indicate that it is widespread. Wage theft is estimated to cost 2.4 million workers billions of dollars in the 10 most populous states in 2015.[2] In California and New York, there are estimated to be hundreds of thousands of minimum wage violations each week, depriving workers of $10.2 to $28.7 million of earned wages in each state for FY 2011.[3] In a survey of thousands of low-wage workers in 3 large cities in 2008, 68% of surveyed workers were victims of at least 1 pay-related violation in the previous week.[4] A 2008 survey of hundreds of restaurant workers in Chinatown in San Francisco, California, found that close to 60% of workers reported experiencing 1 or more forms of wage theft.[5]

Wage theft increases poverty and economic inequity. One estimate found that wage theft, on average, reduced affected workers' earnings by more than one quarter.[2] Wage theft violations can also increase poverty rates,[3] as wages are the largest source of income for the bottom fifth of households by income.[6] Women, Black, Hispanic, and noncitizen workers are disproportionately affected by wage theft.[2] Undocumented women are at a nearly 3 times greater risk of wage theft than their US citizen counterparts.[4] Those working in the service industry, particularly those who work in leisure and hospitality, are more likely to experience wage theft.[2]

Although there is a sizeable literature on minimum wage and health,[7] research more specifically on wage theft has been limited.[8] In minimum wage studies, minimum wage increases were associated with better mental and overall health and lower smoking prevalence.[7,9] Minimum wage, though, is not synonymous with wage theft. Minimum wage violations are a kind of wage theft. Wage theft, however, often amounts to more than the difference between a lower and higher minimum wage.

Wage theft is associated with increased odds of poor self-rated health and psychological distress and increased stress and burnout among workers.[10,11] Furthermore, a simulation study found that preventing wage theft would have eliminated up to 10% of the observed increases in inequities in expected age at death between the highest and lowest household income deciles from 2001 to 2014.[12]

It is better established that income and workplace exploitation influence health. Low incomes can be correlated with health problems and premature death because individuals are less able to afford materials and services to stay healthy, live in healthier neighborhoods, experience lower levels of stress, and have better access to health care.[13] Workplace exploitation, too, is associated with poor health outcomes, particularly negative mental health outcomes.[14,15]

Despite being illegal, wage theft violations persist. In general, wage theft laws are designed to help workers obtain redress while stopping employers from committing wage theft. The problem, however, is the lack of robust enforcement by federal and state agencies, including because of inadequate personnel and resources.[16,17] Furthermore, these agencies have not been able to keep up with the growth of precarious low-wage jobs and an increasing number of workers unaware of their rights.[18]

At the federal level, Congress has not enacted any laws to solve the problem. In response, local policymakers have explored new approaches to address wage theft. Stronger and more innovative wage theft policies could help address the problem.[5,15,17,19,20] Cities have been at the forefront of enacting or amending wage theft laws, by providing mechanisms to facilitate worker complaints and by penalizing violating employers. These legal mechanisms are the necessary precursor to having localities engage in enforcement. State preemption, however, can block these local policies that could potentially improve health and health equity.[21,22]

Every resident of a city is exposed to both their city and state wage theft laws. Absent preemption, city laws can work in a complementary manner with state laws. To date, there has been no research evaluating the effectiveness of local wage theft laws in reducing wage theft for workers. This study begins to fill the gap by creating 4 scientific legal data sets that measured how workers in the 40 largest US cities were exposed to city and state wage theft laws in effect from January 1, 2010, to April 15, 2023. These data sets and our findings can be used to further target public health evaluations of these legal interventions.

METHODS

Using legal epidemiology methods, the research team conducted a legal mapping survey of wage theft laws applicable to workers in the 40 most populous cities.[23] The research team consisted of 4 law student researchers supervised by a JD law professor.

The 4 longitudinal data sets of wage theft laws that we created were (1) city minimum wage laws, (2) city nonpayment laws, (3) state minimum wage laws, and (4) state nonpayment laws. The 40 most populous cities in the United States were identified by using population estimates from July 1, 2021.[24] Residents in such cities constitute one sixth of the US population. The data sets do not include any minimum wage or nonpayment of wages laws that solely applied to a particular subset of employees (e.g., municipal employees) or that applied to nonemployees (e.g., freelancers).

Collecting the Law

We identified and recorded relevant citations within the city ordinances and state statutes. For the city data sets, 2 law student researchers used American Legal Publishing or Municode Library to identify whether localities had minimum wage and nonpayment of wages laws. For the state data sets, the team primarily used state government websites to identify whether jurisdictions had minimum wage and nonpayment of wages laws. The team also sometimes used Westlaw Next or Google to look at state law amendments.

Keyword searches for the minimum wage data sets were "wage," "minimum," and "overtime." Keyword searches for the nonpayment of wages data sets were "wage" and "wage theft." Keyword searches were supplemented by reviewing the table of contents of the city code or statutory compilation and the chapters concerning labor, employment, crimes, and business licensing. After an initial review of sample laws, the supervisor developed a question development table composed of coding questions for each data set. The coding questions track different features of the law and vary slightly according to the data set. The team referenced the question development table when collecting the relevant legal texts for each jurisdiction.

Once the relevant laws were identified for a jurisdiction, 2 researchers created master sheets for each jurisdiction to document the legislative history and effective date for each iteration of the law during the study period. These researchers repeated the process in batches of 10 jurisdictions until all relevant laws were collected. The supervisor resolved any divergences.

Coding the Legal Text

The coding questions for each data set were uploaded in MonQcle (Version 3.0, Center for Public Health Law Research, Philadelphia, PA), a software-coding platform. The team added the text of each iteration of relevant law to MonQcle within the study period, coding 10 jurisdictions at a time. When the written law was unclear, researchers called or e-mailed the jurisdiction to clarify statutory language. Coding conventions were recorded in a protocol and in notations in the data set.

Quality Control Measures

All jurisdictions were 100% redundantly researched and coded by 2 researchers. Each researcher independently recorded the relevant citations from every jurisdiction in each data set and created a master sheet or redundant master sheet for each jurisdiction. The supervisor reviewed these master sheets, resolved divergences, and created a final version for each jurisdiction to collect the relevant laws. Similarly, these researchers coded each jurisdiction independently, comparing results of each batch of 10. The team resolved all divergences between the original and redundant coding through discussion.

RESULTS

We examined how workers in the 40 largest cities were exposed to wage theft laws, which include minimum wage or nonpayment of wages laws.

These workers resided in 25 states, covered by 46 state wage theft laws. In 35 cities, workers were subject to both minimum wage and nonpayment of wages laws at the state level. Residents in 16 of those cities were also covered by 22 city wage theft laws (Figure 1). Although almost all state wage theft laws existed before January 1, 2010, the prevalence of city wage theft laws has more than tripled from 6 to 22 laws in the study period.

Twenty of the 40 largest cities sit in states that either partially or totally preempt localities from enacting wage theft laws (Figure 2). Preemption occurs when states, as a higher-level authority, prohibit cities from enacting a specific kind of law. Partial preemption is when state law preempts either local minimum wage or nonpayment of wages laws. Total preemption is when state law preempts both kinds of laws. Only 4 out of the 40 cities were totally preempted from enacting both kinds of wage theft laws, whereas 16 cities were partially preempted from enacting a minimum wage law. Over the data set's time frame, new state preemption laws covered an additional 8 cities, whereas 2 cities saw a preemption repeal. Despite preemption, many of the 40 largest cities without a wage theft law could possibly enact one.

Facilitating Worker Complaints

Wage theft laws have features that help workers to file complaints. Such features are (1) informing workers of their rights, (2) protecting workers from retaliation, and (3) facilitating a worker's evidentiary burden (Table 1).

Workers in 13 cities were covered by laws that require education to workers about their rights, which may include information about complaint filing.

Wage theft laws also protect workers from retaliation for having asserted their rights. Retaliation is when employers take some kind of negative action, such as firing, demoting, or harassing a worker, in response to their complaint about wage theft. To avoid such retaliation, there are before-the-fact retaliation protections that support workers. They are (1) anonymous or confidential complaint filing, (2) authorizing a third party to file a complaint on the worker's behalf, or (3) workplace-wide investigations based on a single complaint (e.g., a wall-to-wall investigation). Twenty-one cities had such protections.

AJPH April 2026, Vol. 116, No. 4

FIGURE 1— **Distribution of City Wage Theft Laws: United States, 2010–2023**

[a]Nonpayment laws regulate the failure to pay agreed-upon wages.
[b]Minimum wage laws regulate the failure to pay minimum wage and overtime.

Once workers have filed a complaint, they have access to mechanisms that help them prove their case. Workers may lack official documentation of wage theft because their employer failed to keep payroll records. In those instances, the agency will shift the burden of proof onto the employer to show that wage theft has not occurred. Twelve cities had this burden-shifting provision. Furthermore, wage theft laws commonly have penalties for retaliation

AJPH April 2026, Vol. 116, No. 4

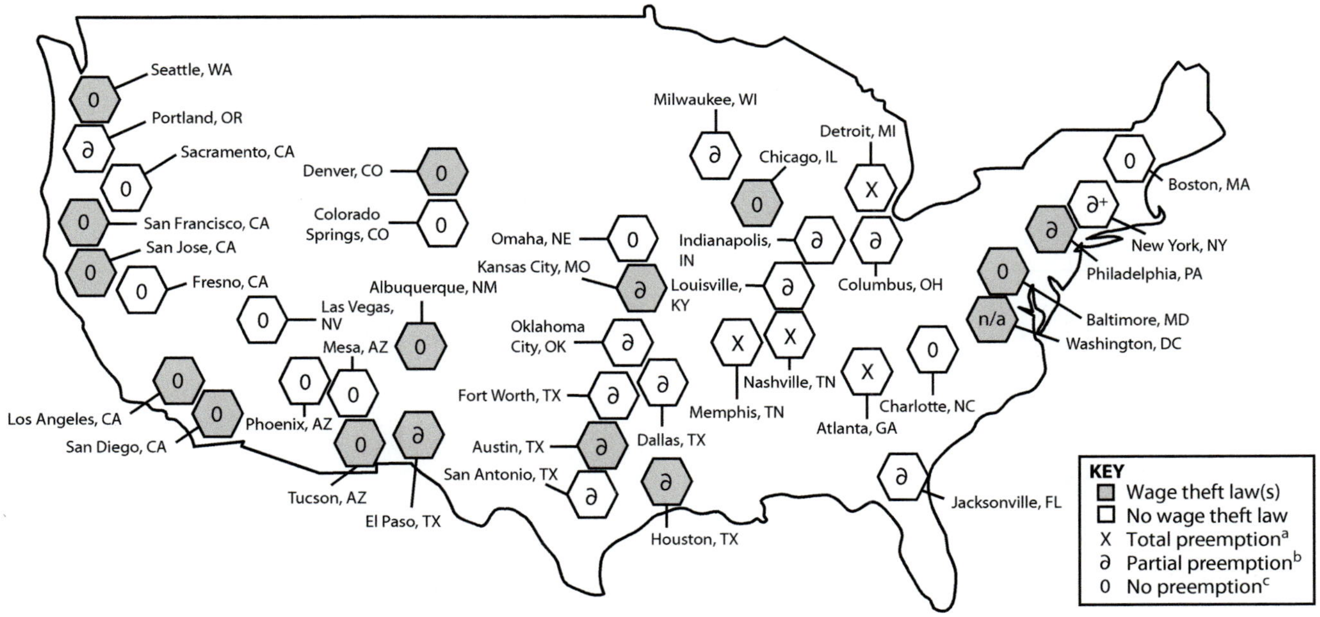

FIGURE 2— **Forty Largest US Cities With Wage Theft Laws and State Wage Theft Preemption: 2023**

Note. n/a = not applicable.
[a]"Total preemption" is when state law preempts both local minimum wage and nonpayment of wages laws.
[b]"Partial preemption" is when state law preempts either local minimum wage or nonpayment of wages laws.
[c]"No preemption" is when state law does not preempt either kind of law.
+Preemption by court decision.

AJPH April 2026, Vol. 116, No. 4

TABLE 1— Cities Covered by Laws With Features Facilitating Worker Complaints and Preventing Wage Theft by Employers: United States, 2023

	Facilitating Worker Complaints					Preventing Wage Theft by Employers					
City	Education: Targeting Workers	Retaliation: Before-the-Fact Protections	Proving Case: Burden Shifting	Proving Case: Presumption of Retaliation	Complaint: City Agency Process	Monetary Penalties: Treble Damages or Daily Fines $50–$120/d	Nonmonetary Penalties: Criminal	Nonmonetary Penalties: Negative Publicity	Nonmonetary Penalties: Revoke License	Education: Targeting Employers	Investigation: City Agency
Albuquerque, NM						X	X	X			
Atlanta, GA											
Austin, TX	X				X		X	X		X	
Baltimore, MD		X			X	X	X			X	X
Boston, MA	X					X	X	X			
Charlotte, NC											
Chicago, IL			X		X	X	X		X		X
Colorado Springs, CO		X				X	X				
Columbus, OH		X				X	X				
Dallas, TX	X						X			X	
Denver, CO		X	X	X	X	X	X				X
Detroit, MI		X					X				
El Paso, TX	X				X		X		X	X	X
Fort Worth, TX	X						X			X	
Fresno, CA		X		X			X				
Houston, TX	X						X		X	X	
Indianapolis, IN						X	X				
Jacksonville, FL											
Kansas City, MO						X	X				
Las Vegas, NV							X				
Los Angeles, CA	X	X		X	X	X	X	X	X	X	X
Louisville, KY		X									
Memphis, TN							X				
Mesa, AZ		X	X	X		X	X				
Milwaukee, WI		X					X				
Nashville, TN							X				
New York, NY		X	X				X	X			
Oklahoma City, OK		X					X				

Continued

TABLE 1— Continued

City	Facilitating Worker Complaints					Preventing Wage Theft by Employers					
	Education: Targeting Workers	Retaliation: Before-the-Fact Protections	Proving Case: Burden Shifting	Proving Case: Presumption of Retaliation	Complaint: City Agency Process	Monetary Penalties: Treble Damages or Daily Fines $50–$120/d	Nonmonetary Penalties: Criminal	Nonmonetary Penalties: Negative Publicity	Nonmonetary Penalties: Revoke License	Education: Targeting Employers	Investigation: City Agency
Omaha, NE							X	X			
Philadelphia, PA	X	X	X		X		X		X	X	X
Phoenix, AZ		X	X	X		X	X				
Portland, OR							X				
Sacramento, CA		X		X			X				
San Antonio, TX	X						X			X	
San Diego, CA		X	X	X	X	X	X				
San Francisco, CA	X	X	X	X	X	X	X		X		X
San Jose, CA		X	X	X	X	X	X	X	X		X
Seattle, WA	X	X	X	X	X	X	X		X	X	X
Tucson, AZ	X	X	X	X	X	X	X		X	X	X
Washington, DC	X	X	X	X	X	X	X		X	X	X
Totals	13	21	12	12	13	18	36	7	11	12	12

if a worker can prove they were retaliated against. Some laws provide a rebuttable presumption that retaliation has occurred if an employer takes negative action against a worker within 180 days or less of the worker having complained about wage theft. A rebuttable presumption is an evidentiary presumption that puts the onus on the employer to disprove retaliation. Workers in 12 cities were covered by laws that have this rebuttable presumption.

For filing complaints, workers in 36 cities (except for Atlanta, Georgia; Indianapolis, Indiana; Jacksonville, Florida; and Kansas City, Missouri) were covered by wage theft laws that allowed workers to file a complaint with a state agency. Within 13 cities, workers could file a complaint with a city agency.

In raw numbers, there were more city than state laws that had features to help workers file complaints (Figure 3). As a percentage of total city (22) or state laws (46), city laws were proportionally much more likely than state laws to have these features. Nine city laws had an educational provision for workers, whereas only Texas's minimum wage law had this provision (41% vs 2%). With before-the-fact retaliation protections, 9 city laws had more than 1 of these protections, versus 4 state laws (41% vs 9%). For evidentiary burden shifting, 12 city laws had this provision versus 3 state laws (55% vs 7%). With the rebuttable presumption of retaliation, 10 city laws had this provision versus 2 state laws (45% vs 4%).

Preventing Wage Theft by Employers

Wage theft laws vary in their features for preventing wage theft by employers. Such features are (1) monetary penalties, (2) nonmonetary penalties, and

FIGURE 3— Percentage of Wage Theft Laws at the City vs State Level in the 40 Largest US Cities With Worker Complaint and Prevention Features: 2023

(3) education (Table 1). Penalties are intended to deter employers because the risk of detection and subsequent monetary or nonmonetary penalties could make engaging in wage theft a losing proposition.

Monetary penalties can vary in amount, but the largest penalties are either treble damages or daily fines. Treble damages require employers to pay back wages and a penalty of 200% of wages owed. Daily fines are based on a fixed amount ranging from $50 to $120 per day for every day of wage theft, which can lead to the accrual of large penalties. Workers in 18 cities were covered by treble damages or these kinds of daily fines to the worker.

Furthermore, wage theft laws have different kinds of nonmonetary penalties: criminal, licensing, and negative publicity. Workers in 36 cities were covered by laws that had criminal penalties. Workers in 7 cities were covered by negative publicity penalties. Negative publicity penalties involve either posting a notice of violation at the workplace or placing the employer in a public "bad actors" database. Finally, workers in 11 cities were covered by laws that authorized the revocation of a business license based on wage theft violations.

In 12 cities, wage theft laws provided education to employers. Education involves notifying employers about the wage theft law.

Finally, stopping employers from committing wage theft relies on agencies having enforcement provisions. The data tracked whether government agencies had enforcement powers. Workers in 38 cities were covered by state laws that authorize a government agency to investigate wage theft (except Jacksonville and Kansas City). In 12 cities, a city agency had authority to investigate wage theft.

In raw numbers, city laws only sometimes have more features than state laws that are intended to prevent employers from committing wage theft (Figure 3). As a percentage of total city (22) or state laws (46), city laws were proportionally more likely than state laws to have these features, except for criminal penalties. Twelve city laws had treble damages or daily fine provisions of $50 to $120 per day to the worker, and 11 state laws had similar provisions (55% vs 24%). Only 6 city laws versus 35 state laws had criminal penalties (27% vs 76%). Three city laws had negative publicity penalties, whereas 5 state laws had such a provision (18% vs 11%). Fourteen city laws had licensing penalties but only Massachusetts's nonpayment of wages law had this provision (64% vs 2%). Eight city laws had an educational provision for employers, but only Texas' minimum wage law had such a provision (36% vs 2%).

DISCUSSION

Wage theft laws constitute an important form of legal protection, but the utilization of such laws is the key to making such laws effective. To utilize a law, workers must be able to recognize that wage theft is occurring ("name"), fault their employer for the wage theft ("blame"), and make a complaint about wage theft ("claim").[25]

City wage theft laws proportionally have more robust features that support workers to name, blame, and make claims against their employers. Providing education to workers about their rights can help them name wage theft and blame their employers.

City wage theft laws also have more protections than state laws that help workers to make a claim against their employers for wage theft by addressing their fear of retaliation. These protections help circumvent employer retaliation by allowing workers to file a complaint confidentially, anonymously, or through a third party or by authorizing a wall-to-wall investigation of the entire workplace that does not require workers to come forward.

Furthermore, city wage theft laws have evidentiary provisions that are more likely to support workers making claims. Providing for evidentiary burden shifting in favor of the worker if the employer has failed to keep records—a common problem for workers who need to prove wage theft[26]—helps workers to prove claims. A rebuttable presumption for retaliation also makes it easier to prove retaliation given how difficult it can be to show that retaliation occurred because of a wage theft complaint.[26]

Having the ability to file a complaint with a city agency can also help workers make claims, as opposed to having to file in court. Although workers in most cities can already file a wage theft claim with a state agency, city agencies can be more readily accessible to workers because they are arguably more responsive to local residents.[27]

In terms of enforcement provisions, city wage theft laws are proportionally more likely to contain innovations that are intended to strengthen enforcement, except when it comes to criminal penalties.

Proportionally, more city versus state laws have large monetary penalties, such as treble damages or daily fines. At least 1 study suggests that larger wage theft penalties against employers can increase employer compliance.[18]

With the nonmonetary penalties of licensing and negative publicity, city laws proportionally have more of these features than state laws. Nonmonetary penalties can have a larger impact on employers compared with monetary penalties.[28] Licensing penalties, if imposed, could shut down an employer's business. Negative publicity penalties, too, have the potential to cause reputational harm to an employer's business.[19]

Criminal penalties are the one exception. State versus city laws are proportionally more likely to have criminal penalties. Most criminal law is regulated at the state level.[29] Cities, however, have begun to enact these provisions, given the more recent trend of prosecuting wage theft violations.[28] These provisions are intended to encourage local district attorneys to take on wage theft.

City versus state laws are proportionally more likely to provide education to employers. Educational efforts targeting regulated business entities can be successful for increasing compliance.[20]

Effective enforcement depends on active investigation. City laws provide authority to city-level agencies to investigate wage theft. The efficacy of such agencies will depend on whether they are well-resourced. However, providing city agencies with such power holds promise for increased enforcement powers beyond state agencies.

Thus, workers residing in cities with at least 1 local wage theft law are more likely to be exposed to innovative features that support complaint filing or motivate employer compliance. Although many of these features have the potential to more effectively address wage theft, educational programs to improve employer compliance and harsher monetary penalties against employers may have the biggest effects given past compliance studies.[18–20]

Innovative features need not be exclusive to local law; more states' laws could be amended to include them. This trend of city wage theft laws also need not end with 16 of the 40 largest cities in the United States. Apart from those 4 cities that are totally preempted, an additional 20 of the 40 largest cities could possibly enact some kind of wage theft law.

Ultimately, this study examined existing features in the law on the books, which do not necessarily translate into how the law is implemented on the ground. These open-source legal data sets, however, can be used to study implementation by investigating the relative efficacy of the specific features of the law and the overall effectiveness of wage theft laws in reducing wage theft and its health consequences.

Conclusions

Local laws can more robustly address wage theft. Such city laws are proportionally more likely than state laws to include features that facilitate the filing of worker complaints and prevent employers from committing wage theft. Workers in these cities, therefore, have access to these additional protections. As total preemption of wage theft laws is not widespread, it suggests that more of the 40 largest US cities could enact wage theft laws.

Public Health Implications

Given the likely association between wage theft and poor health outcomes, legal regulation of wage theft can be an important way to address health and health equity. By longitudinally tracking policy changes that naturally create treatment and control groups, these data sets lend themselves to studies for understanding the public health impacts of wage theft regulation. All data sets are publicly available on https://lawatlas.org and include citations, legal text, and effective dates. As localities consider whether to enact wage theft regulation, they can help illuminate the more effective legal forms of wage theft regulation. AJPH

ABOUT THE AUTHORS

Jennifer J. Lee is with the Sheller Center for Social Justice and the Center for Public Health Law Research at the Temple University Beasley School of Law, Philadelphia, PA. Maggie O'Connor and Jiahui Shen were with the Center for Public Health Law Research at the Temple University Beasley School of Law at the time of this study.

CORRESPONDENCE

Correspondence should be sent to Jennifer J. Lee, Sheller Center for Social Justice, Temple University Beasley School of Law, 1719 N Broad St, Philadelphia, PA 19122 (e-mail: jenniferjlee@temple.edu). Reprints can be ordered at https://ajph.org by clicking the "Reprints" link.

PUBLICATION INFORMATION

Full Citation: Lee JJ, O'Connor M, Shen J. Protecting low-wage workers from exploitation: a mapping study of wage theft laws in the 40 largest US cities. *Am J Public Health*. 2026;116(4):492–501.

Acceptance Date: October 20, 2025.

DOI: https://doi.org/10.2105/AJPH.2025.308351

ORCID iDs:

Jennifer J. Lee https://orcid.org/0000-0002-5411-9512

Maggie O'Connor https://orcid.org/0009-0003-9066-7721

CONTRIBUTORS

J. Lee conceptualized and designed the work, oversaw the acquisition of the data, analyzed and interpreted the data, drafted the work, and critically revised it. M. O'Connor and J. Shen participated in the acquisition of data and conducted data analysis. All authors provided final approval of the version to be published.

ACKNOWLEDGMENTS

The authors would like to thank Livia Luan and Adalberto Rosado, 2 members of the original research team. We are also indebted to Alexandra Hess at the Center for Public Health Law Research for guiding us throughout the process of legal mapping. Special thanks to Scott Burris, Lindsay Cloud, and Bethany Saxon, at the Center for Public Health Law Research, for all their support. Finally, we extend our appreciation to Noa Kaumeheiwa, Jessica Li, and Julie Randolph for research assistance.

CONFLICTS OF INTEREST

The authors have no conflicts of interest to declare.

HUMAN PARTICIPANT PROTECTION

This study did not involve human participants.

REFERENCES

1. Bobo K. *Wage Theft in America: Why Millions of Working Americans Are Not Getting Paid—And What We Can Do About It.* New York, NY: New Press; 2008.
2. Cooper D, Kroeger T. Employers steal billions from workers' paychecks each year. Economic Policy Institute. 2017. Available at: https://www.epi.org/publication/employers-steal-billions-from-workers-paychecks-each-year. Accessed June 7, 2025.
3. Eastern Research Group. *The Social and Economic Effects of Wage Violations: Estimates for California and New York*. US Department of Labor. 2014. Available at: https://www.dol.gov/resource-library/social-and-economic-effects-wage-violations-estimates-california-and-new-york. Accessed June 7, 2025.
4. Bernhardt A, Theodore N, Milkman R, et al. Broken Laws, Unprotected Workers: Violations of Employment and Labor Laws in America's Cities. Center for Urban Economic Development. 2009. Available at: https://www.nelp.org/app/uploads/2015/03/BrokenLawsReport2009.pdf. Accessed June 7, 2025.
5. Minkler M, Salvatore AL, Chang C, et al. Wage theft as a neglected public health problem: an overview and case study from San Francisco's Chinatown district. *Am J Public Health*. 2014;104(6):1010–1020. https://doi.org/10.2105/AJPH.2013.301813
6. Mishel L, Gould E, Bivens J. Wage stagnation in nine charts. Economic Policy Institute. 2015. Available at: https://www.epi.org/publication/charting-wage-stagnation. Accessed June 7, 2025.
7. Leigh JP, Leigh WA, Du J. Minimum wages and public health: a literature review. *Prev Med*. 2019;118:122–134. https://doi.org/10.1016/j.ypmed.2018.10.005
8. Meixell B, Eisenbrey R. An epidemic of wage theft is costing workers hundreds of millions of dollars a year. Economic Policy Institute. 2014. Available at: https://www.epi.org/publication/epidemic-wage-theft-costing-workers-hundreds. Accessed October 11, 2025.
9. Leigh JP, De Vogli R. Low wages as occupational health hazards. *J Occup Environ Med*. 2016;58(5):444–447. https://doi.org/10.1097/JOM.0000000000000717
10. Lee KF, Nakphong MK, De Trinidad Young M. The legacy of immigration policies and employment exclusion: assessing the relationship between employment exclusions and immigrant health. *SSM Popul Health*. 2024;26:101676. https://doi.org/10.1016/j.ssmph.2024.101676
11. Shahidi FV, Tracey M, Gignac MAM, Oudyk J, Smith PM. Unpaid overtime and mental health in the Canadian working population. *Am J Ind Med*. 2024;67(8):741–752. https://doi.org/10.1002/ajim.23622
12. Eisenberg-Guyot J, Keyes KM, Prins SJ, et al. Wage theft and life expectancy inequities in the United States: a simulation study. *Prev Med*. 2022;159:107068. https://doi.org/10.1016/j.ypmed.2022.107068
13. Finkelstein DM, Harding JF, Paulsell D, English B, Hijjawi GR, Ng'andu J. Economic well-being and health: the role of income support programs in promoting health and advancing health equity. *Health Aff (Millwood)*. 2022;41(12):1700–1706. https://doi.org/10.1377/hlthaff.2022.00846
14. Moyce SC, Schenker M. Migrant workers and their occupational health and safety. *Annu Rev Public Health*. 2018;39(1):351–365. https://doi.org/10.1146/annurev-publhealth-040617-013714
15. Hargreaves S, Rustage K, Nellums LB, et al. Occupational health outcomes among international migrant workers: a systematic review and meta-analysis. *Lancet Glob Health*. 2019;7(7):e872–e882. https://doi.org/10.1016/S2214-109X(19)30204-9
16. Kim JJ, Allmang S. Wage theft in the United States: toward new research agendas. *Econ Labour Relat Rev*. 2021;32(4):534–551. https://doi.org/10.1177/10353046211025194
17. Levine M. Behind the minimum wage fight, a sweeping failure to enforce the law. *Politico*. Available at: https://www.politico.com/story/2018/02/18/minimum-wage-not-enforced-investigation-409644. Accessed June 7, 2025.
18. Galvin DJ. Deterring wage theft: alt-labor, state politics, and the policy determinants of minimum wage compliance. *Perspect Polit*. 2016;14(2):324–350. https://doi.org/10.1017/S1537592716000050
19. Johnson M. Regulation by shaming: deterrence effects of publicizing violations of workplace safety and health laws. *Am Econ Rev*. 2020;110(6):1866–1904. https://doi.org/10.1257/aer.20180501
20. Schell-Busey N, Simpson SS, Rorie M, Alper M. What works? A systemic review of corporate crime deterrence. *Am Soc Criminol*. 2016;15(2):387–416. https://doi.org/10.1111/1745-9133.12195
21. Melton-Fant C. Corporate influenced state preemption and health: a legal mapping analysis of workers' rights preemption bills in the US South. *Soc Sci Med*. 2023;336:116255. https://doi.org/10.1016/j.socscimed.2023.116255
22. Carr D, Adler S, Winig BD, Montez JK. Equity first: conceptualizing a normative framework to assess the role of preemption in public health. *Milbank Q*. 2020;98(1):131–149. https://doi.org/10.1111/1468-0009.12444

23. Anderson ED, Tremper C, Thomas S, Wagenaar AC. Measuring statutory law and regulations for empirical research. In: Wagenaar AC, Burris S, eds. *Public Health Law Research: Theory and Methods.* San Francisco, CA: Jossey-Bass; 2013: 237–259.
24. US Census Bureau. City and town population totals: 2020–2024. Annual estimates of resident population incorporated places of 20,000 or more, ranked by July 1, 2023 population: April 1, 2020 to July 1, 2023. Available at: https://www.census.gov/data/tables/time-series/demo/popest/2020s-total-cities-and-towns.html. Accessed June 7, 2025.
25. Felstiner LF, Abel RL, Sarat A. The emergence and transformation of disputes: naming, blaming, and claiming. *Law Soc Rev.* 1981;15(3-4):631–654. https://doi.org/10.2307/3053505
26. Lee JJ, Smith A. Regulating wage theft. *Wash Law Rev.* 2019;94(2):759–822.
27. Davidson N. Localist administrative law. *Yale Law J.* 2017;126:564–634.
28. Gerstein T. How district attorneys and state attorneys general are fighting workplace abuses. Economic Policy Institute. 2021. Available at: https://www.epi.org/publication/fighting-workplace-abuses-criminal-prosecutions-of-wage-theft-and-other-employer-crimes-against-workers. Accessed June 9, 2025.
29. Berris PG, Foster MA. Components of Federal Criminal Law. Congressional Research Service. 2024. Available at: https://www.congress.gov/crs-product/R48177. Accessed June 9, 2025.

US Black Women's Health Before and After the COVID-19 Pandemic: Socioeconomic and Temporal Patterns

Beza A. Taddess, MA, Jolene Tan, PhD, and Sanyu A. Mojola, PhD

Objectives. To examine how socioeconomic status (SES) shaped intraracial health disparities among Black women before, during, and after the COVID-19 pandemic.

Methods. Using Behavioral Risk Factor Surveillance System data (2018–2023; n = 89 634 Black women), we analyzed temporal trends in self-rated health, days of poor physical and mental health, and SES (education, income, employment).

Results. Educational disparities in self-rated health temporarily compressed during the pandemic (health disparity decreased by 3.9%) before partially reexpanding after the pandemic. Income-based physical health disparities persisted: the lowest-income women reported 7.48 poor physical health days before the pandemic versus 2.38 days for highest-income peers. Mental health decreased universally, with lowest-income women reporting 7.00 poor mental health days per year after the pandemic versus 6.09 days before the pandemic. Unemployed women experienced temporary pandemic-period health improvements ($b = -2.07$; $P = .05$)

Conclusions. Although the pandemic temporarily compressed educational disparities, income and employment-based inequities persisted or widened, underscoring SES as a partial buffer and site of structural health inequality.

Public Health Implications. Sustaining pandemic-era protections (expanded health care, income supports) and prioritizing mental health equity are critical to addressing systemic inequities exacerbated by crises. (*Am J Public Health*. 2026;116(4):502–511. https://doi.org/10.2105/AJPH.2025.308348)

AJPH April 2026, Vol. 116, No. 4

Research on health disparities during the COVID-19 pandemic has primarily focused on differences between racial groups, particularly comparing Black Americans to other racial/ethnic populations.[1–4] However, far less attention has been paid to variations in health outcomes within racial groups. This gap is particularly evident for Black women, whose health experiences lie at the intersection of race, gender, and socioeconomic inequality.[5] Widening socioeconomic inequality among Black Americans since the post–Civil Rights era,[6] coupled with socioeconomic status (SES) as a fundamental cause of health disparities,[7] raises critical questions about preexisting disparities that may have been exacerbated or reshaped by the pandemic.

The COVID-19 pandemic provides a crucial context for examining how socioeconomic resources shape health outcomes during crises. Although Black Americans faced disproportionately higher mortality and hospitalization rates,[8] these impacts varied significantly across socioeconomic strata. Early evidence highlighted disparities in physical health, mental well-being, and health care access among Black women during the pandemic.[9–11] Yet, limited research has explored how these outcomes varied by SES within racial groups or how they evolved over time.

This study examines temporal changes in Black women's health outcomes before, during, and after the pandemic. We ask: How do education, income, and employment influence health outcomes for Black women during public health crises? Fundamental Cause Theory posits that higher SES buffers against adverse health outcomes through resources like health care access, enhanced health literacy, and greater material resources.[7] However, studies suggest diminishing returns to SES for Black Americans compared with other racial groups,[12] challenging assumptions about SES as a universal protective factor during crisis periods. Thus, SES may not be as protective a buffer for Black Americans during health crises.

Drawing on data from the 2018–2023 Behavioral Risk Factor Surveillance System (BRFSS), we analyzed 3 key dimensions of health: self-rated health, physical health days, and mental health days. Self-rated health is a robust predictor of future morbidity and mortality,[13] making it critical for understanding layered inequities. By centering Black women and examining socioeconomic variations within this population, our study moves beyond homogenized narratives of racial disparities that often mask significant internal stratification.[14,15] Understanding these intraracial variations in health outcomes during crisis periods can inform more nuanced policy interventions that address the diverse needs across socioeconomic strata within marginalized populations.

METHODS

The study utilized data from the BRFSS, a state-based, cross-sectional telephone health survey of noninstitutionalized US adults aged 18 years and older. We analyzed data from 5 annual surveys (2018–2023), focusing on Black women (n = 89 634). The BRFSS employs a complex sampling design and is administered by state health departments in collaboration with the Centers for Disease Control and Prevention (CDC). Survey data and detailed methodology are publicly available at www.cdc.gov/brfss. Our analysis focused on self-identified Black women in all 50 US states and the District of Columbia. To examine temporal changes in health outcomes, the study periods were categorized as prepandemic (2018–2019), pandemic (2020–2021), and postpandemic (2022–2023). We define the postpandemic period as beginning in 2022, reflecting the end of pandemic-era housing, unemployment, and Medicaid policies, as well as widespread vaccine availability in 2021 (see footnote 1 to Appendix Table A, available as a supplement to the online version of this article at http://www.ajph.org).

Variables and Measurements

We examined 3 dimensions of health outcomes. We measured self-rated health on a 5-point scale and dichotomized as poor or fair versus good, very good, or excellent. We assessed physical and mental health using the number of days per month respondents reported poor physical and mental health days, respectively.

Our main predictors were 3 socioeconomic measures: household income (low income [< $20 000], lower-middle income [$20 000 to $34 999], middle income [$35 000 to $49 999], upper-middle income [$50 000 to $74 999], and high income [≥$75 000]); educational attainment (less than high school, high school graduate or GED, some college or technical school, college graduate or higher); and employment status (employed, unemployed, unable to work, retired, and homemaker or student).

Statistical Analysis

We examined health outcomes across socioeconomic measures during 3 time periods: prepandemic (2018–2019), pandemic (2020–2021), and postpandemic (2022–2023). We employed logistic regression models for binary outcomes (e.g., poor or fair health) and linear regression for continuous outcomes (e.g., poor health days) to verify the descriptive patterns. All analyses incorporated BRFSS survey weights and design variables to account for the complex sampling design. We assessed statistical significance at $P < .05$ using survey-adjusted Wald tests. Analysis code and documentation are available from the first author for replication.

RESULTS

Table 1 presents the demographic and health characteristics of 89 634 Black women across 3 time periods: prepandemic (2018–2019; n = 31 052), pandemic (2020–2021; n = 28 806), and postpandemic (2022–2023; n = 29 776). The age distribution remained relatively stable, with the proportion of adults aged 65 years and older increasing slightly, from 28.7% to 31.3%. Educational attainment increased substantially: those with less than a high school education decreased from 8.7% to 5.8%, whereas college graduates rose from 32.7% to 39.2%. Income distribution shifted markedly upward, with participants earning less than $20 000 decreasing from 31.4% to 17.3%, whereas those earning $75 000 or more increased from 18.2% to 26.9%. Employment improved from 48.7% before the pandemic to 51.4% after the

TABLE 1— Characteristics of Black Women in Regression Analysis Sample Before, During, and After the COVID-19 Pandemic: United States, Behavioral Risk Factor Surveillance System, 2018–2023

	Before Pandemic (2018–2019), No. (%)	During Pandemic (2020–2021), No. (%)	After Pandemic (2022–2023), No. (%)
Age, y			
18–34	5 696 (18.3)	5 005 (17.4)	4 763 (16.0)
35–49	6 939 (22.3)	7 026 (24.4)	7 098 (23.8)
50–64	9 510 (30.6)	8 428 (29.3)	8 606 (28.9)
≥ 65	8 907 (28.7)	8 347 (29.0)	9 309 (31.3)
Education			
< high school	2 698 (8.7)	2 056 (7.1)	1 718 (5.8)
High school graduate/GED	9 077 (29.2)	7 778 (27.0)	7 656 (25.7)
Some college	9 109 (29.3)	8 477 (29.4)	8 728 (29.3)
College graduate	10 168 (32.7)	10 495 (36.4)	11 674 (39.2)
Income, $			
< 20 000	9 749 (31.4)	6 974 (24.2)	5 161 (17.3)
20 000–34 999	7 761 (25.0)	7 086 (24.6)	7 148 (24.0)
35 000–49 999	4 086 (13.2)	4 191 (14.5)	4 726 (15.9)
50 000–74 999	3 792 (12.2)	4 138 (14.4)	4 734 (15.9)
≥ 75 000	5 664 (18.2)	6417 (22.3)	8 007 (26.9)
Employment status			
Employed	15 128 (48.7)	14 371 (49.9)	15 307 (51.4)
Homemaker/student	1 886 (6.1)	1 617 (5.6)	1 595 (5.4)
Retired	7 800 (25.1)	7 220 (25.1)	8 035 (27.0)
Unable to work	4 343 (14.0)	3 286 (11.4)	3 111 (10.4)
Unemployed	1 895 (6.1)	2 312 (8.0)	1 728 (5.8)
Self-rated health			
Excellent/very good/good	23 032 (74.3)	22 274 (77.5)	22 492 (75.7)
Fair/poor	7 962 (25.7)	6 468 (22.5)	7 225 (24.3)
Mental health			
Mean days of poor mental health	4.5	4.9	5.2
≥ 14 days of poor mental health	4 267 (14.0)	4 371 (15.4)	4 826 (16.5)
Physical health			
Mean days of poor physical health	4.9	4.0	4.5
≥ 14 days of poor physical health	4 583 (15.1)	3 508 (12.5)	4 045 (13.9)

Note. GED = general educational development. No. indicates the sample size. This table presents characteristics of the analytical sample restricted to complete cases with nonmissing values for all study variables.

pandemic, with unemployment peaking during the pandemic (8.0%) before decreasing to 5.8%.

Health outcomes showed distinct temporal patterns. Fair or poor self-rated health decreased from 25.7% before to 22.5% during the pandemic, then increased to 24.3% after the pandemic. Mental health deteriorated consistently, with mean poor mental health days increasing progressively from 4.5 days per year before the pandemic to 4.9 days during the pandemic and 5.2 days after the pandemic. Physical health followed a V-shaped pattern: the mean number of poor physical health days decreased from 4.9 before the pandemic to 4.0 during the pandemic, then rose to 4.5 after the pandemic.

Educational Disparities in Self-Rated Health

Figure 1 illustrates self-rated health disparities among Black women across different educational attainment levels

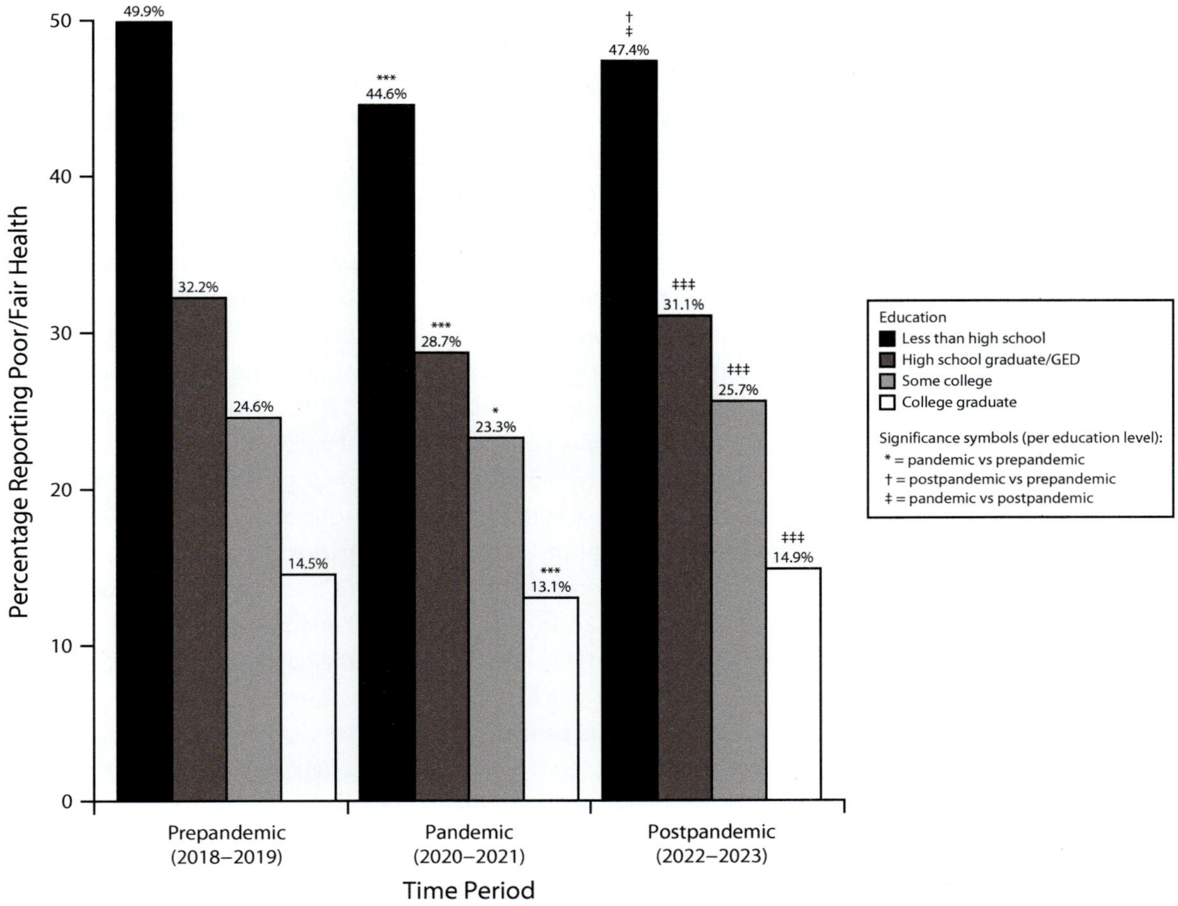

FIGURE 1— **Percentage of Black Women Reporting Poor or Fair Health, by Educational Attainment: United States, 2018–2023**

Note. GED = general educational development. ***$P<.001$; **$P<.01$; *$P<.05$. († ‡ Variation of *)

during the study periods. A clear and consistent educational gradient in fair or poor health ratings is evident across all time periods, with substantial compression of disparities during the pandemic followed by partial reexpansion after the pandemic.

Before the pandemic, nearly half (49.9%) of Black women with less than a high school education reported fair or poor health, decreasing progressively across educational levels: 32.2% among high school graduates, 24.6% among those with some college, and only 14.5% among college graduates, yielding a disparity gap of 35.4 percentage points between the lowest and highest education groups. During the pandemic, this educational gradient persisted but compressed to 31.5 percentage points, as fair or poor health reporting decreased significantly across all education levels. The most substantial improvements occurred among those with less than a high school education (from 49.9% to 44.6%; $P<.001$), followed by high school graduates (32.2% to 28.7%; $P<.001$), those with some college (24.6% to 23.3%; $P=.04$), and college graduates (14.5% to 13.1%; $P<.001$).

The postpandemic period revealed a partial reversal of these gains, with the educational gradient widening again to 32.5 percentage points. Those with less than a high school education experienced the most pronounced decrease, with fair or poor health reports increasing to 47.4% ($P=.05$ compared with pandemic levels), though remaining below prepandemic levels. High school graduates also showed increases (31.1%; $P<.001$ compared with pandemic levels), as did those with some college (25.7%; $P<.001$ compared with pandemic levels). Notably, this intermediate educational group surpassed their prepandemic levels of poor health. College graduates demonstrated the greatest stability, with fair or poor health reporting rising only marginally, from

13.1% during the pandemic to 14.9% after the pandemic, statistically similar to prepandemic levels (14.5%).

Income Gradients in Mental and Physical Health Days

Figure 2 illustrates the number of poor mental and physical health days by income category. Consistent income gradients are evident for mental and physical health, with different temporal patterns. Mental health universally deteriorated: the $20 000–$34 999 group increased from 4.97 to 5.10 poor mental health days per month, the $35 000–$49 999 group from 3.62 to 4.31 days, and the $50 000–$74 999 group from 3.03 to 4.04 days; even the highest income group (≥ $75 000) experienced a 40% increase, from 2.38 days before to 3.75 days after the pandemic. The income gradient persisted throughout all periods, with the lowest income group (< $20 000) consistently reporting the highest burden. Among this group, poor mental health days increased steadily, from 6.09 days (SE = 0.10) before the pandemic to 6.58 days (SE = 0.13) during the pandemic and 7.00 days (SE = 0.15) after the pandemic. The income gradient remained stable across time periods, with approximately 3.5 to 4 days separating the lowest and highest income groups.

By contrast, physical health exhibited a distinctly different temporal pattern: temporary improvement during the pandemic, followed by partial return to prepandemic levels, with income gradients remaining consistently strong. The lowest income group (< $20 000) reported 7.48 poor physical health days (SE = 0.11) before the pandemic, decreasing to 6.72 days (SE = 0.13) during the pandemic and then increasing to 7.68 days (SE = 0.15) after the pandemic. This pattern was consistent across all income categories: the $20 000–$34 999 group decreased from 4.97 to 4.46 days during the pandemic before rising to 5.63 days; the $35 000–$49 999 group from 3.62 to 3.21 days, then to 4.89 days; the $50 000–$74 999 group from 3.61 to 2.73 days, then to 3.49 days; and the highest income group from 2.38 to 2.04 days, then to 2.53 days. The income gradient in physical health was particularly pronounced and stable across time periods. Those earning $75 000 or more consistently reported the fewest poor physical health days throughout all periods, maintaining a substantial advantage—a disparity gap exceeding 5 days in both prepandemic (5.1 days) and postpandemic (5.2 days) periods, narrowing only slightly during the pandemic (4.7 days).

Table 2 presents the results of survey-weighted regression models examining the associations between socioeconomic factors and 3 health outcomes: self-rated health (logistic regression), poor mental health days

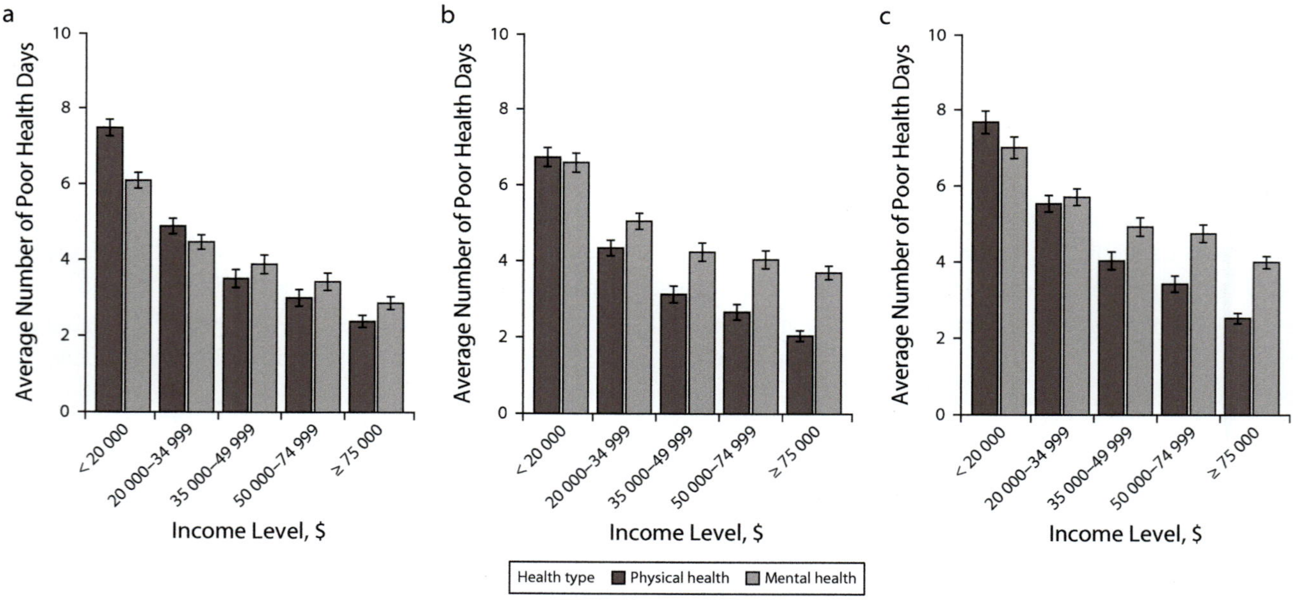

FIGURE 2— Mean Number of Poor Physical and Mental Health Days in the Past 30 Days Among Black Women, by Income Level and (a) Prepandemic (2018–2019), (b) Pandemic (2020–2021), and (c) Postpandemic (2022–2023): United States

Note. Error bars represent 95% confidence intervals.

TABLE 2— Regression Results for Self-Rated Health, Mental Health Days, and Physical Health Days Among Black Women: United States, Behavioral Risk Factor Surveillance System, 2018–2023

	Self-Rated Health, b (SE)	Mental Health Days, b (SE)	Physical Health Days, b (SE)
Education (Ref: < high school)			
High school graduate/GED	−0.58** (0.18)	−0.42 (0.78)	−1.13 (0.64)
Some college	−1.08*** (0.19)	−0.77 (0.77)	−1.67** (0.64)
College graduate	−1.36*** (0.19)	−2.05** (0.77)	−3.16*** (0.64)
Income, $ (Ref: < 20 000)			
20 000–34 999	−0.56*** (0.13)	−1.29** (0.50)	−2.23*** (0.41)
35 000–49 999	−1.16*** (0.19)	−2.18*** (0.63)	−2.91*** (0.51)
50 000–74 999	−1.09*** (0.19)	−2.50*** (0.66)	−3.84*** (0.54)
≥ 75 000	−1.91*** (0.22)	−3.05*** (0.59)	−4.31*** (0.48)
Employment status (Ref: unemployed)			
Unemployed	0.67** (0.20)	2.59*** (0.77)	3.08*** (0.61)
Unable to work	1.93*** (0.14)	5.52*** (0.57)	8.14*** (0.46)
Retired	0.87*** (0.20)	1.32 (0.82)	2.88*** (0.67)
Homemaker/student	0.34 (0.21)	0.84 (0.71)	1.31* (0.57)
Education × time period interactions			
High school × pandemic	−0.11 (0.23)	−2.68** (0.97)	−1.72* (0.80)
Some college × pandemic	0.35 (0.23)	−1.64 (0.96)	−0.37 (0.79)
College graduate × pandemic	−0.12 (0.24)	−1.25 (0.95)	−0.61 (0.79)
High school × postpandemic	0.10 (0.24)	−1.06 (1.02)	−0.68 (0.84)
Some college × postpandemic	0.54* (0.24)	0.03 (1.01)	0.23 (0.83)
College graduate × postpandemic	0.15 (0.25)	−0.51 (1.01)	0.40 (0.83)
Income × time period interactions			
$20 000-$34 999 × pandemic	−0.04 (0.16)	−0.57 (0.62)	0.90 (0.51)
$35 000-$49 999 × pandemic	0.10 (0.22)	−0.49 (0.75)	0.13 (0.62)
$50 000-$74 999 × pandemic	−0.01 (0.23)	−0.25 (0.78)	1.13 (0.64)
≥ $75 000 × pandemic	0.12 (0.25)	0.19 (0.69)	0.80 (0.56)
$20 000–$34 999 × postpandemic	0.24 (0.16)	−0.04 (0.65)	0.69 (0.53)
$35 000–$49 999 × postpandemic	0.35 (0.22)	−0.13 (0.77)	0.36 (0.64)
$50 000–$74 999 × postpandemic	0.19 (0.23)	0.17 (0.80)	0.88 (0.66)
≥ $75 000 × postpandemic	0.24 (0.25)	−0.41 (0.70)	0.46 (0.58)
Employment × time period interactions			
Unemployed × pandemic	−0.19 (0.24)	−2.07* (0.87)	−2.03** (0.70)
Unable to work × pandemic	−0.08 (0.18)	−1.10 (0.72)	−1.19* (0.58)
Retired × pandemic	0.03 (0.22)	−0.25 (0.90)	−0.02 (0.74)
Homemaker/student × pandemic	0.13 (0.25)	−0.00 (0.85)	−0.42 (0.68)
Unemployed × postpandemic	−0.10 (0.24)	−0.41 (0.89)	−1.27 (0.71)
Unable to work × postpandemic	−0.01 (0.18)	−0.53 (0.73)	0.01 (0.60)
Retired × postpandemic	−0.10 (0.23)	−0.32 (0.93)	−0.70 (0.76)
Homemaker/student × postpandemic	−0.29 (0.26)	0.70 (0.86)	−0.76 (0.69)

Note. GED = general educational development; Log-OR = log-odds ratio. All models are adjusted and control for age group, number of children, marital status, and health insurance. The self-rated health model is a logistic regression predicting poor or fair health (log-odds coefficients). All interaction terms shown are included in the same model for each outcome.
*$P < .05$; **$P < .01$; ***$P < .001$.

(linear regression), and poor physical health days (linear regression), with interactions between each socioeconomic factor and time period.

After adjustment for age, number of children, marital status, and health insurance, strong educational gradients persisted across all 3 health outcomes in the prepandemic reference period (unadjusted models; Appendix Table A). Compared with those with less than a high school education, those with higher education reported progressively better health. For self-rated health, high school graduates had significantly lower log-odds of reporting poor or fair health (b = −0.58; SE = 0.18; $P < .01$), as did those with some college (b = −1.08; SE = 0.19; $P < .001$) and college graduates (b = −1.36; SE = 0.19; $P < .001$). For mental health, college graduates reported 2.05 fewer poor mental health days compared with those with less than a high school education (b = −2.05; SE = 0.77; $P < .01$). Differences for high school graduates (b = −0.42) and those with some college (b = −0.77) were not statistically significant. Physical health showed the strongest educational gradient, with high school graduates reporting 1.13 fewer poor physical health days (b = −1.13; SE = 0.64; $P < .10$), those with some college reporting 1.67 fewer days (b = −1.67; SE = 0.64; $P < .01$), and college graduates reporting 3.16 fewer days (b = −3.16; SE = 0.64; $P < .001$) compared with the lowest education group.

Clear income gradients also emerged across all health outcomes, with each ascending income category associated with better health compared with those earning less than $20 000 annually. For self-rated health, those earning $20 000 to $34 999 had lower log-odds of poor or fair health (b = −0.56; SE = 0.13; $P < .001$) than those earning $35 000 to $49 999 (b = −1.16; SE = 0.19; $P < .001$), $50 000 to $74 999 (b = −1.09; SE = 0.19; $P < .001$), and $75 000 or more (b = −1.91; SE = 0.22; $P < .001$). Mental health showed similarly strong income gradients. Compared with the lowest income group, those earning $20 000 to $34 999 reported 1.29 fewer poor mental health days (b = −1.29; SE = 0.50; $P < .01$), those earning $35 000 to $49 999 reported 2.18 fewer days (b = −2.18; SE = 0.63; $P < .001$), those earning $50 000 to $74 999 reported 2.50 fewer days (b = −2.50; SE = 0.66; $P < .001$), and those earning $75 000 or more reported 3.05 fewer days (b = −3.05; SE = 0.59; $P < .001$). Physical health gradients were even more pronounced, with the $20 000–$34 999 group reporting 2.23 fewer days (b = −2.23; SE = 0.41; $P < .001$), the $35 000–$49 999 group reporting 2.91 fewer days (b = −2.91; SE = 0.51; $P < .001$), the $50 000–$74 999 group reporting 3.84 fewer days (b = −3.84; SE = 0.54; $P < .001$), and those earning $75 000 or more reporting 4.31 fewer days (b = −4.31; SE = 0.48; $P < .001$) compared with the lowest income group.

Employment status showed significant associations with all health outcomes. Those unable to work faced the most significant health burden: they had significantly higher log-odds of reporting poor or fair health (b = 1.93; SE = 0.14; $P < .001$), and reported 5.52 more poor mental health days (b = 5.52; SE = 0.57; $P < .001$) and 8.14 more poor physical health days (b = 8.14; SE = 0.46; $P < .001$) compared with the employed. Unemployed individuals also showed worse outcomes, with increased log-odds of poor or fair health (b = 0.67; SE = 0.20; $P < .01$), 2.59 more poor mental health days (b = 2.59; SE = 0.77; $P < .001$), and 3.08 more poor physical health days (b = 3.08; SE = 0.61; $P < .001$).

The interaction effects show that the pandemic period saw a significant compression of educational disparities, particularly for mental and physical health. High school graduates showed improved mental health during the pandemic (b = −2.68; SE = 0.97; $P < .01$) and improved physical health (b = −1.72; SE = 0.80; $P < .05$) compared with those with less than a high school education relative to prepandemic patterns. Those with some college education also showed non–statistically significant improvements in mental health during the pandemic (b = −1.64; SE = 0.96; $P < .10$). Self-rated health interactions during the pandemic were not significant for any education group. However, the postpandemic period revealed the reexpansion of disparities along specific dimensions. Those with some college education showed significantly worse self-rated health after the pandemic (b = 0.54; SE = 0.24; $P < .05$) compared with prepandemic patterns.

Income-based interactions were largely nonsignificant across all 3 health outcomes and both pandemic and postpandemic periods, indicating that income gradients remained relatively stable throughout the study period. During the pandemic, physical health interactions approached but did not reach significance for the $20 000–$34 999 group (b = 0.90; SE = 0.51; $P < .10$) and the $50 000–$74 999 group (b = 1.13; SE = 0.64; $P < .10$). In the postpandemic period, although several interaction coefficients were positive, suggesting a potential rewidening of income disparities, none reached statistical significance.

Employment-based disparities showed compression during the pandemic, particularly among individuals who were unemployed or unable to work. Unemployed Black women experienced notable improvements during the pandemic in both mental health (b = −2.07; SE = 0.87; $P < .05$) and physical health (b = −2.03; SE = 0.70; $P < .01$) compared with employed individuals relative to prepandemic patterns. Those unable to work also showed improved physical health during this period (b = −1.19; SE = 0.58; $P < .05$). The postpandemic period showed attenuation of these benefits, with the unemployment × postpandemic interaction for physical health trending toward significance (b = −1.27; SE = 0.71; $P < .10$), suggesting some persistence of reduced employment-based health disparities.

DISCUSSION

This study addresses a critical gap in pandemic-era health disparities research by examining variations within rather than between racial groups, specifically focusing on socioeconomic stratification among Black women. Although much attention has focused on racial disparities during COVID-19, our findings reveal critical insights into how SES shapes health disparities among Black women during public health crises, challenging assumptions about the inevitability of inequity and the limits of policy intervention. Three key findings stand out.

First, our findings suggest that self-rated health improved during the pandemic, with significant decreases in fair or poor health reports during the 2020–2021 period. On the one hand, this appears contrary to expectations given the disproportionate burden of COVID-19 on Black communities[1,2] and the substantial health consequences documented during this period.[3,4] However, this pattern suggests that pandemic-era policy interventions may have had positive effects on overall well-being. Research examining specific policy impacts has documented improvements in child poverty,[25] food security among Supplemental Nutrition Assistance Program (SNAP) participants,[26] reduced food insecurity among unemployment insurance recipients,[27] and health benefits from eviction moratoriums.[27] Our research suggests that these improvements may have extended to self-rated health among Black women, as these measures capture overall well-being, including social and economic circumstances, rather than just the absence of disease.[13] The temporal pattern we observed is consistent with potential benefits from expanded Medicaid access,[16] eviction moratoriums,[17] and direct economic relief[18] that likely disproportionately benefited the most vulnerable groups. This aligns with Fundamental Cause Theory's[7] premise that SES shapes health through flexible resources like income and housing security. Critically, these findings show that such resources are not static: when governments actively redistribute support during crises, health inequities can be temporarily ameliorated.[19,20] Yet, the partial rebound of disparities after the pandemic, as policies expired and fair or poor health reports increased, underscores the fragility of these gains and the need for permanent structural safeguards to sustain equity.

Second, contrary to literature positing limited health returns to SES for Black Americans,[21,22] our findings reveal that higher education and income provided substantial, though temporally dynamic, protection. College graduates consistently reported better self-rated health and fewer poor health days than their less-educated peers, and the highest-income Black women experienced a persistent advantage in physical health compared with low-income counterparts. However, these benefits fluctuated across pandemic phases: educational disparities compressed during the acute crisis (as reflected in significant interaction terms for high school graduates [b = −2.68; $P < .01$]) but began reemerging after the pandemic, particularly for those with some college education. This health gradient across education is characterized by worsening health among those with some college education, whose reported postpandemic health now resembles that of high school graduates more than that of college graduates for both self-rated health and physician-diagnosed conditions, including cardiovascular disease, renal disease, and cancer (Appendix Figure B). This suggests that SES matters for health but operates within broader structural constraints that shift during societal disruptions.

Lastly, across all socioeconomic groups, mental health burdens increased during and after the pandemic, with low-income Black women experiencing substantially more poor mental health days (6.09 prepandemic, 6.58 during pandemic, 7.00 postpandemic) compared with high-income women (2.86, 3.70, and 4.00 days, respectively) while maintaining a stable relative gradient (adjusted b = −3.05; $P < .001$). This persistent mental health disparity contrasts with the pattern observed in physical health metrics, where disparities temporarily compressed during the pandemic before reexpanding. This differential pattern suggests a lack of effective mental health policy responses to counter the large psychosocial toll of gendered racism, caregiving burdens, and grief,[24] factors disproportionately affecting Black women. The continued increase in poor mental health days after the pandemic signals that without sustained investment mental health care, crises will continue to exacerbate this invisible toll.

Limitations

Our study has important limitations. First, BRFSS response rates decreased substantially during 2020 and 2021 (from 50% prepandemic to 44%; Appendix Table C). Although individuals with worse health may have been less likely to participate because of illness or caregiving responsibilities, 3 validation analyses suggest that our findings reflect genuine patterns: temporal improvement in self-rated health was evident in states with the highest response rates (≥ 51.3%; Appendix Table D, Figure A), strong educational gradients (4.3-fold) persisted when response rates were lowest (Appendix Figure B), and nonresponse to the self-rated health question remained very low (< 1.5%) across all socioeconomic groups (Appendix Table D and Figure C).

Second, the cross-sectional BRFSS design limits causal inference. Third, we chose 2022 to 2023 as our postpandemic period. Although vaccine availability and policy-initiative changes occurred in 2021 and emergency responses became focused on recovery by 2022, the World Health Organization and the CDC declared an end to the pandemic in May 2023. We conducted sensitivity analyses using only 2023 data (n = 14 858 observations) for the postpandemic period and our findings were confirmed. As such, our temporal categorization captures meaningful distinctions in pandemic phases even though it does not align perfectly with all intervention timelines.

Finally, all health measures remain self-reported, subject to recall bias and potential reporting differences across socioeconomic groups. Although physician-diagnosed self-reported conditions validate observed educational gradients (Appendix Figure B), these too rely on participant recall rather than clinical assessment. Despite these limitations, our analysis of more than 89 000 Black women across all 50 states documents meaningful health variation during a critical public health crisis, with consistent patterns across multiple outcomes and socioeconomic measures.

Public Health Implications

Our findings underscore that health crises are not merely moments of catastrophe but critical opportunities for equity. The pandemic's temporary compression of disparities, via policies that disproportionately benefited lower-income groups, demonstrates the possibility that intentional state action can narrow inequities.[25–27] To leverage such opportunities, we must institutionalize pandemic-era protections (e.g., expanded Medicaid, permanent Earned Income Tax Credit enhancements[23]) to address fundamental causes of health inequity rather than treating them as temporary measures. In addition, mental health supports must be integrated into safety-net programs, prioritizing community-driven care tailored to Black women's lived experiences, especially given the consistently high burden of mental health challenges across all socioeconomic strata.[9]

By examining intraracial disparities, this study illuminates how crises can both narrow and widen inequities across intersectional lines. For Black women, SES remains a vital determinant of health, but its power is mediated by policy choices. Our results show substantial protective effects of education and income among Black women while revealing how these protections vary across crisis periods. Sustained equity demands that we treat crises not as exceptions but as revelations of where systemic change is most urgent. AJPH

ABOUT THE AUTHORS

Beza A. Taddess is with the Department of Sociology, Princeton University, Princeton, NJ. Jolene Tan is with the Office of Population Research, Princeton University, Princeton, NJ. Sanyu A. Mojola is with the Department of Sociology, School of Public and International Affairs, and Office of Population Research, Princeton University, Princeton, NJ.

CORRESPONDENCE

Correspondence should be sent to Beza Taddess, MA, Wallace Hall, Princeton NJ 08540 (e-mail: beza.taddess@princeton.edu). Reprints can be ordered at https://www.ajph.org by clicking the "Reprints" link.

PUBLICATION INFORMATION

Full Citation: Taddess BA, Tan J, Mojola SA. US Black women's health before and after the COVID-19 pandemic: socioeconomic and temporal patterns. *Am J Public Health*. 2026;116(4): 502–511.

Acceptance Date: October 14, 2025.

DOI: https://doi.org/10.2105/AJPH.2025.308348

ORCID iDs:

Beza A. Taddess https://orcid.org/0009-0007-9009-0650

Jolene Tan https://orcid.org/0000-0003-4968-3482

Sanyu A. Mojola https://orcid.org/0000-0002-2610-2625

CONTRIBUTORS

B. A. Taddess conducted statistical analyses and drafted the manuscript. J. Tan and S. A. Mojola reviewed data analyses and manuscript drafts and contributed to revisions of the manuscript. S. A. Mojola supervised the study. All authors conceptualized the study, interpreted the results, and approved the final manuscript.

CONFLICTS OF INTEREST

J. Tan and S. A. Mojola have funding from the National Institute on Minority Health Disparities (National Institutes of Health), but this particular study was not funded by that grant.

HUMAN PARTICIPANT PROTECTION

This research did not involve human participants; therefore, institutional review board oversight was not sought.

REFERENCES

1. Zalla LC, Mulholland GE, Filiatreau LM, Edwards JK. Racial/ethnic and age differences in the direct and indirect effects of the COVID-19 pandemic on US mortality. *Am J Public Health.* 2022;112(1): 154–164. https://doi.org/10.2105/AJPH.2021.306541
2. Wilder JM. The disproportionate impact of COVID-19 on racial and ethnic minorities in the United States. *Clin Infect Dis.* 2021;72(4):707–709. https://doi.org/10.1093/cid/ciaa959
3. Quan D, Wong LL, Shallal A, et al. Impact of race and socioeconomic status on outcomes in patients hospitalized with COVID-19. *J Gen Intern Med.* 2021;36(5):1302–1309. https://doi.org/10.1007/s11606-020-06527-1
4. Boserup B, McKenney M, Elkbuli A. Disproportionate impact of COVID-19 pandemic on racial and ethnic minorities. *Am Surg.* 2020;86(12):1615–1622. https://doi.org/10.1177/0003134820973356
5. Chinn JJ, Martin IK, Redmond N. Health equity among Black women in the United States. *J Womens Health (Larchmt).* 2021;30(2):212–219. https://doi.org/10.1089/jwh.2020.8868
6. Wilson WJ. *The Truly Disadvantaged: The Inner City, the Underclass, and Public Policy.* Chicago, IL: University of Chicago Press; 1996.
7. Link BG, Phelan J. Social conditions as fundamental causes of disease. *J Health Soc Behav.* 1995;35: 80–94. https://doi.org/10.2307/2626958
8. Tai DBG, Sia IG, Doubeni CA, et al. Disproportionate impact of COVID-19 on racial and ethnic minority groups in the United States: a 2021 update. *J Racial Ethn Health Disparities.* 2022;9: 2334–2339. https://doi.org/10.1007/s40615-021-01170-w
9. Gibson B, Schneider J, Talamonti D, Forshaw M. The impact of inequality on mental health outcomes during the COVID-19 pandemic: a systematic review. *Can Psychol.* 2021: 62(1):101–126. https://doi.org/10.1037/cap0000272
10. Hudson KD, Azhar S, Rahman R, et al. Dual pandemics or a syndemic? Racism, COVID-19, and opportunities for antiracist social work. *J Ethn Cult Divers Soc Work.* 2022;31(3–5):198–211. https://doi.org/10.1080/15313204.2022.2070895
11. Brooks Stephens JR, Douglas RD, Burrow, et al. And still, we rise: a mixed-methods study examining derailment, posttraumatic stress, and resilience among Black adults during the COVID-19 pandemic. *Cult Divers Ethnic Minor Psychol.* 2025; Epub ahead of print. https://doi.org/10.1037/cdp0000781
12. Bell CN, Sacks TK, Thomas Tobin CS, Thorpe RJ. Racial non-equivalence of socioeconomic status and self-rated health among African Americans and Whites. *SSM Popul Health.* 2020;10:100561. https://doi.org/10.1016/j.ssmph.2020.100561
13. Idler EL, Benyamini Y. Self-rated health and mortality: a review of twenty-seven community studies. *J Health Soc Behav.* 1997;38(1):21–37. https://doi.org/10.2307/2955359
14. Woods-Giscombé CL. Superwoman schema: African American women's views on stress, strength, and health. *Qual Health Res.* 2010;20(5):668–683. https://doi.org/10.1177/1049732310361892
15. Farmer MM, Ferraro KF. Are racial disparities in health conditional on socioeconomic status? *Soc Sci Med.* 2005;60(1):191–204. https://doi.org/10.1016/j.socscimed.2004.04.026
16. Auty SG, Aswani MS, Wahbi RN, Griffith KN. Changes in health care access by race, income, and Medicaid expansion during the COVID-19 pandemic. *Med Care.* 2023;61(1):45–49. https://doi.org/10.1097/MLR.0000000000001788
17. Leifheit SL, Linton J, Raifman GL, et al. Expiring eviction moratoriums and COVID-19 incidence and mortality. *Am J Epidemiol.* 2021;190(12): 2503–2510. https://doi.org/10.1093/aje/kwab196
18. Asebedo SD, Liu Y, Gray B, Hasan Quadria T. How Americans used their COVID-19 economic impact payments. *Financial Planning Rev.* 2020; 3(4):e1101. https://doi.org/10.1002/cfp2.1101
19. Rees-Jones A, D'Attoma J, Piolatto A, Salvadori L. Experience of the COVID-19 pandemic and support for safety-net expansion. *J Econ Behav Organ.* 2022;200:1090–1104. https://doi.org/10.1016/j.jebo.2022.07.002
20. Warner ME, Zhang X. Social safety nets and COVID-19 stay home orders across US states: a comparative policy analysis. *J Comp Policy Anal Res Pract.* 2021;23(2):176–190. https://doi.org/10.1080/13876988.2021.1874243
21. Myerson J, Rank MR, Raines FQ, Schnitzler MA. Race and general cognitive ability: the myth of diminishing returns to education. *Psychol Sci.* 1998;9(2):139–142. https://doi.org/10.1111/1467-9280.00026
22. Assari S, Cobb S, Saqib M, Bazargan M. Diminished returns of educational attainment on heart disease among Black Americans. *Open Cardiovasc Med J.* 2020;14:5–12. https://doi.org/10.2174/1874192402014010005
23. Snowden LR, Graaf G. COVID-19, social determinants, and African American–White disparities: policy response and pathways forward. *J Public Health Policy.* 2025;46(1):8–21. https://doi.org/10.1057/s41271-024-00528-8
24. Walton QL, Campbell RD, Blakey JM. Black women and COVID-19: the need for targeted mental health research and practice. *Qual Soc Work.* 2021;20(1-2):247–255. https://doi.org/10.1177/1473325020973349
25. Parolin Z. *Poverty in the Pandemic: Policy Lessons from COVID-19.* New York, NY: Russell Sage Foundation; 2023.
26. Brady PJ, Harnack L, Widome R, Berry KM, Valluri S. Food security among SNAP participants 2019 to 2021: a cross-sectional analysis of current population survey food security supplement data. *Public Health Nutr.* 2023;26(8):1532–1540. https://doi.org/10.1017/jns.2023.32
27. Raifman J, Bor J, Venkataramani A. Association between receipt of unemployment insurance and food insecurity among people who lost employment during the COVID-19 pandemic in the United States. *JAMA Netw Open.* 2021;4(1): e2035884. https://doi.org/10.1001/jamanetworkopen.2020.35884

Disaggregating Gestational Diabetes and Hypertension Among Hispanic Mothers in Florida by Nativity and Country of Birth: 2004–2022

Cynthia N. Lebron, PhD, MPH, Michaela Larson, MPH, Mary Mitsdarffer, PhD, MPH, and Tayla von Ash, ScD, MPH

AJPH April 2026, Vol. 116, No. 4

Objectives. To examine differences in the prevalence of gestational diabetes and gestational hypertension by maternal nativity and country of birth among Hispanic mothers in Florida.

Methods. We conducted a retrospective analysis of 1 130 250 births from Florida birth certificate data between 2004 and 2022. We compared Hispanic maternal health outcomes by nativity (US-born vs foreign-born) and country of birth using descriptive statistics and nested log-binomial regression models, adjusting for sociodemographic covariates.

Results. Foreign-born Hispanic mothers had a higher prevalence of gestational diabetes (5.3%) but lower rates of gestational hypertension (4.3%) than did US-born mothers (4.7% and 5.3%, respectively). Foreign-born mothers from Mexico, Guatemala, Honduras, and Nicaragua had significantly lower adjusted risks for gestational diabetes. Gestational hypertension risk was also lower for most foreign-born groups. However, foreign-born Puerto Rican and Cuban mothers had elevated risks for gestational diabetes compared with their US-born counterparts.

Conclusions. Maternal health risks vary substantially in the Hispanic population by nativity and heritage, underscoring the need to disaggregate data to identify disparities.

Public Health Implications. Policies and interventions should account for subgroup-specific risks to effectively address maternal health inequities in Hispanic communities. (*Am J Public Health*. 2026;116(4): 512–521. https://doi.org/10.2105/AJPH.2025.308359)

Latinos and Hispanics, hereafter referred to as Hispanics, make up approximately 19% of the US population.[1] From 2010 to 2020, Hispanics accounted for more than half of the total US population growth, a trend driven more by births than immigration. Today, about two thirds of Hispanics living in the United States are US-born citizens.[2] Notably, Hispanic children now make up nearly 1 in 4 children younger than 18 years.[3] As the United States faces the prospect of negative population growth, the health and well-being of Hispanics is of particular importance for the future growth and health of the nation.[4] Therefore, it is imperative that the focus of Hispanic health research shift to include the diverse demographic makeup of the population—US-born and immigrant alike.

To date, much research on Hispanics has focused on the Hispanic health paradox, the phenomenon by which health indicators for Hispanics tend to be more favorable than their socioeconomic status would predict. Hispanic perinatal and maternal health outcomes are often compared with those of non-Hispanic White mothers and infants, in which health outcomes typically match at a rate of 1 to 1 despite disparities and associated risk factors.[5] For example, Hispanic women are less likely to receive early, adequate prenatal care, which is critical for reducing complications and ensuring healthy infants.[6] Despite this, Hispanic mothers and infants are similarly likely to experience positive outcomes as their non-Hispanic White counterparts.[6] However, stratifying perinatal outcomes by Hispanic subgroup reveals important disparities. De Sisto and McDonald showed that infants of US-born Hispanic women had higher rates of preterm birth, low birth weight, and being small for gestational age than did those of foreign-born women.[7] Such findings illustrate that when accounting for origin subgroup or generational status, important disparities in perinatal and maternal birth outcomes emerge—differences that, once identified, could inform better, targeted intervention and prevention strategies.

Building on this evidence of subgroup differences in prenatal care and birth outcomes, it is equally important to examine how risks for specific maternal health conditions, such as gestational diabetes and hypertension, also vary by nativity and heritage in the Hispanic population. Hispanic women have the highest prevalence of gestational diabetes in the United States, with rates increasing more quickly for Hispanic women than for those of other ethnoracial groups.[8] Gestational hypertension, although relatively low among Hispanic women, is the most common cause of pregnancy-related death among foreign-born Hispanic women and the second most common among US-born Hispanic women.[9,10] Both gestational diabetes and hypertension are associated with an increased risk of severe maternal morbidity and poorer infant outcomes as well as a long-term risk of cardiovascular disease among mothers.

Given changing US demographics, high Hispanic birthrates, and the heterogeneity of the Hispanic population, it is essential to study variation in Hispanic maternal and infant health outcomes. Our study is among the first to investigate the incidence of gestational diabetes and gestational hypertension among US-born and foreign-born Hispanic mothers. Specifically, we aimed to, first, compare maternal health outcomes among US-born and foreign-born Hispanic mothers; second, describe maternal health outcomes in Hispanic foreign-born mothers by country of origin; and third, investigate maternal health outcomes in Hispanic heritage groups by comparing US-born mothers to their foreign-born counterparts (e.g., Cuban American vs Cuban).

METHODS

We performed a retrospective, quasiexperimental study in which we examined Florida birth certificate data of January 2004 to May 2022. Florida has the third largest Hispanic population in the United States, behind California and Texas, with approximately 5.6 million people.[11] Hispanics make up 26.5% of Florida's population and include both US-born and foreign-born individuals.[2] Although Cubans have historically been the dominant Hispanic group, particularly in South Florida, recent changes in migration patterns have diversified the state's Hispanic population: a significant number of Venezuelan, Colombian, and Dominican immigrants have arrived in recent years. Among Florida's Hispanic population, the largest subgroup is Cuban (28%), followed by Puerto Rican (21%), South American (18%), Mexican (14%), and Dominican (4%).[12]

Our initial data set included 4 009 855 live births from January 2004 to May 2022. Of these, we included 1 130 250 births in our analyses. We included data in this sample if the mother identified as Hispanic and had available information on the location of her birth (i.e., US-born vs foreign-born). We excluded births based on the following criteria: (1) unknown location of maternal nativity, (2) unknown number of weeks of gestation or gestation less than 20 weeks or greater than 42 weeks, (3) nonsingleton births, and (4) missing information on covariates and outcomes (i.e., age, education, marital status, smoking status, gestational diabetes, or gestational hypertension). A consort diagram of the excluded cases is shown in Figure A (available as a supplement to the online version of this article at http://www.ajph.org). Overall, we excluded less than 5% of cases. There were no meaningful differences in the proportion of covariates or outcomes between excluded and included cases by nativity (US-born vs foreign-born).

Measures

Florida birth certificate data contains medical history and birthing information related to both mother and infant. The main outcomes of interest in our analyses were any diagnosis of gestational diabetes (yes/no) or gestational hypertension (yes/no) during the pregnancy related to each birth.

We explored relevant covariates for both outcomes. Maternal sociodemographic variables included year of birth, maternal education, maternal marital status at birth, maternal smoking status, maternal age at birth, and principal payment source for birth. We coded year of birth as a continuous sequential variable beginning at 1 for 2004 and ending at 19 for 2022. We categorized maternal education as less than high school, high school diploma or equivalent, some college (no degree or associate's degree), bachelor's degree, and master's degree or doctorate.

We defined maternal marital status at birth as not married at time of birth (including widowed and unmarried) or married at time of birth. We defined maternal smoking status as never or ever (which included current or former smokers). We used payment source as a measure of socioeconomic status and included the following: Medicaid, private insurance, self-pay, other (including Indian Health Service, TRICARE, or other government insurance), and unknown.

We determined maternal nativity (US-born vs foreign-born) by the country or territory of maternal birth. We categorized Hispanic mothers born in the United States as US-born, and those born outside the United States or in a US territory (e.g., Puerto Rico) as foreign-born. Although Puerto Ricans are US citizens by birth, their social, economic, and health experiences often align more closely with those of foreign-born Hispanic populations. We included place of birth as a separate variable for some analyses. Origin countries and territories included Colombia, Cuba, Dominican Republic, Guatemala, Honduras, Mexico, Nicaragua, Puerto Rico, Venezuela, other Latin American countries, and other non-Latin American countries. Other Latin American countries included Argentina, Belize, Bolivia, Brazil, Chile, Ecuador, El Salvador, Guyana, Panama, Paraguay, Peru, Uruguay, and unspecified Central or South America. We were also interested in maternal health outcomes by Hispanic heritage. Heritage was available for Cuban American, Mexican American, and Puerto Rican mothers, and our analyses represented US-born Cuban mothers versus Cuba-born mothers, US-born Mexican versus Mexico-born mothers, and US-born Puerto Rican versus Puerto Rico–born mothers.

Analyses

We conducted descriptive analyses, including the χ^2 test of independence and the independent-samples *t*-test to examine differences in covariates and outcomes by nativity (US-born vs foreign-born). We also provide frequencies and proportions of covariates and outcomes by country of birth for foreign-born mothers.

To estimate the relative risk of gestational hypertension and gestational diabetes by origin groups (US-born vs foreign-born of the same heritage, e.g., Cuban American vs native Cuban), we fitted nested Poisson regression models with a log link and robust (sandwich) SEs. Model 1 included only the maternal country of birth. To estimate the adjusted relative risk (ARR) of gestational hypertension and gestational diabetes, model 2 adjusted for marital status, education, maternal age, country of birth, and an interaction term between country of birth and maternal age. Model 3 additionally adjusted for smoking status (ever/never), insurance status, year of birth, and an interaction between country of birth and year of birth. We report estimated relative risks (RRs), ARRs, and 95% confidence intervals (CIs). US-born mothers served as the reference group for all analyses examining maternal heritage.

To estimate the RR of gestational hypertension and gestational diabetes by maternal nativity (US-born vs foreign-born) among Cuban, Mexican, and Puerto Rican mothers, we conducted similar nested Poisson regression models with a log link and robust (sandwich) SEs. We report RRs, ARRs, and 95% CIs. We included interaction terms between country of birth and year of birth and between country of birth and maternal age to adjust for observed potential joint confounding. We checked variance inflation factors to ensure that there was no multicollinearity between covariates.

We conducted all analyses in RStudio version 2025.05.1 + 496 (RStudio, Boston, MA).

RESULTS

Demographic and descriptive statistics by maternal nativity are shown in Table 1. Overall, a lower proportion of Hispanic mothers born in the United States had gestational diabetes (4.7%) compared with foreign-born mothers (5.3%), but a higher proportion had gestational hypertension (5.3% vs 4.3%, respectively). On average, US-born mothers were younger (mean age = 26.6 years; SD = 5.9) than were foreign-born mothers (mean age = 29.1 years; SD = 6.0) at the time of birth. US-born mothers were also more likely to have ever been smokers (2.9% and 0.7%, respectively) and unmarried at the time of birth (53.1% and 48.0%, respectively) than were foreign-born mothers.

Table 2 shows frequencies and proportions of outcomes and covariates by country of birth for foreign-born mothers. Briefly, the proportion of births in which the mother was diagnosed with gestational diabetes ranged from 3.9% (Colombia) to 6.5% (Mexico). For gestational hypertension, the proportion of births in which the mother was diagnosed ranged from 3.0% (Guatemala) to 5.5% (Puerto Rico). Use of private insurance ranged from a high of 50.6% (Colombia) to a low of 6.4%

TABLE 1— Demographics and Descriptive Statistics by Hispanic Mothers' Birthplace: Florida Birth Certificate Data, 2004–2022

	Mean ±SD or No. (%)				
	US-Born (n = 390 156)	Foreign-Born (n = 740 094)	Total (n = 1 130 250)	χ^2 or t^a	P
Average maternal age, y	26.6 ±5.9	29.1 ±6.04	28.2 ±6.1	−212.20	< .001
Education				28 553.00	< .001
< high school diploma	60 103 (15.4)	203 961 (27.6)	264 064 (23.4)		
High school graduate/general equivalency diploma	128 425 (32.9)	235 610 (31.8)	364 035 (32.2)		
Some college	82 865 (21.2)	94 568 (12.8)	177 433 (15.7)		
Associate's/bachelor's degree	94 146 (24.1)	165 379 (22.3)	259 525 (23.0)		
Master's degree/PhD	24 617 (6.3)	40 576 (5.5)	65 193 (5.8)		
Marital status				25 820.20	< .001
Not married	207 079 (53.1)	355 608 (48.0)	562 687 (59.8)		
Married	183 077 (46.9)	384 486 (52.0)	567 563 (50.2)		
Smoking status				90 470.10	< .001
Ever	11 227 (2.9)	4 819 (0.7)	16 046 (1.4)		
Never	378 929 (97.1)	735 275 (99.3)	1 114 204 (98.6)		
Payment source				85 086.00	< .001
Medicaid	214 830 (55.1)	328 355 (44.4)	543 185 (48.1)		
Private insurance	156 681 (40.2)	216 275 (29.3)	372 956 (33.0)		
Self-pay	7 764 (2.0)	162 734 (22.0)	170 498 (15.1)		
Other	7 695 (2.0)	25 785 (3.5)	33 480 (3.0)		
Unknown	3 186 (0.8)	6 945 (0.9)	10 131 (0.9)		
Gestational diabetes				175.69	< .001
Yes	18 367 (4.7)	39 106 (5.3)	57 473 (5.1)		
No	371 789 (95.3)	700 988 (94.7)	1 072 777 (94.9)		
Gestational hypertension				605.03	< .001
Yes	20 649 (5.3)	31 605 (4.3)	52 254 (4.6)		
No	369 507 (94.7)	708 489 (95.7)	1 077 996 (95.4)		

Note. Participants were either US-born or foreign-born.
[a] χ^2 for age; all other = *t*.

(Guatemala). The proportion of births in which mothers were ever smokers was overall quite low, with a high of 1.8% (Puerto Rico and other non-Latin American countries).

Table 3 presents the RR and ARRs for gestational diabetes by maternal country of birth compared with Hispanic US-born mothers. In the unadjusted model, there are significant associations between several countries and gestational diabetes. Foreign-born mothers from Colombia (RR = 0.84; 95% CI = 0.80, 0.88) and Venezuela (RR = 0.72; 95% CI = 0.68, 0.75) had significantly lower risks of gestational diabetes than did US-born Hispanic mothers. By contrast, mothers born in Cuba (RR = 1.16; 95% CI = 1.13, 1.19), the Dominican Republic (RR = 1.09; 95% CI = 1.04, 1.15), Guatemala (RR = 1.09; 95% CI = 1.04, 1.13), Honduras (RR = 1.08; 95% CI = 1.04, 1.12), Mexico (RR = 1.39; 95% CI = 1.35, 1.42), and Puerto Rico (RR = 1.27; 95% CI = 1.23, 1.31) had significantly higher risks.

After partial adjustment, mothers born in Colombia (ARR = 0.54; 95% CI = 0.42, 0.69), Guatemala (ARR = 0.43; 95% CI = 0.36, 0.53), Honduras (ARR = 0.54; 95% CI = 0.44, 0.65), Mexico (ARR = 0.67; 95% CI = 0.60, 0.75), Nicaragua (ARR = 0.42; 95% CI = 0.31, 0.56), and Venezuela (ARR = 0.52; 95% CI = 0.38, 0.72) were seen to have significantly lower risks of gestational diabetes than were US-born mothers.

In the fully adjusted model, mothers born in Colombia (ARR = 0.67; 95%

TABLE 2— Description by Country of Birth for Hispanic Foreign-Born Mothers: Florida Birth Certificate Data, 2004–2022

	Mean ±SD or No. (%)										
	Colombia (n = 56 513)	Cuba (n = 138 945)	Dominican Republic (n = 30 793)	Guatemala (n = 46 188)	Honduras (n = 49 364)	Mexico (n = 149 997)	Nicaragua (n = 28 105)	Puerto Rico (n = 85 970)	Venezuela (n = 47 717)	Other Latin American Country (n = 93 917)	Non-Latin American Country (n = 12 585)
Maternal Age, y	31.1 ±5.7	29.3 ±5.7	29.6 ±5.8	27.3 ±6.1	28.5 ±6.1	27.7 ±6.1	29.6 ±5.8	27.5 ±6.0	31.4 ±5.3	30.7 ±5.9	29.8 ±6.0
Education											
Some high school	2753 (4.9)	11 030 (7.9)	3142 (10.2)	35 952 (77.8)	22 094 (44.8)	94 637 (63.1)	5137 (18.3)	10 834 (12.6)	1257 (2.6)	15 965 (17.0)	1160 (9.2)
High school graduate/ general equivalency diploma	14 572 (25.8)	66 606 (47.9)	10 280 (33.4)	6817 (14.8)	17 498 (35.4)	39 366 (26.2)	10 455 (37.2)	29 149 (33.9)	9025 (18.9)	28 363 (30.2)	3479 (27.6)
Some college	10 019 (17.7)	20 005 (14.4)	6423 (20.9)	1409 (3.1)	4195 (8.5)	6570 (4.4)	4745 (16.9)	17 077 (19.9)	7218 (15.1)	14 527 (15.5)	2380 (18.9)
Associate's/bachelor's degree	22 908 (40.5)	34 745 (25.0)	8713 (28.3)	1629 (3.5)	4761 (9.6)	7933 (5.3)	6546 (23.3)	23 421 (27.2)	22 985 (48.2)	27 609 (29.4)	4129 (32.8)
Master's degree/PhD	6261 (11.1)	6559 (4.7)	2235 (7.3)	381 (0.8)	816 (1.7)	1491 (1.0)	1222 (4.3)	5489 (6.4)	7232 (15.2)	7453 (7.9)	1437 (11.4)
Marital status											
Not married	16 089 (28.5)	78 548 (56.5)	12 232 (39.7)	30 915 (66.9)	30 926 (62.6)	82 444 (55.0)	12 279 (43.7)	44 596 (51.9)	10 509 (22.0)	32 584 (34.7)	4486 (35.6)
Married	40 424 (71.5)	60 397 (43.5)	18 561 (60.3)	15 273 (33.1)	18 438 (37.4)	67 553 (45.0)	15 826 (56.3)	41 374 (48.1)	37 208 (78.0)	61 133 (65.3)	8099 (64.4)
Mother's smoking status											
Ever	199 (0.4)	1073 (0.7)	202 (0.7)	58 (0.1)	149 (0.3)	522 (0.3)	84 (0.3)	1586 (1.8)	184 (0.4)	597 (0.6)	221 (1.8)
Never	56 314 (99.6)	137 928 (99.3)	30 591 (99.3)	46 130 (99.9)	49 215 (99.7)	149 475 (99.7)	28 021 (99.7)	84 385 (98.2)	47 533 (99.6)	93 320 (99.4)	12 364 (98.2)
Payment source											
Medicaid	17 308 (30.6)	89 104 (64.1)	14 410 (46.8)	21 180 (45.9)	19 150 (38.8)	59 858 (39.9)	11 206 (39.9)	52 469 (61.0)	10 585 (22.2)	28 684 (30.5)	4401 (35.0)
Private insurance	28 596 (50.6)	43 846 (31.6)	11 839 (38.6)	2957 (6.4)	6555 (13.3)	14 434 (9.6)	9873 (35.1)	29 997 (34.9)	23 803 (49.9)	38 101 (40.6)	6220 (49.4)
Self-pay	8926 (15.8)	3828 (2.8)	3655 (11.9)	18 327 (39.7)	19 714 (39.9)	64 590 (43.1)	5860 (20.9)	1445 (1.7)	11 950 (25.0)	23 054 (24.5)	1385 (11.0)
Other	1411 (2.5)	1179 (0.8)	731 (2.4)	3137 (6.8)	3520 (7.1)	8232 (5.5)	1024 (3.6)	1396 (1.6)	1158 (2.4)	3486 (3.7)	510 (4.1)
Unknown	272 (0.5)	988 (0.7)	104 (0.3)	587 (1.3)	425 (0.9)	2883 (1.9)	142 (0.5)	663 (0.8)	221 (0.5)	592 (0.6)	67 (0.5)
Gestational diabetes											
Yes	2232 (3.9)	7612 (5.5)	1584 (5.1)	2366 (5.1)	2507 (5.1)	9778 (6.5)	1308 (4.7)	5148 (6.0)	1609 (3.4)	4381 (4.7)	581 (4.6)
No	54 281 (96.1)	131 333 (94.5)	29 209 (94.9)	43 822 (94.9)	46 857 (94.9)	140 219 (93.5)	26 797 (95.3)	80 822 (94.0)	46 108 (96.6)	89 536 (95.3)	12 004 (95.4)
Gestational hypertension											
Yes	1913 (3.4)	7445 (5.4)	1561 (5.1)	1386 (3.0)	2156 (4.4)	5172 (3.4)	1296 (4.6)	4746 (5.5)	1941 (4.1)	3461 (3.7)	528 (4.2)
No	54 600 (96.6)	131 500 (94.6)	29 232 (94.9)	44 802 (97.0)	47 208 (95.6)	144 825 (96.6)	26 809 (95.4)	81 224 (94.5)	45 776 (95.9)	90 456 (96.3)	12 057 (95.8)

TABLE 3— Relative Risk of Gestational Diabetes and Gestational Hypertension by Country of Birth Among Hispanic Mothers: Florida Birth Certificate Data, 2004–2022

	Gestational Diabetes			Gestational Hypertension		
Origin Country	Model 1, RR (95% CI)	Model 2, ARR[a] (95% CI)	Model 3, ARR[b] (95% CI)	Model 4, RR (95% CI)	Model 5, ARR[a] (95% CI)	Model 6, ARR[b] (95% CI)
Colombia	0.84 (0.80, 0.88)	0.54 (0.42, 0.69)	0.67 (0.51, 0.87)	0.64 (0.61, 0.67)	0.60 (0.45, 0.78)	0.66 (0.50, 0.88)
Cuba	1.16 (1.13, 1.19)	1.02 (0.90, 1.17)	0.78 (0.68, 0.91)	1.01 (0.99, 1.04)	0.82 (0.72, 0.95)	0.67 (0.57, 0.77)
Dominican Republic	1.09 (1.04, 1.15)	0.99 (0.76, 1.28)	1.08 (0.82, 1.43)	0.96 (0.91, 1.01)	0.85 (0.65, 1.12)	0.88 (0.66, 1.17)
Guatemala	1.09 (1.04, 1.13)	0.43 (0.36, 0.53)	0.64 (0.52, 0.79)	0.57 (0.54, 0.60)	0.36 (0.28, 0.48)	0.46 (0.35, 0.62)
Honduras	1.08 (1.04, 1.12)	0.54 (0.44, 0.65)	0.73 (0.59, 0.90)	0.83 (0.79, 0.86)	0.49 (0.39, 0.62)	0.58 (0.46, 0.75)
Mexico	1.39 (1.35, 1.42)	0.67 (0.60, 0.75)	1.02 (0.90, 1.14)	0.65 (0.63, 0.67)	0.57 (0.49, 0.66)	0.77 (0.66, 0.90)
Nicaragua	0.99 (0.94, 1.04)	0.42 (0.31, 0.56)	0.58 (0.42, 0.78)	0.87 (0.83, 0.92)	0.47 (0.35, 0.65)	0.65 (0.47, 0.89)
Puerto Rico	1.27 (1.23, 1.31)	1.10 (0.96, 1.27)	1.11 (0.95, 1.29)	1.04 (1.01, 1.08)	0.72 (0.62, 0.84)	0.67 (0.57, 0.79)
Venezuela	0.72 (0.68, 0.75)	0.52 (0.38, 0.72)	0.53 (0.38, 0.75)	0.77 (0.73, 0.80)	0.88 (0.66, 1.17)	0.66 (0.49, 0.90)
Other Latin American country	0.99 (0.96, 1.02)	0.93 (0.78, 1.11)	1.25 (1.04, 1.50)	0.70 (0.67, 0.72)	0.72 (0.59, 0.88)	0.79 (0.64, 0.97)
Other non-Latin American country	0.98 (0.90, 1.06)	0.74 (0.48, 1.14)	0.86 (0.55, 1.34)	0.79 (0.73, 0.86)	0.73 (0.48, 1.13)	0.81 (0.52, 1.28)

Note. ARR = adjusted relative risk; CI = confidence interval; RR = relative risk.
[a]Models 2 and 4 include marital status, education, country, maternal age, and country × maternal age.
[b]Models 3 and 6 include everything in model 2 (for diabetes) or model 4 (for hypertension), plus smoking status, payment source, year of birth, and country × year of birth.

CI = 0.51, 0.87), Cuba (ARR = 0.78; 95% CI = 0.68, 0.91), Guatemala (ARR = 0.64; 95% CI = 0.52, 0.79), Honduras (ARR = 0.73; 95% CI = 0.59, 0.90), Nicaragua (ARR = 0.58; 95% CI = 0.42, 0.56), and Venezuela had significantly lower risks of gestational diabetes than did US-born Hispanic mothers. Mothers from other Latin American countries exhibited significantly higher risk (ARR = 1.25; 95% CI = 1.04, 1.50) of gestational diabetes than did US-born Hispanic mothers.

Table 3 also presents the RR for gestational hypertension by maternal origin country. In the unadjusted model, mothers born in all countries and territories except for Cuba and the Dominican Republic showed a significantly reduced risk of gestational hypertension compared with US-born mothers. After partial adjustment, mothers born in all countries except for the Dominican Republic and Venezuela had a significantly lower risk of gestational hypertension than did US-born mothers. In model 3, mothers from all countries except for the Dominican Republic and other non-Latin American countries had a significantly lower risk of gestational hypertension than did US-born mothers. Results of all other covariates in each model for Table 3 are presented in Table A (available as a supplement to the online version of this article at http://www.ajph.org).

Finally, Table 4 shows our comparison of maternal origin groups of the same heritage and their association with gestational diabetes and hypertension outcomes for Puerto Rican, Cuban, and Mexican mothers. In the unadjusted model, native Puerto Rican (RR = 1.14; 95% CI = 1.10, 1.18), Cuban (RR = 1.38; 95% CI = 1.33, 1.44), and Mexican (RR = 1.23; 95% CI = 1.19, 1.27) mothers had significantly higher risks of gestational diabetes than did their US-born counterparts.

However, after adjusting for maternal characteristics in models 2 and 3, Mexico-born mothers exhibited significantly lower risk of gestational diabetes than did US-born Mexican mothers only in model 2 (ARR = 0.90; 95% CI = 0.86, 0.93). By contrast, Cuba-born mothers continued to show elevated risks in both the partially adjusted model (ARR = 1.23; 95% CI = 1.18, 1.29) and the fully adjusted model (ARR = 1.17; 95% CI = 1.12, 1.22), as did Puerto Rico–born mothers (model 2: ARR = 1.04; 95% CI = 1.01, 1.09; model 3: ARR = 1.04; 95% CI = 1.00, 1.08).

For gestational hypertension, Cuba-born mothers had a slightly lower risk in the fully adjusted model (ARR = 0.94; 95% CI = 0.91, 0.98) than did US-born Cuban mothers. Mexico-born mothers

TABLE 4— Relative Risk of Gestational Diabetes and Gestational Hypertension by Hispanic Heritage and Nativity: Florida Birth Certificate Data, 2004–2022

	Gestational Diabetes			Gestational Hypertension		
Hispanic Heritage	Model 1, RR (95% CI)	Model 2, ARR[a] (95% CI)	Model 3, ARR[b] (95% CI)	Model 4, RR (95% CI)	Model 5, ARR[a] (95% CI)	Model 6, ARR[b] (95% CI)
Puerto Rican	1.14 (1.10, 1.18)	1.04 (1.01, 1.09)	1.04 (1.00, 1.08)	1.04 (1.01, 1.08)	1.01 (0.98, 1.05)	1.01 (0.98, 1.05)
Cuban	1.38 (1.33, 1.44)	1.23 (1.18, 1.29)	1.17 (1.12, 1.22)	1.03 (0.99, 1.07)	0.98 (0.94, 1.01)	0.94 (0.91, 0.98)
Mexican	1.23 (1.19, 1.27)	0.90 (0.86, 0.93)	0.96 (0.92, 1.00)	0.65 (0.62, 0.67)	0.64 (0.61, 0.67)	0.72 (0.69, 0.76)

Note. ARR = adjusted relative risk; CI = confidence interval; RR = relative risk.
[a]Models 2 and 4 include marital status, education, and maternal age.
[b]Models 3 and 6 include everything in model 2 (for diabetes) or model 4 (for hypertension) plus smoking status (ever/never), payment, and year of birth.

exhibited a significantly reduced risk for gestational hypertension in all models (ARR = 0.65; 95% CI = 0.62, 0.67; 0.64; 95% CI = 0.61, 0.67; 0.72; 95% CI = 0.69, 0.76) compared with US-born Mexican mothers. Table B (available as a supplement to the online version of this article at http://www.ajph.org) presents results of all other covariates in each model for Table 4.

DISCUSSION

We examined the risk of gestational diabetes and gestational hypertension among Hispanic mothers in Florida by nativity and heritage using more than 1 million birth records from 2004 to 2022. Our findings underscore significant heterogeneity in maternal health outcomes in the Hispanic population, highlighting how aggregated data may obscure subgroup-specific disparities. We found that risks of both gestational diabetes and gestational hypertension varied not only between US-born and foreign-born Hispanic mothers but also in major heritage groups, such as Puerto Rican, Cuban, and Mexican mothers.

Given the close cultural, geographic, and trade ties between the United States and countries in Central America, migration to the United States and within Central America has been a long-standing phenomenon. Migration from the 4 largest Central American sending countries (i.e., El Salvador, Guatemala, Honduras, and Nicaragua) has largely been driven by escalating violence and deteriorating economic conditions,[13] factors that have been shown to negatively affect birth outcomes in other populations.[14] However, evidence indicates that women born in these countries who migrate to the United States tend to experience better birth outcomes than do their counterparts who remain in their country of origin.[7]

Consistent with previous research, we found lower gestational diabetes risk among Hispanic foreign-born mothers from these countries than among those born in the United States. Conversely, mothers born in Mexico, Puerto Rico, and the Dominican Republic initially had a higher risk of gestational diabetes than did US-born Hispanic mothers (although this was attenuated after adjusting for sociodemographic factors).

A previous study examining Florida's live birth certificate data between 2004 and 2007 among Hispanics found that the prevalence of gestational diabetes was highest among those with Mexican or Puerto Rican heritage compared with those with Central or South American or Cuban heritage; however, sociodemographic and nativity factors were not adjusted for.[15] Our analyses illustrated that both sociodemographics as well as nativity are crucial elements to consider, further complicating generalized notions of Hispanic maternal health outcomes being better than expected.

We found that most foreign-born Hispanic mothers had a significantly lower risk of gestational hypertension than did US-born Hispanic mothers, even after adjusting for sociodemographic characteristics. This finding aligns with previous research showing that immigrant women generally experience lower rates of pregnancy-related hypertensive disorders than do their US-born counterparts.[16–18] A recent study similarly reported a lower prevalence of hypertensive disorders among foreign-born mothers, both overall and in racial and ethnic subgroups, including Black and Hispanic women.[19] Although genetic predispositions may contribute to disparities in maternal hypertension, the consistently lower risk among immigrant women relative to US-born women of the same ethnicity underscores the importance of social environments, health behaviors, and structural determinants.

When comparing US-born Hispanic mothers to mothers from their heritage countries, we found that gestational diabetes risk was higher and gestational hypertension risk was lower in foreign-born women. Foreign-born Cuban and Puerto Rican mothers had a significantly higher risk of gestational diabetes than did their US-born counterparts, even after adjusting for sociodemographic factors. By contrast, being foreign-born showed a protective effect for Mexican mothers, with a lower risk of gestational diabetes in fully adjusted models. A recent Hispanic Community Health Study/Study of Latinos study found that Mexican heritage women had the highest prevalence of gestational diabetes (11.3%), followed by women of Puerto Rican (10.1%) and then Cuban (5.0%) descent.[20]

However, that study was not disaggregated by nativity, which may contribute to the findings being contrary to ours. For gestational hypertension, in our study, Puerto Rico–born mothers had no significant difference in risk compared with US-born Puerto Ricans. However, Cuba-born mothers had a slightly reduced risk in adjusted models, and Mexico-born mothers had a consistently and significantly lower risk of gestational hypertension across all models. The differing risks may be related to distinct migration histories, differing access to health care, or varying levels of socioeconomic integration in the United States.[21]

The contrasting patterns in gestational diabetes and gestational hypertension rates by place of birth in the same population suggest that additional, unmeasured factors, beyond those captured in this data set, are likely influencing these outcomes.[22,23] Some studies that apply the Hispanic health paradox as a theoretical lens contend that as Hispanics acculturate[24] and as successive generations are born into the United States, protective immigrant factors begin to decrease. However, health and health outcomes are complicated by much more than adopting new behaviors or national identities: there are complex cultural factors that must be accounted for, such as structural inequities, racial climate, and protective social factors.

For example, after the first Trump administration, Latina mothers, regardless of nativity, experienced higher risks of negative birth outcomes.[25] Moreover, protective factors, such as familial or social bonds, play a large role in Hispanic health. *Familismo* (i.e., the centering of family)[26] has been shown to mitigate negative health outcomes.[27] So, although nativity does play an important role in maternal health, so too might context. Florida has one of the largest Hispanic populations in the United States. Consequently, there may be greater social benefits and more protective factors for foreign-born Hispanic mothers (e.g., more family, culturally enriching neighborhoods and environments).[28–30]

Strengths and Limitations

Our study has several important strengths. Most notably, the use of 1 million births across an 18-year period provides robust statistical power to detect differences across Hispanic subgroups. The use of rich sociodemographic covariate data, including maternal education, marital status, insurance type, and nativity, enhances the ability to explore disparities in maternal health outcomes in greater detail. Furthermore, the application of nested, adjusted regression models allowed us to isolate the effects of maternal nativity and country of birth while accounting for confounding variables, thus strengthening the internal validity of our findings.

Several limitations should also be acknowledged. First, the data do not include information on the length of residence in the United States or acculturation, both of which are important mediators of maternal health risk and may explain variations among groups born outside the United States. Second, there is potential for reporting bias or misclassification, particularly in the documentation of clinical conditions, such as gestational diabetes and hypertension, on birth certificates. Third, the data set lacks information on behavioral factors such as diet, physical activity, and stress, which may play a critical role in shaping maternal health but could not be directly assessed in our study. Finally, although the long study period provided a rich historical data set, it may also have obscured temporal contextual factors—including shifts in immigration policy, sociopolitical climate, or health care access—that could influence maternal and infant outcomes over time.

Public Health Implications

Our study highlights significant variation in gestational diabetes and hypertension shaped by nativity and heritage among Hispanic mothers in Florida. Our findings challenge the assumption of uniform maternal health outcomes in the Hispanic population and underscore the importance of disaggregating data to uncover subgroup-specific disparities. Mexico-born mothers consistently demonstrated lower risk for both gestational diabetes and hypertension, whereas Puerto Rico– and Cuba-born mothers showed elevated risks for gestational diabetes. These differences point to the critical influence of social, cultural, and structural factors on maternal health. Public health efforts and clinical interventions must move beyond aggregated ethnic labels and adopt tailored, equity-focused strategies that reflect the diverse experiences and risks in Hispanic communities, especially in light of the growing proportion of Hispanics in the US population. Addressing maternal health disparities is essential for improving maternal and infant health outcomes and advancing health equity and overall population health. AJPH

ABOUT THE AUTHORS

Cynthia N. Lebron is with the School of Nursing and Health Sciences, University of Miami, Coral Gables, FL. Michaela Larson is with the Robert Stempel College of Public Health and Social Work, Florida International University, Miami, FL. Mary Mitsdarffer is with the Department of Sociology and Anthropology, Rowan University, Glassboro, NJ. Tayla von Ash is with the Department of Behavioral and Social Sciences and the Center for Health Promotion and Health Equity, Brown University School of Public Health, Providence, RI.

CORRESPONDENCE

Correspondence should be sent to Cynthia Lebron, 5030 Brunson Dr, Coral Gables, FL 33146 (e-mail: clebron@miami.edu). Reprints can be ordered at https://www.ajph.org by clicking the "Reprints" link.

PUBLICATION INFORMATION

Full Citation: Lebron CN, Larson M, Mitsdarffer M, von Ash T. Disaggregating gestational diabetes and hypertension among Hispanic mothers in Florida by nativity and country of birth: 2004–2022. *Am J Public Health*. 2026;116(4):512–521.

Acceptance Date: November 9, 2025.

DOI: https://doi.org/10.2105/AJPH.2025.308359

ORCID iDs:

Cynthia N. Lebron https://orcid.org/0000-0002-2506-572X

Michaela Larson https://orcid.org/0000-0003-1821-1239

Mary Mitsdarffer https://orcid.org/0000-0001-9670-224X

CONTRIBUTORS

C. N. Lebron and M. Larson made substantial contributions to the conceptualization and design of the work. M. Mitsdarffer and T. von Ash drafted the work and revised it critically for important intellectual content. All authors gave final approval of the version to be published.

ACKNOWLEDGMENTS

This study was funded by the National Heart, Lung, and Blood Institute (NLHBI) PRograms to Increase Diversity among Individuals Engaged in Health-related Research (grant 5R25HL105446-15).

Note. The contents of this article are solely the responsibility of the authors and do not necessarily represent the official views of the NLHBI.

CONFLICTS OF INTEREST

The authors have no conflicts of interest to disclose.

HUMAN PARTICIPANT PROTECTION

The Florida Department of Health institutional review board approved this study.

REFERENCES

1. US Census Bureau. QuickFacts United States. Population. Available at: https://www.census.gov/quickfacts/fact/table/US/PST045221. Accessed January 28, 2026.
2. Piña G, Martinez G. Key facts about US Latinos. October 22, 2025. Available at: https://www.pewresearch.org/short-reads/2025/10/22/key-facts-about-us-latinos. Accessed January 28, 2026.
3. Ramirez L, Lina G, Alvira-Hammond M. Latino children represent at least 1 in 4 kids nationwide, and more than 40 percent in 5 states and Puerto Rico. October 9, 2024. Available at: https://www.hispanicresearchcenter.org/research-resources/latino-children-represent-1-in-4-kids-nationwide. Accessed July 10, 2025.
4. Colby SL, Ortman JM. Projections of the size and composition of the US population: 2014 to 2060. March 3, 2015. Available at: https://www.census.gov/library/publications/2015/demo/p25-1143.html. Accessed January 27, 2026.
5. Lebron CN, Mitsdarffer M, Parra A, Chavez JV, Behar-Zusman V. Latinas and maternal and child health: research, policy, and representation. *Matern Child Health J*. 2025;29(8):1167–1176. https://doi.org/10.1007/s10995-023-03662-z
6. Montoya-Williams D, Williamson VG, Cardel M, Fuentes-Afflick E, Maldonado-Molina M, Thompson L. The Hispanic/Latinx perinatal paradox in the United States: a scoping review and recommendations to guide future research. *J Immigr Minor Health*. 2021;23(5):1078–1091. https://doi.org/10.1007/s10903-020-01117-z
7. DeSisto CL, McDonald JA. Variation in birth outcomes by mother's country of birth among Hispanic women in the United States, 2013. *Public Health Rep*. 2018;133(3):318–328. https://doi.org/10.1177/0033354918765444
8. Florida Department of Health. Data on pregnancy complications. Available at: https://www.cdc.gov/reproductivehealth/maternalinfanthealth/pregnancy-complications-data.htm. Accessed July 13, 2022.
9. Ananth CV, Keyes KM, Wapner RJ. Pre-eclampsia rates in the United States, 1980–2010: age-period-cohort analysis. *BMJ*. 2013;347:f6564. https://doi.org/10.1136/bmj.f6564
10. Creanga AA, Berg CJ, Syverson C, Seed K, Bruce FC, Callaghan WM. Race, ethnicity, and nativity differentials in pregnancy-related mortality in the United States: 1993–2006. *Obstet Gynecol*. 2012;120(2, pt 1):261–268. https://doi.org/10.1097/AOG.0b013e31825cb87a
11. US Census Bureau. Quick facts. Florida. Available at: https://www.census.gov/quickfacts/FL. Accessed January 27, 2026.
12. Ahn T, De Leon H, Galdámez M, et al. 15 facts about Latino well-being in Florida. June 28, 2022. Available at: https://latino.ucla.edu/research/15-facts-latinos-florida. Accessed June 4, 2025.
13. Dasema R, Batalova J. Central American immigrants in the United States. August 14, 2025. Available at: https://www.migrationpolicy.org/article/central-american-immigrants-united-states. Accessed January 28, 2026.
14. Messer LC, Kaufman JS, Dole N, Herring A, Laraia BA. Violent crime exposure classification and adverse birth outcomes: a geographically defined cohort study. *Int J Health Geogr*. 2006;5:22. https://doi.org/10.1186/1476-072X-5-22
15. Kim SY, England L, Sappenfield W, et al. Racial/ethnic differences in the percentage of gestational diabetes mellitus cases attributable to overweight and obesity, Florida, 2004–2007. *Prev Chronic Dis*. 2012;9:110249. https://doi.org/10.5888/pcd9.110249
16. Singh GK, Siahpush M, Liu L, Allender M. Racial/ethnic, nativity, and sociodemographic disparities in maternal hypertension in the United States, 2014–2015. *Int J Hypertens*. 2018;2018:7897189. https://doi.org/10.1155/2018/7897189
17. Singh GK, Hiatt RA. Trends and disparities in socioeconomic and behavioural characteristics, life expectancy, and cause-specific mortality of native-born and foreign-born populations in the United States, 1979–2003. *Int J Epidemiol*. 2006;35(4):903–919. https://doi.org/10.1093/ije/dyl089
18. Gong J, Savitz DA, Stein CR, Engel SM. Maternal ethnicity and pre-eclampsia in New York City, 1995–2003. *Paediatr Perinat Epidemiol*. 2012;26:45–52. https://doi.org/10.1111/j.1365-3016.2011.01222.x
19. Fram MR, Denney JM, Quinn KH. Nativity, race, ethnicity, and hypertensive disorders during pregnancy. *J Clin Med*. 2025;14(13):4594. https://doi.org/10.3390/jcm14134594
20. Casagrande SS, Avilés-Santa ML, Sotres-Alvarez D, et al. Association between gestational diabetes and 6-year incident diabetes: results from the Hispanic Community Health Study/Study of Latinos (HCHS/SOL). *BMJ Open Diabetes Res Care*. 2022;10:e002980. https://doi.org/10.1136/bmjdrc-2022-002980
21. Carvajal DN, Anaya YB, McLean I, et al. We are not all the same: implications of heterogeneity among Latiné/e/x/o/a, Hispanic, and Spanish origin people. *Ann Fam Med*. 2024;22(3):254–258. https://doi.org/10.1370/afm.3103
22. Shah NS, Harrington KA, Huang X, Cameron NA, Yee LM, Khan SS. Trends in de novo hypertensive disorders of pregnancy among Asian and Hispanic population subgroups in the United States, 2011–2019. *JAMA Cardiol*. 2022;7(7):742–746. https://doi.org/10.1001/jamacardio.2022.1378
23. Shah NS, Wang MC, Freaney PM, et al. Trends in gestational diabetes at first live birth by race and ethnicity in the US, 2011–2019. *JAMA*. 2021;326(7):660–669. https://doi.org/10.1001/jama.2021.7217

24. Gordon MM. *Assimilation in America: Theory and Reality.* New York, NY: Oxford University Press; 1964.
25. Gutierrez C, Dollar NT. Birth and prenatal care outcomes of Latina mothers in the Trump era: analysis by nativity and country/region of origin. *PLoS One.* 2023;18(3):e0281803. https://doi.org/10.1371/journal.pone.0281803
26. Lopez C, Vazquez M, McCormick AS. Familismo, respeto, and bien educado: traditional/cultural models and values in Latinos. In: Gonzalez JE, Liew J, Curtis GA, Zou Y, eds. *Family Literacy Practices in Asian and Latinx Families: Educational and Cultural Considerations.* Cham, Switzerland: Springer; 2022:87–102.
27. Stein GL, Cupito AM, Mendez JL, Prandoni J, Huq N, Westerberg D. Familism through a developmental lens. *J Lat Psychol.* 2014;2(4):224–250. https://doi.org/10.1037/lat0000025
28. Bécares L, Shaw R, Nazroo J, et al. Ethnic density effects on physical morbidity, mortality, and health behaviors: a systematic review of the literature. *Am J Public Health.* 2012;102(12):e33–e66. https://doi.org/10.2105/AJPH.2012.300832
29. Shaw RJ, Pickett KE, Wilkinson RG. Ethnic density effects on birth outcomes and maternal smoking during pregnancy in the US linked birth and infant death data set. *Am J Public Health.* 2010; 100(4):707–713. https://doi.org/10.2105/AJPH.2009.167114
30. Shaw RJ, Pickett KE. The health benefits of Hispanic communities for non-Hispanic mothers and infants: another Hispanic paradox. *Am J Public Health.* 2013;103(6):1052–1057. https://doi.org/10.2105/AJPH.2012.300985

Effectiveness of a Participatory Voice Intervention on Psychological Well-Being Among Warehouse Workers: Results From the Fulfillment Center Intervention Study, United States, 2021–2023

Kirsten F. Siebach, MSW, Yaminette Díaz-Linhart, PhD, Laura D. Kubzansky, PhD, Lisa F. Berkman, PhD, Molin Wang, PhD, Lin Ge, PhD, Alexander M. Kowalski, PhD, Hazhir Rahmandad, PhD, and Erin L. Kelly, PhD

AJPH April 2026, Vol. 116, No. 4

Objectives. To examine whether a novel workplace intervention designed to increase worker voice can reduce psychological distress and improve emotional vitality at 6- and 12-month follow-up.

Methods. We conducted a cluster-randomized controlled trial in 16 fulfillment centers throughout the United States between 2021 and 2023. Data were collected at 3 time points; 2813 workers participated in at least 1 survey. Treated fulfillment centers established a new, participatory committee called the Health and Well-Being Committee. We compared differences in psychological distress and emotional vitality and explored differential treatment effects by gender.

Results. At baseline, 51% of the participants reported moderate or severe psychological distress. Intervention sites had lower average psychological distress at the 6-month follow-up compared with control sites, with no significant differences at 12-month follow-up. Gender moderation analyses suggest the Health and Well-Being Committee was particularly effective in reducing psychological distress among men at 6-month follow-up.

Conclusions. Our findings suggest that opportunities for workers to share concerns with a committee of their peers tasked with identifying solutions can support mental health. Our study contributes important experimental evidence on workplace interventions that improve the well-being of low-wage US populations.

Trial Registration. Clinicaltrials.gov identifier: NCT05199415. (*Am J Public Health*. 2026;116(4):522–532. https://doi.org/10.2105/AJPH.2025.308352)

The work environment is a critical social determinant of health, including mental health.[1–3] Workers exposed to poor working conditions, including low job control, excessive job demands, unsupportive work relationships, and limited schedule control, are at higher risk for poor mental health, including anxiety, depression, and psychological distress.[4,5] Poor mental health contributes to increased risk of chronic disease and premature mortality,[6] strain on family and other relationships,[7] and work absenteeism and work disability,[8,9] which negatively impact firms' functioning and productivity. The work environment may also support positive psychological well-being, which has been associated with reduced heart disease,[10,11] diabetes,[12] and stroke risk,[13] and is a public health target in its own right.

Workplace interventions that aim to change the conditions of work represent a primary prevention approach that may reduce psychological distress and improve psychological well-being, in addition to supporting physical and cardiometabolic health.[14–20] Interventions to increase job control, which refers to "decision-making freedom (discretion) available to the worker,"[21] or decision latitude are among the most commonly tested,[22] with demonstrated benefits to mental health.[23–25]

We extend the job control literature to consider employee voice. While job control interventions aim to give workers more say about how they do their jobs, a voice intervention aims to increase workers' input within the workplace beyond their specific job tasks or role. Voice has been defined as "the ways and means through which employees attempt to have a say about, and influence, their work and the functioning of their organization."[26(p5)] We define a voice channel as a structure or initiative enabling such voice or input. A union would constitute a strong voice channel, but other channels (e.g., engagement surveys, "town hall" meetings) can encourage employees to share their ideas and to work toward changing work conditions.[27,28]

Economic and organizational theories suggest employee voice can prompt organizational changes that improve health, safety, and other work conditions, meaning voice may directly improve job quality.[29–31] In addition, the opportunity to share one's perspective, contribute ideas, and be respected (or colloquially, "heard") may support well-being. Having a voice may affirm individuals' basic psychological needs of autonomy, competence, and relatedness.[32–37] Employees who voice more are more engaged at work[38] and report more energy[33,39,40] and lower burnout,[36,37] suggesting positive effects on well-being.

Empirical research on voice channels' impact on well-being is limited, with no studies identified that causally examine the psychological well-being outcomes evaluated here. One cross-sectional study found an association between employees' reports that managers seek their input and well-being, indicated by an anxiety–contentment scale and job satisfaction.[39] A longitudinal study found that certain bundles of high-involvement practices are associated with job satisfaction, fatigue, and self-reported health.[34] Fox et al. found that some participatory interventions improved well-being; these interventions bring employees together to identify problems and pursue changes, which can be conceptualized as a strategy to increase voice.[22] One randomized trial of an employee survey serving as a novel voice channel in Indian garment factories found reduced absenteeism, but a quasi-experimental analysis of a new voice channel, required by Finnish law, found no effect on sickness spells, perhaps because other opportunities for voice already existed in this highly unionized context.[41,42]

Our primary aim was to evaluate the hypothesis that a new voice channel will improve psychological well-being using a cluster-randomized controlled trial in fulfillment centers (FCs). The voice channel involved a new committee that solicited employees' ideas and concerns and then developed action projects to change the work environment. This intervention created opportunities for all nonsupervisory employees to share ideas and concerns but involved a smaller committee (primarily nonsupervisory employees) in the participatory process of prioritizing and developing action plans. We prespecified the hypotheses that workers in sites randomized to the intervention would have lower levels of psychological distress and higher levels of emotional vitality compared with workers in sites that continued operations as usual.

An exploratory analysis assessed gender differences in effects. Previous research found men showed a stronger association between low job control or high job strain and depressive symptoms,[43] psychological distress,[44] and long-term spells of depression[45] than women. Pohrt et al. noted that low job control conflicts with "cultural ideals of masculinity emphasizing power and dominance. Low job control may, therefore, contribute to lower self-esteem and risk of depressive symptoms in men."[46(p384)] A longitudinal study found the effect of cumulative union membership (i.e., exposure to an important voice channel) on self-rated health, functional limitations, and chronic health conditions in late adulthood was stronger for men than women.[47] We therefore hypothesize that a new voice channel may have greater effects on men's psychological well-being. This exploratory hypothesis is not preregistered.

METHODS

The Fulfillment Center Intervention study was a 2-arm cluster-randomized controlled trial conducted between July 2021 and August 2023 in 16 FCs throughout the United States. We partnered with the supply chain division of a midsized retailer, referred to as its pseudonym "Sigma." In the study period, Sigma operated 24 FCs, which are warehouses that prepare packages for online orders and employed approximately 4800 nonsupervisory workers, with a median FC size of 175 employees. The most common job is "picking," where employees select products and place them in shipping boxes. In 2021, Sigma's nonsupervisory employees earned approximately $19 per hour. Working within an FC is physically taxing, and workers face some time pressure, with individual productivity tracked using technology.

The main objective was to assess the effects of a novel voice intervention on psychological distress and emotional vitality. The randomization unit was the FC, and the analysis unit was the individual. We used an open cohort design, as opposed to a closed cohort design, which is appropriate given the high turnover of this workforce (about 45% annually) and because new hires are "exposed" to the committee even if they arrive after its launch.[48] We assessed study outcomes at 3 time-points: at baseline and before randomization and intervention launch (T1), at 6 months (T2), and at 12 months (T3). Spillover concerns were minimal given the geographic distribution of FCs and limited communication between nonsupervisory employees across sites (see "Industry information" on page 1 of the Appendix, available as a supplement to the online version of this article at https://ajph.org).

Before the cluster-randomized controlled trial, we piloted the intervention in 1 site. Among the remaining 23 FCs, 8 sites were excluded before randomization based on the following criteria: fewer than 15 workers at the worksite, site closure planned, changes in site leadership during the planned baseline survey window, or a union contract in 1 FC, which might have required negotiated intervention adaptation for that single site. There was a 3-stage rollout of the study. After conducting the baseline survey, sites were matched based on their main picking technology (cart, conveyor, or robotics picking systems) and the number of hourly workers (small, medium, large, or very large). Within each stratum, we randomized FCs to receive the intervention or maintain operations as usual (see "Randomization procedures" on page 2 of the Appendix for randomization procedures and study rollout). Because of the participatory nature of the intervention, blinding was not possible.

Recruitment and Data Collection

All Sigma employees in these FCs were eligible to participate at each survey time point. Because nonsupervisory employees did not have work e-mail addresses, individuals received an individualized invitation packet at each time point with a bilingual (English and Spanish) study description, a unique survey ID, and a unique URL and QR code linking to their electronic survey administered on Qualtrics.[49] Flyers were posted and frontline supervisors were provided talking points to announce the survey. Employees could complete the 15- to 20-minute survey (in English and Spanish) during work time on their smartphone, Sigma computers, or electronic tablets provided, or could take the survey outside of work. Participants received $10 (T1, T2) and $15 (T3) incentive gift cards. Each building also conducted weekly $25 to $150 raffles for participants.

Intervention

FCs randomized to the intervention arm established a new, participatory committee called the Health and Well-Being Committee (HaWC). Following randomization, researchers met with managers at intervention sites to plan intervention roll-out. HaWCs included 6 to 14 nonsupervisory employees representing different departments and shifts and were led by 1 nonsupervisory employee and 1 supervisor, called "coleads." Coleads participated in a 4- to 6-hour training on HaWC processes. HaWCs provided a formal voice channel to which nonsupervisory employees could submit their concerns pertaining to safety, the psychosocial work environment, and work organization. Workers submitted concerns anonymously via comment boxes located in the warehouse or verbally to HaWC members. HaWCs then utilized continuous improvement strategies to document concerns, define problems, brainstorm possible solutions, and coordinate solution implementation, using bulletin boards and other announcements to share action projects.[50,51] HaWCs met 1 or 2 times a month for 1 hour, but less frequently during peak business periods (e.g., Black Friday) or if there was a change in coleads. All HaWC activities were conducted on the clock.

Importantly, this analysis investigated the potential broad effects of a voice channel. Not all nonsupervisory employees engaged directly with the intervention (e.g., submitted concerns, attended HaWC meetings), but all could experience changes attributable to HaWC activities. For more information on the development and details of the intervention, see Kelly et al.[52] The Appendix

("Cost" on page 3) provides information on costs and potential adverse effects.

Measures

The primary outcomes for this study were self-reported psychological distress and emotional vitality in the previous 30 days. Psychological distress was measured continuously and dichotomously using the Kessler-6 Psychological Distress Scale.[53] The scale provides a measure of global well-being, rather than work-related well-being (e.g., job satisfaction or burnout), and was designed to maximize case discrimination of serious mental illness.[53] Participants indicated frequency of symptoms of psychological distress on a 5-point scale ranging from 0 ("none of the time") to 4 ("all of the time"). Items were summed to create an overall score (range = 0–24), with higher scores indicating higher levels of psychological distress. For dichotomous models, we used pre-established cutoffs; scores of 5 or higher were considered indicative of moderate or severe psychological distress, and scores of 13 or higher were considered severe psychological distress.[53,54]

Emotional vitality is characterized by a sense of energy, positive well-being, and effective emotional regulation.[6] It was measured using an existing 6-item scale[6] wherein participants indicated how often they woke up fresh and rested; their daily life had been full of things that were interesting to them; they felt in firm control of their behavior, thoughts, emotions, or feelings; and they felt emotionally stable and sure of themselves; and their sense of energy and vitality. Responses ranged from 0 ("not at all") to 5 ("a lot or all of the time"), though the energy item ranged from 0 ("no energy at all, listless") to 10 ("very energetic, dynamic"). We summed items to create an overall score (range = 0–35), with higher scores indicating higher emotional vitality.

Covariates. Covariates spanned demographic and work characteristics, including gender, age, race and ethnicity, tenure, shift, department, full- versus part-time status, and wage changes from Sigma's administrative data. We included county-level unemployment rate and county-level proportion of deaths attributed to COVID-19 during the month of survey administration using data from the US Bureau of Labor Statistics and the Centers for Disease Control and Prevention. Both COVID-19 risk and unemployment varied significantly across time and locations, and each is plausibly related to psychological well-being.

Statistical analysis. All analyses followed the intention-to-treat principle. Before regression analyses, we conducted bivariate analyses to assess baseline balance across study arms using the Wilcoxon signed-rank test and Pearson χ^2 test. To assess response and attrition bias, we explored differences in baseline characteristics between survey participants, survey nonparticipants, and those who exited the firm. Predictors of response and attrition were included as covariates in the main analyses.

As planned,[52] we used separate multilevel linear regression models to estimate the effects of the HaWC intervention on psychological distress and emotional vitality across the 3 time points, each measured as a continuous variable. We included random effects for individuals clustered within buildings and for buildings. We used multilevel logistic models to estimate the intervention effects on the severity of psychological distress (none or mild vs moderate or severe).[53,54] See Appendix ("Methods," page 2) for the regression equations. In all multilevel models we included treatment status, randomization strata, time (T1, T2, and T3), and covariates. Fewer covariates were included in the logistic regression for model convergence and optimizing model fit. The interaction between treatment status and the indicator for follow-up time captures the treatment effect over time. To assess differential intervention effects by gender, we conducted multilevel linear regression for continuous outcomes or logistic regression for dichotomous outcomes, including a 3-way interaction term among intervention status, time point, and gender. We then computed the intervention effect within each time point as a linear combination of coefficients. We defined statistical significance as $P<.05$. We used the LMER and GLMER packages in R (version 2024.04.2) to perform continuous and logistic multilevel regression analyses.[55]

RESULTS

Figure 1 shows the participant flowchart. Sixteen sites were randomized to receive the intervention or continue business operations as usual. In total, 2813 workers participated in at least 1 survey for a total of 4527 observations; 1234 (44%) participants answered at least 2 surveys. The number of workers who joined or left the organization between waves is noted in Figure 1. A total of 114 observations (2.5%) were excluded for missing outcome or demographic data. The final analytic sample included 4413 observations. At baseline, intervention and control sites were unbalanced with respect to

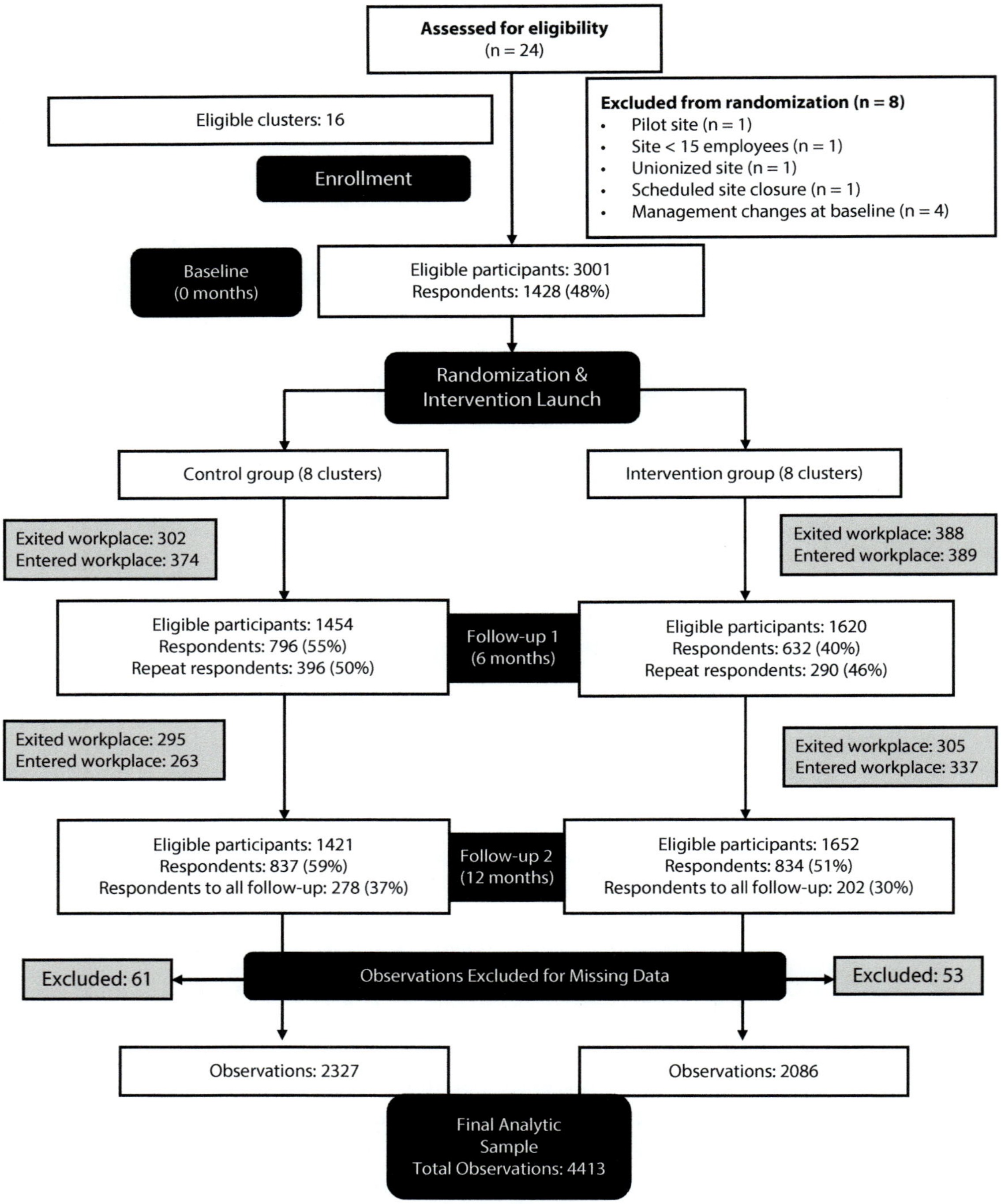

FIGURE 1— Participant Flowchart for the Fulfillment Center Intervention Study, an Open Cohort Cluster-Randomized Controlled Trial: United States, 2021–2023

race/ethnicity, full or part-time status, and tenure. Male gender, full-time status, lower wages, higher tenure, some departments, and racialized minorities were associated with lower odds of survey response. Regression analyses included these covariates.

Table 1 shows characteristics and psychological well-being of participants by time point and intervention condition. The study baseline mean psychological distress for all groups was 5.6 (SD = 4.8), and baseline mean emotional vitality was 22.3 (SD = 7.8), with no significant differences across condition. Baseline

TABLE 1— Characteristics of the Fulfillment Center Intervention Study Participants, by Time Point and Study Arm: United States, 2021–2023

Characteristic	Baseline				Follow Up 1 (6 Months)				Follow Up 2 (12 Months)			
	Overall (n = 1389), Mean ±SD or No. (%)	Intervention (n = 657), Mean ±SD or No. (%)	Control (n = 732), Mean ±SD or No. (%)	P	Overall (n = 1391), Mean ±SD or No. (%)	Intervention (n = 616), Mean ±SD or No. (%)	Control (n = 775), Mean ±SD or No. (%)	P	Overall (n = 1633), Mean ±SD or No. (%)	Intervention (n = 813), Mean ±SD or No. (%)	Control (n = 820), Mean ±SD or No. (%)	P
Age, y	40.16 ±13.33	39.85 ±13.08	40.45 ±13.55	.48	40.61 ±13.62	40.88 ±13.00	40.39 ±14.09	.33	40.53 ±13.43	40.46 ±13.19	40.61 ±13.67	.97
Psychological distress (0–24)	5.63 ±4.84	5.75 ±5.06	5.52 ±4.64	.75	5.44 ±4.83	5.11 ±4.83	5.70 ±4.82	.007	5.23 ±4.85	5.23 ±4.93	5.23 ±4.77	.8
Psychological distress (moderate or severe)	712 (51)	338 (51)	374 (51)	.9	683 (49)	278 (45)	405 (52)	.008	765 (47)	370 (46)	395 (48)	.28
Psychological distress (severe)	140 (10)	67 (10)	73 (10)	.89	119 (9)	53 (9)	66 (9)	.95	140 (9)	71 (9)	69 (8)	.82
Emotional vitality (0–35)	22.25 ±7.83	21.89 ±8.00	22.58 ±7.67	.12	22.90 ±7.85	22.75 ±7.72	23.01 ±7.95	.39	23.34 ±7.78	23.06 ±7.76	23.61 ±7.80	.13
Gender				.09				.021				.029
Female	666 (48)	299 (46)	367 (50)		642 (46)	263 (43)	379 (49)		723 (44)	338 (42)	385 (47)	
Male	723 (52)	358 (54)	365 (50)		749 (54)	353 (57)	396 (51)		910 (56)	475 (58)	435 (53)	
Race/ethnicity				<.001				<.001				<.001
Non-Hispanic White	639 (46)	342 (52)	297 (41)		570 (41)	275 (45)	295 (38)		638 (39)	341 (42)	297 (36)	
Hispanic	498 (36)	164 (25)	334 (46)		537 (39)	188 (31)	349 (45)		629 (39)	241 (30)	388 (47)	
Non-Hispanic AI/PI/AN/MR	74 (5.3)	49 (8)	25 (3)		93 (7)	57 (9)	36 (5)		104 (6)	73 (9)	31 (4)	
Non-Hispanic Black	178 (13)	102 (16)	76 (10)		191 (14)	96 (16)	95 (12)		262 (16)	158 (19)	104 (13)	
Tenure, y	6.44 ±7.16	6.62 ±7.02	6.28 ±7.28	.012	6.11 ±7.14	6.53 ±7.09	5.78 ±7.16	<.001	6.36 ±7.31	6.27 ±7.24	6.45 ±7.37	.4
Job status				.009				<.001				.013
Full time	1120 (81)	549 (84)	571 (78)		1164 (84)	550 (89)	614 (79)		1418 (87)	723 (89)	695 (85)	
Part time	269 (19)	108 (16)	161 (22)		227 (16)	66 (11)	161 (21)		215 (13)	90 (11)	125 (15)	
Shift				.005				<.001				<.001
1	597 (43)	272 (41)	325 (44)		626 (45)	298 (48)	328 (42)		729 (45)	362 (45)	367 (45)	
2	662 (48)	306 (47)	356 (49)		612 (44)	236 (38)	376 (49)		564 (35)	319 (39)	245 (30)	
3	130 (9.4)	79 (12)	51 (7)		153 (11)	82 (13)	71 (9)		340 (21)	132 (16)	208 (25)	
Department				.013				.035				.4
Breakpack	641 (46)	296 (45)	345 (47)		554 (40)	221 (36)	333 (43)		590 (36)	295 (36)	295 (36)	
Admin	29 (2)	16 (2)	13 (2)		23 (2)	14 (2)	9 (1)		35 (2)	18 (2)	17 (2)	
Bulk picks	138 (9.9)	68 (10)	70 (10)		123 (9)	56 (9)	67 (9)		209 (13)	112 (14)	97 (12)	
Inbound	148 (11)	79 (12)	69 (9)		206 (15)	103 (17)	103 (13)		232 (14)	107 (13)	125 (15)	

Continued

TABLE 1— Continued

Characteristic	Baseline				Follow Up 1 (6 Months)				Follow Up 2 (12 Months)			
	Overall (n = 1389), Mean ±SD or No. (%)	Intervention (n = 657), Mean ±SD or No. (%)	Control (n = 732), Mean ±SD or No. (%)	P	Overall (n = 1391), Mean ±SD or No. (%)	Intervention (n = 616), Mean ±SD or No. (%)	Control (n = 775), Mean ±SD or No. (%)	P	Overall (n = 1633), Mean ±SD or No. (%)	Intervention (n = 813), Mean ±SD or No. (%)	Control (n = 820), Mean ±SD or No. (%)	P
Replenishment	169 (12)	88 (13)	81 (11)		206 (15)	96 (16)	110 (14)		262 (16)	141 (17)	121 (15)	
Shipping	110 (8)	35 (5)	75 (10)		114 (8)	44 (7)	70 (9)		112 (7)	51 (6)	61 (7)	
Support	154 (11)	75 (11)	79 (11)		165 (12)	82 (13)	83 (11)		193 (12)	89 (11)	104 (13)	

Note. AI/PI/AN/MR = American Indian, Pacific Islander, Alaska Native, or multiracial. Statistical significance of the estimates comparing the treatment and control arms at each time point are obtained from a Pearson χ^2 test when the variable is dichotomous and Wilcoxon signed-rank test when continuous.

prevalence of moderate or severe psychological distress was 51% (n = 712), and baseline prevalence of severe distress was 10% (n = 140), again with no significant differences across study conditions. Prevalence of psychological distress in this workforce sample was notably higher than the general working population. The 2021 National Health Interview Survey showed a prevalence of 19.1% of moderate or severe psychological distress among working adults aged 18 to 64 years.[56]

Psychological Distress and Emotional Vitality

Table 2 presents intervention effects on psychological distress and emotional vitality with 95% confidence intervals (CIs). When psychological distress was modeled continuously using multilevel linear regression (see model 1), there was a significant interaction between treatment arm and T2 (b = −0.55; 95% CI = −1.09, −0.01), but the interaction of treatment and T3 was not significant (b = −0.03; 95% CI = −0.57, 0.51). Based on Cohen's guidelines,[57] the effect magnitude on continuously measured psychological distress at T2 was small ($d = 0.11$; $P = .045$). Full regression results are available in Appendix Table A. Appendix Figure A shows the distribution of psychological distress by intervention status and time.

When moderate or severe distress was modeled dichotomously using multilevel logistic regression (model 2), there was a nonsignificant interaction effect at T2 (ratio of odds ratio = 0.67; 95% CI = 0.43, 1.05; $P = .08$) and T3 (ratio of odds ratio = 0.84; 95% CI = 0.54, 1.30; $P = .44$). Too few participants met the threshold for severe psychological distress (sum score ≥ 13) to allow for model convergence; an alternative model is presented in Table B (available as a supplement to the online version of this article at https://ajph.org).

There were no significant interaction effects for emotional vitality (model 3), suggesting that the intervention had no effect on this measure of psychological well-being. Across arms, emotional vitality increased significantly between T1 and T2 (b = 2.34; 95% CI = 0.62, 4.06), but this increase was not sustained after T2.

As sensitivity analyses, we first conducted regression analyses for continuous outcomes using an autoregressive correlation structure to account for potential decaying of correlation among repeated measures. We found very similar results (Appendix Table E). We then conducted an analysis of study outcomes among participants completing all survey waves (n = 480), which also showed results consistent with the primary analyses (Appendix Tables F and G).

Intervention Effects by Gender

Table 3 shows the within-gender differences in psychological distress across arms. The linear combination of coefficients suggests men in intervention sites had improved psychological distress compared with men in control sites at T2 (difference = −0.89; 95% CI = −1.68, −0.09), adjusting for the same covariates in the intention-to-treat analysis (see Appendix Table D for full regression results). Results also show that men in intervention sites were 57% less likely to have moderate or severe psychological distress compared with men in control sites at T2 (OR = 0.43; 95% CI = 0.26, 0.74). Neither of these results were sustained at T3. There were no significant differences

TABLE 2— Analysis of the Impact of the Health and Well-Being Committee Intervention on Psychological Well-Being: Intention-to-Treat, United States, 2021–2023

Intention-to-Treat, Main Effects	Model 1[a]: Psychological Distress (n = 4413), b (95% CI)	Model 2[b]: Moderate or Severe Psychological Distress (n = 4413), AOR (95% CI)	Model 3[a]: Emotional Vitality (n = 4398), b (95% CI)
Intervention (Ref = control)	0.02 (−0.68, 0.72)	0.95 (0.63, 1.42)	−0.34 (−1.21, 0.53)
Time (Ref = T1)			
T2	−0.50 (−1.84, 0.84)	1.02 (0.75, 1.41)	2.34 (0.52, 4.06)
T3	−0.14 (−0.90, 0.61)	0.75 (0.53, 1.04)	0.71 (−0.31, 1.73)
Intervention × T2	−0.55 (−1.09, −0.01)	0.67 (0.42, 1.05)	0.20 (−0.64, 1.04)
Intervention × T3	−0.03 (−0.57, 0.51)	0.84 (0.54, 1.30)	−0.02 (−0.88, 0.83)

Note. AOR = adjusted odds ratio; CI = confidence interval; T1 = baseline; T2 = 6 months; T3 = 12 months.
[a]Model adjusted for strata, age, race/ethnicity, gender, tenure, job status, department, shift, month of survey, wage difference from previous survey, county-level proportion of deaths attributed to COVID-19 during the month of survey, local unemployment rate, and building volume.
[b]Model adjusted for strata, age, race/ethnicity, gender, tenure, job status, and wage difference from previous survey.

in psychological distress across arms among women. Gender subgroup analysis did not reveal interaction effects for emotional vitality.

TABLE 3— Estimated Within-Gender Difference in Psychological Distress Across Health and Well-Being Committee Intervention Arms and by Time Point: Fulfillment Center Intervention Study, United States, 2021–2023

Time and Gender	
Psychological distress, estimated difference between arms (95% CI)	
T1 (n = 1389)	
Male (n = 723)	−0.27 (−1.09, 0.54)
Female (n = 666)	0.43 (−0.42, 1.29)
T2 (n = 1391)	
Male (n = 749)	−0.89 (−1.68, −0.09)
Female (n = 642)	−0.01 (−0.85, 0.83)
T3 (n = 1633)	
Male (n = 910)	−0.44 (−1.17, 0.29)
Female (n = 723)	0.52 (−0.26, 1.31)
Odds of psychological distress, OR (95% CI)	
T1 (n = 1389)	
Male (n = 723)	0.95 (0.56, 1.61)
Female (n = 666)	0.97 (0.56, 1.69)
T2 (n = 1391)	
Male (n = 749)	0.43 (0.26, 0.74)
Female (n = 642)	1.03 (0.58, 1.82)
T3 (n = 1633)	
Male (n = 910)	0.65 (0.40, 1.05)
Female (n = 723)	1.07 (0.63, 1.83)

Note. CI = confidence interval; OR = odds ratio; T1 = baseline; T2 = 6 months; T3 = 12 months.

DISCUSSION

The Fulfillment Center Intervention study used a rigorous design to evaluate a new, participatory voice intervention in an important workforce. We built upon limited nonexperimental evidence suggesting a positive association between voice and well-being[22,34,39] and provide experimental evidence that a new voice channel can improve workers' mental health. In the intention-to-treat analyses, workers in intervention sites had lower average psychological distress compared with control sites at T2. These findings support the idea that new voice channels can improve well-being, extending the existing literature on job control to consider the benefits of having a say on work conditions more broadly.

These results were not sustained at T3. An ongoing process evaluation suggests growing variation in the implementation of the intervention (e.g., number of meetings, projects pursued) after the initial phase, reflecting a common challenge in sustaining workplace interventions.[58,59] Furthermore, in both study arms, the firm implemented new initiatives unrelated to our study but focused on worker safety and engagement between T2 and T3. These changes could explain shifts in the control sites between T2 and T3, effectively "catching up" to intervention sites, or dilute or mask the HaWC effect. It is also possible that participant turnover between T2 and T3 contributed to the diminished intervention effect.

Results suggest that men particularly benefited from the HaWC intervention, with lower average psychological distress compared with men in the control arm at T2, though mean levels of psychological well-being also improved for women in intervention sites (Appendix Table C). Men in intervention sites also had 57% lower odds of moderate or severe psychological distress compared with men in control sites at T2. As noted previously, one possibility is that men respond more strongly to the voice channel because it allows them to act in ways that are psychologically rewarding (e.g., to behave more like the ideal of agentic, powerful men at work).[43] Other plausible alternative explanations for gender differences, including voicing behavior, are reviewed in the Appendix ("Discussion," page 5).

Limitations and Future Research Directions

This study is not without limitations. First, as with most field trials, variation in implementation and competing organizational priorities create challenges for fidelity and sustainability, although the intention-to-treat effects here provide conservative evidence of short-term impact even with substantial variation. Second, the number of clusters meeting the study's eligibility criteria was relatively small. While our study includes more clusters (n = 16) than the generally accepted minimum for a 2-arm trial (n = 8),[60] future cluster-randomized controlled trials should test similar interventions in organizations with more work establishments to identify minimal effects and in other populations to increase generalizability. Lastly, our analyses relied on self-reported mental health measures. Self-report data may be subject to recall bias and social desirability bias, the latter being particularly relevant given persistent stigma associated with mental illness.

This study identified important directions for future research. First, additional process research can identify the barriers and facilitators to implementation to improve the effectiveness of workplace interventions, and to address important questions of sustainability beyond initial benefits.[61] Second, the intervention effects on psychological distress, though small, are notable. The initiative did not involve activities specifically targeting mental health (e.g., mental health awareness campaigns or resources), and workers may not have engaged directly with the HaWC problem-solving but nonetheless benefited from the voice channel. These are promising results for a low-cost workplace intervention and point to the value of additional research on voice interventions. Third, future research should continue to investigate gender differences and consider the relationship between voice and well-being among workers in different industry contexts, including those with different demographic compositions (e.g., female-dominated industries such as health care). Lastly, though this study found no intervention effect for emotional vitality, future studies should continue investigating how workplace interventions may affect positive psychological well-being.

Conclusions

With the renewed emphasis from public health leaders on workplace mental health,[62] it is crucial to identify feasible strategies to improve the psychological well-being of nonsupervisory and low-wage employees. Our findings suggest that providing opportunities for workers to share their concerns with a committee of their peers who seek to identify solutions can provide mental health benefits, even if workers are not members of the committee. Our study contributes important experimental evidence on workplace interventions that improve well-being of low-wage US populations. AJPH

ABOUT THE AUTHORS

Kirsten F. Siebach is with the Department of International Health at the Johns Hopkins Bloomberg School of Public Health, Baltimore, MD. Yaminette Díaz-Linhart was with the Institute of Work and Employment Research, Massachusetts Institute of Technology Sloan School of Management, Cambridge, MA, at the time of the study. Laura D. Kubzansky is with the Department of Social and Behavioral Sciences, Harvard T. H. Chan School of Public Health, Boston, MA. Lisa F. Berkman is with the Department of Global Health and Population, Harvard T. H. Chan School of Public Health. Molin Wang and Lin Ge are with the Department of Epidemiology, Harvard T. H. Chan School of Public Health. Alexander M. Kowalski is with Human Resource Studies, Cornell University School of Industrial and Labor Relations, Ithaca, NY. Hazhir Rahmandad is with System Dynamics at the Massachusetts Institute of Technology Sloan School of Management. Erin L. Kelly is with Work and Organization Studies, the Institute of Work and Employment Research, Massachusetts Institute of Technology Sloan School of Management.

CORRESPONDENCE

Correspondence should be sent to Kirsten F. Siebach, Johns Hopkins Bloomberg School of Public Health, 615 N Wolfe St, Baltimore, MD 21205 (e-mail: ksiebac1@jhu.edu). Reprints can be ordered at https://www.ajph.org by clicking the "Reprints" link.

PUBLICATION INFORMATION

Full Citation: Siebach KF, Díaz-Linhart Y, Kubzansky LD, et al. Effectiveness of a participatory voice intervention on psychological well-being among warehouse workers: results from the Fulfillment Center Intervention study, United States, 2021–2023. *Am J Public Health*. 2026;116(4):522–532.

Acceptance Date: October 20, 2025.

DOI: https://doi.org/10.2105/AJPH.2025.308352

ORCID iDs:
Kirsten F. Siebach https://orcid.org/0000-0002-2532-7814

Yaminette Díaz-Linhart https://orcid.org/0000-0003-1380-713X

Laura D. Kubzansky https://orcid.org/0000-0002-4039-2235

Lin Ge https://orcid.org/0000-0002-8180-9615

Alexander M. Kowalski https://orcid.org/0000-0002-4636-5449

Hazhir Rahmandad https://orcid.org/0000-0002-2784-9042

Erin L. Kelly https://orcid.org/0000-0003-2168-5611

CONTRIBUTORS

E. L. Kelly, L. D. Kubzansky, L. F. Berkman, H. Rahmandad, M. Wang, and A. M. Kowalski originated the study. K. F. Siebach, A. M. Kowalski, H. Rahmandad, and E. L. Kelly were involved in original data collection. K. F. Siebach, Y. Díaz-Linhart, L. D. Kubzansky, L. F. Berkman, A. M. Kowalski, H. Rahmandad, and E. L. Kelly were involved in analysis and writing the article. M. Wang and L. Ge were involved in statistical analysis and writing the article.

ACKNOWLEDGMENTS

This study was supported by the Harvard Center for Work, Health, and Well-being and the National Institute of Occupational Safety and Health (grant: U19-OH008861), the MIT Good Companies, Good Jobs Initiative, the MIT Sloan Health Systems Initiative, and the Washington Center for Equitable Growth.

The authors thank all research participants from Sigma and all members of the research team, including Meg Lovejoy, Dena Javadi, and Grace DeHorn.

Note. The contents of this publication are solely the responsibility of the authors and do not necessarily represent the official views of any of these institutions or offices.

CONFLICTS OF INTEREST

The authors declare no conflicts of interest.

HUMAN PARTICIPANT PROTECTION

Ethics approval was given by the Committee on the Use of Humans as Experimental Subjects at Massachusetts Institute of Technology (protocol: 200800024).

REFERENCES

1. Ahonen EQ, Fujishiro K, Cunningham T, Flynn M. Work as an inclusive part of population health inequities research and prevention. *Am J Public Health.* 2018;108(3):306–311. https://doi.org/10.2105/AJPH.2017.304214
2. Landsbergis PA, Choi B, Dobson M, et al. The key role of work in population health inequities. *Am J Public Health.* 2018;108(3):296–297. https://doi.org/10.2105/AJPH.2017.304288
3. Frank J, Mustard C, Smith P, et al. Work as a social determinant of health in high-income countries: past, present, and future. *Lancet.* 2023;402(10410):1357–1367. https://doi.org/10.1016/S0140-6736(23)00871-1
4. Lovejoy M, Kelly EL, Kubzansky LD, Berkman LF. Work redesign for the 21st century: promising strategies for enhancing worker well-being. *Am J Public Health.* 2021;111(10):1787–1795. https://doi.org/10.2105/AJPH.2021.306283
5. Laditka JN, Laditka SB, Arif AA, Adeyemi OJ. Psychological distress is more common in some occupations and increases with job tenure: a thirty-seven year panel study in the United States. *BMC Psychol.* 2023;11(1):95. https://doi.org/10.1186/s40359-023-01119-0
6. Kubzansky LD, Thurston RC. Emotional vitality and incident coronary heart disease: benefits of healthy psychological functioning. *Arch Gen Psychiatry.* 2007;64(12):1393–1401. https://doi.org/10.1001/archpsyc.64.12.1393
7. Kupferberg A, Bicks L, Hasler G. Social functioning in major depressive disorder. *Neurosci Biobehav Rev.* 2016;69:313–332. https://doi.org/10.1016/j.neubiorev.2016.07.002
8. de Graaf R, Tuithof M, van Dorsselaer S, ten Have M. Comparing the effects on work performance of mental and physical disorders. *Soc Psychiatry Psychiatr Epidemiol.* 2012;47(11):1873–1883. https://doi.org/10.1007/s00127-012-0496-7
9. Kessler RC, Frank RG. The impact of psychiatric disorders on work loss days. *Psychol Med.* 1997;27(4):861–873. https://doi.org/10.1017/S0033291797004807
10. Boehm JK, Peterson C, Kivimaki M, Kubzansky L. A prospective study of positive psychological well-being and coronary heart disease. *Health Psychol.* 2011;30(3):259–267. https://doi.org/10.1037/a0023124
11. Boehm JK, Kubzansky LD. The heart's content: the association between positive psychological well-being and cardiovascular health. *Psychol Bull.* 2012;138(4):655–691. https://doi.org/10.1037/a0027448
12. Boehm JK, Kivimaki M, Trudel-Fitzgerald C, Kubzansky LD. The prospective association between positive psychological well-being and diabetes. *Health Psychol.* 2015;34(10):1013–1021. https://doi.org/10.1037/hea0000200
13. Lambiase MJ, Kubzansky LD, Thurston RC. Positive psychological health and stroke risk: the benefits of emotional vitality. *Health Psychol.* 2015;34(10):1043–1046. https://doi.org/10.1037/hea0000228
14. Sorensen G, Peters S, Nielsen K, et al. Improving working conditions to promote worker safety, health, and well-being for low-wage workers: the workplace organizational health study. *Int J Environ Res Public Health.* 2019;16(8):1449. https://doi.org/10.3390/ijerph16081449
15. Chari R, Chang CC, Sauter SL, et al. Expanding the paradigm of occupational safety and health: a new framework for worker well-being. *J Occup Environ Med.* 2018;60(7):589–593. https://doi.org/10.1097/JOM.0000000000001330
16. VanderWeele TJ, Chen Y, Long K, Kim ES, Trudel-Fitzgerald C, Kubzansky LD. Positive epidemiology? *Epidemiology.* 2020;31(2):189–193. https://doi.org/10.1097/EDE.0000000000001147
17. Hammer LB. The interplay of workplace redesign and public policy in the 21st century. *Am J Public Health.* 2021;111(10):1784–1786. https://doi.org/10.2105/AJPH.2021.306368
18. Mäkikangas A, Aunola K, Seppälä P, Hakanen J. Work engagement-team performance relationship: shared job crafting as a moderator. *J Occup Organ Psychol.* 2016;89(4):772–790. https://doi.org/10.1111/joop.12154
19. Schulte PA, Guerin RJ, Schill AL, et al. Considerations for incorporating "well-being" in public policy for workers and workplaces. *Am J Public Health.* 2015;105(8):e31–e44. https://doi.org/10.2105/AJPH.2015.302616
20. Berkman LF, Kelly EL, Hammer LB, et al. Employee cardiometabolic risk following a cluster-randomized workplace intervention from the Work, Family and Health Network, 2009–2013. *Am J Public Health.* 2023;113(12):1322–1331. https://doi.org/10.2105/AJPH.2023.307413
21. Karasek RA. Job demands, job decision latitude, and mental strain: implications for job redesign. *Adm Sci Q.* 1979;24(2):285. https://doi.org/10.2307/2392498
22. Fox KE, Johnson ST, Berkman LF, et al. Organisational- and group-level workplace interventions and their effect on multiple domains of worker well-being: a systematic review. *Work Stress.* 2022;36(1):30–59. https://doi.org/10.1080/02678373.2021.1969476
23. Egan M, Bambra C, Petticrew M, Whitehead M. Reviewing evidence on complex social interventions: appraising implementation in systematic reviews of the health effects of organisational-level workplace interventions. *J Epidemiol Community Health.* 2009;63(1):4–11. https://doi.org/10.1136/jech.2007.071233
24. Kossek EE, Thompson RJ, Lawson KM, et al. Caring for the elderly at work and home: can a randomized organizational intervention improve psychological health? *J Occup Health Psychol.* 2019;24(1):36–54. https://doi.org/10.1037/ocp0000104
25. Rugulies R, Aust B, Greiner BA, et al. Work-related causes of mental health conditions and interventions for their improvement in workplaces. *Lancet.* 2023;402(10410):1368–1381. https://doi.org/10.1016/S0140-6736(23)00869-3
26. Wilkinson A, Dundon T, Donaghey J, Freeman RB. Employee voice: bridging new terrains and disciplinary boundaries. In: *Handbook of Research on Employee Voice.* Cheltenham, England: Edward Elgar Publishing; 2020:2–18. https://doi.org/10.4337/9781788971188.00007
27. Boxall P, Macky K. Research and theory on high-performance work systems: progressing the high-involvement stream. *Human Res Mgmt Journal.* 2009;19(1):3–23. https://doi.org/10.1111/j.1748-8583.2008.00082.x
28. Avgar AC, Sekwao S, Strom P. Voice in the mutual gains organization. In: Wilkinson A, Donaghey J, Dundon T, Freeman RB, eds. *Handbook of Research on Employee Voice.* 2nd ed. Cheltenham, England: Edward Elgar Publishing; 2020:362–377.
29. Hirschman AO. *Exit, Voice, and Loyalty: Responses to Decline in Firms, Organizations, and States.* Cambridge, MA: Harvard University Press; 1970.
30. Appelbaum E, ed. *Manufacturing Advantage: Why High-Performance Work Systems Pay Off.* Ithaca, NY: Cornell University Press; 2000.

31. Díaz-Linhart Y, Kochan T, Minster A, Park D, Yang D. Does voice gap influence workers' job attitudes and well-being? Measuring voice as a dimension of job quality. *Br J Ind Relat.* 2025;63(3):429–444. https://doi.org/10.1111/bjir.12866

32. Ryan RM, Deci EL. Self-determination theory and the facilitation of intrinsic motivation, social development, and well-being. *Am Psychol.* 2000;55(1):68–78. https://doi.org/10.1037//0003-066x.55.1.68

33. Budd JW. *Employment With a Human Face: Balancing Efficiency, Equity, and Voice.* Ithaca, NY: Cornell University Press; 2004.

34. Böckerman P, Bryson A, Ilmakunnas P. Does high involvement management improve worker well-being? *J Econ Behav Organ.* 2012;84(2):660–680. https://doi.org/10.1016/j.jebo.2012.09.005

35. Deci EL, Ryan RM. Autonomy and need satisfaction in close relationships: relationships motivation theory. In: Weinstein N, ed. *Human Motivation and Interpersonal Relationships: Theory, Research, and Applications.* Dordrecht, Netherlands: Springer; 2014:53–73. https://doi.org/10.1007/978-94-017-8542-6_3

36. Kerrissey MJ, Hayirli TC, Bhanja A, Stark N, Hardy J, Peabody CR. How psychological safety and feeling heard relate to burnout and adaptation amid uncertainty. *Health Care Manage Rev.* 2022;47(4):308–316. https://doi.org/10.1097/HMR.0000000000000338

37. Shipton H, Kougiannou N, Do H, Minbashian A, Pautz N, King D. Organisational voice and employee-focused voice: two distinct voice forms and their effects on burnout and innovative behavior. *Human Res Mgmt Journal.* 2024;34(1):177–196. https://doi.org/10.1111/1748-8583.12518

38. Weiss M, Zacher H. Why and when does voice lead to increased job engagement? The role of perceived voice appreciation and emotional stability. *J Vocat Behav.* 2022;132:103662. https://doi.org/10.1016/j.jvb.2021.103662

39. Wood S. Job characteristics, employee voice and well-being in Britain. *Ind Relat J.* 2008;39(2):153–168. https://doi.org/10.1111/j.1468-2338.2007.00482.x

40. Röllmann LF, Weiss M, Zacher H. Does voice benefit or harm occupational well-being? The role of job insecurity. *British J of Management.* 2021;32(3):708–724. https://doi.org/10.1111/1467-8551.12471

41. Adhvaryu A, Molina T, Nyshadham A. Expectations, wage hikes and worker voice. *Econ J.* 2022;132(645):1978–1993. https://doi.org/10.1093/ej/ueac001

42. Harju J, Jager S, Schoefer B. Voice at work. Cambridge, MA: National Bureau of Economic Research; 2024. https://doi.org/10.3386/w28522

43. Pudrovska T, Karraker A. Gender, job authority, and depression. *J Health Soc Behav.* 2014;55(4):424–441. https://doi.org/10.1177/0022146514555223

44. Vermeulen M, Mustard C. Gender differences in job strain, social support at work, and psychological distress. *J Occup Health Psychol.* 2000;5(4):428–440. https://doi.org/10.1037//1076-8998.5.4.428.

45. Clumeck N, Kempenaers C, Godin I, et al. Working conditions predict incidence of long-term spells of sick leave due to depression: results from the Belstress I prospective study. *J Epidemiol Community Health.* 2009;63(4):286–292. https://doi.org/10.1136/jech.2008.079384

46. Pohrt A, Fodor D, Burr H, Kendel F. Appreciation and job control predict depressive symptoms: results from the Study on Mental Health at Work. *Int Arch Occup Environ Health.* 2022;95(2):377–387. https://doi.org/10.1007/s00420-021-01735-6

47. Han X, VanHeuvelen T, Mortimer JT, Parolin Z. Cumulative unionization and physical health disparities among older adults. *J Health Soc Behav.* 2024;65(2):162–181. https://doi.org/10.1177/00221465231205266

48. Poupin P, Caille A, Gana W, Fougère B, Giraudeau B. Cluster randomized trials in nursing homes should better be planned as open-cohort than as closed-cohort. *J Clin Epidemiol.* 2023;161:1–7. https://doi.org/10.1016/j.jclinepi.2023.06.016

49. Sabbath EL, Lovejoy M, Schneider DK, Diaz-Linhart Y, DeHorn G, Peters SE. Engaging low-wage workers in health and well-being survey research: strategies from 5 occupational studies. *Am J Public Health.* 2025;115(2):201–208. https://doi.org/10.2105/AJPH.2024.307875

50. Milgate N, Innes E, O'Loughlin K. Examining the effectiveness of health and safety committees and representatives: a review. *Work.* 2002;19(3):281–290. https://doi.org/10.3233/WOR-2002-00263

51. von Thiele Schwarz U, Augustsson H, Hasson H, Stenfors-Hayes T. Promoting employee health by integrating health protection, health promotion, and continuous improvement: a longitudinal quasi-experimental intervention study. *J Occup Environ Med.* 2015;57(2):217–225. https://doi.org/10.1097/JOM.0000000000000344

52. Kelly EL, Siebach KF, DeHorn G, Lovejoy M. The Fulfillment Center Intervention Study: protocol for a group-randomized control trial of a participatory workplace intervention. *PLoS One.* 2024;19(7):e0305334. https://doi.org/10.1371/journal.pone.0305334

53. Kessler RC, Barker PR, Colpe LJ, et al. Screening for serious mental illness in the general population. *Arch Gen Psychiatry.* 2003;60(2):184–189. https://doi.org/10.1001/archpsyc.60.2.184

54. Prochaska JJ, Sung H, Max W, Shi Y, Ong M. Validity study of the K6 scale as a measure of moderate mental distress based on mental health treatment need and utilization. *Int J Methods Psychiatr Res.* 2012;21(2):88–97. https://doi.org/10.1002/mpr.1349

55. R Core Team. R: A Language and Environment for Statistical Computing. 2023. Available at: https://www.R-project.org. Accessed March 1, 2025.

56. National Center for Health Statistics. National Health Interview Survey. 2021. Available at: https://www.cdc.gov/nchs/nhis/documentation/2021-nhis.html. Accessed January 15, 2025.

57. Cohen J. *Statistical Power Analysis for the Behavioral Sciences.* 2nd ed. London, England: Taylor and Francis; 2013.

58. Karanika-Murray M, Biron C, eds. *Derailed Organizational Interventions for Stress and Well-Being: Confessions of Failure and Solutions for Success.* Dordrecht, Netherlands: Springer; 2015. https://doi.org/10.1007/978-94-017-9867-9

59. Rojatz D, Merchant A, Nitsch M. Factors influencing workplace health promotion intervention: a qualitative systematic review. *Health Promot Int.* 2017;32(5):831–839. https://doi.org/10.1093/heapro/daw015

60. Hayes RJ, Moulton LH. *Cluster Randomised Trials.* 2nd ed. London, England: CRC Press; 2017. https://doi.org/10.4324/9781315370286

61. Nielsen K, Randall R. Opening the black box: presenting a model for evaluating organizational-level interventions. *Eur J Work Organ Psychol.* 2013;22(5):601–617. https://doi.org/10.1080/1359432X.2012.690556

62. *The US Surgeon General's Framework for Workplace Mental Health & Well-Being.* Washington, DC: The Office of the US Surgeon General; 2022.

Context and Disclosure of Sexual Orientation and Gender Identity Information Among US Adults, 2021

Thomas E. Schlechter, MS, Bradley T. Conner, PhD, Asher C. Allen, Anthony T. Pho, PhD, Nancy Bates, MS, Rachel Logan, PhD, MPH, Annesa Flentje, PhD, Micah E. Lubensky, PhD, Mitchell R. Lunn, MD, MAS, and Juno Obedin-Maliver, MD, MPH

Objectives. To investigate if anticipated survey context (e.g., national government health survey, local community health survey, health care provider form) would affect participants' likelihood of (1) responding to sexual orientation, gender identity, sex assigned at birth, and intersex status (SOGISI) questions or (2) changing their responses to SOGISI questions.

Methods. We performed an online study of people across sexual orientations and gender identities in the United States (n = 851) testing the hypotheses that individuals with minoritized identity would be less likely to respond and more likely to change their responses to questions about their SOGISI identity.

Results. Overall, results were significant and in the expected direction, indicating that there was a dependent relation between identities and type of question being asked.

Conclusions. Within this sample, participants with minoritized sexual and gender identities were more likely to change their answer on the basis of the context of data collection, highlighting important considerations for individuals who utilize surveys to collect SOGISI data.

Public Health Implications. Results from this study can be used to provide recommendations for questions to use in surveys for collection of SOGISI data and important considerations when collecting data from sexual and gender minorities. (*Am J Public Health*. 2026;116(4):533–543. https://doi.org/10.2105/AJPH.2025.308376)

AJPH April 2026, Vol. 116, No. 4

Sexual orientation, gender identity, sex assigned at birth, and intersex status (hereafter referred to as SOGISI) are key demographics in research, health care, and administrative contexts. Increasing evidence demonstrates important health and social differences among those who are sexual or gender minority (SGM; i.e., those who are not exclusively heterosexual or not cisgender, often commonly referred to as lesbian, gay, bisexual, transgender, and queer plus [LGBTQ+] community members) and non-SGM populations.

Little work has addressed how SOGISI disclosure may differ among SGM and non-SGM populations across different contexts. Identity disclosure can carry risks such as discrimination or harassment not experienced by non-SGM populations.[1] Previous research found that SGM people were more likely to report concerns regarding personal safety and the potential to change their answers compared with non-SGM individuals.[2] In addition, some people may express unwillingness to provide SOGISI information because of concerns around data privacy and distrust of the group conducting the survey.[1,2] With these risks of disclosure and the importance of delineating SGM people from non-SGM people for health and social research, it is important to understand if people may choose not to disclose or choose to change their answers to SOGISI questions depending on the context in which SOGISI questions are being asked.

SGM communities face unique stressors related to being SGM in a society that centers cisgender and heterosexual people.[3,4] Research on SGM people's willingness to disclose SOGISI information has found identity concealment, expectations of rejection, experiences of identity-based discrimination, and violence as additional motivations for SGM people to not answer SOGISI questions or not answer them truthfully.[1,5–7] SGM communities experience stress in unique ways,[8–11] and as such, different SGM communities appear to navigate disclosure differently. Existing research has found that plurisexual (e.g., bisexual, pansexual, and queer) individuals report less willingness to disclose SOGISI information compared with monosexual (e.g., gay and lesbian) individuals.[5,6,12–14]

Gender minority individuals face unique barriers compared with sexual minority individuals in disclosing their gender identity, especially in socially gendered spaces (e.g., athletics, gender-segregated facilities).[7,15] Studies have found a decreased willingness to disclose SOGISI among people who are SGM and from minoritized racial/ethnic groups compared with SGM–White individuals.[7,16] SOGISI disclosure research found contextual factors, such as the setting of data collection or the question format, to affect individuals' willingness to disclose.[7,13,17,18] One method that participants may choose to not disclose their SGM identity is by changing their answers to SOGISI questions to not endorse a minoritized sexual or gender identity.[19]

THE PRESENT STUDY

To investigate if and how context may influence participants' intention to change their answers to SOGISI questions, we conducted a study of SGM and non-SGM people to understand if the anticipated survey context (e.g., national government health survey, local community health survey, health care provider form) would affect participants' likelihood of (1) responding to the questions or (2) changing their response to SOGISI questions in light of anticipated context. Considering previous research on SOGISI disclosure across contexts and identities, we hypothesized that the anticipated context would influence the response habits of all participants but that it would be most significant for SGM participants. We also predicted that there would be significant differences in such effects between subgroups within SGM communities. We hypothesized that SGM individuals would report a significantly higher likelihood of changing their answers depending on context and would have a significantly lower likelihood of answering identity questions compared with their nonminoritized peers.

METHODS

This study was part of a larger study working to refine SOGISI questions for large sample data collection in the United States (NIH R21MD015878). Participants for this study were recruited through a convenience sample of adults (aged 18 years or older) in the United States with a diverse representation of sexual orientations, gender identities, ages, races, ethnicities, geographic regions, and socioeconomic statuses. Inclusion criteria for this substudy were being aged 18 years or older, having the ability to read and write in English, having a valid e-mail address, having completed the screening survey, and having provided participation consent. People were excluded if they were participants in a concurrent cohort study led by the study principal investigator (PI), if they had completed cognitive interviews associated with this study, or if they were members of the PI's longitudinal cohort, because that cohort was exposed to other study components apart from the work described here.

Procedure

The sample for this online survey was drawn from a convenience sample that was constructed through digital Internet periodicals (e.g., newspapers, magazines) and social media (i.e., Facebook, Instagram, Twitter) advertisements. Participants were informed that, after a screening survey, they may be invited to participate in an interview (60–90 minutes) or an online survey (15 minutes)—mutually exclusive. If selected to participate in the online survey, individuals would be compensated with a $5 gift card upon completion. Interested participants were presented with consent materials, and those wishing to proceed completed an eligibility screening survey. All prospective screening survey results were reviewed, and those who met eligibility criteria were invited to participate in the online survey. Upon completion of the online survey, after the removal of duplicate and implausible entries, the study staff then distributed $5 electronic gift cards to eligible study participants.

Survey and Measures

The survey was developed and piloted among a group of adult study staff, trainees, researchers, and community members.[20] In addition to demographics, participants were presented with 5 different identity domain questions described in the next section. After each identity question (total of 10 questions in 5 domains), participants were asked follow-up questions, including "Would you change your answer to this question depending on the setting?"

Identity Domains

Sexual and gender minority status questions. The 2 versions of questions asking participants if they identify as a SGM person were "Do you identify as LGBTQ?" and "Are you LGBTQ?" Participants could answer "yes," "no," or "decline to answer" to each question.

Sexual orientation questions. The 2 versions of questions asking participants to describe their sexual orientation were "What is your current sexual orientation? (Select all that apply)" and "What is your sexual orientation? (Select all that apply)." Participants were given 11 answer choices and could select as many as personally appropriate. The answer options were *"asexual," "bisexual," "gay," "lesbian," "pansexual," "queer," "questioning," "same gender loving," "straight/heterosexual," "Two-Spirit," and "another sexual orientation."* Two-Spirit was included in both sexual orientation and gender identity for this study after we consulted with Indigenous researchers. Community members noted that, as a concept, Two-Spirit is different from either sexual orientation or gender identity alone but is related to both concepts and should thus be included within both domains.[21] Participants who indicated the "another sexual orientation" answer choice could provide a write-in answer. Participants could also decline to answer either question.

Gender identity questions. The 2 versions of questions asking participants to describe their gender identity were "What is your current gender identity? (Select all that apply)" and "What is your gender? (Select all that apply)." Participants were given 12 answer choices and could select as many as appropriate. Answer options were agender, cisgender man, cisgender woman, genderqueer, man, nonbinary, questioning, transgender man, transgender woman, Two-Spirit, woman, another gender identity, and an option to decline to answer. Participants who indicated the "another gender identity" answer choice could provide a write-in answer.

Sex assigned at birth questions. The 2 versions of questions asking participants to describe their sex assigned at birth were "What sex were you assigned at birth, for example on your original birth certificate?" (answer options: female, male, another [please specify], or decline to answer) and "What sex were you assigned at birth?" (answer options: female, intersex, male, or decline to answer).

Intersex questions. The 2 versions of questions asking participants to indicate whether they were intersex were "Do you identify as intersex?" (answer options: yes, no, or decline to answer) and "Are you intersex?" (answer options: yes, no, or decline to answer). These questions were developed and have been in use by the coauthors in a related but distinct longitudinal cohort study, The PRIDE Study, since 2017.[20–23] These measures were developed in collaboration and consultation with intersex-identifying individuals as part of long-standing community-engaged research work and specifically aim to address intersex identity rather than variations in sex characteristics as described by anatomic, physiologic, or socio-clinical practice characteristics (e.g., sex assignment at birth).[20,23]

Change answer questions. Participants were asked the following 4 questions for each of the question stems for SGM status as noted previously: (1) "Would you change your answer to this question depending on the setting," (2) "I would answer the question, [question stem] on a national government health survey," (3) "I would answer the question, [question stem] on a local community health survey," and (4) "I would answer the question, [question stem] on a health care provider form." For question 1, participants could answer yes, no, or decline to answer. For questions 2 through 4, they were given a 5-point Likert-type scale with 1 anchored at strongly agree and 5 anchored at strongly disagree, and the option to decline to answer the questions.

Analyses

We analyzed all data using SPSS version 29.0.[24] Initial analyses indicated less than 5% missing data on all variables, so missing data were addressed using listwise deletion. Given that participants were not randomly assigned to identities and that many of the outcome variables were highly skewed, we used nonparametric methods for independent samples to analyze all data.[25] When the outcome variable was dichotomous, we ran χ^2 analyses to determine the dependency between identity and propensity to answer the identity question. When the predictor variable had only 2 levels, we ran Mann–Whitney *U* analyses. When the predictor variable had more than 2 levels, we ran Kruskal–Wallis analyses.

For each of 5 identity domains (i.e., SGM status, sexual orientation, gender identity, sex assigned at birth, and intersex status), we analyzed differences in responses to the follow-up questions. The predictor variable was based on the identity domain question version being analyzed. For example, when the dependent variable pertained to SGM identity domain, the 2-level predictor variable was LGBTQ+ versus non-LGBTQ+ identity. Furthermore, when the questions pertained to sexual orientation identity domain, the 2-level predictor variable was exclusively heterosexual versus nonheterosexual sexual orientation. Within the sexual orientation variable, we also compared nonheterosexual individuals with those who identified as exclusively gay or lesbian versus identified with a plurisexual identity. When the questions pertained to gender identity domain, the 2-level predictor variable was exclusively cisgender versus gender minority identity. When the questions pertained to the domain of sex assigned at birth, the 3-level predictor variable was another, female, or male as response options for the first question or female, intersex, and male as the response options for the second question (Table D, available as a supplement to the online version of this article at https://www.ajph.org). When the questions pertained just to intersex, the 2-level predictor variable was intersex versus nonintersex. Interpretation of significant χ^2s in the χ^2 analyses suggested dependence between the variables in the analysis, and directionality was interpreted by comparing observed and expected values. Given the number of analyses run, α was set to 0.01.

RESULTS

A total of 2001 people initiated the screening survey. Among those, 1463 were deemed eligible and invited to participate in the online survey. A total of 851 completed the online survey sufficiently for inclusion in this analysis. The median time survey completion time was 10.9 minutes.

Demographic data are presented in Table 1. Descriptive data for the collapsed identities are presented in Table 2. Proportions for responses to all prompts are presented in Table 3. Frequencies for responses can be found in Table A (available as a supplement to the online version of this article at https://ajph.org). Results from χ^2 analyses indicated significant dependencies between all identities of interest and participants' willingness to

TABLE 1— Demographic Variables for the Total Sample: United States, 2021

	Mean ±SD or No. (%)
Age (range = 18–71; median = 36), y	36.8 ±12.7
Gender identity	
Agender	2 (0.2)
Cisgender man/man[a]	59 (6.9)
Cisgender woman/woman[a]	139 (16.3)
Genderqueer	7 (0.8)
Man[a]	186 (21.9)
Nonbinary	15 (1.8)
Questioning	1 (0.1)
Transgender man/man[a]	8 (0.9)
Transgender woman/woman[a]	1 (0.1)
Two-Spirit	0 (0)
Woman[a]	336 (39.5)
Another gender	1 (0.1)
More than 1 gender	52 (6.1)
Decline to answer	2 (0.2)
Sex assigned at birth	
Female	546 (66.4)
Intersex	10 (1.2)
Male	258 (31.3)
Decline to answer	9 (1.1)

Continued

TABLE 1— Continued

	Mean ±SD or No. (%)
Sexual orientation	
Asexual	20 (2.4)
Bisexual	98 (11.5)
Gay	61 (7.2)
Lesbian	33 (3.9)
Pansexual	18 (2.1)
Queer	18 (2.1)
Questioning	4 (0.5)
Same-gender loving	1 (0.1)
Straight/heterosexual	510 (58.9)
Two-Spirit	0 (0)
Another sexual orientation	1 (0.1)
More than 1 sexual orientation	96 (11.2)
Decline to answer	0 (0)
Race/ethnicity	
American Indian/Alaska Native	8 (0.9)
Asian	115 (13.5)
Black	170 (20)
Hispanic, Latino/x, or Spanish	44 (5.2)
Middle Eastern or North African	3 (0.4)
Native Hawaiian or other Pacific Islander	1 (0.1)
White	426 (50.1)
More than 1 race and/or ethnicity	81 (9.5)
None of these describe me	3 (0.4)
Decline to answer	0 (0)

Note. Categories are mutually exclusive though participants were allowed to check as many identities as they wanted. The "More than 1" category for each demographic variable is a count of every participant who checked more than 1 box for that variable. The sample size was n = 851.
[a]For gender identity, the cisgender man/man category represents all participants who checked either cisgender man or cisgender man and man, man represents participants who checked only man, and transgender man/man represents participants who checked transgender man or transgender man and man; the cisgender woman/woman category represents all participants who checked either cisgender woman or cisgender woman and woman, woman represents participants who checked only woman, and transgender woman/woman represents participants who checked transgender woman or transgender woman and woman.

answer questions in different contexts, except when comparing plurisexual to gay or lesbian (monosexual). In the analysis among these nonheterosexual groups (plurisexual compared with monosexual), the directionality was in the expected direction, but *P* values were greater than .01 (Table 4). All significant results were in the expected direction, with the minoritized identity significantly associated with a higher likelihood of changing their answer to identity questions.

Results from Mann–Whitney *U* analyses when the predictor variable was LGBTQ+ identity indicated no significant differences between those who identified as LGBTQ+ and those who did not on the likelihood that they would answer all 3 of the context questions regardless of the 2 types of question prompts (Table C, available as a supplement to the online version of this article at https://ajph.org).

By contrast, when the predictor variable was sexual orientation, results from Mann–Whitney *U* analyses indicated significant differences between those who identify as exclusively heterosexual and those who do not on the likelihood that they would answer all 3 of the context questions regardless of the 2 types of question prompts (Table C). Results were inconsistent when comparing those who identified as plurisexual with those who exclusively identified as gay or lesbian. Although results were in the expected direction, with significant findings showing

TABLE 2— Descriptive Information for Combined Demographic Categories: United States, 2021

	No. (%)
SGM	
LGBTQ+	344 (41.0)
Non-LGBTQ+	496 (59.0)
Gender identity	
Cisgender	741 (87.1)
Gender minority	99 (11.6)
Intersex	
Intersex	27 (3.4)
Non-intersex/endosex	758 (96.6)
Sexual orientation	
Straight/heterosexual	350 (41.1)
Nonheterosexual	490 (57.6)
Plurisexual	207 (66.8)
Monosexual (gay/lesbian)	103 (33.2)

Note. LGBTQ+ = lesbian, gay, bisexual, transgender, and queer plus; SGM = sexual and gender minority. LGBTQ+ was coded as a combination of sexual orientation and gender identity so that non-LGBTQ+ was composed of those who identified as exclusively straight/heterosexual and cisgender whereas LGBTQ+ was composed of all participants who endorsed expansive sexual orientation and expansive gender identity. Gender identity was dichotomized into cisgender versus gender minority, which was composed of all gender identities other than cisgender man, cisgender man and man, cisgender woman, and cisgender woman and woman. Sexual orientation was dichotomized into straight/heterosexual versus all expansive sexual orientations, labeled nonheterosexual. Among those in the nonheterosexual group, further analyses were run for those who identified as monosexual, defined as identifying as gay or lesbian, versus those who identified as plurisexual, which is composed of those in the nonheterosexual group who identified as having an expansive sexual orientation identity (note that asexual, questioning straight/heterosexual, and same-gender-loving were excluded from these categorizations).

plurisexual people being more likely to change their answers depending on context, this was different by prompt. Plurisexual participants reported being more likely to change their answers when anticipating a health care provider form for prompt 1 and when anticipating either a health care provider form or national government survey for prompt 2.

Results from Mann–Whitney *U* analyses when the predictor variable was gender identity indicated significant differences in the expected direction between those who identified as exclusively cisgender and those who did not on the likelihood that they would answer all 3 of the questions regardless of the 2 types of questions (Table C).

Results from Kruskal–Wallis analyses when the predictor variable was sex assigned at birth indicated significant anticipated disclosure differences by location between those who were presumably endosex (i.e., not intersex)[26] and identified as female or male and those who identified as intersex regardless of the 2 question prompts (Table C). Results were in the anticipated direction with those who identified as intersex reporting a lower likelihood of answering questions across all types of surveys for the first prompt but not the second compared with those assigned female and male.

Results from Mann–Whitney *U* analyses when the predictor variable was intersex indicated significant differences between those who identified as intersex and those who did not identify as intersex on the likelihood that they would answer some of the 3 questions for both prompts (Table C). Results were generally in the anticipated direction with those who identified as intersex reporting a higher rate of not answering the question on a health care provider form for the first prompt and the national health survey and health care provider form for the second prompt compared with those who did not identify as intersex (presumably endosex).

DISCUSSION

In the present study, we sought to investigate if and how anticipated SOGISI question context may influence whether participants intend to change their answers to SOGISI questions. Results supported most of our hypotheses in that the anticipated context (i.e., health care provider form, national government survey, or local community health survey) had some amount of influence for all respondents but was more significant for SGM individuals. All comparisons between non-SGM and SGM folks highlighted that context played a more significant role in whether the participant would answer the question for SGM individuals. Most subgroup analyses supported previous research that has illuminated multiple marginalized subgroups within the LGBTQ+ community such as transgender, intersex, and gender-expansive communities may be more likely to not answer or change their answers on the basis of context.[7,13,27] Across contexts, the propensity for participants to change answers and the willingness to answer questions were consistent across SGM

TABLE 3— Proportions of Responses to Identity Status Questions by 2 Different Question Prompts: United States, 2021

	Answer to Follow-Up Context Question 1: "Would You Change Your Answer to This [Question Stem] Depending on the Setting?",[a] % Yes/% No
SGM	
Prompt 1: "Do you identify as LGBTQ?"	
LGBTQ+	49.1/49.4
Non-LGBTQ+	10.3/89.7
Prompt 2: "Are you LGBTQ?"	
LGBTQ+	48.3/51.7
Non-LGBTQ+	11.7/88.3
Sexual orientation	
Prompt 1: "What is your current sexual orientation?"	
Heterosexual	15.7/84.3
Nonheterosexual	50.9/49.1
SM: plurisexual	55.4/44.6
SM: gay/lesbian	45.5/54.5
Prompt 2: "What is your sexual orientation?"	
Heterosexual	15.2/84.8
Nonheterosexual	51.0/49.0
SM: plurisexual	53.9/46.1
SM: gay/lesbian	44.6/55.4
Gender identity	
Prompt 1: "What is your current gender identity?"	
Cisgender	13.5/86.5
Gender minority	64.6/31.3
Prompt 2: "What is your gender?"	
Cisgender	15.2/84.8
Gender minority	66.0/34.0
Sex assigned at birth	
Prompt 1: "What sex were you assigned at birth, for example on your original birth certificate?"	
Female	15.1/84.9
Another (please specify)	80.0/20.0
Male	10.3/89.7
Prompt 2: "What sex were you assigned at birth?"	
Female	12.9/87.1
Intersex	70.0/30.0
Male	10.5/89.5
Intersex	
Prompt 1: "Do you identify as intersex?"	
Intersex	48.1/51.9
Nonintersex/endosex	8.7/91.3
Prompt 2: "Are you intersex?"	
Intersex	33.3/66.7
Nonintersex/endosex	9.0/91.0

Note. LGBTQ+ = lesbian, gay, bisexual, transgender, and queer plus; SGM = sexual and gender minority; SM = sexual minority. Group composition is described in the notes for Table 2. Additional data for follow-up questions can be found in Table B (available as a supplement to the online version of this article at https://ajph.org).
[a]Answers were "Yes," "No," or "Decline to Answer."

TABLE 4— Association Between Probability of Changing an Answer to a Question About SOGISI identity and Respondent Identity Status: United States, 2021

	No. of Responses		
	Yes, Observed (Expected)	No, Observed (Expected)	χ^2 (*df* = 1); *P*
SGM			
Prompt 1: "Do you identify as LGBTQ+?"			158.26; <.001
LGBTQ+	172 (93.1)	173 (251.9)	
Non-LGBTQ+	49 (127.9)	425 (346.1)	
Prompt 2: "Are you LGBTQ?"			135.44; <.001
LGBTQ+	167 (93.8)	179 (252.2)	
Non-LGBTQ+	56 (129.2)	421 (347.8)	
Sexual orientation			
Prompt 1: "What is your current sexual orientation?"			
Heterosexual	75 (144.5)	403 (333.5)	115.95; <.001
Nonheterosexual	171 (101.5)	165 (234.5)	
SM: plurisexual	112 (105.3)	46 (52.7)	2.65; <.1
SM: gay/lesbian	90 (96.7)	55 (48.3)	
Prompt 2: What is your sexual orientation?"			
Heterosexual	73 (140.2)	408 (340.8)	109.95; <.001
Nonheterosexual	166 (98.8)	173 (240.2)	
SM: plurisexual	110 (103.7)	94 (100.3)	2.37; .08
SM: gay/lesbian	45 (51.3)	56 (49.7)	
Gender identity			
Prompt 1: "What is your current gender identity?"			152.26; <.001
Cisgender	97 (142.1)	619 (573.9)	
Gender minority	64 (18.9)	31 (76.1)	
Prompt 2: "What is your gender?"			131.63; <.001
Cisgender	56 (152.4)	608 (564.6)	
Gender minority	64 (20.6)	33 (76.4)	
Sex assigned at birth			
Prompt 1: "What sex were you assigned at birth, for example on your original birth certificate?"			33.83; <.001
Another	4 (0.5)	0 (3.5)	
Female	44 (33.8)	220 (230.2)	
Male	56 (69.7)	488 (474.3)	
Prompt 2: "What sex were you assigned at birth?"			109.95; <.001
Female	30.6 (255.0)	222 (224.4)	
Intersex	7 (1.2)	3 (8.8)	
Male	57 (65.2)	487 (478.8)	
Intersex			
Prompt 1: "Do you identify as intersex?"			59.64; <.001
Intersex	18 (3.9)	19 (33.1)	
Nonintersex/endosex	65 (79.1)	684 (669.9)	
Prompt 2: "Are you intersex?"			88.07; <.001
Intersex	18 (3.0)	9 (24.0)	
Nonintersex/endosex	67 (82.0)	681 (666.0)	

Note. LGBTQ+ = lesbian, gay, bisexual, transgender, and queer plus; SGM = sexual and gender minority; SM = sexual minority; SOGISI = sexual orientation, gender identity, sex assigned at birth, and intersex status. Results are from χ^2 analyses. Groups are mutually exclusive, such that, if participants checked more than 1 identity for any demographic variable, they are in the minoritized group (e.g., the heterosexual group is composed of those participants who checked only heterosexual, whereas the nonheterosexual group is composed of anyone who checked anything other than heterosexual even if they also checked heterosexual, the cisgender group is composed of those participants who only selected cisgender, the gender minority group is composed of those participants who checked anything other than cisgender even if they also checked cisgender).

status, sexual orientation questions, and gender identity questions. However, the likelihood changed with sex assigned at birth and intersex questions by individual setting. Such results are likely attributable to low within-group sample size, but it does provide evidence of lower disclosure rates among intersex and transgender individuals.

Such results point to the importance of the questions used and the setting in which the questions are being asked when collecting SOGISI information. Although this has been explored in previous work,[7,13,19] the results reported here provide quantitative evidence from a large sample that SGM individuals are taking these contextual factors into account when deciding if and how to answer SOGISI questions. These findings support previous findings from focus groups and cognitive interviews that have identified the potential for SGM individuals to consider changing their answers on the basis of the setting and question stems used.[19,28] It is essential for researchers and others collecting SOGISI information to consider these contextual factors when selecting SOGISI questions. Previous research on the setting of data collection has highlighted that individuals across genders and sexualities may be more comfortable sharing SOGISI information when they feel it is relevant, such as to a health care provider as compared with a federal survey.[17] Our results provide further evidence of the potential that SGM individuals may anticipate changing their answers to these questions on the basis of context, and thus, survey designers, administrators, and those reviewing the results of surveys need to be aware of this phenomenon. Furthermore, more work needs to be done to understand how to bolster participant feelings of comfort, safety, and, thus, stability of answer choices to build meaningful population-based and health-related estimates.

Strengths and Limitations

The results of this study are strengthened by its large sample size, which is diverse in terms of race, ethnicity, age, and SGM status. It is also one of the first studies to examine how the question stems used may influence participants' willingness to answer and likelihood to change their answers. However, the sample was a cross-sectional convenience sample and, thus, may not be generalizable to all parts of the population; nor would it capture changes in identities over time that may also influence identity disclosure patterns. In addition, there are more contextual factors that may have an impact on disclosure such as what governmental or community agency is conducting the survey (e.g., Department of Health and Human services vs Department of Defense; a local non-profit organization vs a national one). Future research in this area should include more contextual factors to address these current limitations. Future research should also test other versions of intersex status questions as current recommendations provide other questions to utilize that incorporate defining intersex as well as using language of "variations of sex development" or "difference of sex development" into the question.[1,29] Our results about intersex communities are limited by the fact that the questions utilized required a participant to identify with the label "intersex." Future work should ensure including the diversity of terms utilized by people within the intersex umbrella.

While the sample included diversity across demographic characteristics, there were some sexual orientations (e.g., questioning, same-gender loving), gender identities (e.g., agender, genderqueer, Two-Spirit), and races/ethnicities (e.g., Middle Eastern/North African, American Indigenous communities) that were poorly represented compared with others, and thus, interpretation of results for such communities should be done with caution. Future research should be conducted that includes more robust representation of these communities to better understand how their individual experiences may differ.

Furthermore, disclosure of SOGISI status may be influenced by how "out" someone is with their identity or identities before the influence of context,[30] and as such, this study may not capture those who are less likely to disclose at all. Future research should consider additional ways to examine participant response patterns to address these limitations.

Lastly, all participants were given the option to decline to respond to any question. Given the lack of data that accompanies this choice and the difficulty with interpreting why someone may have chosen not to respond, these data were treated as missing and excluded from all analyses. Future research may want to address this response option differently to determine how refusing to answer questions is associated with minoritized identities.

Conclusion

Results from this study underscore the importance of considering the context and question stems used to collect SOGISI data in survey research. Analyses revealed a higher likelihood of SGM individuals across identities to not answer or change their answers on the basis of anticipated contextual factors, which poses an issue for researchers in terms of participant inclusion and data validity. Researchers must understand such factors that may increase the likelihood that SGM participants are not answering or changing their answers to SOGISI questions to continue conducting accurate, inclusive research. This is especially relevant to health-related research in the current context of attacks on gender-affirming health care and ensuring that transgender and gender-expansive experiences are accurately collected and represented in data analysis and dissemination. The results of this study can be utilized to help inform better ways to include SOGISI-related questions in survey research to better collect and create knowledge about SGM communities and their needs. AJPH

ABOUT THE AUTHORS

Thomas E. Schlechter and Bradley T. Conner are with the Department of Psychology at Colorado State University, Fort Collins. Asher Allen is with Stanford University, Stanford, CA. Anthony T. Pho was with Division of Nephrology, Department of Medicine at Stanford University School of Medicine, Stanford, CA. Nancy Bates was with the US Census Bureau (ret.), Washington, DC. Rachel Logan was with The Equity Experience LLC, Tampa, FL. Annesa Flentje and Micah E. Lubensky were with the Department of Community Health Systems at the School of Nursing at University of California, San Francisco. Mitchell R. Lunn is with Division of Nephrology, Department of Medicine at Stanford University School of Medicine. Juno Obedin-Maliver is with the Department of Obstetrics and Gynecology at Stanford University School of Medicine.

CORRESPONDENCE

Correspondence should be sent to be sent to Thomas E. Schlechter, Department of Psychology, 1876 Campus Delivery, Colorado State University, Fort Collins, CO 80523-1876 (e-mail: thomas.schlechter@colostate.edu). Reprints can be ordered at https://www.ajph.org by clicking the "Reprints" link.

PUBLICATION INFORMATION

Full Citation: Schlechter TE, Conner BT, Allen AC, et al. Context and disclosure of sexual orientation and gender identity information among US adults, 2021. *Am J Public Health*. 2026;116(4):533–543.

Acceptance Date: November 30, 2025.

DOI: https://doi.org/10.2105/AJPH.2025.308376

ORCID iDs:

Thomas E. Schlechter https://orcid.org/0000-0003-4969-7825

Bradley T. Conner https://orcid.org/0000-0001-6069-4401

Asher C. Allen https://orcid.org/0009-0007-3308-8423

Micah E. Lubensky https://orcid.org/0000-0001-8882-0967

Mitchell R. Lunn https://orcid.org/0000-0002-0068-0814

Juno Obedin-Maliver https://orcid.org/0000-0002-0945-2842

CONTRIBUTORS

T. E. Schlechter was involved with writing the original draft and reviewing and editing the final article. B. T. Conner was involved with formal analyses, supervision, writing the original draft, and reviewing and editing the final draft. N. Bates was involved in conceptualization, methodology, data acquisition, and reviewing the final draft. A. Flentje and M. R. Lunn were involved with providing resources and reviewing the final draft. J. Obedin-Maliver was involved with conceptualization, funding acquisition, investigation and methodology, project administration, supervision, and writing the original and final drafts. A. T. Pho, R. Logan, and M. E. Lubensky were involved with data acquisition and reviewing and editing the final draft. A. C. Allen was involved with reviewing and editing the final draft.

ACKNOWLEDGMENTS

Research reported in this publication was supported by the National Institutes of Minority Health and Health Disparities under award R21MD015878 to J. Obedin-Maliver, and a Patient-Centered Outcomes Research Institute (PCORI) award (PPN-1501-26848) to M. R. Lunn.

We acknowledge the courage and dedication of all participants for sharing their experiences. We also appreciate the enthusiastic engagement of PRIDEnet, a community-engaged network dedicated to enhancing the enrollment of lesbian, gay, bisexual, transgender, queer, intersex, asexual, and other sexual and gender minority (LGBTQIA+) people in research in reviewing, promotion, recruitment, and engagement materials.

Note. The statements in this article are solely the responsibility of the authors and do not necessarily represent the views of PCORI, its Board of Governors or Methodology Committee, or the National Institutes of Health.

CONFLICTS OF INTEREST

M. R. Lunn receives consulting fees from Hims Inc (2019–present), Folx Inc (2020), Otsuka Pharmaceutical Development and Commercialization Inc (2023), and the American Dental Association (2024). J. Obedin-Maliver receives consulting fees from Sage Therapeutics (2017), Ibis Reproductive Health (2017–2018, 2020–present), Hims Inc (2019–present), Folx Inc (2019–present), and Upstream Inc (2024).

HUMAN PARTICIPANT PROTECTION

This study was approved by the institutional review board at Stanford University School of Medicine.

REFERENCES

1. National Academies of Sciences, Engineering, and Medicine. *Measuring Sex, Gender Identity, and Sexual Orientation.* Washington, DC: The National Academies Press; 2022. https://doi.org/10.17226/26424
2. Pho AT, Bates N, Snow A, et al. Asking sexual orientation and gender identity on health surveys: findings from cognitive interviews in the United States across sexual orientations and genders. *SSM Qual Res Health.* 2023;4:100344. https://doi.org/10.1016/j.ssmqr.2023.100344
3. Brooks VR. *Minority Stress and Lesbian Women.* Lanham, MD: Lexington Books; 1981.
4. Meyer IH. Prejudice, social stress, and mental health in lesbian, gay, and bisexual populations: conceptual issues and research evidence. *Psychol Bull.* 2003;129(5):674–697. https://doi.org/10.1037/0033-2909.129.5.674
5. Barringer MN, Sumerau JE, Gay DA. Examining differences in identity disclosure between monosexuals and bisexuals. *Sociol Spectrum.* 2017;37(5):319–333. https://doi.org/10.1080/02732173.2017.1348276
6. Baldwin A, Dodge B, Schick V, Herbenick D, Sanders SA, Dhoot R, Fortenberry JD. Health and identity-related interactions between lesbian, bisexual, queer, and pansexual women and their healthcare providers. *Cult Health Sex.* 2017;19(11):1181–1196. https://doi.org/10.1080/13691058.2017.1298844
7. Garvey JC, Mobley SD, Summerville KS, Moore GT. Queer and trans* students of color: navigating identity disclosure and college contexts. *J Higher Educ.* 2019;90(1):150–178. https://doi.org/10.1080/00221546.2018.1449081
8. Hendricks ML, Testa RJ. A conceptual framework for clinical work with transgender and gender nonconforming clients: an adaptation of the Minority Stress Model. *Prof Psychol Res Pr.* 2012;43(5):460–467. https://doi.org/10.1037/a0029597
9. Feinstein BA, Dyar C. Bisexuality, minority stress, and health. *Curr Sex Health Rep.* 2017;9(1):42–49. https://doi.org/10.1007/s11930-017-0096-3
10. Matsuno E, Israel T. Psychological interventions promoting resilience among transgender individuals: Transgender Resilience Intervention Model (TRIM). *Couns Psychol.* 2018;46(5):632–655. https://doi.org/10.1177/0011000018787261
11. Millar K, Brooks CV. Double jeopardy: minority stress and the influence of transgender identity and race/ethnicity. *Int J Transgend Health.* 2022;23(1-2):133–148. https://doi.org/10.1080/26895269.2021.1890660

12. Durso LE, Meyer IH. Patterns and predictors of disclosure of sexual orientation to healthcare providers among lesbians, gay men, and bisexuals. *Sex Res Social Policy.* 2013;10(1):35–42. https://doi.org/10.1007/s13178-012-0105-2
13. Keene LC, Heath RD, Bouris A. Disclosure of sexual identities across social-relational contexts: findings from a national sample of Black sexual minority men. *J Racial Ethn Health Disparities.* 2022;9(1):201–214. https://doi.org/10.1007/s40615-020-00944-y
14. Feinstein BA, Hurtado M Jr, Dyar C, Davila J. Disclosure, minority stress, and mental health among bisexual, pansexual, and queer (Bi+) adults: the roles of primary sexual identity and multiple sexual identity label use. *Psychol Sex Orientat Gend Divers.* 2023;10(2):181–189. https://doi.org/10.1037/sgd0000532
15. Catalano DCJ. "Trans enough?": the pressures trans men negotiate in higher education. *Transgender Stud Q.* 2015;2(3):411–430. https://doi.org/10.1215/23289252-2926399
16. Szymanski DM, Sung MR. Asian cultural values, internalized heterosexism, and sexual orientation disclosure among Asian American sexual minority persons. *J LGBT Issues Couns.* 2013;7(3):257–273. https://doi.org/10.1080/15538605.2013.812930
17. Ferlatte O, Hottes TS, Trussler T, Marchand R. Disclosure of sexual orientation by gay and bisexual men in government-administered probability surveys. *LGBT Health.* 2017;4(1):68–71. https://doi.org/10.1089/lgbt.2016.0037
18. Lee S, Fredriksen-Goldsen KI, McClain C, Kim HJ, Suzer-Gurtekin ZT. Are sexual minorities less likely to participate in surveys? An examination of proxy nonresponse measures and associated biases with sexual orientation in a population-based health survey. *Field Methods.* 2018;30(3):208–224. https://doi.org/10.1177/1525822X18777736
19. Suen LW, Lunn MR, Sevelius JM, et al. Do ask, tell, and show: contextual factors affecting sexual orientation and gender identity disclosure for sexual and gender minority people. *LGBT Health.* 2022;9(2):73–80. https://doi.org/10.1089/lgbt.2021.0159
20. Obedin-Maliver J, Hunt C, Flentje A, et al. Engaging sexual and gender minority (SGM) communities for health research: building and sustaining PRIDEnet. *J Community Engagem Scholarsh.* 2024;16(2):1–34. https://doi.org/10.54656/jces.v16i2.484
21. Pruden H, Salway T. Meet the Methods Series: "What and who is Two-Spirit" in health research. CIHR Institute for Gender and Health. October 2020;2. Available at: https://cihr-irsc.gc.ca/e/documents/igh_two_spirit-en.pdf. Accessed July 8, 2024.
22. Lunn MR, Lubensky M, Hunt C, et al. A digital health research platform for community engagement, recruitment, and retention of sexual and gender minority adults in a national longitudinal cohort study—The PRIDE Study. *J Am Med Inform Assoc.* 2019;26(8-9):737–748. https://doi.org/10.1093/jamia/ocz082
23. PRIDEnet. Community listening sessions with intersex persons: summary report. 2023. Available at: https://static1.squarespace.com/static/5dabba582ea9cc041d48f549/t/661d5befdafc0f404342b213/1713200112122/PRIDEnet_Intersex_CLS_Summary_Report_2023-02-23.pdf. Accessed July 8, 2024.
24. IBM SPSS Statistics for Windows, Version 29.0.2.0. Armonk, NY: IBM Corp; 2023.
25. Leech NL, Onwuegbuzie AJ. A call for greater use of nonparametric statistics. Presented at: The Annual Meeting of the Mid-South Educational Research Association; November 6–8, 2002; Chattanooga, TN. Available at: https://files.eric.ed.gov/fulltext/ED471346.pdf. Accessed July 8, 2024.
26. Carpenter M, Dalke KB, Earp BD. Endosex. *J Med Ethics.* 2023;49(3):225–226. https://doi.org/10.1136/medethics-2022-108317
27. McKay TR, Watson RJ. Gender expansive youth disclosure and mental health: clinical implications of gender identity disclosure. *Psychol Sex Orientat Gend Divers.* 2020;7(1):66–75. https://doi.org/10.1037/sgd0000354
28. Suen LW, Lunn MR, Katuzny K, et al. What sexual and gender minority people want researchers to know about sexual orientation and gender identity questions: a qualitative study. *Arch Sex Behav.* 2020;49(7):2301–2318. https://doi.org/10.1007/s10508-020-01810-y
29. Lindahl H. Intersex data collection: your guide to question design. interACT. August 24, 2020. Available at: https://interactadvocates.org/intersex-data-collection. Accessed May 25, 2025.
30. Morris JF, Rothblum ED. Who fills out a "lesbian" questionnaire? The interrelationship of sexual orientation, years "out," disclosure of sexual orientation, sexual experience with women, and participation in the lesbian community. *Psychol Women Q.* 1999;23(3):537–557. https://doi.org/10.1111/j.1471-6402.1999.tb00380.x

Navigating "Wicked" Disagreement in Public Health

Safura Abdool Karim, PhD, LLM, Ruth Faden, PhD, MPH, Anne Barnhill, PhD, Virginia A. Brown, PhD, MA, Jeff Kahn, PhD, MPH, Nancy Kass, ScD, Anna Mastroianni, JD, MPH, Stephanie Morain, PhD, MPH, Vardit Ravitsky, PhD, and Reed Tuckson, MD

Public health has long grappled with moral and epistemic disagreement—conflicts over values and facts that shape decisions about how best to protect population health. While these forms of disagreement are not new, recent years have seen a shift toward a more entangled and intractable form, which we term "wicked" disagreement.

This wicked disagreement, adapted from the concept of wicked problem, sees political identity as shaping both factual beliefs and moral commitments, rendering traditional tools of public health persuasion—such as appeals to evidence or shared values—ineffective. Wicked disagreement is not defined by what is disputed but by the polarized context in which facts, values, and identity are deeply fused.

In this essay, we argue that public health must develop new strategies for navigating this terrain, including sustained engagement with a wide range of communities, transparent communication about uncertainty, and a willingness to revise guidance publicly. Navigating wicked disagreement is not about achieving consensus. It is about finding trustworthy ways to protect life and advance health in a fractured public sphere. (*Am J Public Health*. 2026;116(4):544–551. https://doi.org/10.2105/AJPH.2025.308350)

AJPH April 2026, Vol. 116, No. 4

Public health, and what public health ought to do, is often a contested space.

Historically, debates in public health have often centered on whether the government ought to implement a particular intervention or how restrictive public health policies should be in the name of protecting the public's health. People generally agree that sodas are bad for health, but not all agree that the government should tax sodas. Proponents of soda taxes believe soda taxes represent a legitimate use of government authority to protect public health and discourage soda consumption.[1] Opponents believe that what people eat is a matter of individual choice and that taxation is an unjustifiable burden, especially on the poor.[1] This disagreement centers on what values should be prioritized in policy: public welfare and health promotion or individual choice and economic fairness. In public health ethics, this is termed "moral disagreement."[2]

Yet sometimes there is a disagreement about facts, what is termed "epistemic disagreement."[3] Here, the debate is about how public health should act, but the disagreement is about facts, evidence, and what sources of knowledge are legitimate.[4] Epistemic disagreement occurs regularly among public health professionals who share core epistemic assumptions about, for example, the relevant hierarchy of evidence but disagree about whether the available data in a particular case are robust enough to justify public health action. There is also, however, a deeper kind of epistemic disagreement, exemplified in the measles vaccine context. Despite long-standing scientific consensus on the safety and efficacy of measles vaccines, some communities believe these vaccines are unsafe and cause autism.[5] Those with different views do not share the same epistemic assumptions about what counts as good evidence, about either the nature of the threat or the safety and effectiveness of the intervention. This deeper form of epistemic disagreement is not amenable to adjudication in the way scientific disagreement is typically resolved.[3,6]

Moral disagreements are not easy to navigate. Public health has spent decades grappling with tensions in values and making trade-offs, accommodations, or compromises when conflicts arise.[7–9] Tools and frameworks have been developed to provide ethics guidance in public health. These frameworks help public health professionals identify tensions between, for example, individual liberties, justice, and the government's responsibility to protect the public's health and assist them in making considered choices about which values to prioritize based on defensible justifications that can be shared with the public. Some tools also emphasize the importance of engaging with the public, especially when the moral dimensions of decisions are difficult.[8,9]

Both moral disagreement and epistemic disagreement are long-standing challenges for public health, and both figured prominently during the COVID-19 pandemic and in after-action analyses of pandemic policymaking. Recent debates seem to be characterized as much if not more by contested facts than contested values.[10] Epistemic disagreement poses a different challenge to public health decision-making and is less frequently addressed in existing ethical guidance.[11] This disagreement about facts has become a more common reason for some to oppose public health interventions, with even widespread scientific consensus increasingly challenged by both decision-makers and laypeople.[12] Rejection of both the scientific method and robust evidence has intensified, making epistemic disputes especially difficult to resolve.[12] Furthermore, the advent of artificial intelligence has increased the ease of creating convincing but false information, making discerning the "truth" more difficult.[13]

Throughout the COVID-19 pandemic, epistemic disagreement created challenges for public health efforts.[4,12] Some groups rejected vaccines, not only because they prioritized liberty and opposed vaccine mandates but also because they believed vaccines were harmful, were ineffective, or had not been sufficiently tested.[4] Epistemic disagreement may emanate from a mistrust of institutions, exposure to alternative sources of information, and divergent views about who counts as a legitimate epistemic authority.[14] Scientific uncertainty and evolving information can often exacerbate epistemic disagreement and reinforce the seeming unreliability of mainstream science.[15]

Although disagreements about public health policy are not new, it seems that, in recent years, this disagreement has intensified, worsened, and become more widespread—not just within the United States, which is the focus of this article, but globally.[12] Although we present moral disagreement and epistemic disagreement as distinct (Box 1), they are often intertwined and can be mutually reinforcing. Debates may begin as factual disputes but escalate into value conflicts, and vice versa, with or without the source of disagreement articulated. People on both sides of contested

BOX 1— Characterizing Disagreement in Public Health

Types of Disagreement	Explication	Example
Substantial agreement	There is broad agreement that, as a matter of values and of facts, measures should be adopted.	There is agreement that access to clean water prevents disease and is essential for life and agreement that it is appropriate for governments to use certain powers to maintain functional water and sanitation systems.
Moral disagreement	There is broad agreement about the facts and evidence underpinning an intervention but disagreement about whether, as a matter of values, the government should adopt the measure.	There is agreement that access to prenatal care reduces infant mortality but disagreement about the ethically right way to allocate limited prenatal care funding (e.g., prioritizing pregnant women living in disadvantaged communities that have particularly high infant mortality rates or pregnant women living in any community where infant mortality continues to be a concern).
Epistemic disagreement	There is broad agreement about the appropriateness of the role of government to secure a particular public health objective but disagreement about the facts and evidence underpinning specific interventions.	There is agreement about the moral importance of promoting the health and development of children but disagreement about the extent to which the current childhood immunization schedule advances child health.
Intertwined disagreement	There is disagreement about both the facts related to the intervention and whether, as a matter of values, the government should be taking action.	There is debate about the scientific evidence concerning the benefits and harms of cannabis and disagreement about whether it is ethically appropriate for governments to control access to a recreational drug like cannabis.

debates may hold particular views based on their values and seek evidence to support their preferred course of action.[11] An individual who places high value on individual liberty and freedom may require more evidence to justify incursions on freedoms than someone who places a high value on protecting themselves or others from threats to health. Where a person disagrees with the evidence or doubts the effectiveness of an intervention, they will be less likely to find limitations on freedoms justifiable.[16] Thus, when moral and epistemic disagreement intersect, they frequently compound each other.

These instances of intertwined disagreement have been exacerbated by how the internet and artificial intelligence facilitate the flow of information, with few checks and balances for rigor or accuracy.[13] Individuals can more easily selectively seek evidence that reinforces their preexisting beliefs and values, something perpetuated by bias-enforcing social media algorithms.[11] Public health faces a substantial challenge: its primary tools for navigating disagreements—such as appeals to expert authority or shared values—are increasingly ineffective, particularly as what counts as expertise and its importance are increasingly contested.

Disagreement may also drive coercive responses from policymakers. If members of the public cannot be persuaded to follow an intervention on their own, policymakers may feel compelled to implement mandates or coercion to compel compliance and achieve public health objectives.[17] For example, vaccine mandates are sometimes employed because much of the population needs to be immunized to secure the public health benefit, and too many people do not believe in the benefit of the vaccine for a voluntary policy to be effective. This is what drove increasingly coercive childhood immunization policies in Australia, France, and Italy.[18]

Yet, this coercion may itself cause a hardening of disagreement and distrust, fueling further division. The adoption of smallpox vaccination mandates and community water fluoridation were contentious and the subject of much disagreement.[19] This disagreement did not abate with time but, in certain segments of the population, has hardened, demonstrating this long-standing trade-off between short-term public health gains and long-term risks of festering mistrust in public health.

FROM INTERTWINED TO WICKED DISAGREEMENT

Disagreement, whether moral, epistemic, or intertwined, is an expected and often navigable feature of public health decision-making. People may differ on the moral permissibility of coercive health interventions, prioritization of resources, or interpretation of emerging scientific evidence. These kinds of disagreements are more tractable when the disputing parties share some basic moral and epistemic commitments—for example, that all persons are deserving of equal respect or that bacteria and viruses can cause disease.[9]

As Figure 1 illustrates, disagreement in the current moment is distinct from the kinds of disagreements discussed previously. This is not simply disagreement over values or facts but a complex form of disagreement created by a context in which political commitments, ideology, and identity are entangled so as to shape both what individuals perceive as factually true and what they consider morally right.[14] This is a kind of wicked disagreement (as we term it): defined not by the substance of the dispute or the nature of disagreement as moral or epistemic (or both) but by the context in which disagreement unfolds, where political identity, facts, and values become so deeply intertwined that disentanglement is nearly impossible. The term "wicked" disagreement is adapted from the concept of a "wicked" problem as described by Horst Rittel and Melvin Webber[20] and refers to a complex issue with no clear solution, where stakeholders often disagree on the causes, facts, and appropriate responses. These problems are deeply interconnected with other social, political, and economic systems, and any attempted solution can create new challenges.

Unlike traditional disagreements, where parties debate values or facts within a shared framework, wicked disagreement destabilizes public health decision-making by centering widely divergent political commitments and ideologies. These political commitments may shape not only moral intuitions about state authority or individual freedom but also epistemic commitments such as acceptance and trust of scientific consensus or beliefs in germ theory.[21] Here, disagreement becomes more than a clash of values or evidence; it is a site of ideological expression and political alignment. Individual positions are evaluated not just on merit but on their source and convergence with wider political and world views.[11,16] Even if the disagreements themselves are resolvable, they become intractable in practice because participants reflexively disavow the facts of the matter as understood by those on the other side, reject the legitimacy of opposing values, and dismiss

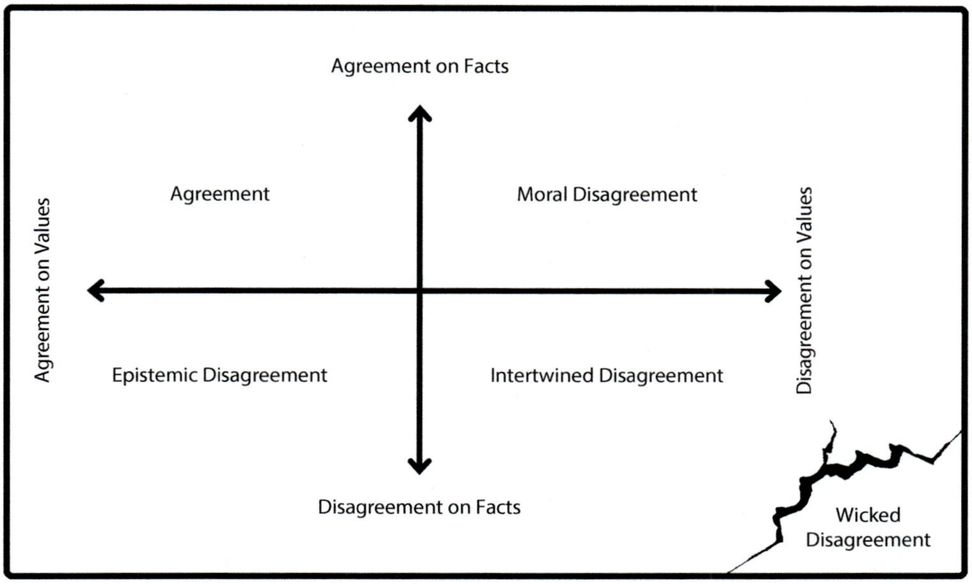

FIGURE 1— The Matrix of (Dis)Agreement: A Framework Mapping Disagreement Across Facts and Values

any institutional authority not aligned with their own worldview.

While this kind of disagreement is not novel in the history of public health, the political dimension of the context that drives wicked disagreement seems to us, as authors, particularly heightened in the current US climate in which political polarization continues to intensify. This polarization has far-ranging impact across a number of sectors, but public health is one of several areas of policy-making that has been particularly targeted and negatively affected by this polarized political climate.[22,23] The impact of polarization on health has been so significant that it has been described as a determinant of health.[23,24] We also acknowledge that this contestation of public health policy is not happening purely as a consequence of politically influenced epistemic or moral disagreement; it may also be influenced by other considerations that are similarly bound in the political moment, including financial or commercial interests.[25]

The dynamic relationship between identity, political viewpoint, and the acceptance or rejection of evidence is not exclusive to one end of the political spectrum. On the political right, we see rejection of long-standing childhood immunization policies on grounds that these vaccines lack sufficient scientific evidence of safety and are likely harmful; emphatic claims to the contrary by professional societies are discredited as biased or captured by commercial interests. On the political left, the lab-leak theory of COVID-19's origin was categorically dismissed because it was promoted by figures on the political right, whose values and facts the left deeply distrusted.[26] This open scientific question quickly became a litmus test for political affiliation, and positions became partisan: some conservatives embraced the theory as a way to discredit public health institutions and justify anti-China rhetoric; some progressives rejected it to distance themselves from perceived racist tropes and misinformation—with neither appearing to be moved by evidence or reasoned argument.[26]

In this wicked context, disagreements are resolved through the political system, and the "truth" can change as political power shifts, not because of new evidence. Wicked disagreement can lead to some absurd consequences such as how, under President Joe Biden, scientific agencies reaffirmed natural origin explanations of severe acute respiratory coronavirus 2 (SARS-CoV-2) while, under President Donald Trump's administration, the lab-leak theory has been adopted as the federal government's official position.[27]

This is the hallmark of a wicked disagreement: its structure is not resolvable by the usual approaches adopted in public health, not because the facts are unknowable or the values irreconcilable but because the political context ensures that disagreement is interpreted as threat; evidence as subjective, contested, and political; and solutions as the imposition of ideology. Even when a policy or claim is epistemically credible and ethically defensible, its acceptability turns on who proposes it, rather than what is proposed. This kind of disagreement cannot be easily resolved through traditional appeals to reason, evidence, or shared values—particularly in an increasingly polarized political climate.

RESOLVING DISAGREEMENT IN A WICKED CONTEXT

The wicked context also makes it difficult to rely on traditional means to resolve disagreement, such as adjudication of the evidence, persuasion, and participatory decision-making.[28] Political processes, including going directly to the public through referenda and "ballot box" measures, like voting on soda taxes, may offer a pragmatic means to resolve wicked disagreements that aligns with majoritarian commitments of many democracies.[29] One concern with this approach is that it may yield policies divorced from scientific evidence, but the principal limitation is that the public cannot, practically, directly vote on every, or even most, public health decisions. Another strategy is ceding decision-making entirely to public health experts, which could potentially lead to (but would not guarantee) more evidence-based policies.[30] However, allowing technical experts this much authority on policy risks marginalizing other values, besides the promotion of health, that are important to the public and that should be taken into account in evaluating policy options, and makes policies appear top-down and unaccountable.[30]

Another option is deliberative democracy processes that enable diverse groups of citizens to learn about policies, deliberate, and make policy recommendations.[28] These processes may encourage respectful dialogue among citizens and experts, promoting mutual understanding. However, they rely on positions being movable, and views changeable based on new evidence or engagement on values.[29] They are also time- and resource-intensive, limiting their scalability to only a handful of the enormous number of public health decisions that must be made.

We see no silver bullet for disagreement in a wicked context. Wicked disagreement, by its nature, resists tidy solutions. To respond, public health must do more than aim to resolve disagreement; it must equip public health actors to navigate and manage disagreement effectively within a polarized landscape.

A WAY FORWARD FOR PUBLIC HEALTH

There is no doubt that the current times are challenging, particularly for public health. We have seen public health policies and public health infrastructure eroded.[31,32] Federal public health agencies continue to be downsized, federal funding to state and local agencies is reduced, and there is a "splintering" of federal scientific leadership.[31–33] Once-fringe ideas, such as the growing move to end school vaccine mandates in some states, are displacing and ending long-standing policies, something celebrated by antivaccination movements while being decried by public health.[21,34,35]

Yet, public health cannot retreat, and it cannot afford to disengage. Public health must find a path forward that holds firm to its core purpose: protecting life and advancing well-being. To this end, we propose five principles that public health (in all its forms: institutional, professional, bureaucratic, academic, and others who aim to advance public health research, policy, practice, and education) ought to adopt as a starting point for navigating wicked disagreement. Rather than aiming for universal consensus, these principles offer a strategic framework for preserving trustworthiness, advancing public health goals, and sustaining engagement amid polarization. We recognize that adherence to these principles will not eliminate wicked disagreement, but we suggest that the "something" proposed in these principles is a step in the right direction that is, at minimum, better than nothing.

Stay in Common Cause With Science

Public health must avoid compromising science to make itself more palatable in a polarized climate. To this end, it is imperative that public health remains actively engaged in generating and evaluating evidence and, in doing so, remains committed to improving the clarity, relevance, and robustness of that evidence, even if it is contested.[36] There should also be renewed efforts to define what kinds of evidence are sufficient or required for what kind of public health decisions. This is especially important when public discourse becomes polarized, as public health professionals have the responsibility to rely on and pursue the best available knowledge in service of human health and well-being.

Fulfill the Obligation to Save and Protect Lives

While we advocate staying in common cause with science, we do not equate this with a "follow the science" approach to policymaking. Public health officials should identify what impact on health different public health policy options may have, but policy decisions—particularly cross-sectoral policies—should not be based solely on health-specific evidence.[7,9] These kinds of decisions ought to involve attention to other important values alongside health, including respect for individual rights, justice, and promoting well-being beyond health.[7,9]

Nevertheless, as technical experts, public health professionals (especially when not the final decision-maker) have a distinct and nonnegotiable obligation in the policymaking process: to provide the best assessment of available scientific evidence about how alternative options fare in terms of their likely impact on health so that these outcomes can be considered along with other socially valued considerations in the policy process.[36]

Be Clear When Sure, Humble When Uncertain

The COVID-19 pandemic highlighted the importance of recognizing scientific uncertainty and the responsibility public health has to communicate clearly and honestly about this uncertainty.[37] When the evidence is close to incontrovertible, there is an ethical duty to be clear and unambiguous about this evidence and its role in justifying public health recommendations and policies.[38] However, where there is uncertainty about the quality or sufficiency of the evidence, there is an ethical duty to openly acknowledge that uncertainty to both the public and political decision-makers.[21,38] This includes being transparent about the limitations of evidence and the provisional nature of certain recommendations.[37] We need to understand better the relationship between acknowledging scientific uncertainty and public trust, but, regardless, scientific humility is an important virtue in its own right. We suspect that overconfidence in uncertain science can erode trust just as much as misinformation.

Engage With Communities (Plural)

Public health should avoid retreating into a technocratic approach anchored solely in scientific evidence and public health officials' own values. While it is tempting in times of polarization to abandon those who disagree, public health must engage proactively and continuously with communities to establish and sustain relationships with diverse communities before, during, and after crises.[22,23] This involves engaging broadly, not selectively, in respectful and honest conversations about values and facts, to, at minimum, earn and build trust and in some cases even reach some level of shared vision. We harbor no illusions about how difficult respectful engagement is in the current climate, but we do not see a morally acceptable alternative. To do otherwise risks exacerbating this already-polarized climate, something public health must avoid at all costs.[23,24]

Learn and Revise Publicly and Rigorously

One of the most damaging consequences of wicked disagreement is the entrenchment of ideological positions, including within public health itself.[39] Public health must model a willingness to revisit assumptions and revise recommendations in light of new evidence, even in the midst of a crisis, and to do so in ways that demonstrate accountability and intellectual integrity. Saying "We were wrong" or "We've learned" is not a weakness; it is professional obligation, one that is arguably critical to ensuring the trustworthiness of public health institutions.[37,38] There are always learnings that can be drawn from a public health crisis, such as COVID-19, yet these learnings are not always sufficiently discussed publicly or drawn upon in the next crisis. Observations and learnings were offered in debates following the severe acute respiratory syndrome 1 and Middle East respiratory syndrome outbreaks, but these were not necessarily well taken up in the COVID-19 response.[40,41]

CONCLUSION

Disagreement has always been part of public health, but the current moment presents a particular challenge that requires us to revisit the principles that should guide our practice. As moral and epistemic disagreements increasingly intertwine and become shaped by political identity, these disagreements become entrenched and resistant to resolution, with traditional tools often falling short. Public health must adapt by remaining committed to evidence, engaging diverse communities with respect, communicating with both clarity and humility, and learning openly. Public health must evolve to navigate wicked disagreement, not by striving for consensus but by maintaining trustworthiness, integrity, and a steadfast commitment to protecting health in an increasingly fragmented world. AJPH

ABOUT THE AUTHORS

Safura Abdool Karim is with the Centre for the AIDS Programme of Research in South Africa, University of KwaZulu-Natal, Durban. Ruth Faden,

Anne Barnhill, Jeff Kahn, Nancy Kass, Anna Mastroanni, and Stephanie Morain are with the Berman Institute of Bioethics, Johns Hopkins University, Baltimore, MD. Virginia A. Brown and Vardit Ravitsky are with the Hastings Center for Bioethics, Garrison, NY. Reed Tuckson is with Tuckson Health Connections LLC, Atlanta, GA.

CORRESPONDENCE

Correspondence should be sent to Safura Abdool Karim, Centre for the AIDS Programme of Research in South Africa, Private Bag X7, Congella, 4013, South Africa (e-mail: safura.abdoolkarim@caprisa.org). Reprints can be ordered at https://ajph.org by clicking the "Reprints" link.

PUBLICATION INFORMATION

Full Citation: Karim SA, Faden R, Barnhill A, et al. Navigating "wicked" disagreement in public health. *Am J Public Health*. 2026;116(4):544–551.

Acceptance Date: October 20, 2025.

DOI: https://doi.org/10.2105/AJPH.2025.308350

ORCID iDs:
Safura Abdool Karim https://orcid.org/0000-0002-4843-9907

Anne Barnhill https://orcid.org/0000-0003-1478-6609

Jeff Kahn https://orcid.org/0000-0003-2493-2016

Nancy Kass https://orcid.org/0000-0003-3833-8456

Anna Mastroianni https://orcid.org/0000-0002-6127-1993

Stephanie Morain https://orcid.org/0000-0001-7278-7517

CONTRIBUTORS

R. Tuckson conceptualized the work with J. Kahn, V. Ravitsky, and R. Faden. S. Abdool Karim led the drafting of the article. All authors contributed to the conceptualization of the work and the drafting of the article, reviewed and critically revised the article, and approved the final version.

ACKNOWLEDGMENTS

S. Abdool Karim was supported by a grant from the Wellcome Trust, as part of the Oxford–Johns Hopkins Global Infectious Disease Ethics Collaborative (grant 221719).

CONFLICTS OF INTEREST

The authors have no conflicts of interest to declare.

HUMAN PARTICIPANT PROTECTION

No institutional review board review was required because this study did not involve human participants.

REFERENCES

1. Barnhill A, King KF. Ethical agreement and disagreement about obesity prevention policy in the United States. *Int J Health Policy Manag.* 2013;1(2):117–120. https://doi.org/10.15171/ijhpm.2013.21
2. Cosker-Rowland R. *Moral Disagreement.* London, England: Routledge; 2020. https://doi.org/10.4324/9780429491375
3. Smith PS, Lynch MP. Varieties of deep epistemic disagreement. *Topoi.* 2021;40(5):971–982. https://doi.org/10.1007/s11245-020-09694-2
4. Casselman-Hontalas A, Adams-Santos D, Watkins-Hayes C. Discourses of distrust: how lack of trust in the US health-care system shaped COVID-19 vaccine hesitancy. *RSF.* 2024;10(4):154–172. https://doi.org/10.7758/RSF.2024.10.4.07
5. Dubé E, Laberge C, Guay M, Bramadat P, Roy R, Bettinger JA. Vaccine hesitancy: an overview. *Hum Vaccin Immunother.* 2013;9(8):1763–1773. https://doi.org/10.4161/hv.24657
6. Bistagnino G. Epistemology of disagreement: mapping the debate. Working Paper-LPF no. 6. Gli Annali di LPF-Laboratorio di Politica Comparata e Filosofia Pubblica. 2011:159–187. Available at: https://www.centroeinaudi.it/images/abook_file/wp6_11_bistagnino.pdf. Accessed January 21, 2026.
7. Childress JF, Faden RR, Gaare RD, et al. Public health ethics: mapping the terrain. *J Law Med Ethics.* 2002;30(2):170–178. https://doi.org/10.1111/j.1748-720X.2002.tb00384.x
8. Faden R, Bernstein J, Shebaya S. Public health ethics. *Stanford Encyclopedia of Philosophy*. April 2010. Available at: https://plato.stanford.edu/Entries/publichealth-ethics. Accessed June 11, 2025.
9. Kass NE. Public health ethics: from foundations and frameworks to justice and global public health. *J Law Med Ethics.* 2004;32(2):232–242. https://doi.org/10.1111/j.1748-720X.2004.tb00470.x
10. Shapiro RY, Bloch-Elkon Y. Do the facts speak for themselves? Partisan disagreement as a challenge to democratic competence. *Critical Review.* 2008;20(1-2):115–139. https://doi.org/10.1080/08913810802316373
11. Hornsey MJ. Why facts are not enough: understanding and managing the motivated rejection of science. *Curr Dir Psychol Sci.* 2020;29(6):583–591. https://doi.org/10.1177/0963721420969364
12. Furman K, Goldenberg MJ. Disagreement and public health. In: Baghramian M, Adam Carter J, Cosker-Rowland R, eds. *The Routledge Handbook of Philosophy of Disagreement.* London, England: Routledge; 2024.
13. Li Y, Chiu CY. Redefining truth in the context of AI-truth era: a practice-led research of "from post-truth to AI-truth." In: Rau PLP, ed. *Cross-Cultural Design.* Cham, Switzerland: Springer Nature Switzerland; 2024:245–257. https://doi.org/10.1007/978-3-031-60913-8_17
14. Levy N. It's our epistemic environment, not our attitude toward truth, that matters. *Crit Rev.* 2023;35(1-2):94–111. https://doi.org/10.1080/08913811.2022.2149108
15. Brooks P. On the origin of conspiracy theories. *Philos Stud.* 2023;180(12):3279–3299. https://doi.org/10.1007/s11098-023-02040-3
16. Lewandowsky S, Oberauer K. Worldview-motivated rejection of science and the norms of science. *Cognition.* 2021;215:104820. https://doi.org/10.1016/j.cognition.2021.104820
17. Abdool Karim S, Smith MJ, Silva DS, et al. Coercing for public health: reflections on the role of coercion in public health emergencies. *Monash Bioeth Rev.* 2025;43(2):384–397. https://doi.org/10.1007/s40592-025-00245-2
18. Attwell K, Hannah A. Convergence on coercion: functional and political pressures as drivers of global childhood vaccine mandates. *Int J Health Policy Manag.* 2022;11(11):2660–2671. https://doi.org/10.34172/ijhpm.2022.6518
19. Carstairs C, Elder R. Expertise, health, and popular opinion: debating water fluoridation, 1945–80. *Can Hist Rev.* 2008;89(3):345–371. https://doi.org/10.3138/chr.89.3.345
20. Rittel HW, Webber MM. Dilemmas in a general theory of planning. *Policy Sci*. 1973;4(2):155–169. https://doi.org/10.1007/BF01405730
21. Hughes R, Gostin LO. When science splinters: vaccine federalism and the erosion of national standards. The Hastings Center for Bioethics. September 2025. Available at: https://www.thehastingscenter.org/when-science-splinters-vaccine-federalism-and-the-erosion-of-national-standards. Accessed October 5, 2025.
22. Dew K, Donovan S. Vaccines, polarising divides and the role of public health. *Crit Public Health.* 2020;30(1):1–3. https://doi.org/10.1080/09581596.2020.1702286
23. Van Bavel JJ, Gadarian SK, Knowles E, Ruggeri K. Political polarization and health. *Nat Med.* 2024;30(11):3085–3093. https://doi.org/10.1038/s41591-024-03307-w
24. Hiam L. Political polarisation: an overlooked determinant of health. *BMJ.* 2025;390:r1858. https://doi.org/10.1136/bmj.r1858
25. Gilmore AB, Fabbri A, Baum F, et al. Defining and conceptualising the commercial determinants of health. *Lancet.* 2023;401(10383):1194–1213. https://doi.org/10.1016/S0140-6736(23)00013-2
26. Stolberg SG, Mueller B. Lab leak or not? How politics shaped the battle over Covid's origin. *New York Times*. March 19, 2023. Available at: https://www.nytimes.com/2023/03/19/us/politics/covid-origins-lab-leak-politics.html. Accessed June 11, 2025.
27. Taylor L. Trump turns government's COVID websites into pages promoting lab leak claims. *BMJ.* 2025;389:r806. https://doi.org/10.1136/bmj.r806
28. Sunstein CR. Deliberation, democracy, disagreement. In: Kaempfer E, Stepaniants M, eds. *Justice and Democracy: Cross-Cultural Perspectives.* Honolulu, HI: University of Hawaii Press; 1997:93–118.
29. Gutmann A, Thompson D. Moral disagreement in a democracy. *Soc Phil Pol.* 1995;12(1):87–110. https://doi.org/10.1017/S026505250000457X
30. Landwehr C. Democratic and technocratic policy deliberation. *Crit Policy Stud.* 2010;3(3-4):434–439. https://doi.org/10.1080/19460171003619865
31. The Lancet Public Health. Public health under Trump 2.0: the first 50 days. *Lancet Public Health.* 2025;10(4):e264. https://doi.org/10.1016/S2468-2667(25)00071-4
32. Benjamin GC. Decimated public health systems, a depleted federal workforce and the deletion of safety nets that maintain the health security of America are all outcomes of President Trump's

first 100 days. American Public Health Association. April 29, 2025. Available at: https://www.apha.org/news-and-media/news-releases/apha-news-releases/public-health-outcomes-of-president-trump-s-first-100-days. Accessed September 29, 2025.

33. Ungar L, Smith MR. Trump administration's deep cuts to public health leave system reeling. PBS News. May 31, 2025. Available at: https://www.pbs.org/newshour/health/trump-administrations-deep-cuts-to-public-health-leave-system-reeling. Accessed September 29, 2025.

34. Kundu A. Why Florida's plan to end vaccine mandates will likely spread to other conservative states. *The Conversation*. September 18, 2025. https://doi.org/10.64628/AAI.hkwwwwcr7

35. Goldman M. Idaho restricts vaccine mandates. *Axios*. April 9, 2025. Available at: https://www.axios.com/2025/04/09/idaho-restricts-vaccine-mandates. Accessed September 29, 2025.

36. Brownson RC, Fielding JE, Maylahn CM. Evidence-based public health: a fundamental concept for public health practice. *Annu Rev Public Health*. 2009;30:175–201. https://doi.org/10.1146/annurev.publhealth.031308.100134

37. Oxman AD, Fretheim A, Lewin S, et al. Health communication in and out of public health emergencies: to persuade or to inform? *Health Res Policy Syst*. 2022;20(1):28. https://doi.org/10.1186/s12961-022-00828-z

38. Keohane RO, Lane M, Oppenheimer M. The ethics of scientific communication under uncertainty. *Polit Philos Econ*. 2014;13(4):343–368. https://doi.org/10.1177/1470594X14538570

39. Williams JH, Hooker C, Gilbert GL, Hor S, Degeling C. Disagreement among experts about public health decision making: is it polarisation and does it matter? *BMJ Glob Health*. 2023;8(3):e011182. https://doi.org/10.1136/bmjgh-2022-011182

40. Heymann DL, Rodier G. SARS: a global response to an international threat. *Brown J World Aff*. 2003;10(2):185–197.

41. Smith RD. Responding to global infectious disease outbreaks: lessons from SARS on the role of risk perception, communication and management. *Soc Sci Med*. 2006;63(12):3113–3123. https://doi.org/10.1016/j.socscimed.2006.08.004

Who Counts, Who's Accountable: Independent Scholarship and the Future of Carceral Mortality Oversight

David H. Cloud, PhD, JD, Zaire Cullins, BS, Andrea Armstrong, JD, and Lauren Brinkley-Rubinstein, PhD

Deaths in jails and prisons are rising, yet the federal government lacks a reliable system to track or prevent them. This essay examines the Department of Justice's failure to implement the Death in Custody Reporting Act and produce accurate and timely data on deaths behind bars.

We call for transferring responsibility for carceral mortality monitoring to public health systems with capacity to identify multilevel drivers of death and support interventions that promote prevention and accountability. Shifting this responsibility affirms the value of lives lost and moves surveillance from error-prone, passive recordkeeping to epidemiological systems better equipped to account for how carceral institutions contribute to premature death and population health disparities.

Amid political interference and instability in public health, independent scholars must help lead this transition. We outline a path forward focused on strengthening data integrity, improving timely public data access, expanding oversight, and building sustained research infrastructure rooted in public health. Until public health systems are fully empowered, independent scholars, advocates, and journalists remain essential to resisting the erasure of, and holding systems accountable for, preventable deaths behind bars. (*Am J Public Health*. 2026;116(4):552–560. https://doi.org/10.2105/AJPH.2025.308360)

AJPH April 2026, Vol. 116, No. 4

Jails and prisons, plagued by overcrowding, violence, isolation, and inadequate health care, expose individuals to heightened risks of disease, disability, and premature death.[1–3] Thousands of incarcerated people die each year,[4] and mortality rates continue to rise. In 2018, at least 4135 people died in state prisons, the highest rate recorded from 2001 to 2019.[5] Studies and independent reporting have documented spikes in preventable deaths, including suicides and overdoses, during and since the COVID-19 pandemic.[6–9]

Despite this crisis, the United States lacks critical information necessary to save lives behind bars because it lacks a reliable system for tracking carceral deaths.[10,11] Congress enacted the Death in Custody Reporting Act (DCRA) to promote transparency and accountability,[12] but incomplete data and weak enforcement undercut its effectiveness.[10] Public health systems track mortality across populations, yet carceral deaths remain largely excluded.[13] Instead, the US Department of Justice (DOJ) collects these data. More than 2 decades after the DCRA's enactment, the DOJ has yet to publish complete, verifiable, or timely data on carceral deaths,[14] constraining efforts to measure the scale of mortality, identify clusters of preventable deaths and their causes, and mobilize effective interventions.[10,13,15]

We describe how the existing carceral mortality surveillance system is structurally flawed. Fixing it requires more than technical adjustments; it demands rethinking where, how, and by whom data on deaths in custody are collected, analyzed, and disseminated. We outline law enforcement's failures in implementing the DCRA and offer recommendations for creating a carceral mortality surveillance system rooted in transparency, accountability, and prevention. We also emphasize embedding the DCRA within public health infrastructures while sustaining the work of independent scholars, journalists, and activists filling critical gaps amid political uncertainty.

A BRIEF TIMELINE OF FLAWED IMPLEMENTATION

The DCRA was first enacted in 2000 in response to journalists' and activists' growing concerns about unacknowledged deaths in the criminal legal system.[13] The law mandates reporting all deaths in custody, including during police interactions and in jails, juvenile detention centers, and prisons.[12] The DCRA was amended and reenacted in 2014 to include a nominal financial penalty for states that failed to submit data.[12]

For nearly 2 decades, the DOJ's Bureau of Justice Statistics (BJS) collected, analyzed, and published data on carceral deaths via the Mortality in Correctional Institutions program, which sought data from most state prison systems and local jail jurisdictions.[16,17] Persistent concerns about incomplete, inaccurate, and delayed reporting, however, raised questions about the data's reliability.[11] The analyses were bare, lacked contextual details, and offered no strategies to prevent premature deaths. The BJS also refused to release facility-level data, undermining efforts to compare mortality rates across prisons, identify outliers, and hold states accountable.[15] In 2016, citing the financial penalty in the reenacted DCRA, the DOJ transferred responsibility for state and local data collection from the BJS to the Bureau of Justice Assistance (BJA), a technical assistance and funding subagency. The BJS ended its state data collection efforts at the end of 2019.[14] That October, the BJA began collecting DCRA data using less precise methods. For example, the BJA's new survey did not ask for the total average daily population of facilities, which is essential for calculating mortality rates. Facilities with zero deaths were not required to report, making it difficult to learn from those facilities.[11]

In May 2022, amid growing public pressure, President Biden directed the FBI and federal prosecutors to improve DCRA enforcement. That September, a bipartisan Senate report revealed that the DOJ had failed to report at least 990 custodial deaths in 2021, confirming long-standing warnings about flawed data collection and underreporting. Rather than penalize noncompliant states, the DOJ deflected accountability by calling for new legislation to fix problems it already has the statutory power to address.[11]

In November 2024, the BJA released summary deaths in custody data for the first time. The tables reported deaths by facility type, fiscal year (2020–2023), manner of death, demographics, and jurisdiction. Notably, at the time of release, the tables on the BJA website were linked to underlying data files, providing access to detailed individual-level records for all 25 393 reported deaths over this span, including 15 915 in state prisons, 3828 in local jails, 3716 in police custody, 109 in community corrections, and 1825 categorized as "unknown."[18] The BJA issued a disclaimer stating that the data "does not constitute official statistics of the federal government nor comport with the Information Quality Guidelines of the Department of Justice."[19] Still, the release offered a rare chance to analyze facility-level mortality patterns and further scrutinize the data's completeness and accuracy to bolster calls to transform carceral mortality surveillance.

Indeed, the November 2024 BJA data are riddled with errors. For example, the BJA's tables recorded no deaths in Washington's state prisons, which is easily refuted by state data.[18,20] They reported 18 executions carried out by states between 2020 and 2023, whereas the Death Penalty Information Center recorded 70 during the same period.[21] The Marshall Project found that hundreds of deaths were either missing or labeled with incorrect or vague causes, and about 75% failed to meet the BJA's own reporting guidelines.[18]

Currently, official carceral death reporting remains fragmented and unreliable. Jurisdictions differ in how they define "in custody" and "natural" deaths, and many omit critical contextual information, such as housing conditions, access to medical care, or institutional responses.[22] Deaths occurring in hospitals, in other states, or misclassified by cause often go uncounted. These inconsistencies undermine efforts to investigate individual cases, detect system-level vulnerabilities, and implement effective oversight and policy interventions.[13]

More generally, prison and jail systems remain shrouded in secrecy. Most lack independent oversight, hold few public meetings, and bar media access.[23] Even elected officials have been denied entry to monitor prison conditions.[24,25] Courts have developed doctrines that defer to carceral administrators and impose unusually stringent proof standards on incarcerated people pursuing civil rights claims.[26,27] Incarcerated individuals face punishment for basic advocacy, like circulating petitions or staging work slowdowns to protest conditions of confinement.[28,29] Although researchers, activists, and journalists have managed to extract some information on deaths in custody, the process is resource intensive. In a national study of post–COVID-19 prison mortality, Sugie et al. revealed the labor required to collect, verify, and standardize data through repeated public records requests across states with inconsistent laws and data systems.[9,30]

These barriers reveal the criminal legal system's inability to reliably monitor and report deaths in custody. They also point to a missed opportunity: public health institutions, despite their expertise in mortality surveillance and population-level data systems, have remained largely absent from this work. As a result, the scope, causes, and disparities of carceral mortality remain hidden, undermining accountability and delaying interventions to address the conditions and policies driving carceral mortality.[13,31,32]

Reframing carceral deaths as a public health issue centers the inherent value of the lives lost and shifts the focus from passive recordkeeping to active prevention. Embedding carceral death surveillance into public health systems would enhance data quality, illuminate structural drivers of mortality, and enable earlier intervention, ensuring that preventable deaths in custody are met with the urgency, transparency, and accountability afforded to other public health crises.

SHIFTING CARCERAL MORTALITY OVERSIGHT TO PUBLIC HEALTH

When we began writing this article, our aim was to call for the full transition of carceral death data collection, reporting, and oversight from the DOJ to the Centers for Disease Control and Prevention (CDC). Historically, the CDC has been better equipped to manage mortality surveillance through standardized definitions, epidemiological analysis, and timely dissemination.

Transferring this responsibility from the DOJ to the CDC remains the most structurally sound pathway to creating a credible carceral mortality surveillance system. Unlike the DOJ, public health has the infrastructure to steward mortality data using standardized definitions, electronic reporting, and validated coding systems like the *International Classification of Diseases, 10th Revision* (*ICD-10*) and the *ICD-11*. The CDC oversees the National Vital Statistics System, the primary repository of US mortality data. In collaboration with 57 jurisdictions, the agency standardizes death certification, ensures the validity of cause-of-death reporting, and supports the timely collection of high-quality data.[33] Specialized systems such as the National Violent Death Reporting System and the State Unintentional Drug Overdose Reporting System show that multisource, incident-level data can be integrated and adapted to produce timely reports on suicides, violence, and drug-related deaths behind bars.[31,34,35] By integrating medical and legal records, such platforms can support analysis that the DOJ has consistently failed to produce, such as how facility conditions and policies contribute to premature deaths.

Any paradigm shift must also contend with the current strain on the nation's public health infrastructure, which faces defunding, politicization, and operational instability. On April 1, 2025, the CDC lost roughly 18% of its workforce through layoffs, retirements, and reassignments.[35] In this vacuum, independent researchers, journalists, and advocates are more vital than ever. For decades, they have led efforts to expose the toll of carceral deaths—challenging official narratives, building alternative data systems, and using public records laws to shed light on what carceral institutions often obscure.[11] The following section offers a dual path forward: holding firm to the goal of shifting carceral mortality surveillance to public health systems while sustaining investment in the researchers and community-based organizations that have always been at the heart of campaigns for transparency and justice around carceral deaths.

RECOMMENDATIONS

Here, we outline strategies for shifting oversight of deaths in custody away from carceral authorities and into the stewardship of public health systems. Drawing on established tools in population health sciences, these recommendations provide insights into documenting, analyzing, and reporting carceral mortality in ways that enhance data integrity, strengthen independent oversight, support public accountability, and establish a research infrastructure for confronting the carceral forces that produce premature death and health disparities.

Strengthen Integrity Through Independent Verification

Accurate, complete, and timely data are essential for understanding and preventing deaths in custody. Public health agencies should collaborate with independent academic and community partners to verify official data, harmonize definitions, and pilot improved reporting systems that can inform federal standards.

Researchers with expertise in public health, carceral systems, or legal accountability are well positioned to lead this work. Through independent verification, they can identify discrepancies in official records and uncover overlooked deaths that might otherwise evade scrutiny. This work often draws on multiple sources, including state and local vital records, media investigations, documents obtained through the Freedom of Information Act (e.g., autopsy reports or internal communications), and interviews with families, attorneys, or formerly incarcerated individuals.[36]

Scholars can also support standardization by piloting revised classifications for manner and cause of death, identifying misapplied terms, and developing reporting templates to guide future adoption. For example, the Incarceration Transparency Project at Loyola University New Orleans and the Third City Project at Duke University maintain parallel data sets that can support reforms by flagging inconsistent definitions and serving as testing grounds for new data categories and reporting protocols.[7,37]

Federal public health agencies already have infrastructure for partnering with local, tribal, and state entities to collect and standardize data. Programs such as the National Electronic Disease Surveillance System and the Treatment Episode Data Set provide shared definitions, reporting instruments, and technical guidance to support consistent data collection across jurisdictions. Adapting a similar model for deaths in custody could enhance the accuracy, comparability, and coordination of carceral mortality surveillance nationwide.

Improving how carceral deaths are tracked requires updating vital records protocols. Mitchell and Aronson propose adding a checkbox to the US Standard Death Certificate to indicate whether a death occurred in custody. This change, which falls within the authority of the National Center for Health Statistics, would increase the visibility of carceral deaths and support more standardized and timely reporting.[12] Health scholars can advance this proposal through federal advocacy and partnerships with state health departments to pilot and standardize this reform.

Implement a Data-to-Action Framework

Transferring carceral mortality surveillance to public health systems will require replacing the DOJ's recordkeeping practices with protocols that ensure timely collection and release of deaths-in-custody data to the public. Implementing a data-to-action framework[38] means collecting and using carceral death data to support oversight, enable rapid responses to emergent risks, and empower communities to pursue structural change. During the COVID-19 pandemic, academic researchers stepped in where government surveillance fell short. The UCLA Law COVID Behind Bars Data Project and the COVID Prison Project, for example, scraped daily data from corrections websites, press releases, media, and other public sources to document the scale of disease, death, and neglect behind bars. Their analyses showed that COVID-19–related deaths in prisons far exceeded those in the general population, amplifying calls for emergency responses and decarceration.[39]

Timely public access to mortality data is imperative. With appropriate infrastructure, carceral mortality data could be released on a timeline and with accessibility comparable to the CDC WONDER system.[40] Several independent entities compile and display carceral death data on their own dashboards.[7,41,42] These organizations can help verify public data by using established collection methods to flag gaps or inaccuracies and build open-access platforms that complement government reporting and expand transparency.

Achieving this requires routine, near–real-time release of carceral death data, disaggregated by facility, cause of death, and demographics, and formatted for analysis. Public health researchers can support this objective by developing open-access dashboards, downloadable data sets, and clear documentation of data limitations. The Third City Project, for example, mitigates DCRA delays by collecting press releases in states that routinely issue them, providing a near-real-time view of deaths in custody and demonstrating the value of open-source data for verification and accountability when official systems fall short.[3] Some states have launched dashboards to comply with the DCRA. South Carolina, for instance, publishes quarterly reports sortable by date, facility, location, and demographics yet requires log-in credentials, with no clear process for obtaining them . Other states impose similar restrictions. Dashboards controlled by carceral authorities do little to advance transparency because they constrain independent analysis, and instead reinforce a model of minimal compliance and weak accountability.[43] In the long run, placing carceral mortality oversight within public health agencies offers a more durable solution to the persistent concerns about data access, reliability, and integrity.[44]

Through rigorous peer-reviewed research, scholars can generate credible evidence to inform policy and illuminate the multilevel drivers of carceral mortality. Sykes et al.[31] exemplify the kind of theory-driven work needed to document disparities by race, place, and gender while situating mortality patterns in historical, sociopolitical, and institutional contexts. Drawing on federal data from 2000 to 2014, the authors found that declines in prison mortality following the Great Recession coincided with bipartisan reforms and reductions in imprisonment; however, these gains were uneven across racial groups and may have been overstated because of underreporting of deaths. A closer analysis of California further showed that, even after court-mandated health care reforms and substantial state investments to improve conditions, the state's prison mortality remained high. This finding suggests that institutional reforms, although necessary, are unlikely to produce lasting reductions in carceral deaths without addressing the broader social determinants of health in hypermarginalized communities.[31,45]

Partnering with journalists can further extend the reach and impact of this scholarship. Reuters' Dying Inside series exemplifies the power of such partnerships. Working with local journalists, the investigation filed more than 1500 public records requests across 523 jails and documented 7571 deaths from 2008 to 2019, nearly two thirds involving people who had not been convicted. The resulting data were subsequently leveraged by researchers to conduct facility-level analyses linking all-cause jail mortality to population turnover, jail size, racial stratification within jail populations, and the privatization of health care services,[2,46] and to study the interplay between individual-, facility-, and community-level factors shaping suicide rates in jails.[47]

Advance Research Methods

Standard methods for tracking deaths in custody, often limited to static aggregate tables, offer only a partial view of the forces driving preventable mortality. Reducing these deaths requires more than tracking trends; it calls for deeper inquiry into the structural forces, carceral policies, and facility conditions that contribute to premature death among incarcerated people.[11,13,44] Mixed-methods research is a powerful tool to connect population-level data to the lived realities of incarceration. By combining quantitative analysis with interviews, case reviews, legal records, and facility documents, researchers can better contextualize how conditions such as overcrowding, solitary confinement, heatwaves, lockdowns, or access to medical care shape mortality risk. These methods can help explain why deaths cluster in certain facilities and how carceral conditions erode health over time. Qualitative research allows directly affected people and families to speak to the realities behind the numbers. The Texas Jail Project, for example, supports families in challenging official narratives, humanizing data, and building public understanding of how and why carceral deaths occur.[48]

In-depth case studies offer another mixed-methods approach for understanding and addressing carceral mortality. Some examine individual deaths, piecing together timelines, records, and testimony to reveal institutional failures such as delayed care, misclassification, or negligence. Others may examine clusters of deaths—such as suicides during prolonged lockdowns, fatalities linked to extreme heat,[49] drug supply contaminants,[50] or preventable outcomes following shifts to privatized health care, uncovering patterns often obscured in aggregate data.

Improving carceral mortality surveillance requires methods that capture the influence of both acute events and longer-term, structural forces. One priority is developing metrics that reflect the health vulnerabilities and conditions specific to carceral settings. Standard mortality rates often miss critical context such as population turnover, housing arrangements, and facility size. More precise indicators—such as deaths per 1000 occupied beds, mortality per admission, or time to death after intake—can help flag facilities where intervention is most needed. When stratified by unit type, custody status, or demographic risk, and paired with institutional factors such as staff ratios, lockdown frequency, health care access, or heat exposure, these measures give a clearer picture of facility-level strain. Such linkages can reveal drivers of mortality and clarify how incarceration shapes health over time.

Accurate prison mortality rates require denominators that reflect the population at risk—measured over time and at the level of states, facilities, and housing units. This granularity is essential for identifying where deaths cluster, such as in solitary confinement or medical units, and for linking outcomes to specific policies or conditions. Yet available population data are often limited to annual state totals, without breakdowns by age, gender, race, facility, or housing unit. These gaps hinder estimation of age-standardized rates, obscure racial and gender disparities, and mask facility-level risks. Sykes et al. developed a replicable method that integrates state imprisonment rates with census and national corrections data to generate annual population estimates and support more valid epidemiological analyses of prison mortality.[31]

Methodological innovations such as natural language processing and early warning systems can improve how carceral deaths are tracked and prevented. Natural language processing helps researchers analyze unstructured data, such as incident reports or legal filings, to identify how deaths are documented and where harm may be underreported.[51–53] These insights can inform early warning systems designed to detect spikes in suicides, overdoses, or lapses in medical care. Drawing on lessons from overdose surveillance, scholars have cautioned that such systems must go beyond short-term outbreak models to capture slow-building institutional factors that produce premature deaths behind bars.[54]

Strengthen Independent Oversight

Health scholars have critical roles to play in reinforcing carceral oversight systems, many of which remain fragmented, underfunded, or entirely absent.[55,56] This work includes supporting independent civilian review boards, ombuds programs, external audits, and family-informed case reviews. Carceral health scholars can help identify where oversight is lacking, document disparities in investigative practices, and evaluate how external monitoring influences transparency and policy. They can also help define clear thresholds for triggering investigations, such as suicides, overdoses, withdrawal complications, or deaths shortly after intake, and develop protocols for timely access to key materials such as medical records, incident reports, and autopsy findings.

Another important area for academic involvement is advancing forensic investigation standards, such as those recommended by the National Association of Medical Examiners, which call for consistent use of autopsies, toxicology screening, and full reviews of medical and correctional records.[57] Researchers can contribute by assessing how consistently these standards are implemented , analyzing links between investigation protocols and case outcomes, and advocating broader adoption at state and federal levels. Without rigorous, independent investigation and documentation, official data may obscure patterns of neglect, violence, or systemic failure.

Sustain Infrastructure to Prevent Carceral Deaths

We recommend developing a long-term research infrastructure, within public health institutions focused on preventing carceral deaths by identifying systemic causes, evaluating policies, and translating evidence into action. Although incarceration has long been linked to poor health and premature death, existing evidence in explaining how facility conditions, correctional policies, and structural determinants shape mortality during and after incarceration and at a community level is limited.

A key pillar of this infrastructure is shifting responsibility for analyzing deaths in custody data from the DOJ to federal public health agencies. Although the DCRA directs the DOJ to analyze carceral death data to identify preventable causes, this mandate has largely gone unmet, resulting in mostly descriptive tables and technical reports, with little insight into how carceral institutions and their policies shape health outcomes.[58]

Making this shift will require federal investment in research capacity and independent expertise. Incarcerated people are excluded from national health surveys,[59] and a negligible share of National Institutes of Health (NIH) funding supports carceral health research.[60] This exclusion distorts national health statistics and conceals the health inequities produced by mass incarceration.[31,59] Transferring responsibility for collecting and analyzing carceral mortality data to public health agencies is therefore essential for reversing the erasure of incarcerated people from population health research.

The NIH and CDC should establish dedicated funding streams for carceral mortality prevention and support interdisciplinary teams of public health researchers, legal scholars, forensic scientists, and community-based investigators. Priority should go to studies linking death records with correctional, clinical, and environmental data to show how overcrowding, solitary confinement, racialized punishment, and inadequate care shape mortality risk. Expanding existing grant mechanisms to include carceral settings within broader health portfolios, including overdose, suicide, cardiovascular disease, and maternal health, would help establish incarceration as a health determinant in mainstream public health discourse.[61]

Such infrastructure is also essential for advancing understanding of the so-called mortality paradox, in which incarceration appears to raise mortality for White men but lower it for Black men.[62] The disparity reflects conditions in marginalized communities, where structural racism shapes exposure to violence, unsafe environments, and other threats to health, rather than any protective effect of prisons.[63] This line of research also needs a preventive approach that situates prison mortality within the broader determinants of health[61] and advances structural interventions to counter societal inequities produced by decades of organized abandonment that render prisons sites of premature death.[31,64] Sustaining long-term capacity requires investment in early-stage researchers. Many junior scholars are committed to studying the health impacts of mass incarceration but face limited institutional support. Mentored career awards and postdoctoral fellowships can help build a durable pipeline of researchers focused on carceral systems, public health, and racial justice.

As research universities face political attacks and public health institutions remain underfunded, carceral health scholars urgently need support from private foundations, individual donors, and state governments. These researchers are already uncovering unreported deaths, challenging official data, and developing open-source tools that allow the public to track and verify deaths in custody, often without support from federal public health agencies. Philanthropic funding is therefore crucial to sustaining scholarship that acknowledges incarceration as a sociostructural driver of health inequities and confronts barriers that shield carceral systems from accountability.

CONCLUSION

Mortality surveillance is a cornerstone of public health. It provides the empirical foundation for calculating life expectancy, identifying premature and preventable deaths, tracking disease outbreaks, and measuring disparities by race, ethnicity, gender, age, geography, and class. When deaths behind bars are excluded or misclassified in official data, it distorts our understanding of population health disparities, conceals the burden of carceral violence, and undermines efforts to allocate resources toward interventions that extend life expectancy and advance health equity.

The DOJ's long-standing failure to produce timely, accurate, and actionable data on deaths in custody—and its unwillingness to penalize states that fail to comply with the Death in Custody Reporting Act—reflects a structural failure of our nation's public health infrastructure: an abdication of core responsibilities to carceral institutions built not for transparency or care but for punishment, secrecy, and control—without the tools, training, or ethical mandate to protect population health.

Solving this crisis requires more than improving data systems. It calls for a fundamental shift in who holds responsibility for carceral mortality oversight. Transferring this role to public health systems is a necessary step toward reversing the erasure of incarcerated people from how we define, measure, and respond to population health inequalities. Public health agencies have the infrastructure and expertise to collect, analyze, and disseminate mortality data with transparency and rigor—and to identify the drivers of preventable deaths behind bars that carceral institutions are incentivized to obscure.

Creating a just and credible mortality surveillance system for the future means giving public health agencies the authority to conduct oversight, fund preventive interventions, and provide scholars and community organizations with the independence to uncover what governments cannot or will not reveal. Although federal health agencies provide scale and regulatory power, independent scholars contribute the speed, innovation, and critical perspective needed to break institutional silence and contest state violence. Until (and when) public health systems are fully empowered to take on this role, independent researchers must continue the work of bearing witness, exposing harm, and holding carceral systems accountable for their contributions to premature death. AJPH

ABOUT THE AUTHORS

David H. Cloud, Zaire Cullins, and Lauren Brinkley-Rubinstein are with the Bellwether Collaborative for Health Justice, Department of Population Health Sciences, Duke University School of Medicine, Durham, NC. Andrea Armstrong is with the College of Law, Loyola University New Orleans, New Orleans, LA.

CORRESPONDENCE

Correspondence should be sent to David H. Cloud, 215 Morris St, Durham, NC 27701 (e-mail: david.cloud@duke.edu). Reprints can be ordered at https://www.ajph.org by clicking the "Reprints" link.

PUBLICATION INFORMATION

Full Citation: Cloud DH, Cullins Z, Armstrong A, Brinkley-Rubinstein L. Who counts, who's accountable: independent scholarship and the future of carceral mortality oversight. *Am J Public Health*. 2026;116(4):552–560.

Acceptance Date: November 9, 2025.

DOI: https://doi.org/10.2105/AJPH.2025.308360

ORCID iDs:

David H. Cloud https://orcid.org/0000-0001-5270-4171

Andrea Armstrong https://orcid.org/0009-0002-7390-9269

CONTRIBUTORS

D. H. Cloud and L. Brinkley-Rubinstein co-conceptualized the essay. D. H. Cloud led the research, writing, and development of the manuscript. L. Brinkley-Rubinstein contributed to writing and editing and provided guidance throughout. Z. Cullins supported background research, early drafting, and revisions. A. Armstrong contributed legal insight, particularly on the Death in Custody Reporting Act, and helped shape key sections through writing and editing. All authors contributed to the essay's development, reviewed the final manuscript, and take responsibility for its content.

ACKNOWLEDGMENTS

This essay draws in part on research conducted through the Third City Project, supported by the Robert Wood Johnson Foundation.

Note. The views expressed here do not necessarily reflect those of the Robert Wood Johnson Foundation.

CONFLICTS OF INTEREST

The authors declare no conflicts of interest.

HUMAN PARTICIPANT PROTECTION

This essay did not involve human participant research and was therefore not subject to institutional review board approval or exemption.

REFERENCES

1. Cloud DH, Garcia-Grossman IR, Armstrong A, Williams B. Public health and prisons: priorities in the age of mass incarceration. *Annu Rev Public Health.* 2023;44(1):407–428. https://doi.org/10.1146/annurev-publhealth-071521-034016
2. Adler JL, Chen W. Jail conditions and mortality: death rates associated with turnover, jail size, and population characteristics. *Health Aff (Millwood).* 2023;42(6):849–857. https://doi.org/10.1377/hlthaff.2022.01229
3. Brinkley-Rubinstein L, Berk J, Williams BA. Carceral health care. *N Engl J Med.* 2025;392(9):892–901. https://doi.org/10.1056/NEJMra2212149
4. Armstrong A, Booker M, Grant J. Data, deference, and non-disclosure: shedding light on Louisiana's deaths behind bars from 2015–2019. *Loy J Pub Int L.* 2021;23:105.
5. Carson EA, Cowhig M. *Mortality in State and Federal Prisons, 2001–2016 Statistical Tables.* Washington, DC: US Dept of Justice, Office of Justice Programs, Bureau of Justice Statistics; 2020.
6. Burkhalter E. Fentanyl is killing people inside Alabama's largest, most expensive law enforcement agency—the Alabama Department of Corrections. Alabama Appleseed Center for Law & Justice. 2023. Available at: https://alabamaappleseed.org/home-page-updates/death-by-incarceration-is-far-higher-in-alabama-than-anywhere-else-in-the-united-states. Accessed December 5, 2025.
7. Armstrong A. Incarceration Transparency. Available at: https://www.incarcerationtransparency.org. Accessed March 31, 2025.
8. Dolovich S. The UCLA Law COVID Behind Bars Data Project: doing social justice work from inside a law school. *UCLA Crim Just Law Rev.* 2023;7(1):211–249. https://doi.org/10.5070/CJ8712085
9. Sugie NF, Turney K, Reiter K, Tublitz R, Kaiser D, Goodsell R, Jiménez M. Excess mortality in US prisons during the COVID-19 pandemic. *Sci Adv.* 2023;9(48):eadj8104. https://doi.org/10.1126/sciadv.adj8104
10. Fliss MD, Lao J, Behne F, Brinkley-Rubinstein L. Few prison systems release individual death data: death in custody reporting act completeness, speed, and compliance. *J Public Health Manag Pract.* 2024;30(3):424–428. https://doi.org/10.1097/PHH.0000000000001893
11. Gall M, Janovsky D, Spencer B. A matter of life and death: the importance of the Death in Custody Reporting Act. 2023. Available at: https://www.pogo.org/reports/matter-of-life-and-death-the-importance-of-the-death-in-custody-reporting-act. Accessed May 7, 2025.
12. Mitchell RA Jr, Aronson JD. *Death in Custody: How America Ignores the Truth and What We Can Do About It.* Baltimore, MD: Johns Hopkins University Press; 2023.
13. US Senate. Uncounted deaths in America's prisons and jails: how the Department of Justice failed to implement the Death in Custody Reporting Act. 2022. Committee on Homeland Security & Governmental Affairs. Available at: https://www.congress.gov/event/117th-congress/senate-event/333126. Accessed May 15 2025.
14. Armstrong A. Testimony before the US Senate Permanent Subcommittee on Investigations: uncounted deaths in America's prisons and jails: how the Department of Justice failed to implement the Death in Custody Reporting Act. *US Senate Committee on Homeland Security & Governmental Affairs.* 2022. Available at: https://www.hsgac.senate.gov/wp-content/uploads/imo/media/doc/Armstrong%20Testimony.pdf. Accessed September 15, 2025.
15. Death in Custody Reporting Act of 2013. Pub L No. 113-242, Section 2(c)(2). 2014.
16. Carson EA. Mortality in Correctional Institutions (MCI) (Formerly Deaths in Custody Reporting Program (DCRP)). US Dept of Justice. Available at: https://bjs.ojp.gov/data-collection/mortality-correctional-institutions-mci-formerly-deaths-custody-reporting-program. Accessed March 31, 2025.
17. *Gannett Satellite Information Network, LLC v US Department of Justice.* No. 22-475, 2023 WL 2682121 (DDC March 29, 2023) (Howell, J.).
18. Mahajan I, Flagg A, Sankin A. Why doesn't the US government know how many people die in custody? The Marshall Project. Available at: https://www.themarshallproject.org/2025/08/07/deaths-in-custody-reporting-act-problems. Accessed August 7, 2025.
19. Bureau of Justice Assistance. State reported deaths in custody interactive tables. November 2024. Available at: https://bja.ojp.gov/program/dcra/reported-data. Accessed September 15, 2025.
20. Washington State Dept of Corrections, Unexpected Fatality Review Committee. Unexpected Fatality Review Committee Report: Unexpected Fatality UFR-25-019, Report to the Legislature. Publication No. 600-SR001. Olympia, WA. December 1, 2025. Available at: https://app.leg.wa.gov/ReportsToTheLegislature/Home/GetPDF?fileName=600-SR001%20R.%2012-01-2025%20UFR-25-019_b9ce8368-761c-47c2-a989-6262a4ef5bd2.pdf. Accessed October 17, 2025.
21. Death Penalty Information Center. Executive database. Available at: https://deathpenaltyinfo.org/facts-and-research/data/executions. Accessed March 28, 2025.
22. Shapiro N, Bhatia N, LeMasters K, Smith R, Armstrong A. The complexity of "natural" deaths behind bars. *Acad Forensic Pathol.* 2023;13(3-4):90–91. https://doi.org/10.1177/19253621231211952
23. Armstrong AC. No prisoner left behind? Enhancing public transparency of penal institutions. *Stanford Law & Policy Rev.* 2014;25(2):435–475.
24. Boone C. State lawmakers barred from touring Arrendale prison. *Atlanta Journal-Constitution.* August 11, 2021. Available at: https://www.ajc.com/news/crime/state-lawmakers-barred-from-touring-arrendale-prison/Z6OTITDHOVDX3G5RTKM7ZTXXNU. Accessed July 11, 2025.
25. Keller R. Turned away from visiting prison, lawmakers voice concerns about spate of inmate deaths. *Missouri Independent.* October 7, 2021. Available at: https://missouriindependent.com/2021/10/07/turned-away-from-visiting-prison-lawmakers-voice-concerns-about-spate-of-inmate-deaths. Accessed July 11, 2025.
26. Library of Congress. *Turner et al. v Safley et al.*, 482 US 78 (1987). Available at: https://www.loc.gov/item/usrep482078. Accessed April 23 2025.
27. *Estelle v Gamble*, 429 US 97 (1976). Available at: https://www.loc.gov/item/usrep429097. Accessed April 23 2025.
28. Covert B. Louisiana prisoners demand an end to "modern-day slavery." *The Appeal.* August 8, 2023. Available at: https://theappeal.org/louisiana-prisoners-demand-an-end-to-modern-day-slavery. Accessed July 11, 2025.
29. Smith M. Prison strike organizers aim to improve conditions and pay. *New York Times.* August 26, 2018. Available at: https://www.nytimes.com/2018/08/26/us/national-prison-strike-2018.html. Accessed July 11, 2025.
30. Feldman JM, Bassett MT. Monitoring deaths in police custody: public health can and must do better. *Am J Public Health.* 2021;111(S2):S69–S72. https://doi.org/10.2105/AJPH.2021.306213
31. Sykes BL, Chavez EK, Strong JD. Death and disappearance: measuring racial disparities in mortality and life expectancy among people in state prisons, United States 2000–2014. *PLoS One.* 2025;20(2):e0314197. https://doi.org/10.1371/journal.pone.0314197
32. Centers for Disease Control and Prevention. National Vital Statistics System (NVSS). 2025. Available at: https://www.cdc.gov/nchs/nvss/index.htm. Accessed April 1, 2025.
33. Nguyen BL, Lyons BH, Forsberg K, et al. Surveillance for violent deaths—National Violent Death Reporting System, 48 states, the District of Columbia, and Puerto Rico, 2021. *MMWR Surveill Summ.* 2024;73(5):1–44. https://doi.org/10.15585/mmwr.ss7305a1
34. Nguyen A, Wang J, Holland KM, et al. Trends in drug overdose deaths by intent and drug categories, United States, 1999–2022. *Am J Public Health.* 2024;114(10):1081–1085. https://doi.org/10.2105/AJPH.2024.307745
35. Branswell H, Owermohle S. At CDC, Trump administration's job cuts wipe out wide array of specialists. STAT News. Available at: https://www.statnews.com/2025/04/01/cdc-rif-2400-layoffs-rfk-jr-hhs-reorganization-rapid-response-capability-weakened. Accessed May 7, 2025.
36. Levintow SN, Remch M, LeMasters K, Rice DK. The role of epidemiologists in addressing the public health consequences of the United States criminal legal system. *Am J Epidemiol.* 2025;194(5):1173–1178. https://doi.org/10.1093/aje/kwae477
37. Brinkley-Rubinstein L. Third City Project. Available at: https://3rdcityproject.com/index.php/mortality_data. Accessed April 2, 2025.
38. Zakocs R, Hill JA, Brown P, Wheaton J, Freire KE. The Data-to-Action Framework: a rapid program improvement process. *Health Educ Behav.*

2015;42(4):471–479. https://doi.org/10.1177/1090198115595010

39. Saloner B, Parish K, Ward JA, DiLaura G, Dolovich S. COVID-19 cases and deaths in federal and state prisons. *JAMA*. 2020;324(6):602–603. https://doi.org/10.1001/jama.2020.12528
40. Centers for Disease Control and Prevention. CDC WONDER. 2025. Available at: https://wonder.cdc.gov. Accessed May 7, 2025.
41. Correctional Association of New York. Deaths in custody. Available at: https://www.correctionalassociation.org/data/dashboard-deaths-in-custody. Accessed April 5, 2025.
42. Texas Justice Initiative. Deaths in custody: interactive data tools. Available at: https://texasjusticeinitiative.org. Accessed April 2, 2025.
43. South Carolina Dept of Public Safety. SC deaths in custody dashboard. Available at: https://scdps.maps.arcgis.com/apps/dashboards/007fe103761b4b38bb9be9ff48a9c821. Accessed August 17, 2025.
44. Cullins Z, Behne MF, Brinkley-Rubinstein L. The current state of carceral health data: an analysis of "listening sessions" with stakeholders. *Health Justice*. 2023;11(1):40. https://doi.org/10.1186/s40352-023-00239-4
45. Sykes BL, Chavez E, Strong J. Mass incarceration and inmate mortality in the United States—death by design? *JAMA Netw Open*. 2021;4(12):e2140349. https://doi.org/10.1001/jamanetworkopen.2021.40349
46. Reuters. Dying Inside: Jail deaths dataset. 2020. Available at: https://www.reuters.com/investigates/special-report/usa-jails-graphic. Accessed May 7, 2025.
47. Kim M, St John VJ, Szkola J. Preventing suicide in jails: examining community, facility, and individual differences. *Crim Justice Behav*. 2025; Epub ahead of print. https://doi.org/10.1177/00938548251376919.
48. Texas Jail Project. Texas Jail Project: custody deaths. Available at: https://www.texasjailproject.org. Accessed May 7, 2025.
49. Cloud DH, Williams B, Haardörfer R, Brinkley-Rubinstein L, Cooper HL. Extreme heat and suicide watch incidents among incarcerated men. *JAMA Netw Open*. 2023;6(8):e2328380. https://doi.org/10.1001/jamanetworkopen.2023.28380
50. Hvozdovich JA, Chronister CW, Logan BK, Goldberger BA. Case report: synthetic cannabinoid deaths in state of Florida prisoners. *J Anal Toxicol*. 2020;44(3):298–300. https://doi.org/10.1093/jat/bkz092
51. Goodman-Meza D, Shover CL, Medina JA, Tang AB, Shoptaw S, Bui AA. Development and validation of machine models using natural language processing to classify substances involved in overdose deaths. *JAMA Netw Open*. 2022;5(8):e2225593. https://doi.org/10.1001/jamanetworkopen.2022.25593
52. Leeson W, Resnick A, Alexander D, Rovers J. Natural language processing (NLP) in qualitative public health research: a proof of concept study. *Int J Qual Methods*. 2019;18:1609406919887021. https://doi.org/10.1177/1609406919887021
53. Omar M, Brin D, Glicksberg B, Klang E. Utilizing natural language processing and large language models in the diagnosis and prediction of infectious diseases: a systematic review. *Am J Infect Control*. 2024;52(9):992–1001. https://doi.org/10.1016/j.ajic.2024.03.016
54. Rhodes T, Lancaster K. Early warnings and slow deaths: a sociology of outbreak and overdose. *Int J Drug Policy*. 2023;117:104065. https://doi.org/10.1016/j.drugpo.2023.104065
55. Deitch M. But who oversees the overseers? The status of prison and jail oversight in the United States. *Am J Crim L*. 2020;47:207.
56. Dolovich S. The failed regulation and oversight of American prisons. *Annu Rev Criminol*. 2022;5(1):153–177. https://doi.org/10.1146/annurev-criminol-011518-024445
57. Mitchell RA, Jr Diaz F, Goldfogel GA, et al. National Association of Medical Examiners position paper: recommendations for the definition, investigation, postmortem examination, and reporting of deaths in custody. *Acad Forensic Pathol*. 2017;7(4):604–618. https://doi.org/10.23907/2017.051
58. Planty M, Jonhson N, Couzens L, Weimer B. Understanding and reducing deaths in custody: analysis of the Bureau of Justice Assistance Death in Custody Reporting Act (DCRA) data. Prepared for Benjamin Adams, program manager, National Institute of Justice Office of Justice Programs, US Dept of Justice. September 2024. Available at: https://www.ojp.gov/pdffiles1/nij/310043.pdf. Accessed May 7, 2025.
59. Ahalt C, Binswanger IA, Steinman M, Tulsky J, Williams BA. Confined to ignorance: the absence of prisoner information from nationally representative health data sets. *J Gen Intern Med*. 2012;27(2):160–166. https://doi.org/10.1007/s11606-011-1858-7
60. Boch SJ, Murnan AW, Pollard JF, Nidey NL, Hardy RY, Iruka IU. Assessment of US federal funding of incarceration-related research, 1985 to 2022. *JAMA Netw Open*. 2023;6(2):e230803. https://doi.org/10.1001/jamanetworkopen.2023.0803
61. Cloud DH, Bassett MT, Graves J, Fullilove RE, Brinkley-Rubinstein L. Documenting and addressing the health impacts of carceral systems. *Am J Public Health*. 2020;110(S1):S5. https://doi.org/10.2105/AJPH.2019.305475
62. Patterson EJ. The dose–response of time served in prison on mortality: New York State, 1989–2003. *Am J Public Health*. 2013;103(3):523–528. https://doi.org/10.2105/AJPH.2012.301148
63. Bovell-Ammon BJ, Xuan Z, Paasche-Orlow MK, LaRochelle MR. Association of incarceration with mortality by race from a national longitudinal cohort study. *JAMA Netw Open*. 2021;4(12):e2133083. https://doi.org/10.1001/jamanetworkopen.2021.33083
64. Gilmore RW. *Golden Gulag: Prisons, Surplus, Crisis, and Opposition in Globalizing California*. Berkeley, CA: University of California Press; 2007.

ISBN 978-0-87553-3599, 220 PP., 2026,
SOFTCOVER, PRINT ON DEMAND

Strategic Skills for Public Health Practice: Advancing Equity and Justice

Jamila M. Porter, DrPH, MPH, and Aysha Dominguez Pamukcu, JD

Strategic Skills for Public Health Practice: Advancing Equity and Justice is a call to reimagine public health as a dynamic social movement rooted in community leadership. Grounded in bold vision and practical application, this book confronts the root causes of health inequities — powerful systems that determine how long and how well we live. *Advancing Equity and Justice* challenges practitioners to move beyond limited technical fixes to embrace the moral clarity and collective action necessary to improve health for all.

APHA 2026

ANNUAL MEETING & EXPO

NOVEMBER 1-4, 2026 • SAN ANTONIO, TX

Together We Thrive: Health Across the Lifespan

Call for Abstracts

Make your mark on public health!

Opening Date
Jan. 5, 2026

Submission Deadline
Mar. 31, 2026

APHA
AMERICAN PUBLIC HEALTH ASSOCIATION
For science. For action. For health.

Learn more at APHA.org/AnnualMeeting.